Creating Applications with Mozilla

Creating Applications with Mozilla

David Boswell, Brian King, Ian Oeschger, Pete Collins, and Eric Murphy

O'REILLY®

Beijing • Cambridge • Farnham • Köln • Paris • Sebastopol • Taipei • Tokyo

Creating Applications with Mozilla
by David Boswell, Brian King, Ian Oeschger, Pete Collins, and Eric Murphy

Published by O'Reilly & Associates, Inc., 1005 Gravenstein Highway North, Sebastopol, CA 95472.

O'Reilly & Associates books may be purchased for educational, business, or sales promotional use. Online editions are also available for most titles (*safari.oreilly.com*). For more information, contact our corporate/institutional sales department: (800) 998-9938 or *corporate@oreilly.com*.

Editor: Laurie Petrycki

Production Editor: Mary Brady

Cover Designer: Ellie Volckhausen

Interior Designer: David Futato

Printing History:

September 2002: First Edition.

ISBN: 0-596-00052-9

[C] [12/02]

Table of Contents

Preface

Mozilla is not just a web browser. It is also a framework for building cross-platform applications using standards such as Cascading Style Sheets (CSS), XML languages such as the XML-based User-interface Language (XUL), eXtensible Binding Language (XBL), and Resource Description Framework (RDF).

Gecko, Mozilla's rendering engine, is used as part of the framework, along with other technologies such as XPConnect and XPCOM, Mozilla's component model. The Mozilla development framework also uses programming languages such as JavaScript, C++, C, Python, and Interface Definition Language (IDL).

The Mozilla framework is used to create Netscape's Mozilla-based browsers (Netscape 6.x and 7.x), other browsers such as Galeon and Chimera, and chat clients like ChatZilla and JabberZilla. Developers also use Mozilla to create development tools, browser enhancements, games, and other types of add-ons and applications.

This book explains how applications are created with Mozilla and provides step-by-step information that shows how to create your own programs using Mozilla's powerful cross-platform development framework. It also includes examples of different existing applications to demonstrate the possibilities of Mozilla development.

Mozilla Background

When Netscape Communications Corporation was founded, it planned to create a better version of NCSA's Mosaic browser, the first application that made accessing the Internet possible for ordinary users. This new application would be a Mosaic Killer. In time, the word "Mozilla" became the shortened version of this phrase and the code word for Netscape's browsers.

Mozilla has become more than a reference to one of Netscape's products. On March 31, 1998, *http://www.mozilla.org/* was launched as the site where the development of Netscape's next-generation Communicator 5.0 browser suite would take place. At that point, Mozilla became an open source project and began to take on a life of its own beyond its origins at Netscape.

When Netscape released its Communicator code to the open source community, it did something that was never done before: no other major software company had given away the source code to a proprietary product. At the time, many people in the software industry and the press debated the wisdom of this decision.

Many other companies have followed Netscape's lead and released their own products to the open source community. Sun Microsystems sponsors several projects, including *http://www.openoffice.org/* and *http://www.netbeans.org/*. Apple also bases the core of its new operating system on an open source project called Darwin, hosted at *http://developer.apple.com/darwin/*.

A year after the Mozilla source code was released, Mike Homer, a senior executive at Netscape, made the following comments: "Mozilla is larger than Netscape, and that was its intention. Mozilla is essentially a collaborative project that was sponsored by a commercial entity. Some of the people that staff mozilla.org are Netscape employees, and the code that was contributed was code previously owned by Netscape. However, it's also true that the code base will take on a life of its own someday."

Since the project's launch, many people outside Netscape have joined the community, although many Netscape (now AOL) employees still contribute to its advancement. The Mozilla community is growing beyond the original home of mozilla.org. Other community resources worth examining include *http://www.mozillazine.org/*, an advocacy and news site, and *http://www.mozdev.org/*, a project-hosting site for Mozilla applications.

Several companies, including IBM, Red Hat, ActiveState, and Sun Microsystems have also contributed to the Mozilla community. For instance, Red Hat has provided support for Mozilla because it wants to help drive development of an open source alternative to the closed source Netscape 4.x browser suite that they had included in their Linux distribution. AOL has also explored the use of Mozilla in its latest CompuServe and AOL clients.

Because all Mozilla source code is made available to anyone who is interested, the community benefits from an increase in the number of suggestions, bug reports, patches, and new developers. Along with the people who were involved with the project when it was first released as open source, the new people and companies that joined the community have helped shape the direction and outcome of the Mozilla project.

The State of Mozilla

Mozilla 1.0 was released on June 5, 2002, after more than four years of development as an open source project. This book was written so that all examples will work with this release and any 1.0.x maintenance release.

After the 1.0 release, two main development branches of Mozilla were created. The stable, long-lived 1.0 branch is dedicated to fixing bugs in the code of the 1.0 release. From this branch, periodic maintenance releases are labeled as Version 1.0.x. Every 1.0.x release is designed to be fully compatible with (though less buggy than) the original 1.0 release.

The other development branch is from the Mozilla CVS trunk. New releases from this development effort are labeled as 1.x and may include new features, changes to architecture, or other additions that help Mozilla evolve as a project.

These new 1.x releases may not be fully compatible with applications created to work with Mozilla 1.0 and the 1.0.x releases, but mozilla.org made a commitment to preserve frozen API compatibility (including XUL and XBL syntax) throughout the 1.x series until a future 2.0 release. See *http://www.mozilla.org/roadmap/mozilla-1.0.html* for details.

Because Mozilla itself is under active development, applications built on the framework may be affected when new versions of Mozilla are released. We recommend that you refer to mozilla.org's development road map for the latest information about the state of Mozilla; see *http://www.mozilla.org/roadmap.html*.

We also recommend that you use Mozilla 1.0.x versions when working with examples in this book. We encourage you to use the latest 1.x release as well so you can stay involved with the latest and greatest that Mozilla has to offer.

Who Should Read This Book

This book is primarily aimed at programmers (and would-be programmers) interested in exploring this brand-new platform—the Mozilla development framework. However, you do not need to be a professional programmer to create your own cross-platform Mozilla-based applications.

As shown in the coming chapters, all you need to get started is a basic understanding of a few technologies that are already familiar to most web developers: CSS, XML, and JavaScript. In fact, this is one of the great advantages to developing a Mozilla-based application: the learning curve isn't as steep as most alternatives, such as C, C++, or even Java.

Your applications will be cross-platform automatically (although you can create platform-specific applications as well) and easily installable over the Internet by anyone running Mozilla on their computer. What more could you ask for in a development platform?

This book assumes that the reader has some level of familiarity with JavaScript, CSS, HTML, and XML. Reading this book in conjunction with other books that are devoted specifically to these topics may be useful if you are not already comfortable using these technologies. Some useful O'Reilly & Associates titles include *JavaScript:*

The Definitive Guide, *Cascading Style Sheets: The Definitive Guide*, *HTML & DHTML: The Definitive Guide*, *Learning XML*, and *XML in a Nutshell, Second Edition*. Concepts and technologies that are new to Mozilla or used with Mozilla in a new way are explained in detail throughout the book.

This book also assumes that the reader has access to a computer with Mozilla 1.0 or later installed on it, plus any text editor or word processor. Mozilla runs on almost any type of personal computer available today, so finding a compatible platform shouldn't be difficult. The full system requirements for any Mozilla release can be found on the mozilla.org site.

Platform and Applications

Some developers work on Mozilla to improve the way it functions and other developers use Mozilla to create new applications. These two approaches reflect the dual nature of Mozilla as a development project and a framework for creating applications, but the line between the two isn't always clear.

People often start developing an application with Mozilla and then notice a way to make Mozilla itself work better, which will in turn make their application work better. In these cases, the developer works on both Mozilla applications and the Mozilla development framework that provides the plumbing those applications run on top of.

This distinction between platform and applications is important. This book provides in-depth information about application development using Mozilla, but it does not directly describe anything relating to the development of Mozilla itself.

If you are interested in learning how to become a Mozilla developer (and actually hacking the code), we can suggest a couple of starting points. *Getting Your Work Into Mozilla* is an article written by two authors who chronicled their own experiences about becoming a part of the Mozilla community, and is available at *http://www.oreillynet.com/pub/a/mozilla/2000/09/29/keys.html*. There is also great information about getting started with development on Mozilla from the mozilla.org site at *http://www.mozilla.org/get-involved.html*.

Structure of the Book

This book is structured so you can create and distribute a simple Mozilla application after reading through Chapter 6. You should read Chapters 1–6 in order and work through the examples. The later chapters provide information about advanced aspects of application development that allow you to take full advantage of what Mozilla has to offer. If you wish, you can read Chapters 7–12 out of order, depending on your needs and interests.

Chapter 1, *Mozilla as Platform*, provides an introduction to Mozilla and its advantages as a development framework. Conceptually, the chapter gives you a thorough understanding of how JavaScript, CSS, and XUL are used to create cross-platform applications.

Chapter 2, *Getting Started*, goes into the initial technical details about creating Mozilla applications. Two "Hello World" examples are presented to show you how to build an application shell.

Chapter 3, *XUL Elements and Features*, introduces the XML-based User-interface Language, shows you how to create custom XUL documents, and explains how to use the XUL tag set to build out your application shell.

Chapter 4, *CSS in Mozilla Applications*, shows how Cascading Style Sheets are used to create the look and feel of an application and how custom CSS files work together with XUL files in your application shell.

Chapter 5, *Scripting Mozilla*, describes how to add functionality to your application by using JavaScript and how custom JS files added to your application shell interact with existing XUL and CSS files.

Chapter 6, *Packaging and Installing Applications*, explains how to package an application so it can be installed on different computers. Once you create your custom XUL, CSS, and JS files, you can package and distribute them to users as your Mozilla application after reading this chapter.

Chapter 7, *Extending the UI with XBL*, is the first of the more advanced chapters that show you how to extend the basic application framework described in Chapters 1–6. This chapter explains how to use the eXtensible Binding Language to create reusable widgets that will help organize a complicated application.

Chapter 8, *XPCOM*, examines Mozilla's cross-platform component object model. After reading this chapter, you should be able to find and use existing scriptable components in your own application and create a simple XPCOM component using JavaScript or C++.

Chapter 9, *XUL Templates*, explains how to include dynamic information in your application that can be updated from a database, user input, or other sources. XUL templates rely on RDF, but it is not necessary to fully understand RDF to be able to use XUL templates.

Chapter 10, *RDF, RDF Tools, and the Content Model*, looks more closely at how Mozilla configures and uses datasources with the Resource Description Framework. RDF is used in XUL templates, but it is also used throughout Mozilla and Mozilla applications. Although it is considered to be one of the most difficult technologies to learn and use, RDF is worth the effort.

Chapter 11, *Localization*, shows how to make your application more accessible by localizing it into any number of different languages. This chapter shows you how to use Document Type Definitions and string bundles to provide translations of your application's interface and other content, such as the Help documents you may provide in your application.

Chapter 12, *Remote Applications*, explores an alternate distribution method that has several advantages over the direct installation method discussed in Chapter 6. By serving your application from a server, you may be able to add extra features that wouldn't be possible otherwise.

The book's three appendixes contain supplemental information not directly applicable to any of the different chapters. Appendix A, *Getting and Building the Mozilla Source*, explains how to start using the Mozilla source code. Appendix B, *Development Tools*, describes projects that will assist you with your application development. Appendix C, *Programmer's Reference*, provides a convenient reference useful for quickly locating specific XUL and XBL elements and event attributes.

This book was written so that a reader who does not want to read about each aspect of application creation can read just the chapters that interest them and still get useful information. For instance, a graphic designer can read the chapters about XUL and CSS and learn how to create an application interface to which a programmer can then add functionality.

How This Book Was Written

This book was created as a collaborative project hosted at *http://books.mozdev.org*. The authors of the book have become aware of the benefits of creating a project in an open source method while working within the Mozilla community and wanted to extend these benefits to the creation of the book itself.

The content of this book was released under the Open Publication License (OPL) and is available at the site mentioned in the previous paragraph and at *http://www.oreilly.com/mozilla/*. Anyone interested in contributing to the further development of this book is encouraged to visit the site; they can help us make sure that this book lives on as an active document that will continue to be useful to the Mozilla community.

The examples used throughout the book contain code fragments that were created specifically as examples to highlight the use of a particular aspect of Mozilla application development. Several existing Mozilla applications are also used as examples and more information about each is provided in the chapters where they are used. All numbered examples in the book can be found online at *http://books.mozdev.org/examples/* and *http://www.oreilly.com/catalog/mozilla/*.

Mozilla Licensing Information

The Mozilla source code is all publicly available and released under several different licenses. The details of Mozilla's licensing scheme aren't discussed here, but we provide information and pointers to where additional information can be found.

Several licenses are used in conjunction with the Mozilla source code, including the Mozilla Public License (MPL), Netscape Public License (NPL), GNU General Public License (GPL), and the GNU Lesser General Public License (LGPL). This wide selection of licenses was chosen to make the source available to as large a group of developers as possible.

Any code that is checked into the Mozilla source code tree needs to comply with mozilla.org's licensing policy. Because Mozilla applications can be created and stored anywhere, however, there are many different options for how to license and distribute a Mozilla-based application. One option is to sell your application with or without making all of the source available.

For more information about Mozilla's licensing scheme and the license options available to Mozilla applications, visit mozilla.org's license page at *http://www.mozilla.org/MPL/*. Questions about licensing issues can also be answered by posting to the license newsgroup *netscape.public.mozilla.license* or the license mailing list *mozilla-license@mozilla.org*.

Conventions

The following conventions are used in this book:

`Constant Width` is used for:

- Code examples and fragments
- Anything that might appear in an HTML document, including element names, tags, attribute values, entity references, and processing instructions
- Anything that might appear in a program, including keywords, operators, method names, class names, commands, and literals

`Constant-Width Bold` is used for:

- User input in code examples
- To highlight certain code in examples

Italics is used for:

- New terms where they are defined
- Host and domain names (*http://www.mozdev.org/*)
- URLs (*http://books.mozdev.org/index.html*)
- Interface names and variable names

Constant Width Italic is used for replaceable items, such as variables or optional elements, within syntax lines of code.

You should pay special attention to notes set apart from the text with the following icons:

This is a tip, suggestion, or a general note. It contains useful supplementary information about the topic at hand.

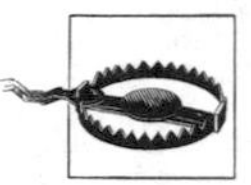

This indicates a warning or caution. It will help you solve and avoid annoying problems.

Significant code fragments, complete programs, and documents are generally placed into a separate paragraph like this:

```
<?xml version="1.0"?>
<!DOCTYPE window>
<window
    xmlns:html="http://www.w3.org/1999/xhtml"
    xmlns="http://www.mozilla.org/keymaster/gatekeeper/there.is.only.xul">
</window>
```

Comments and Questions

Please address comments and questions concerning this book to the publisher:

O'Reilly & Associates, Inc.
1005 Gravenstein Highway North
Sebastopol, CA 95472
1-800-998-9938 (in the United States or Canada)
1-707-829-0515 (international/local)
1-707-829-0104 (fax)

There is a web page for this book, which lists errata, examples, or any additional information. You can access this page at:

http://www.oreilly.com/catalog/mozilla

To comment or ask technical questions about this book, send email to:

bookquestions@oreilly.com

For more information about books, conferences, Resource Centers, and the O'Reilly Network, see the O'Reilly web site:

http://www.oreilly.com/

Acknowledgments

This book was made possible by the help and contributions of many different people. Laurie Petrycki and Paula Ferguson are the editors at O'Reilly who helped create and shape this book. Their guidance and feedback has been crucial throughout this entire process. We would also like to thank Ann Schirmer, Mary Brady, Betsy Waliszewski, and David Chu at O'Reilly for their work on helping to create and promote this book.

Many other people have contributed their suggestions, ideas, and feedback, including Martin Kutschker, Andreas Otte, Andy Edmonds, Mike Potter, Chris Waterson, Mark Murphy, Pavol Vaskovic, Andrew Wooldridge, Doug Turner, Tao Cheng, Michael Ang, Neil Rashbrook, Rob Ginda, Steve Rudman, Kathleen Brade, Zach Lipton, Cameron Barrett, Chiko Chow, Jan Varga, Axel Hecht, David Ascher, Michael Gannon, David McNamara, and Mark Hammond.

Several Mozilla application developers have allowed us to use their projects in the book as examples. We would like to thank Rob Ginda for allowing us to feature his IRC client ChatZilla, his JavaScript Debugger Venkman and his XULKit development tools, David Gillen for his Snake game, Neil Rashbrook for his XULMine game, Andy Edmonds and Pavol Vaskovic for the Optimoz and Mouse Gestures projects, Henrik Lynggaard for MozillaTranslator, David Hyatt and Mike Pinkerton for the Chimera browser, and Gervase Markham for letting us reference Patch Maker.

We would like to thank Joshua Lerner, who helped with the creation of the book's original plans and also helped as a reviewer (Joshua and Kerry Fitzpatrick also let a couple of their employees at Alphanumerica work on Mozilla projects during their day job and funded the first Mozilla Developer Conference). We would like to thank Julia Kleyman for creating several of the illustrations used throughout the book, including the xFly logo (not to mention the FruityGum skin). Thanks also to Eoin Campbell for supporting Mozilla developers and having the vision to use Mozilla for application development from its very early days.

We would also like to thank the people who have supported us during the time this book was written, including Kim Steckler, Rachel Oeschger, and Priscilla, Dylan, and Devon Collins.

CHAPTER 1

Mozilla as Platform

The Mozilla project was started in March 1998 with the goal of developing the successor to Netscape's Communicator 4.x browser suite. Today Mozilla is used by developers as a platform for creating applications that can be installed locally or run remotely over the Internet.

The difference between the Mozilla project's original goal of creating a browser suite and its current use as a cross-platform development framework is not as strange as it may sound at first. A web browser might not seem like an application development framework, but it is. Browsers allow people using any type of computer to access applications such as Yahoo! Mail to send and receive email, Amazon's book ordering service, or eBay's online auction house.

Mozilla has expanded the idea of using a browser to access applications by building on some of the technologies that are used to create web sites, such as CSS and JavaScript. A comparison of web technologies to Mozilla technologies is presented in this chapter and is helpful in explaining how the Mozilla project has turned into a platform for creating cross-platform applications.

Visualizing Mozilla's Front End

> In the beginning, there were 3 front ends: Mac, Windows and Unix. Each took a suite of developers to maintain. Adding a new feature (even just a button) required 3 engineers to waste at least a day (more often a week) slaving away until the feature was complete. This had to change.

This quote is posted on mozilla.org and describes how the Netscape 4.x browsers required a different set of engineers to create and maintain the code for the user interface, even though the browser looked nearly identical on each different supported platform.

For a company committed to creating an application that runs on a wide range of different systems, using platform-specific code was a big waste of time. XPFE, Mozilla's cross-platform front end, was designed to solve this problem by enabling engineers to create one interface that would work on any operating system.

Extreme Portability

Perhaps the biggest advantage Mozilla has for a developer is that Mozilla-based applications are cross-platform, which means that these programs work the same on Windows as they do on Unix or the Mac OS. It's possible to have applications run across different platforms because Mozilla acts as an interpretation layer between the operating system and the application.

As long as Mozilla runs on a given computer, most Mozilla-based applications also run on that computer, regardless of what operating system it uses. Not all Mozilla applications are cross-platform however, since it is possible to create an application with platform-specific code that runs only on certain operating systems, like Chimera (an ultrafast browser that works only on Mac OS X).

The number of different operating system ports of Mozilla gives you an idea of the full range of Mozilla applications. Mozilla runs on Windows, Macintosh (Classic Mac and Mac OS X), and Linux, as well as most types of Unix, including Solaris, FreeBSD, HP-UX, and Irix. Porting projects are under way to bring Mozilla to BeOS, OS/2, Open VMS, Amiga, and other operating systems. More information about most projects is available at *http://www.mozilla.org/ports/*.

In this context, a front end is more than the look and feel of an application, since it also includes the functionality and structure of that application. For example, the Netscape 6.x and 7.x browser suites use XPFE to allow the creation of different themes, but the browser suites are created by using XPFE as well.

This new technology started out as a time-saving technique and turned into one of Mozilla's most powerful innovations. Mike Cornall, in an article published in Linux-Today, summarizes the history of XPFE well when he states, "The application platform capabilities of Mozilla came about through a happy coincidence of open source development, good design, and far-sighted developers who were paying attention."

Mozilla engineers were trying to create a more efficient process that would save them time and effort, but this technology had the unintended advantage of lowering the barriers to entry to application development. To better understand this happy coincidence and why it can be so useful for developers, it is necessary to take a closer look at what XPFE is made of.

XPFE Framework

XPFE uses a number of existing web standards, such as Cascading Style Sheets, JavaScript, and XML (the XML component is a new language called XUL, the XML-based User-interface Language). In its most simple form, XPFE can be thought of as the union of each technology. Viewed together, these technologies can be seen forming the XPFE framework in Figure 1-1.

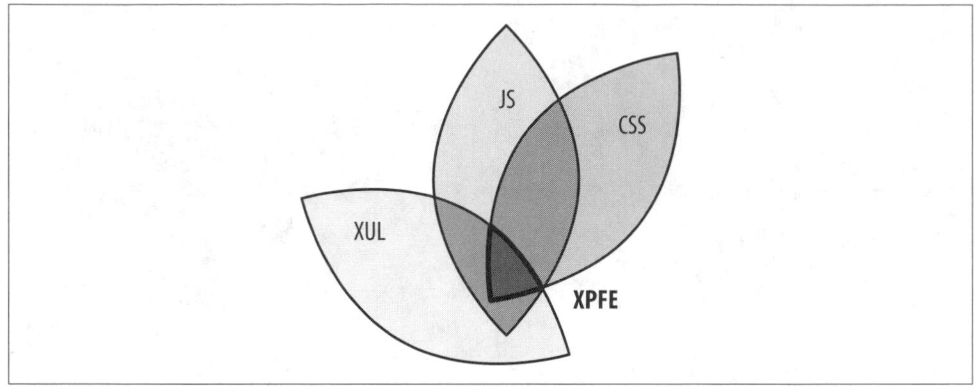

Figure 1-1. XPFE framework

To understand how XPFE works, we can look at how these different components fit together. JavaScript creates the functionality for a Mozilla-based application, Cascading Style Sheets format the look and feel, and XUL creates the application's structure.

Instead of using platform-specific code in languages like C or C++ to create an application, XPFE uses well-understood web standards that are platform-independent by design. Because the framework of XPFE is platform-independent, so are the applications created with it. Since the framework is also made up of some of the technologies used to create web pages, people familiar with creating a web page can learn how to use XPFE to create a cross-platform application.

Comparing XPFE and DHTML

In many ways, XPFE is similar to DHTML. Dynamic HTML is a combination of HTML, JavaScript, and CSS that allows a developer to create an application that is contained within the content area of a browser. XPFE provides a logical evolution to this idea by allowing the creation of applications that are more powerful, more flexible, and that can live outside the browser window as standalone programs.

Figure 1-2 illustrates the similarities between XPFE and DHTML. Both use JavaScript to create functionality, CSS to specify design and layout, and a simple markup language to describe content. The difference between the two is that one of the markup languages is HTML and the other is XUL.

Although HTML has been put to many different uses, it was originally designed as a simple system to link separate documents on the Internet. Later additions to the HTML standard have extended its functionality, but even these enhancements can't make it an appropriate language to use for developing applications. XUL is a language specifically designed for creating user interfaces, so it makes sense that XPFE is better suited for application development than is DHTML.

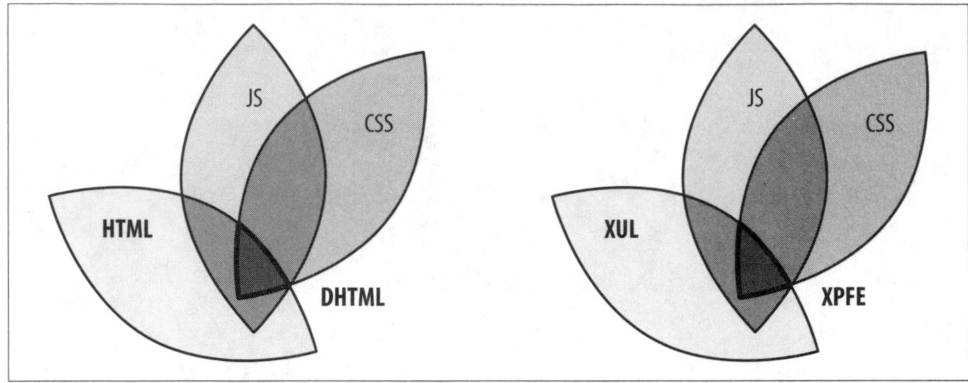

Figure 1-2. Comparison of DHTML and XPFE

Since XUL is structurally similar to HTML, knowledge of building web pages will give you a boost in learning how to create Mozilla applications. Even if you never used HTML, XUL uses a straightforward collection of tags that makes it easy to become comfortable with it in a short period of time. Once you become accustomed to using XUL, you will be ready to start using XPFE to create your own applications.

Components of a Mozilla Application

There is quite a bit more to XPFE than just XUL, CSS, and JavaScript. Now that we've gotten past the basics, we can talk about the rest of the available functionality that makes Mozilla such a powerful framework for creating applications.

At the Second Mozilla Developer Meeting, Rob Ginda, the creator of ChatZilla, led a discussion group about Mozilla as Platform. In this session, he listed all of the following components of a Mozilla application:

XML-based User-interface Language (XUL)
: Used to create the structure and content of an application.

Cascading Style Sheets (CSS)
: Used to create the look and feel of an application.

JavaScript
: Used to create the functionality of an application, although other scripting languages, such as Python, Perl, or Ruby, can be used in place of JavaScript.

Cross-Platform Install (XPInstall)
: Used to package applications so they can be installed on any platform.

eXtensible Binding Language (XBL)
: Used to create reusable widgets with a combination of XUL and JavaScript.

XPCOM/XPConnect
: Used to allow JavaScript, or potentially any other scripting language, to access and utilize C and C++ libraries.

XUL Templates
: Used to create a framework for importing data into an application with a combination of RDF and XUL.

Resource Description Framework (RDF)
: Used to store data and transmit information. Generally regarded as one of the most complicated aspects of XPFE.

Document Type Definition (DTD)
: Used for localization and internationalization; more commonly referred to as L10N and I18N, respectively.

Some of these new technologies are in the process of becoming approved standards. For instance, in 2001, AOL submitted the XBL specification to the W3C on behalf of mozilla.org. Although the W3C has not endorsed or approved the submission, this is the first step that is required to make XBL an official standard. The CSS Working Group within the W3C will now have a chance to evaluate the XBL proposal and may create an official recommendation based on it.

Each technology is important and several deserve to have whole books devoted to them. However, a distinction should be made among them. Some are essential to the creation of a Mozilla application and others provide powerful extra features to the application developer.

For example, it is possible to write an application that does not use DTDs (although a nonlocalized application would have limited usefulness for users around the world). It would be much more difficult to create an application without XUL though, since without XUL, your program wouldn't have a user interface!

Setting Up Your System

Before we look at our first example of a Mozilla application, let's make sure you have everything you need to get Mozilla running on your system along with the tools you need to create your own applications. Every Mozilla application developer will need two main tools: Mozilla itself and a text editor.

If you don't already have Mozilla installed on your computer, it can be easily downloaded from mozilla.org. You have two main choices when picking what to download. You can choose between a precompiled binary or you can grab the source. Either option will work with the examples in this book. Appendix A provides more information about the different available options.

You will also need access to a text editor. Any editor that can save as plain text will do. HTML editors will also work fine. If you normally use HomeSite, BBEdit, or another editor to create HTML files, these programs are suitable for working with the examples in this book as long as they can save files in plain text.

Although there are other tools such as debuggers and specialized editors that you can use to assist with your application development (several of these programs are described in Appendix B), the core tools that you will need are simply Mozilla and a text editor. Once you have these tools up and running, you can start working with the examples in the rest of the book.

Mozilla Applications

The most well-known Mozilla applications are those bundled with Netscape's latest browser suite—including a browser, mail and newsgroup client, an HTML editor, and an Instant Messenger chat program. However, these are just a few of the applications that are already built with Mozilla.

The mozilla.org site hosts the development of several applications, but Mozilla applications can be developed and hosted anywhere. Other locations where Mozilla applications can be found include *http://www.mozdev.org/* (which hosts over 70 different applications at the time of this writing) as well as the web sites for companies that use Mozilla as a part of their products.

Our first look at Mozilla applications entails three different chat clients. In Figure 1-3, you can see an example of ChatZilla, a program that allows you to chat with other users on Internet Relay Chat (IRC) servers (such as *irc.mozilla.org*, where Mozilla developers gather on the *#mozilla* channel). ChatZilla can be installed using the standard Mozilla installer from mozilla.org or installed separately. If it is already installed in your copy of Mozilla, you can launch it by going to Window → IRC Chat. The two other chat clients are AOL's Instant Messenger, which comes bundled with Netscape 7 and JabberZilla (a cross-platform Jabber client).

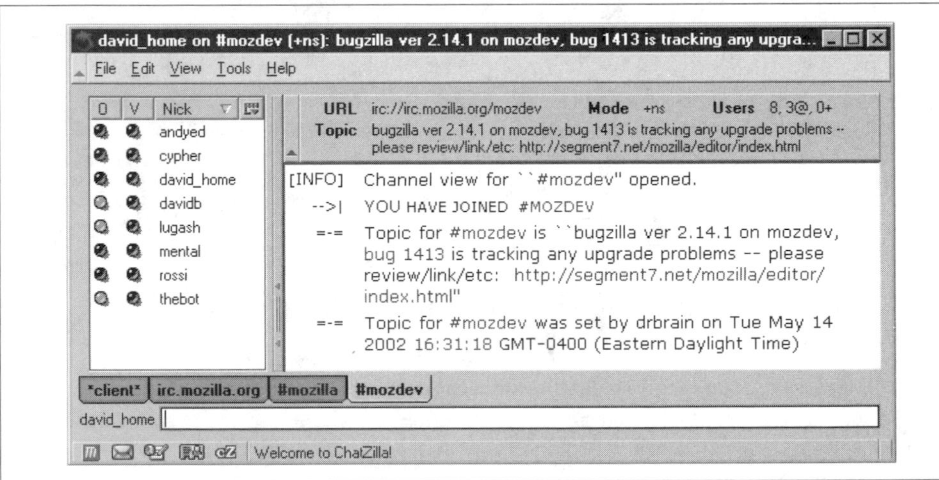

Figure 1-3. ChatZilla, an IRC chat client created by using Mozilla

Browser suites and chat clients are only some possibilities. In the following chapters, you will learn how to use each Mozilla technology to create your own applications. You will find out how to use XUL, CSS, JavaScript, and other technologies and concepts to build your own browser, chat client, blog editor, word processor, adventure game, music player, FTP client, recipe organizer, trip planner, personal calendar, or whatever type of application you are interested in creating.

Let a Hundred Browsers Bloom

Because Mozilla can be used to create any sort of application, there's no reason why it can't be used to create different types of browsers. Several projects are currently under development independently from the work being done on the default Mozilla browser. This variety is a huge asset because the Mozilla community doesn't have to try to create one browser that is all things to all people.

A few of these projects are working on improving the basic Mozilla browser interface. One of the first Mozilla applications, Aphrodite (*http://aphrodite.mozdev.org*), has an interface designed and created by members of the Mozilla community. Another project, called m/b (short for mozilla/browser), addresses shortcomings that some people see with the default browser interface. In many ways, these projects are similar to themes, but they take this idea one step further and use XUL, CSS, and JavaScript to change the layout of the browser interface and not just the look of the browser.

Additional projects are creating different types of alternative browsers, but instead of using Mozilla itself to create the application, they use the native user interface toolkits for different platforms. These projects create stripped-down browsers that use just Gecko, Mozilla's layout engine. Because these projects use platform-specific code, they work only on a specific operating system. Some examples include Chimera (*http://chimera.mozdev.org*) for Mac OS X, Galeon (*http://galeon.sourceforge.net*) for Unix, and K-Meleon (*http://kmeleon.sourceforge.net*) for Windows.

These projects are just a few examples of the different available browsers. Others include Dino!, Beonex, SkipStone, and BrowserG!. If you are interested in learning more about any of these browsers, links to many of them can be found at *http://www.mozdev.org/categories/browsers.html*. If you think of a type of browser that is needed but that is not being developed right now, use Mozilla to create your own browser.

Applications as Web Pages

Mozilla deals with applications web built using XPFE the same way that it handles ordinary web pages. This is not very surprising considering that Mozilla applications are conceptually similar to web pages (both use markup languages in conjunction with stylesheets, JavaScript, and other technologies).

The same rendering engine that lays out a web page inside the content area of the Mozilla browser also lays out Mozilla applications. This concept is usually not apparent since most Mozilla applications are contained inside their own windows instead of inside the browser's content area.

Gecko, the name of Mozilla's rendering engine, doesn't draw a distinction between Mozilla applications and web pages, so it is necessary for application developers to specifically tell Gecko to do something different when rendering a Mozilla application.

As an example of how Gecko renders applications, you can have the Mozilla browser render itself inside its own content area as seen in Figure 1-4. To do this, launch the Mozilla browser and in the location bar where you would type the URL of a web page, type **`chrome://navigator/content`**. In a sense, the browser itself is now a web page.

Figure 1-4. The Mozilla browser rendering itself

It is perfectly acceptable to create an application that lives inside of the browser window, but most developers don't want the extra browser interface surrounding their own application.

In the next chapter, we show you how to create your own custom XUL file that you can display inside of the browser window. Then we show you how to break out of the browser and have your example launch as a standalone window that can serve as the beginning of your own Mozilla application.

CHAPTER 2

Getting Started

To help you start creating applications as quickly as possible, this chapter presents two "Hello World" examples that demonstrate the beginning stages of Mozilla application development.

The first example is a simple XUL file that is loaded into the browser window. This example is then expanded on by adding additional features to the XUL file, such as imported stylesheets and JavaScript functions. The second "Hello World" example shows how to turn files like these into packages, which are the modular, bundled sets of files that fit together to make Mozilla applications or new modules for the Mozilla browser.

These examples provide a context for discussing the development of Mozilla applications. The first example focuses on creating and editing the basic file types, and the second focuses on the organization and distribution of applications on the Mozilla platform.

Simple XUL Example

Like all good "Hello World" applications, Example 2-1 shows one of the simplest possible examples of XUL. Although it is small, it demonstrates some important aspects of XUL programming, including the use of event handlers to add behavior and the use of a box to lay out elements properly within the window. This example also provides a context for discussing more general features of the language, such as the file format, the namespace, and some XUL programming conventions.

Example 2-1. Hello xFly

```
<?xml version="1.0"?>
<!-- Sample XUL file -->
<window xmlns="http://www.mozilla.org/keymaster/gatekeeper/there.is.only.xul">
<box align="center">
  <button label="hello xFly" onclick="alert('Hello World');" />
</box>
</window>
```

Use your text editor to save the code in Example 2-1 in a file called *hello.xul* and then load the file in Mozilla (you can do this by using File → Open File from the browser window and browsing to where you saved the file). You should see a button in the upper-left corner of the browser window that brings up an alert box when clicked. Figure 2-1 shows an example of the alert pop-up window that appears.

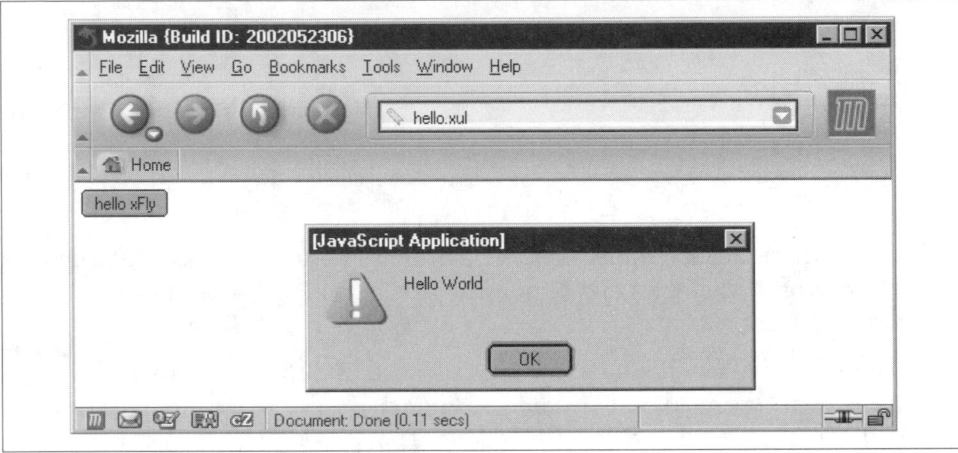

Figure 2-1. The first Hello xFly example

The next few sections describe this sample file in more detail. The covered topics include the file itself, the syntax of the markup, XUL namespaces, and the basic layout of a XUL file.

The xFly Examples

The best way to understand the possible uses of the Mozilla framework is to look more closely at a number of various existing applications. This book highlights several Mozilla development projects, such as ChatZilla and JSLib, as examples of how some people have already started using Mozilla's XPFE technologies.

Along with these applications, you'll note the use of the name "xFly" in many examples in this chapter and elsewhere in this book. The xFly examples are used throughout Chapter 2 to Chapter 6 to show how to create and package a simple Mozilla application.

This simple application is useful because it provides a place to start exploring the new information that you will learn about in this book. As you read more about XUL, CSS, JavaScript, and the other parts of Mozilla's development framework, you can create and edit the xFly files to see how these technologies work in practice.

Basic XUL Concepts

You have already seen many of XUL's basic features at work. When you load the example in the previous example, the browser identifies it as a XUL file, parses the data, creates a new window and draws the button widget, and executes the function you've defined when the button is clicked.

These activities are part of the basic and often transparent interaction between your application files and Mozilla. However, the format of your XUL files, their syntax and namespace, the XUL layout, and the windowing system are all basic to successful XUL programming.

The XUL File Format

A XUL file is a simple text file that contains proper XML syntax and has a *.xul* file extension. Mozilla expects to draw UI widgets when it encounters a file with a *.xul* extension or when it encounters the XUL namespace in other markup files that it recognizes, including HTML and XML.

The MIME type registered for XUL files is *application/vnd.mozilla.xul+xml*. When editing and using XUL files locally, you shouldn't need to worry about setting this on your computer; however, sometimes you may need to set the MIME type, such as when you host XUL files on a server. Chapter 12 provides additional information about how you can set the correct file type for your system.

Conventions

XUL has to follow certain conventions (as does XHTML or any other XML-based file) in order to be valid. Mozilla generates an error when it encounters an invalid XUL file.

The first thing required in a XUL document is the XML declaration.

```
<?xml version="1.0"?>
```

Any comments used to introduce your file can begin on the line after the declaration. Comments in XUL follow the same format used in HTML and XML, delimited by `<!--` and `-->`.

All tag sets must be closed. Empty tags are allowed for some elements, such as the `<label>` element, that are used without nested elements or content. Note that a trailing slash at the end of the tag is required to denote an empty element.

```
<label value="Getting Started" />
```

Another thing to remember is that XUL is case-sensitive. Closing a XUL `<window>` tag with `</Window>` renders it invalid.

These conventions ensure that the rendering engine can parse the XUL file successfully and display the elements defined there. Mozilla does not validate XML files, such as XUL, and it does not resolve externally parsed entities, but it does check for document well-formedness.

Following the XML specification, Mozilla ignores well-formed tags that it does not recognize, which can give your applications extra flexibility, particularly as you begin to use technologies such as XBL. But it can also make debugging a little more difficult, as when you create an element named `<botton>` and don't see why your XUL button doesn't have the typical borders or three-dimensional style.

A good practice to follow when creating XUL files is to use comments, copious whitespace, indentations (but not tabbed indentations where you can avoid them), and XUL widgets you are familiar with.

The XUL Namespace

Like other markup vocabularies, XUL uses a namespace declaration to define the particular elements that may be included in a valid file. Example 2-2 shows a sample of the required namespace declaration. The namespace is an attribute of the root `window` element. The lack of any suffix on the XML namespace declaration (i.e., `xmlns:xul`) indicates that XUL is the default namespace for this file.

Example 2-2. The XUL namespace declaration

```
<window
  xmlns="http://www.mozilla.org/keymaster/gatekeeper/there.is.only.xul" />
  <description>Illustrating the XUL namespace</description>
</window>
```

If you want to include XUL content in documents that use other types of markup, you need to declare more than one namespace. Common namespace declarations for getting other language elements into your code include HTML and RDF, but you can invent your own as well. If you wanted to put the button from Example 2-1 into a vanilla XML file, for example, you could place it into an XML document by using the `xmlns:xul` attribute, as shown in Example 2-3.

Example 2-3. Mixed namespaces in an XML document

```
<flies:flies
  xmlns:flies="http://www.flies.com/come.fly.with.me.xml#"
  xmlns:html="http://www.w3.org/1999/xhtml"
  xmlns:xul="http://www.mozilla.org/keymaster/gatekeeper/there.is.only.xul">
  <flies:wings>
    <xul:box align="center">
      <xul:button label="hello xFly" onclick="alert('hello.');" />
    </xul:box>
    <html:img src="wings.jpg" />
  </flies:wings>
</flies:flies>
```

This file has three types of content: XUL, HTML, and customized markup called `flies`. When you use mixed namespaces, you have to prefix the XUL elements with `xul:` to distinguish them from markup in other namespaces, as with the `xul:box` and `xul:button` shown in Example 2-3.

Basic XUL Layout

Example 2-1 features some very common XUL elements. In this section, each element is dissected to show what it does and how it interacts with other elements. The `<window>` element is the root of individual primary XUL documents (in contrast to dialogs that pop up from windows, which can use `<dialog>` as the root, and XUL documents loaded within other XUL containers, which can use `<page>`).

As in HTML, the root element defines the document into which all elements are drawn, but in XUL, that document is a piece of an application interface and not a web page. We'll have more to say about the window and some of its features in the second example.

A `<box>` element that contains a `<button>` is inside the window in Example 2-1. Although you can use attributes on the window element to lay out and position window children, it's never a bad idea to use the `<box>` as a container, particularly when you add new layout to your document, such as rows of buttons, grids, tabs, or other elements that need to be arranged precisely within the space of the window. The `box` is the basic element for layout in XUL.

The `align` attribute on the box specifies that the children do not stretch and center themselves in the middle of the available space. If the box was omitted and there were multiple children of the root window, they would be laid out vertically by default, one under the other. This setting can be overridden by adding the `orient` attribute to `<window>` and giving it a value of "horizontal."

Using XUL Windows

The foundation of an XPFE application is a window. Each XUL document has to have at least one XUL `<window>` element, and it must be the root of the document—the surrounding, outermost element in the XML document, set apart from the XML declaration itself and other processing "preambles." A basic window with no content looks like this:

```
<?xml version="1.0"?>
<!DOCTYPE window>
<window
    xmlns:html="http://www.w3.org/1999/xhtml"
    xmlns="http://www.mozilla.org/keymaster/gatekeeper/there.is.only.xul">
</window>
```

Commonly, an application has more than one window, with a number of dialogs and secondary windows. Each window is also contained within a `<window>` element (though recent additions to the XUL specification include the `dialog` and `page` elements, which are derived from `window` and can be used in its place as root elements in your XUL files).

As your application becomes more complex, you need a way to keep track of the windows and ensure that they can communicate with one another. In Mozilla, there is a way to do this by using the `type` attribute identifier, which allows you to use special window-opening functions like `toOpenWindowByType()` to manage particular window types.

As with any existing Mozilla functions referred to in this book, you can look up `toOpenWindowByType` by using the LXR web-based source code viewer, described in Appendix A and available at *http://lxr.mozilla.org/*.

Window features

An `id` attribute is present on the `<window>` element. Using this attribute is not necessary to run the windows system, but it is a good idea to give each window a unique identifier because it makes nodes easier to find from script (see the DOM method `getElementByID` in Chapter 5 for information about how to get elements by identifier). This is how to set up an ID attribute:

```
<window
    xmlns:html="http://www.w3.org/1999/xhtml"
    xmlns="http://www.mozilla.org/keymaster/gatekeeper/there.is.only.xul">
    id="xflyMain">
```

Load event handlers such as `onload` and `onunload` are useful and necessary if you want to add behavior to a window, pass input to it, or manipulate its content depending on context:

```
<window
    xmlns:html="http://www.w3.org/1999/xhtml"
    xmlns="http://www.mozilla.org/keymaster/gatekeeper/there.is.only.xul"
    id="xfly-main"
    onload="startUp()"
    onunload="shutdown()"
    onclose="onClose()">
```

When you load a XUL file that begins in this way, the event handler attributes `onload` and `onunload` carry out the functions listed as values (`startUp()` and `shutdown()`). In addition, Mozilla provides an `onclose` event handler that intercepts the upcoming window closure to carry out any extra processing you need. The close event is fired before the `unload` event, so you can stop the window from closing in the `onclose` event handler if necessary. To stop window closure, the close event must return *false*.

Additional handlers are available for dialog windows. They are listed and their use is outlined in the section "Application Windows" in Chapter 3.

Window properties

The window declaration is expanding, but there is still plenty of room for more features. In addition to the *attributes*—the event handlers, the ID, and the namespace that appear within the <window> tag itself—a XUL window also has all of the properties of the DOM window object from HTML. These properties are listed below, along with additional properties for application specific tasks.

Navigator	Document	window	Parent
Top	Scrollbars	name	ScrollX
ScrollY	ScrollTo	scrollBy	GetSelection
ScrollByLines	ScrollByPages	Size ToContent	Dump
SetTimeout	SetInterval	Clear Timeout	ClearInterval
SetResizable	CaptureEvents	Release Events	RouteEvent
Enable External Capture	DisableExternal Capture	prompt	Open
OpenDialog	Frames	find	self
Screen	History	content	Sidebar
Menubar	Toolbar	Locationbar	Personalbar
Statusbar	Directories	closed	Crypto
pkcs11	Controllers	opener	Status
defaultStatus	Location	innerWidth	InnerHeight
outerWidth	OuterHeight	screenX	ScreenY
pageXOffset	PageYOffset	length	FullScreen
alert	Confirm	focus	Blur
back	Forward	home	Stop
print	MoveTo	moveBy	ResizeTo
resizeBy	Scroll	close	UpdateCommands
escape	Unescape	atob	Btoa
AddEvent Listener	RemoveEvent Listener	Dispatch Event	GetComputed Style

Special properties of the XUL window object include:

window.content

Using this property is a quick way to access the content area of your window, if one exists. This property is useful only if your window uses one of the content elements, namely <iframe>, <browser>, and <editor>. Refer to the section "Content Panels" in Chapter 3 for a more detailed discussion. The content property is linked only to the frame you have explicitly declared as the primary area.

```
<browser type="content-primary" ...>
```

Subsequently, you can access and manipulate the content.

```
window.content.focus();
```

window.sizeToContent()

This property is used to ensure intrinsic sizing, which is important in XUL application development, especially in dialog windows. Intrinsic sizing ensures that the window adapts and morphs to fit the content. This is preferable to constraining your window with a fixed width and height when the `onload` handler anticipates changeable content, depends on context, or takes input from another window. The colorpicker in the Mozilla Editor, for example, uses this function to make sure that the window displaying the chosen palette shrinks to fit that palette:

```
function ChangePalette(palette)
{
  gDialog.ColorPicker.setAttribute("palettename", palette);
  window.sizeToContent();
}
```

Interaction between windows

The `nsIWindowMediator` XPCOM component provides several routines for interacting with different windows. Though it's a little too early to discuss using a component like this in the Hello World examples, these routines include:

- Getting the most recent window of a particular type
- Enumerating all open windows
- Registering and unregistering the window
- Updating the window timestamp
- Updating the window title
- Setting the Z-order position

Chapter 8 provides full details of how to understand and use XPCOM components.

Window behavior

Mozilla supports the standard `window.open` JavaScript function, which has its origins in the world of browser scripting and the launching of new browser windows. Mozilla extends the function to provide some features for application development. It also provides the `window.openDialog` function for opening windows in the XPFE scripting environment. The latter function has become the more commonly used method to open a new XUL window, although the two are interchangeable.

The usage of `window.open` is:

```
window.open (url, name, features);
```

`window.openDialog` extends this functionality with a new argument list passed to it, which is optional and can be any number of arguments as needed:

```
window.openDialog (url, type, features, argument1, argument2);
```

Here is a list of some of the features of a XUL window opened using `window.openDialog`:

close
: The window can be created with or without a close widget.

chrome
: The new window has to be treated as a window within the chrome context, rather than in the browser context. It gets its own top-level window. The window itself is the chrome URL passed to the function, and is not to be loaded in a browser window.

dependent
: The new window belongs to the calling window on operating systems that support this behavior. It "floats" on top of the opening window, and you can still access the parent window. It is minimized with its parent.

modal
: The window will be run modally. Control is not given back to the parent window until this window has closed.

titlebar
: The window can be created with or without a titlebar.

centerscreen
: Open the window centered on screen.

A comma delimits the features list and the entire list must be in quotes. The script that handles the new window accesses the arguments list:

```
window.openDialog("chrome://xfly/content/utils/prompt.xul",
                  "xFly_prompt",
                  "chrome,dialog,modal",
                  message);
```

The window created in this example will be modal and use the message that was passed to it in the variable *message*. By default, Mozilla assumes that the `chrome` feature is on when you use either `window.open` or `window.openDialog` in a chrome environment, and creates a new window in the window hierarchy.

Making Mozilla Work for You

The second "Hello World" sample, shown in Example 2-4, adds some important application features and begins to take advantage of the resources that Mozilla provides for you. This section goes over the ways you can import stylesheets and Mozilla scripts to make your XUL more sophisticated and modular. It also prepares you to make an actual application.

You can see this example in action by saving the code in Example 2-4 to a file, *hello2.xul*, and then launching Mozilla and selecting File → Open File → from the browser. This displays the example as content in the Mozilla browser, as shown in Figure 2-2.

Example 2-4. Sample XUL window

```
<?xml version="1.0"?>
<?xml-stylesheet href="chrome://global/skin" type="text/css"?>
<!DOCTYPE window>
<window title="Hello xFly"
  xmlns:html="http://www.w3.org/1999/xhtml"
  xmlns="http://www.mozilla.org/keymaster/gatekeeper/there.is.only.xul"
  style="background-color: white;"
  width="300"
  height="215"
  onload="centerWindowOnScreen()">
<script type="application/x-javascript"
  src="chrome://global/content/dialogOverlay.js" />
<vbox align="left">
  <label style="font-weight: bold;"
      value="Hello, Welcome to the xFly" />
  <image src="http://books.mozdev.org/xfly.gif" />
  <button label="hello xFly" oncommand="alert('Hello World');" />
</vbox>
</window>
```

The difference between Example 2-4 and the first example is the addition of new elements, including the `script` element that brings in Mozilla JavaScript functions for use, additional box layout properties, inline style rules and processing instructions to import stylesheets, and the `DOCTYPE` declaration, which we describe later in this chapter in the section "The xFly DTD."

These extras make your XUL file work more like an application by giving you access to services and features that already exist in Mozilla. They can also help you organize your own work into reusable parts, such as application stylesheets, widgets, and script libraries, as described later in this chapter in the section "Creating a Package."

Figure 2-2. The second Hello xFly example loaded in the browser

Importing Resources from Mozilla

The code in Example 2-4 uses scripts and styles that are already defined in Mozilla. As you'll see in examples in this book and in the Mozilla source code, the *global.css* stylesheet is where many basic styles are defined for XUL widgets. Most XUL widgets have some inherent style, as you can see in Example 2-1, where the button has a button-like look without any explicit style rules or stylesheet imports.

As the XPFE has evolved, XUL widgets have used XBL internally to define some of these inherent looks and behaviors, which has taken some of the responsibility away from *global.css* and other CSS files. But this stylesheet still contains important rules for displaying basic XUL widgets. It's usually a good idea to import this main stylesheet into your application, as described here, and see what it gets you in terms of presentation. If you load Example 2-4 with and without the *global.css* line, you can see the way that the rules in the stylesheet provide styles for the widgets in the XUL.

Similarly, scripts like *globalOverlay.js*, *tasksOverlay.js*, and *dialogOverlay.js*, imported in Example 2-4, provide basic functions you can use in your applications.

Loading stylesheets

In the second line of Example 2-4, the stylesheet declaration uses a *chrome://* URL to refer to and load the *global.css* file. The style rules in that file give the button widget its "widgetness." You can use the stylesheet processing instruction to load Mozilla stylesheets like *global.css*, *navigator.css*, and *toolbar.css*, or you can use it to load your own application stylesheet. In both cases, the *chrome://* URL allows you to refer to packaged files in a flexible way.

```
<!--import the navigator.css stylesheet
    from the Mozilla navigator component-->
<?xml-stylesheet href="chrome://navigator/skin" type="text/css"?>
<!--import xfly.css stylesheet from the xFly package-->
<?xml-stylesheet href="chrome://xfly/skin" type="text/css"?>
```

Also note the use of an inline style in Example 2-4. The `style` property on the `label` widget gives you a place to define CSS rules directly on widgets. In this case, the label is given a bold font so that it shows up better in the window. You could also define this style rule in an external stylesheet and make that stylesheet part of the package for your application, as we do later in this chapter in the section "Separating the Files."

Accessing script in XUL

To access a script in XUL, use the `script` element and a URL value for its `src` attribute:

```
<script type="application/x-javascript"
   src="chrome://xfly/content/xfly.js" />
```

The dialogOverlay.js script imported into your XUL file in Example 2-4 provides access to the CenterWindoOnScreen( ) function. This function is made available to your XUL file with the line:

```
<script type="application/x-javascript"
  src="chrome://global/content/dialogOverlay.js" />
```

All functions in *dialogOverlay.js* are imported into the scope of the XUL file and can be called directly, as CenterWindowOnScreen( ) is in the onload event handler for the XUL window. Note that the functions contained in an imported JavaScript file are not broadcast in any particular way (though you can see them if you use the JavaScript Debugger). You may need to look around in the source code or see how other applications import files to find the functions you need, but the routines you want to use in your application code are probably already available in Mozilla.*

Displaying XUL Files as Chrome

Figure 2-2 shows the XUL file in Example 2-4 loaded into the browser's main content area. The example features a label widget and an image, both situated within a vbox that lays them out properly in the available space. These widgets make up the chrome of your application, the Mozilla user interface that can refer to itself and its resources with the special *chrome://* URL.

This example is starting to show off some of the nice features of XPFE programming, but it still isn't an application yet. Among other things, you probably don't want your code to live inside the browser window forever. As it grows, you may also want to divide it into sensible parts—a XUL file, a separate stylesheet, and a script file, for example. The rest of this chapter explains how to organize and package the code in Example 2-4 and launch it as a standalone window by using the -chrome option when launching Mozilla.

Launching a XUL file by using the chrome switch requires that you register your application in the chrome registry so that Mozilla sees and recognizes it. The "Registering a Package" section later in this chapter provides more information about the chrome environment and how to register this sample application.

Although this example hasn't been registered yet, we want to give you a preview of what it will look like when launched in a standalone window so you can compare it with how the same XUL file looks when loaded into the browser window. When you do launch the example by using the -chrome option (as described later in this chapter in the section "Launching the Application"), you will see the window displayed in Figure 2-3.

* Unfortunately, no good reference exists for the functions defined in the various scripts files you can import. The functions and their locations within the files continue to change, so finding and using the right ones is sometimes a matter of luck, sometimes a matter of whom you know, and often a matter of testing, determination, and patience.

Figure 2-3. The second Hello xFly example launched in its own window

Using the `-chrome` option tells Mozilla to display the specified file (in this case, the code from Example 2-4) as a standalone application rather than as content within a browser window. The file itself is the same regardless of how it is loaded, but the results differ depending on what you tell Mozilla to do with the file.

Displaying a XUL file in its own chrome window makes it more independent and breaks the link to the browser content area that is present when you use the File → Open File... method. Launching standalone windows, accompanied by the JavaScript `window.openDialog` function explained later in this chapter, opens up much more flexible window display options for your application.

Creating a Package

The previous two main sections introduced the concept of chrome and the prospect of creating standalone application windows. The next step is to make the example into an actual package—a modularized collection of files that can be installed in Mozilla as a new application.

In the earlier section "Making Mozilla Work for You," you added features and complexity to your XUL file. In this section, you pull those features into separate files—a CSS file, JS file, and a DTD file—register these files together, and make them installable as a single package.

Only when you have packaged your work will your files have access to Mozilla files, such as CSS and scripts, be accessible from the special *chrome://* type URLs, be able to accept new themes, and be able to get to the XPCOM objects in which much of the application for Mozilla is defined.

Tools are available that help set up the files that form the basis of a new package. Appendix B provides information about XULKit, which is a collection of scripts that automates part of the package creation process. It is recommended that you try to set up your own package by hand first to understand how packages are put together before using the XULKit scripts.

Architecture of a Chrome Package

The architecture of the Mozilla XPFE is component- or layer-based. One of the primary aims of the design was the separation of each different component of an application, namely content, functionality, and layout. This design results in greater modularization, making it easy to create and change a UI—to change skins for your application, for example, update the language in which the user interface is presented, or bring in new script elements.

When a package is modularized like it can be in Mozilla, design determinations can be left to the designer, language in the user interface can be left to writers, and the application framework itself can be handled by software developers (though the programmer handles all of these in many small- to medium-sized projects). The next several sections provide more detail about each component and its content and file types. The way basic packages fit components together can be the basis for your own application development.

A package is a group of directories and related files that make up a Mozilla application. A small, typical package may include a single XUL file, a script file (currently JavaScript, with implementations for Perl, Python, Ruby, and other languages being developed), and a CSS file. However, a single package might include dozens of these files, and may also include XBL files, Image File Types (PNG, JPG, GIF), DTD, HTML, and RDF files. Each has an important role to play in the application.

Package Components

As you will discover, each component in a package is independent. It is possible for your application to exist with just one or two of these components. Yet they all tie together when necessary to create a full featured application, and they are all at your disposal to take advantage of.

Chrome content

The content is the XUL and XBL data, contained in one or more files. This content is pulled in at runtime from files, overlays, and bindings, for display in the window system. The cross-platform implementation ensures consistency in the native system, and fits into the "write once, run anywhere" model. The XUL defines a single set of UI elements for all platforms. The XUL parser is much less tolerant than many HTML parsers; in fact, it's completely intolerant. However, it needs to be because every element in XUL impacts others and affects the layout of the UI—especially in the context of the Box Model, which Chapter 3 describes in detail.

The widget set consists of simple widgets that display by drawing themselves absolutely in their allotted space, and of more complex widgets that act as containers, draw on top of others, or accept input. A `<label>` widget is an example of the former, while <stack> is of the latter, more complex group. If the parser does not find an element in the content files, it fails to load and returns an error. Errors vary by type. An XML syntax error, for example, displays in the window in place of the expected content. It gives you the file the error originated in, along with the line number and column number.

Built as a complementary description language to XUL, XBL allows you to create your own widgets or add new behavior to existing XUL widgets. You may attach scripting and create (anonymous) content in a single binding or in many. With a little imagination, you can extend the content available to you infinitely by adding your own styling and behavior with XBL.

Chrome appearance

Loading up a XUL file with no styles attached to the XUL elements will render the UI as a plain, disproportioned group of widgets. While plain text on a web page can be effective for simply relaying information, the situation is not analogous in user interfaces.

Mozilla user interfaces without style are not very usable. Even to achieve the traditional plain gray interface that so many applications use, you must use CSS to style the Mozilla front end, and subtle effects, such as color grades or 3D button effects, often make even the most basic interface look and work better.

Themes and the ability to customize the look of an application are becoming more prominent. Mozilla developers realized this prominence during the design phase of Mozilla, and it's reflected in the architecture: the appearance of the interface is almost entirely separate from the structural representation in the content.

Chrome behavior

Mozilla currently supports only JavaScript as the bridge between the UI and the application code. JavaScript is the glue that binds the UI and the back end functionality, which is almost entirely written in C++.

Much of the infrastructure is in place for the support of other programming languages, however, and Python and Perl are currently being proposed as the next languages to fit into the framework. Currently, you will see JavaScript associated with XUL content via the following declaration:

```
<script type="application/x-javascript" src="xfly.js" />
```

type replaces the now deprecated language attribute and expects a MIME type for its value. As Mozilla matures and support for other languages arrives, this value may become interchangeable—which fits in with the philosophy, common in open source projects, of there being More Than One Way To Do It. Note that the behavior component of a Mozilla application usually sits in the *content* subdirectory of a package, as described later in the section "Directory Structure."

Chrome locale

Localization is the modification of software to meet the language of a location and the adaptation of resources, such as user interface and documentation, for that region. Widgets such as menu items, buttons, window titlebars, and alert dialogs commonly need to be localized. Beyond these widgets, there can be other localizable content in an application, from HTML pages to install packages.

The formats used by Mozilla are:

- DTD (*.dtd*) files, which contain entities that host the strings to be included in your XUL content.
- Property files (*.properties*), which contain string bundles that are accessed by dynamic content in JavaScript and C++ files or, theoretically, any language.
- HTML files for certain pages installed with the application—e.g., About Mozilla.
- RDF files.

Directory Structure

Files can be organized in many different ways. If your application is small—say a single window with a simple structure that needs to be available only in one language—then having all your files in one directory may be easier. As the size of an application goes over a certain threshold, however, logically grouping your files into subdirectories is a good practice to make the files more accessible.

Most applications use a directory structure that mirrors the package component descriptions described earlier: XUL and JavaScript in a *content* subdirectory, CSS and images in a *skin* subdirectory, and DTDs and other resources for localizing the interface in a *locale* subdirectory. Figure 2-4 shows this common grouping.

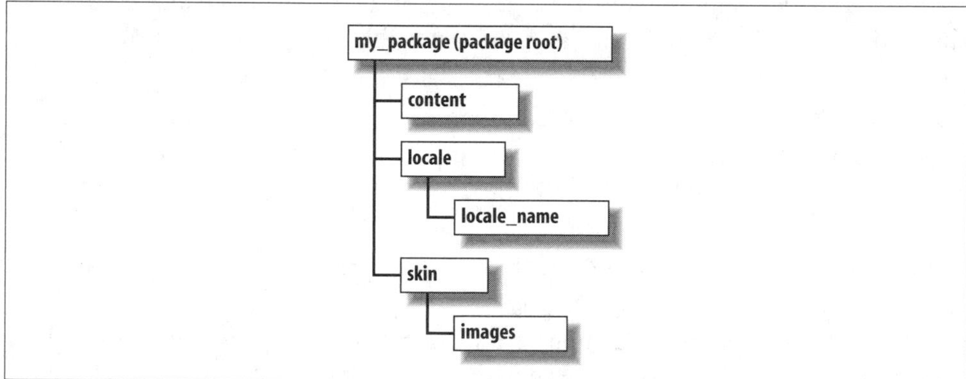

Figure 2-4. A sample package layout in the directory system

These three different directories usually contain the following type of files:

content
: The *content* directory is the home for the XUL files that contain the widgets to be drawn for you application. It is common practice to also place files related to behavior, namely JavaScript files, in this directory.

locale
: This directory contains the files that contain localized strings for your package. Most files are DTD files that contain the entities referenced in XUL files. There is a subdirectory for each language, and the naming convention is *code-region*, such as `en-US`.

skin
: The term "skin" is an internal name for a theme. The *skin* directory contains all CSS files and images that contribute to the appearance of the windows. This is a good place to put the application images—in their own subdirectory.

The xFly application directory structure

The structure of the directories in which an application is defined (whether those directories are in the filesystem or subdirectories in an archive such as a JAR file) is an important part of that application's design and relationship to Mozilla. Use the following steps to make your xFly package self-contained, registerable, and adaptable.

- On your computer, go to the directory where you have installed Mozilla and create a new directory underneath the *chrome* directory called "*xfly*."

  All Mozilla applications live in the *chrome* directory.
- Under that directory, create the three new directories, *content*, *locale*, and *skin*, as shown in Figure 2-5.

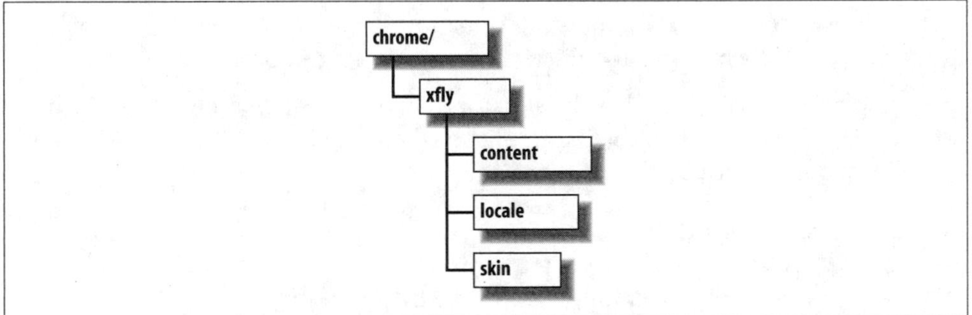

Figure 2-5. xFly package directory structure

Package Manifests

Now that you have created the directories for your package, you must tell Mozilla about them. All Mozilla packages must include manifests that describe their contents and make it possible to register them with Mozilla. A manifest is an RDF file (or series of RDF files) that sits within the package and interacts with Mozilla's *chrome* directory. RDF files are XML files that describe data in a machine-readable form.

Each xFly package subdirectory needs its own manifest file. Mozilla uses these files (in each case, called *contents.rdf*) when registering the application. These files are listed in Examples 2-5, 2-6, and 2-7. Create these files in your xFly *content*, *skin*, and *locale* subdirectories, respectively.

Example 2-5. chrome/xfly/content/contents.rdf file

```
<?xml version="1.0"?>
<RDF:RDF xmlns:RDF="http://www.w3.org/1999/02/22-rdf-syntax-ns#"
         xmlns:chrome="http://www.mozilla.org/rdf/chrome#">
  <!-- list all the packages being supplied -->
  <RDF:Seq about="urn:mozilla:package:root">
    <RDF:li resource="urn:mozilla:package:xfly"/>
  </RDF:Seq>
  <!-- package information -->
  <RDF:Description about="urn:mozilla:package:xfly"
        chrome:displayName="xFly"
        chrome:author="xfly.mozdev.org"
        chrome:name="xfly">
  </RDF:Description>
 </RDF:RDF>
```

In the content manifest in Example 2-5, note the `chrome:name`, `chrome:author`, and the other metadata that the manifest provides to Mozilla. This information can be used by others to identify what your application is and who wrote it. For example, the name, author, and short description information for each browser theme you have installed is viewable by going to Preferences and selecting Appearance → Themes.

In Example 2-6, which describes the skin for xFly only, note that new skin resources for the Classic theme are all that is supplied, as indicated in the `RDF:Seq`, which lists only `classic` as affected by this new package.

Example 2-6. chrome/xfly/skin/contents.rdf file

```
<?xml version="1.0"?>
<RDF:RDF xmlns:RDF="http://www.w3.org/1999/02/22-rdf-syntax-ns#"
         xmlns:chrome="http://www.mozilla.org/rdf/chrome#">
  <RDF:Seq about="urn:mozilla:skin:root">
    <RDF:li resource="urn:mozilla:skin:classic/1.0" />
  </RDF:Seq>
  <RDF:Description about="urn:mozilla:skin:classic/1.0">
    <chrome:packages>
      <RDF:Seq about="urn:mozilla:skin:classic/1.0:packages">
```

Example 2-6. chrome/xfly/skin/contents.rdf file (continued)

```
        <RDF:li resource="urn:mozilla:skin:classic/1.0:xfly"/>
      </RDF:Seq>
    </chrome:packages>
  </RDF:Description>
</RDF:RDF>
```

In Example 2-7, which shows the third kind of manifest, for new locale information, the English language pack (en-US) is augmented with the localizable resources in the xFly package named there. The RDF:Seq structure in a manifest states, "to the package listed here (i.e., the en-US language pack), add the following."

Example 2-7. chrome/xfly/locale/contents.rdf file

```
<?xml version="1.0"?>
<RDF:RDF xmlns:RDF="http://www.w3.org/1999/02/22-rdf-syntax-ns#"
         xmlns:chrome="http://www.mozilla.org/rdf/chrome#">
  <RDF:Seq about="urn:mozilla:locale:root">
    <RDF:li resource="urn:mozilla:locale:en-US"/>
  </RDF:Seq>
  <!-- locale information -->
  <RDF:Description about="urn:mozilla:locale:en-US"
        chrome:displayName="English(US)"
        chrome:author="xfly.mozdev.org"
        chrome:name="en-US"
        chrome:previewURL="http://www.mozilla.org/locales/en-US.gif">
    <chrome:packages>
      <RDF:Seq about="urn:mozilla:locale:en-US:packages">
        <RDF:li resource="urn:mozilla:locale:en-US:xfly"/>
      </RDF:Seq>
    </chrome:packages>
  </RDF:Description>
</RDF:RDF>
```

Manifests are detailed in Chapter 6. For now, it's enough to see that each manifest describes the subdirectory in which it is located, and that the contents of those subdirectories make up the package collectively.

The content describes the content of the xFly package, the XUL, and the JavaScript. The skin describes the theme of xFly, or the CSS and images used to lay out the XUL. The third part describes the locale, or the strings in the UI that can be localized or adapted for various languages or locales.

Separating the Files

Once you have a subdirectory structure set up in accordance with the package component structure of your application, you can pull the pieces of your XUL file out into their own files and modularize your application. These separate files—the basic XUL file and separate CSS, JS, and DTD files—are registered as a single package and can then be launched as a standalone application.

Though the files contain the information you've already seen in the "Hello World" sample shown in Example 2-4, their interaction demonstrates how packages can work together in Mozilla. Each step taken to separate the different components requires editing the base XUL file.

The xFly CSS file

The inline style rule on the label widget can go almost unadulterated into a separate text file called *xfly.css*. Save the code in Example 2-8 in the *chrome/xfly/skin/* directory.

Example 2-8. The contents of the xfly.css file

```
#xlabel { font-weight: bold; }
window  { background-color: white; }
```

Using style rules from an external file is different because you have to specify some way for the style rule to associate itself with the appropriate tags in the XUL file. CSS provides a rich collection of selectors, which bind style data to elements. In this case, where you have two separate elements that need to pick up rules, the `id` attribute on the XUL element is used to bind a unique element to an external style rule and the other style rule is bound by referring to the XUL element directly. Example 2-8 includes the selectors for the two elements, and Example 2-9 shows the updated XUL that uses *xfly.css*.

Example 2-9. XUL using external style data

```
<?xml version="1.0"?>
<?xml-stylesheet href="chrome://global/skin" type="text/css"?>
<?xml-stylesheet href="chrome://xfly/skin" type="text/css"?>
<!DOCTYPE window>
<window title="Hello xFly"
  xmlns:html="http://www.w3.org/1999/xhtml"
  xmlns="http://www.mozilla.org/keymaster/gatekeeper/there.is.only.xul"
  width="300"
  height="215"
  onload="centerWindowOnScreen()">
 <script type="application/x-javascript"
  src="chrome://global/content/dialogOverlay.js" />
 <vbox align="left" id="vb">
  <label id="xlabel"
      value="Hello, Welcome to the xFly" />
  <image src="http://books.mozdev.org/xfly.gif" />
  <button label="hello xFly" oncommand="alert('hello.');" />
 </vbox>
</window>
```

Note the extra stylesheet import statement at the top and the use of the new `id` attribute on the label. When you register the new files in your package with Mozilla, the *xfly* directory in that stylesheet processing instruction will point into your application directory structure (at the *skin* subdirectory, and at a file named after the directory itself, *xfly.css*). The label will pick up the style information in the file that was previously defined directly in its `style` attribute.

The xFly script file

The next step is to take the scripting portion, as simple as it is, out of the XUL file and put it into an external JavaScript file. Example 2-10 shows a XUL file that gets a function for the button from an external script file, given here as *xfly.js*.

Example 2-10. XUL using an external script

```
<?xml version="1.0"?>
<?xml-stylesheet href="chrome://global/skin" type="text/css"?>
<?xml-stylesheet href="chrome://xfly/skin" type="text/css"?>
<!DOCTYPE window>
<window title="Hello xFly"
  xmlns:html="http://www.w3.org/1999/xhtml"
  xmlns="http://www.mozilla.org/keymaster/gatekeeper/there.is.only.xul"
  width="300"
  height="215"
  onload="centerWindowOnScreen()">
<script type="application/x-javascript"
  src="chrome://global/content/dialogOverlay.js" />
<script type="application/x-javascript"
  src="chrome://xfly/content/xfly.js" />
 <vbox align="left" id="vb">
  <label id="xlabel"
      value="Hello, Welcome to the xFly" />
  <image src="http://books.mozdev.org/xfly.gif" />
  <button label="hello xFly" oncommand="greet();" />
 </vbox>
</window>
```

Note that the function `greet()` is used to name the action that is performed when the button is clicked. The `greet()` function is now defined in the *xfly.js* file that the XUL file picks up with the script import statement:

```
<script type="application/x-javascript"
  src="chrome://xfly/content/xfly.js" />
```

Example 2-11 contains all of the code needed for the *xfly.js* file.

Example 2-11. The contents of the xfly.js file

```
function greet() {
  alert("Hello World");
}
```

Save *xfly.js* in the *content* subdirectory of the xFly application (*chrome/xfly/content/*). The script import statement above uses the *chrome://* URL to locate scripts from directories that were registered with Mozilla.

The xFly DTD

The final step in a basic application setup is to generalize parts of the interface that are written in a particular language, such as English. When you create a *locale* subdirectory for your package and place a DTD file that contains the English strings in the user interface, you can refer to and load that DTD just as you do with the CSS and script files.

For example, to localize the text of the label and button elements in the "hello xFly" example, you can use a special syntax to tell Mozilla to use an entity rather than a string. Because that entity is defined in *xfly.dtd* and located in the locale subdirectory, it can easily be swapped for an entity from a different language pack when the user switches languages in Mozilla.

Once again, the external file you create can be very simple. Example 2-12 contains the code needed for the *xfly.dtd* file, which you create and save in the *locale* subdirectory.

Example 2-12. The contents of the xfly.dtd file

```
<!ENTITY label.val        "Hello, Welcome to the xFly " >
<!ENTITY btn.lbl          "hello xFly " >
```

The updated XUL file that uses this external DTD, then, appears in Example 2-13. Once you have made the final changes in the XUL to refer to the external files you've created, save the code in Example 2-13 as *xfly.xul* in the *chrome/xfly/content/* directory.

Example 2-13. XUL using an external DTD file

```
<?xml version="1.0"?>
<?xml-stylesheet href="chrome://global/skin" type="text/css"?>
<?xml-stylesheet href="chrome://xfly/skin" type="text/css"?>
<!DOCTYPE window SYSTEM "chrome://xfly/locale/xfly.dtd" >
<window title="Hello xFly"
  xmlns:html="http://www.w3.org/1999/xhtml"
  xmlns="http://www.mozilla.org/keymaster/gatekeeper/there.is.only.xul"
  width="300"
  height="215"
  onload="centerWindowOnScreen()">
<script type="application/x-javascript"
  src="chrome://global/content/dialogOverlay.js" />
<script type="application/x-javascript"
  src="chrome://xfly/content/xfly.js" />
 <vbox align="left" id="vb">
  <label id="xlabel"
      value="&label.val;" />
  <image src="http://books.mozdev.org/xfly.gif" />
  <button label="&btn.lbl;" oncommand="greet();" />
 </vbox>
</window>
```

Like the CSS and script file imports, the updated `DOCTYPE` definition at the top of the file tells Mozilla to load additional entities as part of the xFly package. Those entities—the English strings that display in the user interface—are defined so they can be localized or internationalized without affecting the application's structure.

All three of these imports use the *chrome://* URL to refer to resources that are internal to the xFly package. These type of URLs can also refer to resources elsewhere in Mozilla, such as image resources, strings that have already been defined in entities, and functions from scripts such as `centerWindowOnScreen()`.

When you finish setting things up in the package directories, you should have a structure that looks like the tree structure in Example 2-14.

Example 2-14. Tree structure of a completed sample xFly package

```
chrome/
       xfly/
           content/
                  xfly.xul
                  xfly.js
                  contents.rdf
           locale/
                  xfly.dtd
                  contents.rdf
           skin/
                  xfly.css
                  contents.rdf
```

Registering a Package

Registering packages in Mozilla can be confusing at first, so don't worry about understanding everything at this point. Later chapters provide more detailed information about packaging and registration, and you can always copy the examples given here to install your own application. In general, to make your package registerable, create manifests that describe your package in terms that Mozilla can understand.

Although it's customary to make registration a part of the installation process by using the XPInstall API and installation scripts, you need a simple way to register the xFly application so you can see your work and test it as it develops. For this purpose, hacking the *installed-chrome.txt* file living in Mozilla's *chrome* directory will do.

The *installed-chrome.txt* file is a list of packages and package parts that Mozilla should find and register on start up. When you add entries to this file, you point to your package and tell Mozilla to register that package when it starts up.

Append the entries in Example 2-15 to the bottom of the *installed-chrome.txt* file in the main chrome directory.

Example 2-15. Additions to the installed-chrome.txt file

```
content,install,url,resource:/chrome/xfly/content/
skin,install,url,resource:/chrome/xfly/skin/
locale,install,url,resource:/chrome/xfly/locale/
```

When Mozilla starts up, it looks for the package manifests, reads them, and registers the xFly package.

When others install your application and use it on their machines (but do not use the hack to *installed-chrome.txt*), you can provide them with a JavaScript installation file that downloads and registers your package from a web page. See Chapter 6 for more information about these installation files and the XPInstall technology they are based upon.

Launching the Application

Once your package is registered, you can use these startup options to access your package directly.

Windows launch

In the Mozilla install directory, launch xFly at the command prompt with:

```
mozilla -chrome chrome://xfly/content/
```

You can also launch xFly from a shortcut on your desktop by right-clicking on the existing Mozilla icon and selecting Properties. In the Target area of the Properties box, add the following text at the end of the line:

```
-chrome chrome://xfly/content/
```

Figure 2-6 shows what the new properties box should look like.

Unix launch

In the Mozilla install directory, launch xFly with:

```
./mozilla -chrome chrome://xfly/content/
```

Macintosh launch

Start xFly by creating a text file on your desktop with the following content:

```
-chrome chrome://xfly/content/
```

You can either drag this text file onto your Mozilla icon to launch the application or set the text file's creator type to `MOZZ`. If you change the creator type, you should be able to double-click on the text file to launch Mozilla.

Once you register your application, you are free to continue developing it in the various component subdirectories and relaunching it as it progresses. You can add new

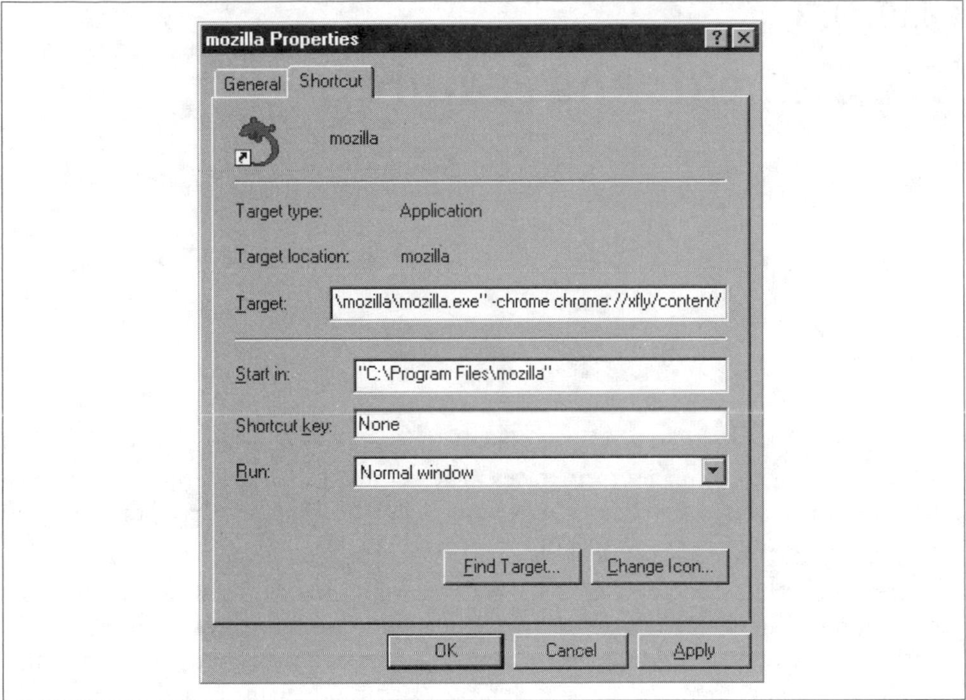

Figure 2-6. Modified shortcut properties

XUL files in the *content* directory, for example, that are invoked from buttons using `window.openDialog()` event handlers.

You can add new widgets to *xfly.xul*, add new styles to *xfly.css* that apply to the XUL, add new functions to *xfly.js*, or use existing functions in the Mozilla source code that you can find new ways to use in your own application.

The steps described in this chapter—creating a basic XUL file, adding features, displaying that XUL file as a standalone window, organizing the code into separate files and a package structure, and registering and launching that package—are the basic building blocks of all Mozilla applications. When you get a feel for what's going on here, you'll be able to quickly understand and use the topics described in the rest of the book.

CHAPTER 3
XUL Elements and Features

The XML-based User-interface Language (XUL) includes all of the basic widgets you need to build application user interfaces. These interfaces include tabs, text areas, buttons, and menus, as well as handy interfaces you may not have thought you needed, such as the `<stack>` widget or `<colorpicker>`.

Chapter 2 introduced some of the XUL elements that make up a window and basic applications. This chapter examines XUL elements and features in more detail, describing the rationale behind them, their look and behavior, and common usage. Though not comprehensive, the chapter provides more than enough information about XUL to get you started on building your own Mozilla applications, particularly when used in conjunction with the XUL reference in Appendix C.

The elements described here, such as menus, buttons, trees, and boxes, are needed in almost any type of application, and most of the examples are generic, so you can plug them into any application or customize them to your needs. We've packed a lot information in this chapter and it be a useful reference as you begin to develop your applications.

The XUL Document Object

At the core of a XUL file is the `document` object. As in HTML, `document` is an object that represents the XUL document itself—the content as opposed to the window that surrounds it. The `document` provides methods for getting individual elements, manipulating the structure of the document, or updating style rules.

A `document` object provides methods such as `getElementById`, `getElementsByTagName`, `createElement`, and `createTextNode` for DOM querying and manipulation of the actual document. Further details about the DOM are available in Chapter 5.

Other types of `document` objects include the width and height of the window, a `popupNode` property that accesses the elements currently displaying a pop up (a XUL widget that attaches to another widget and appears above it holding some content), a `tooltipNode` property that accesses the element currently displaying a tooltip, and a `documentElement` property that accesses the body of the document:

```
var docEl = document.documentElement;
var secondLevelNodes = new Array();
for (var I=0; I<docEl.childNodes.length;I++)  {
    secondLevelNodes[I] = docEl.childNodes[i];
}
```

This example creates an array of all the second-level nodes in relation to the document, and could be extended to walk to the whole tree. Using nodes in the structural representation of the document to get to other nodes in this way allows you to quickly access and change any part of a document with script.

The `document` object is global only for the particular scope that you are working in, so every window, dialog, and page has its own `document` object. To access it, just use the `document.` prefix followed by the name of the property you want to access:

```
var title = document.getElementById("bookTitle");
```

It is possible to access `document` outside the current scope—for example, the window that opened another one using `window.opener`:

```
var title = window.opener.document.getElementById("bookTitle");
```

XUL Parsing and the Document Object Model

Mozilla runs XUL documents through the Expat XML parser to check that they are well-formed. Expat is an XML parser library, written in C, that was integrated into Mozilla at the early stages of the code rewrite when the source was made open.

During parsing, a content model based on the Document Object Model (DOM) is built, allowing access to the content in a way that facilitates dynamic manipulation. Once the XML tags are in the correct namespaces, Mozilla parses the document a second time to ensure that XUL tags themselves are valid. If this fails, or if the document does not conform to the syntax rules, an error appears in your window so you can address the problem.

The parsing process builds an internal tree structure that can be used as a handle for querying, modifying, and copying documents the structure represents. Chapter 5 describes in more detail the relationship between JavaScript (the main scripting engine used in Mozilla) and the DOM, and it goes further with examples of commonly used methods for querying and modifying a XUL document. To view that internal tree, you can use a tool called the DOM Inspector, which is a Mozilla application that lets you view and manipulate the document object model of any XUL file or web page. For more information about the DOM Inspector, see Appendix B.

Application Windows

<window> is just one of the possible root elements of a XUL document, the others being <overlay>, <dialog>, <page>, and <wizard>. Overlays play an especially important role in managing and modularizing the code in your XUL application, so the section "Overlays," later in this chapter, is dedicated to them.

The remaining root elements all have the XUL namespace and XUL window attributes and properties. All have a XUL document object. Yet, added features exist for each. Which element you choose for the XUL document depends on the purpose of the window. A <window> is typically top-level, a <dialog> is secondary, appearing above another window, a <page> is a document that appears in a frame, and a <wizard> stores a set of subsections for loading one at a time through a step-by-step process.

Dialogs

Dialogs usually carry out specific functions like displaying a message or getting information from the user. The <dialog> element was created relatively late in the XUL toolkit development cycle to cater for some special needs of dialog windows, including their position relative to other windows (particularly the main application window) and the existence of buttons for accepting or rejecting a particular operation. A dialog in XUL appears in Example 3-1.

Example 3-1. XUL dialog

```
<dialog id="turboDialog" buttons="accept" buttonpack="center"
        xmlns="http://www.mozilla.org/keymaster/gatekeeper/there.is.only.xul"
        title="Empty the Cache"
        onunload="SetTurboPref();">
```

As you can see, the dialog includes the XUL namespace and the id and title attributes. However, some attributes, such as buttons and buttonpack, don't appear in a regular window context.

Dialogs commonly require the user to take some action or make a choice, so the button attributes are provided for this purpose. In addition to buttons and buttonpack, there are special event handlers on the dialog element—ondialogaccept, ondialogcancel, and ondialoghelp—that correspond to the buttons typically displayed and can execute code in response to user input. As with onunload, you can place a function in the ondialogaccept event handler that executes when the user clicks the OK button:

```
<dialog id="flush" buttons="accept" buttonpack="center"
        xmlns="http://www.mozilla.org/keymaster/gatekeeper/there.is.only.xul"
        title="&exitWarningTitle.label;"
        ondialogaccept="doCacheFlush();">
```

Pages

The <page> element is designed specifically for documents that are loaded in a frame of a higher-level document. They are not top-level windows themselves. In Mozilla, the page element is used often in the preferences dialog to represent the various preference panels.

As with the dialog in Example 3-1, the <page> element in Example 3-2 includes the familiar namespace attribute (xmlns) and load handler (onload). The headertitle attribute is also used for the top of the page, which itself gets loaded into another window that has its own title.

Example 3-2. XUL page

```
<page xmlns="http://www.mozilla.org/keymaster/gatekeeper/there.is.only.xul"
      onload="parent.initPanel('chrome://communicator/content/pref/pref-fonts.xul');"
      headertitle="&lHeader;">
```

An application of the page element in Mozilla is in the global preferences for the whole suite of Mozilla applications. Figure 3-1 shows the layout of this preferences panel. In Example 3-2, the entity in the header title, &lHeader;, resolves to "Languages" and be displayed above the individual preference panel page.

The main preferences window is a XUL dialog, and the content is split in two. On the left is a tree from an overlay that contains the preference topics, and on the right is a XUL page loaded into an <iframe>.

```
<iframe id="panelFrame" name="panelFrame" style="width:0px" flex="1"/>
```

As shown in Figure 3-1, selecting one of the topics in the left panel changes the page that is loaded into the frame. Although the changeover requires quite a bit of scripting in practice, at a basic level, it is just a case of changing the src attribute on the frame.

```
document.getElementById("panelFrame").setAttribute("src", "chrome://communicator/
content/pref/pref-navigator.xul" );
```

Wizards

This type of window is designed for a very specific type of functionality—to walk the user through a step-by-step process, with each step represented by a different screen. Using one window after another can create inconsistencies, including different sizes and performance issues. These can be especially bad when you try to create an interface that guides the user through a new process, such as setting up an account of some kind. Thus, the wizard element was adapted from the wizard paradigm now common in some native toolkits. Example 3-3 shows how Mozilla handles wizard dialogs.

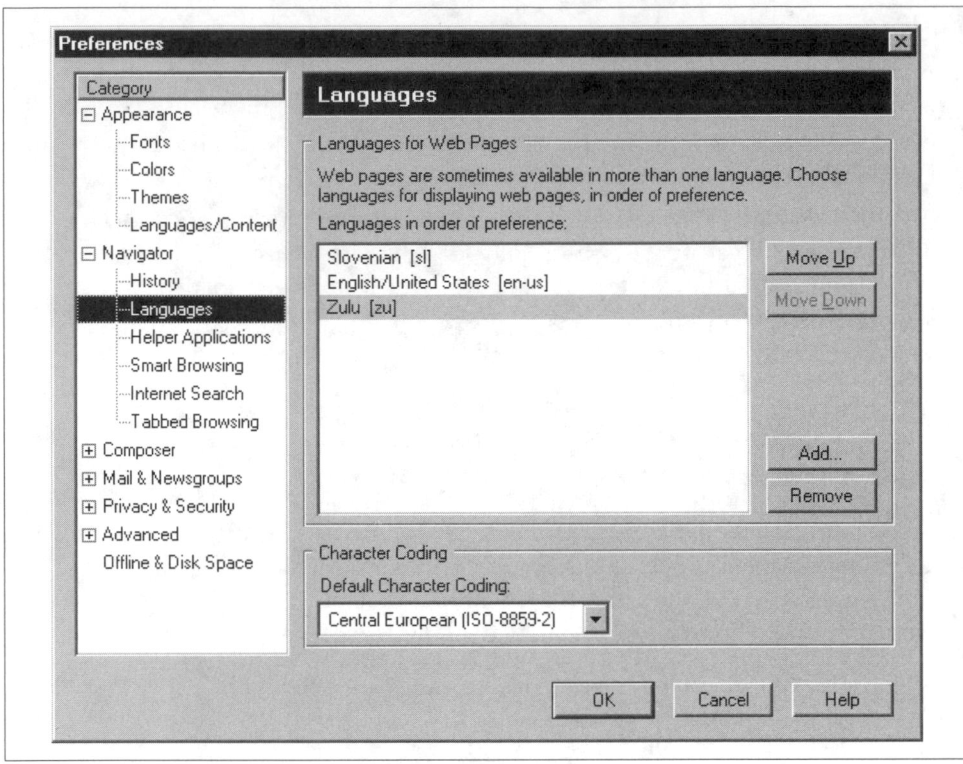

Figure 3-1. Preferences panel loaded as a page

Example 3-3. A XUL wizard

```
<wizard id="NewAccount" title="Account Set-up"
    onwizardcancel="return Cancel();"
    onwizardfinish="return Finish();"
    onload="onLoad();"
    width="44em" height="30em"
    xmlns=http://www.mozilla.org/keymaster/gatekeeper/there.is.only.xul
    xmlns:nc="http://home.netscape.com/NC-rdf#">
  <wizardpage id="wPage1" pageid="page-1" label="New Account"
      onpageshow="return acctNamePageInit();"
      onpageadvanced="nextPage(this)">
    <vbox flex="1">
      <description>Welcome and enjoy the wizardry</description>
      <image src="page1.png">
    </vbox>
  </wizardpage>
  <wizardpage id="wPage2"/>
  <wizardpage id="wPage3"/>
</wizard>
```

A `wizardpage` is similar to a page because it has a surrounding window into which it is loaded. The difference, as shown in Example 3-3, is that in the wizard, the pages exist as a set within the window-level <wizard> element. Order wizardpages in the sequence you want them to appear on the screen. When the user accepts one page, the next one is loaded. In Example 3-3, the content of the first page is text and an image, and the other pages define only id attributes (though this is exactly how you might set them up if their actual content were overlaid into this wizard at runtime). You can use the wizard code in Example 3-3 by including the <?xml version="1.0"?> preamble at the top, adding label attributes to pages two and three, and seeing the pages advance as you click the buttons that guide the wizard process when you load the XUL file into the browser.

Application Widgets

Like most applications, yours may rely on menus and toolbars as part of the basic user interface. Menus and toolbars are common, multipurpose widgets that are familiar to most users. Menus often appear as part of a menu bar that organizes all of the capabilities of the program, or they can be single menus for presenting a simple list of choices. Buttons provide quick access to the most commonly used tasks and help get information back from the user. Beyond these basics, however, XUL provides widgets for creating almost any kind of interface (and the flexibility of Mozilla's presentation layer means you can make even the most prosaic menus look any way you want).

The Toolbox

As your applications grow in complexity and provide more services to the user, the toolbox can be a good way to organize menus, toolbars, and other widgets. A <toolbox> is a special container for holding one or more toolbars and/or menu bars. A Mozilla toolbar implements a toolbargrippy and a box that contains children. The toolbargrippy is a bar on the lefthand side used for collapsing and expanding the bar. This useful method allows users to control the space that is available to them onscreen.

Toolbars

The <toolbar> element shown in Example 3-4 contains buttons used to carry out various application functions. Buttons are the most common children of a toolbar, but they are by no means the only widgets or content you can put in there.

Example 3-4. Toolbar with buttons and spacing

```
<toolbox>
  <toolbar id="fixed-toolbar" class="toolbar-primary"
      tbautostretch="always" persist="collapsed">
    <toolbarbutton id="newfileBtn" label="New" oncommand="doNew();" />
    <toolbarseparator />
```

Example 3-4. Toolbar with buttons and spacing (continued)

```
    <toolbarbutton id="openfileBtn" label="Open" oncommand="doOpen();" />
    <spacer flex="1" />
  </toolbar>
</toolbox>
```

To apply spacing between elements, the <spacer> element can be used. In Example 3-4, all space that remains after the buttons are drawn goes *after* the buttons because the spacer there is flexible and the buttons are not. Space added elsewhere with other <spacer> elements is determined by ratio of the flex values on the elements competing for layout space. Extending the toolbar in Example 3-4, you can add a print button on the far right:

```
<toolbarbutton id="newfileBtn" label="New" oncommand="doNew();" />
<toolbarseparator />
<toolbarbutton id="openfileBtn" label="Open" oncommand="doOpen();" />
<spacer flex="1" />
<toolbarbutton id="printBtn" label="Open" oncommand="doPrint();" />
```

The <toolbarseparator> element does not create additional spacing between the first two toolbarbuttons, but there is space between them and the print button, which is pushed to the far right because the flex attribute of the spacer in between is set to 1.

Menu bar

Among the other most common nested elements within a toolbox is a XUL <menubar>. <menubar> is a container much like the toolbar that has one or more menus as its children.

```
<menubar id="fixed-menubar">
  <menu label="Quantity" />
  <menu label="Color" />
</menubar>
```

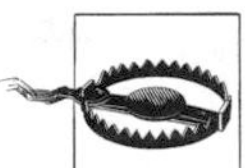

There is one caveat in menubar behavior that you should be aware of. On the Mac OS, application menu bars appear at the top of the screen. If you have any nonmenu elements contained in your menu bar widget, they are ignored because the OS does not know how to display them there.

As Example 3-5 illustrates, it's easy to build up a simple application menu and get the intrinsic look and collapsibility of a menu bar with a few simple lines of code:

Example 3-5. Application menu bar

```
<?xml version="1.0"?>
<window
   xmlns="http://www.mozilla.org/keymaster/gatekeeper/there.is.only.xul">
<menubar id="appbar">
  <menu label="File">
     <menupopup>
```

Example 3-5. Application menu bar (continued)

```
      <menuitem label="New"/>
      <menuitem label="Open"/>
    </menupopup>
  </menu>
  <menu label="Edit" />
</menubar>
</window>
```

The complete XUL file in Example 3-5 produces the menu bar in Figure 3-2.

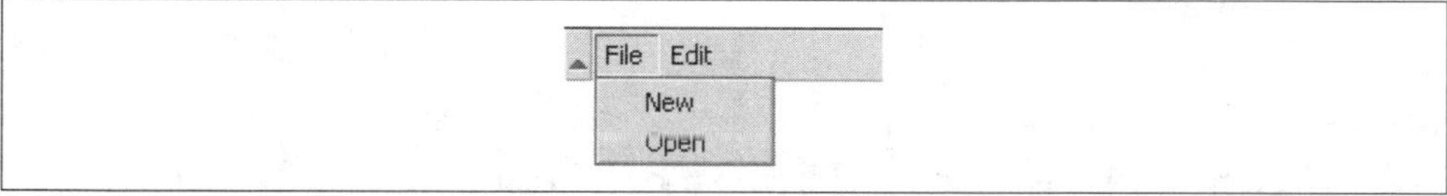

Figure 3-2. Application menu bar

Selection Lists

There are a number of ways to create lists in Mozilla. This section provides three alternative ways of presenting the same choices to the user. The options are illustrated in Figure 3-3. The one thing these three selection list widgets—*menus*, *pop ups*, and *menu lists*—have in common is they all use menu items to display individual choices:

```
<menuitem label="Tachinidae"   oncommand="changeF(1)"/>
<menuitem label="Tanyderidae"   oncommand="changeF(2)"/>
<menuitem label="Tipulidae"   oncommand="changeF(3)"/>
<menuitem label="Syrphidae"   oncommand="changeF(4)"/>
<menuitem label="Tephritidae"   oncommand="changeF(5)"/>
```

When you wrap the `menuitem` elements above in a menu, a menu list, and a pop-up window, you see the variations in Figure 3-3.

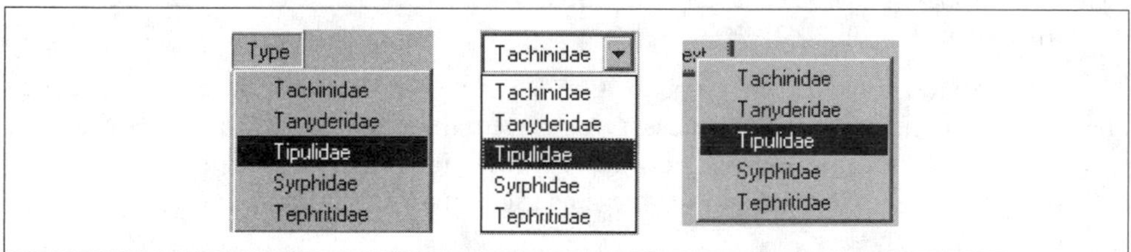

Figure 3-3. Visual comparison of menu widgets

Menus

Menus are much more flexible than they first appear to be. They can appear anywhere in the UI, for one thing, and needn't be stuck at the top of the window. They can be in buttons, trees, or just out on their own. Example 3-6 shows the basic structure of a menu.

Example 3-6. A sample menu

```
<menu label="Quantity">
  <menupopup>
    <!-- menuitems here -->
  </menupopup>
</menu>
```

There is a rigid ordering of nesting in a menu. A menu contains a <menupopup>, which in turn contains one or more menu items. Optionally, you can segregate groups of menu items by using a <menuseparator> in the pop up, which draws a thin line between items.

Pop ups

The pop up manifests as either a <menupopup> or a <popup> element. The latter can be used in a number of different ways, but Example 3-7 focuses on its common use in context menus.

Example 3-7. Context menu using pop up

```
<popup id="FlyContext"
    onpopupshowing="return doThis();"
    onpopuphiding=" return doThat();">
  <!-- menuitems here -->
</popup>
```

A couple of extra steps are needed to prepare a context pop up for activation. First, you must attach the `popup` element to a widget in the UI by using the `id` of the pop up that must correspond to the `context` of the widget:

```
<toolbar id="main-toolbar" context="FlyContext" />
```

When the toolbar is clicked, the pop up that corresponds to that value appears. You can have some script execute when you show and/or hide the pop up by using the `onpopupshowing` and `onpopuphiding` methods, as when you show and hide items in a dynamic menu.

The second step includes the pop up in a set of pop ups, enclosed in a <popupset> element. Though not strictly necessary as a container for pop ups, the pop-up set helps organize the free-floating* pop-up windows in your application and makes it easy to overlay them or overlay into them as the situation requires.

Menu lists

Another manifestation of the pop up is in the use of menu lists. A menu list is a choice of options presented to solicit a single choice, usually in the form of a drop-down menu, for which XUL provides the <menulist> element. Example 3-8 presents

* Free-floating because their location in the interface is not determined by their position in the XUL markup, as it usually is for items like menus and buttons.

a straightforward menu list with a selection of items to choose from. As in the other pop-up examples, selecting an item executes the code defined in the oncommand event handler for that item (e.g., changeF(1) for the menu item "Tachinidae").

Example 3-8. XUL menu list

```
<menulist id="FlyInput">
  <menupopup>
    <!-- menuitems here -->
  </menupopup>
</menulist>
```

The menulist widget provides functionality beyond that of a regular menu. The menu list can be made editable when the user should be allowed to enter a value not represented in the menu items. In this case, the menulist element definition in Example 3-8 would change to something such as:

```
<menulist id="FlyInput" editable="true"
    oninput="onInputFly();"
    onchange="onChangeFly();">
```

A true value on the editable attribute allows input in the list. Input can be validated immediately by using the oninput attribute. The addition of the onchange attribute can be used to carry out an extra script when a new selection is made.

Tabular and Hierarchical Information

Many options exist to display hierarchical information in your user interface. The most common are tree-like and table-like structures, both of which are represented by elements in Mozilla's XPFE toolkit. In this section, we look at list boxes, trees, and grids. With the exception of the tree, these elements are not limited in regard to the content they can contain. Currently, the tree only holds text and image content and grids are designed for holding the more diverse content as shown in upcoming examples.

List Boxes

<listbox> is used to display tabular data. Example 3-9 shows a listbox widget with all the basic features, including the definition of the number of columns (listcol), the listbox header (listhead), and a list item (listitem).

Example 3-9. Listbox widget

```
<listbox rows="5" class="list" id="FlyTree" onselect="SelectFly()">
  <listcols>
    <listcol flex="1"/>
    <splitter class="tree-splitter"/>
    <listcol flex="1"/>
  </listcols>
```

Example 3-9. Listbox widget (continued)

```
  <listhead>
    <listheader label="Name" />
    <listheader label="Type" />
  </listhead>
  <listitem id="type-d">
    <listcell label="Syrphidae" />
    <listcell label="flower" />
  </listitem>
  <!-- More Items -->
</listbox>
```

The first thing of note in the markup in Example 3-9 is the rules for the nesting of elements within a `listbox` structure. The number of columns needs to be set, each with a `<listcol>` element, and all have to be wrapped in a `<listcols>` set. Example 3-9 has two columns. They are separated by a draggable `grippy` item, which also acts as a column separator in the header row. The cells for those columns are contained in a `<listitem>` grouping. The header is optional and has the same structure as a list item. Once you've put a hierarchy like this in place, you can put the content you want into the tabular structure.

The `listbox` does not support multilevel/nested rows. Also note that the class attribute example above is what gives the tree much of its particular appearance. Listboxes and trees often use class-based style rules for their appearance and positioning (e.g., the column splitter in Example 3-9).

Example 3-9 creates the listbox in Figure 3-4.

Name	Type
Syrphidae	flower
Sophocles	dramatist

Figure 3-4. Listbox

High Performance Trees

The `<listbox>` widget is suitable only for certain kinds of content. For better scalability and multilevel capabilities, the `<tree>` was created. `<tree>` is an advanced tree widget that was originally designed for the Mail/News component in Mozilla. In its first incarnation, it was called the outliner widget.

The tree is designed for high performance in large lists, such as newsgroups, message folders, and other applications where the volume of data is expected to be high. The tree widget has a simpler, more lightweight layout, but it is more difficult to use, requiring the addition of special "views" in order to display data.

Tree features

The implementation of the tree widget is unique in the XUL universe in that it displays its content only when it comes into view, which makes it very efficient for long lists of data. Table 3-1 lists some of the main features of the tree.

Table 3-1. Main features of the tree

Row features	Column features	Visual features
Plain or hierarchical rows	Multicolumn	Each cell can display an image preceding text
Multiselection based on selection ranges	Resizing using mouse dragging	Look of each element (row, cell, image, etc.) is defined in CSS
Drag and drop, either on a row or in between rows	Column hiding using pop-up menu in top-right corner	Appearance of the drop feedback during drag-and-drop can be styled
	Reordering using drag-and-drop	Spring loaded containers that open after hovering over a closed container for a second
	Sorting by clicking on a column header; custom views can implement their own sorting	

Even with this rich set of features, however, a `tree` can display only text and image content. The `listbox` is more flexible in the type of content that appears in its cells.

Tree views

In the tree widget, a *view* is a model for the population and display of data. The view is a flexible feature of the tree that can handle everything from simple data in a content view to more dynamic data from a custom view or an RDF datasource (builder view). Table 3-2 shows the main features of each, using general categories of datasource, speed, and type of usage.

Table 3-2. Tree views

Content view	Builder view	Custom view
Rows are built from a content model.	Rows are built from an RDF datasource.	Consumer provides its own tree view implementation.
Fast but not as memory efficient (bigger footprint).	Still fast and efficient.	The fastest and most efficient way.
Suitable for small trees; easiest to use.	Relatively easy to use.	Most difficult to implement.

As already mentioned, the tree is used in the Mail/News thread pane, but there are plenty of other places to look for it in Mozilla. Custom views and tree widgets are implemented for the Address Book results, JS Debugger, DOM Inspector, Bookmarks, and for autocomplete. You can see builder views in History and a content view implementation in Preferences.

The tree content model

The content in a tree is defined with <tree>, <treecols>, <treecol>, and <treechildren> tags. Example 3-10 shows a basic column number definition (two in this instance) and a treechildren placeholder that defines the tree body.

Example 3-10. Tree base model

```
<tree id="tree" flex="1">
  <treecols>
    <treecol id="Col1" label="Col1" flex="1"/>
    <treecol id="Col2" label="Col1" flex="1"/>
  </treecols>
  <treechildren/>
</tree>
```

As in the listbox, a well-defined hierarchy of elements has to be observed. This hierarchy is part of the content model for a tree. The organization of content within a tree enforced by the specific tree elements is listed below.

Unlike listbox, nested children are possible for multilevel trees. An example of nested children appears later in this chapter in Example 3-11.

<treeitem>
: This element contains a single top-level row and all its descendants. The container attribute is used to mark this row as a container and is optional. The open attribute is used for expanded containers.

<treerow>
: The row is contained in the <treeitem> element. You may optionally set the properties attribute on the <treerow> to a whitespace-separated list of properties.

<treeseparator>
: A special element used to draw a horizontal separating line. The properties attribute is used to compute the properties that apply to the separator.

<treecell>
: The <treecell> element must appear within the <treerow> element. It specifies the text and properties that apply for a cell. The label attribute is used to set the text for the cell. The optional properties attribute is used to compute the properties that apply to the cell. The ref attribute correlates a cell within an <treerow> to the column in the tree and is optional.

Tying the concepts presented in this section together allows us to present Example 3-11, which shows a multilevel tree with two columns and two top-level rows.

Example 3-11. Multilevel tree content view

```
<tree id="tree" hidecolumnpicker="true" flex="1">
  <treecols>
    <treecol id="type" label="Type" flex="1" primary="true"/>
    <treecol id="method" label="Method" flex="1"/>
  </treecols>
  <treechildren>
    <treeitem>
      <treerow>
        <treecell label="Bike"/>
        <treecell label="Bicycle"/>
      </treerow>
    </treeitem>
    <treeitem container="true" open="true">
      <treerow>
        <treecell label="Fly"/>
        <treecell label="Wings"/>
      </treerow>
      <treechildren>  <!-- Second level row -->
        <treeitem>
          <treerow>
            <treecell label="Glide"/>
            <treecell label="Hand-Glider"/>
          </treerow>
        </treeitem>
      </treechildren>
    </treeitem>
  </treechildren>
</tree>
```

To create a new sublevel, create another <treechildren> element; inside of it, place a <treeitem>, which, in turn, contains one or more rows and cells. Figure 3-5 illustrates the result of this hierarchy.

Figure 3-5. Multilevel tree hierarchy

Using trees in XUL templates

XUL templates are special built-in structures that allow dynamic updating of XUL elements and that are often used with trees and list boxes. Templates harness the power of the Resource Description Framework (RDF) to pull data from external datasources and dynamically create or update content in the UI. The following code extract shows the basic structure of a XUL template for displaying the browser history in Mozilla:

```
<template>
  <rule>
    <treechildren>
      <treeitem uri="rdf:*" rdf:type="rdf:http://www.w3.org/1999/02/22-rdf-syntax-
            ns#type">
        <treerow>
          <treecell label="rdf:http://home.netscape.com/NC-rdf#Name"/>
          <treecell label="rdf:http://home.netscape.com/NC-rdf#URL"/>
          <treecell label="rdf:http://home.netscape.com/NC-rdf#Date"/>
          <!-- further cells -->
        </treerow>
      </treeitem>
    </treechildren>
  </rule>
</template>
```

For each entry or row in the browser history, the template extracts information from the datasource and renders it in a `treecell`. It then updates it each time a page is visited. For a more detailed discussion, refer to Chapter 9.

Custom tree views

Custom views extend upon the static presentation of data in a tree with more flexibility, different ways to present the same data, and interfaces for defining behavior related to content. The functions include intercepting a `treeitem` selection and carrying out some functionality, populating or getting values from the tree, and returning the number of rows currently in the tree.

The first thing you have to do to build a custom view is instantiate your `tree` and then associate a `view` object with it, commonly known as a view.

```
document.getElementById('main-tree').treeBoxObject.view=mainView;
```

In this example, the view that is exposed in the `nsITreeView` XPCOM object is essentially the lifeline for the tree, supplying the data that populates the view. The view is assigned to the code object that contains all the functions available to it and your implementation of what you need to do when they are activated.

Here is a large subset of the functions available to the view object:

`setTree(tree)`
: Called during initialization and used to connect the tree view to the front end. This connection ensures that the correct tree is associated with the view.

`getCellText (row,column)`
: Returns the text of a particular cell, or an empty string if there's just an image in it.

rowCount
: Set up the number of rows that you anticipate for your tree.

cycleHeader(index)
: Called when you click on the header of a particular column.

toggleOpenState
: Put code in here to be carried out when the view is expanded and collapsed.

setCellText (row, colID, value)
: Called when the contents of the cell have been edited.

performAction (action)
: An event from a set of commands can be invoked when you carry out a certain action on the outliner. The tree invokes this method when certain keys are pressed. For example, when the ENTER key is pressed, `performAction` calls with the "enter" string.

  There are more local conveniences in the form of `PerformActionOnRow` and `performActionOnCell`.

selectionChanged
: Should be hooked up to the `onselect` handler of the <tree> element in the XUL content.

Grid

A `<grid>` is another XUL table structure, designed to be more flexible with the content it can hold than the other tabular widgets. Example 3-12 shows a two-column grid that holds text input boxes and labels for them.

Example 3-12. XUL grid

```
<grid>
  <columns><column flex="1"/><column flex="2"/></columns>
  <rows>
    <row align="center">
      <label value="Title"/>
      <textbox id="title-text" oninput="TextboxInput(this.id)"/>
    </row>
    <row align="center">
      <label value="Author"/>
      <textbox id="author-text" oninput=" TextboxInput(this.id)"/>
    </row>
    <row align="center">
      <label value="About"/>
      <textbox id="about-text" oninput=" TextboxInput(this.id)"/>
    </row>
  </rows>
</grid>
```

In a grid, the number of columns needs to be defined and placed in a <columns> set. In Example 3-12, the first column holds the labels and the second contains the text boxes. These two columns are horizontal to each other and in rows for easy association. The flex is greater on the second column, allowing more space for the text input boxes. As with all examples in this chapter, you can see Example 3-12 in action by adding the XML processing instruction at the top and surrounding the grid in a basic `window` root element.

Words and Pictures

The text widgets described here are used to label other widgets, or simply to display messages or instructions to the user in the interface and include a text input widget. Images can be displayed with the main `image` element or in various ways on other elements, such as buttons or menus.

Text Input

The <textbox> element is a text input box not unlike the HTML <textarea> element. The default <textbox> element has a single line.

```
<textbox id="singleFlyInput" />
```

However, setting the `multiline` attribute makes it into a larger text area.

```
<textbox id="multiFlyInput" value="Fly Name" multiline="true" rows="4" />
```

A multiline textbox defaults to three lines unless constricted by a fixed size on a container or stretched out with flex. To force the number of lines, use the `rows` attribute. If you want to restrict the number of characters inputted, set the `size` attribute to a numeric value.

```
<textbox id="holdtheFlyInput" cols="3" rows="2" />
```

The initial value of an input widget is blank if no `value` is specified. Setting the `readonly` attribute to `true` or `false` can control editing access.

Autocomplete

Autocompletion is the process of automatically finishing a user's input by offering possible choices, or completions, when something is typed in. In Mozilla, this mechanism is simply known as *autocomplete*, and the textbox widget is used for this process in such places as the browser URL bar and in the address area of the mail compose window. Example 3-13 shows the code from the Open Web Location dialog, which provides autocompletion.

Example 3-13. Text autocomplete

```
<textbox id="dialog.input" flex="1" type="autocomplete"
    searchSessions="history" timeout="50" maxrows="6"
    disablehistory="false"
    oninput="doEnabling();">
```

Example 3-13. Text autocomplete (continued)

```
  <menupopup id="ubhist-popup" class="autocomplete-history-popup"
      popupalign="topleft" popupanchor="bottomleft"
      onpopupshowing="createUBHistoryMenu(event.target);"
      oncommand="useUBHistoryItem(event.target)"/>
</textbox>
```

The first thing to note is the nested `<menupopup>`. This pop up holds the choices in a drop-down format. The relevant attribute in this example is `type` on the `<textbox>`, which has a value of `autocomplete`.

Figure 3-6 shows the `autocomplete` widget. As the user types the URL into the textbox, auto completion kicks in and the values are retrieved to show in the pop-up list, from which the user can then choose. When similar values are input regularly, `autocomplete` can be a great time-saving feature.

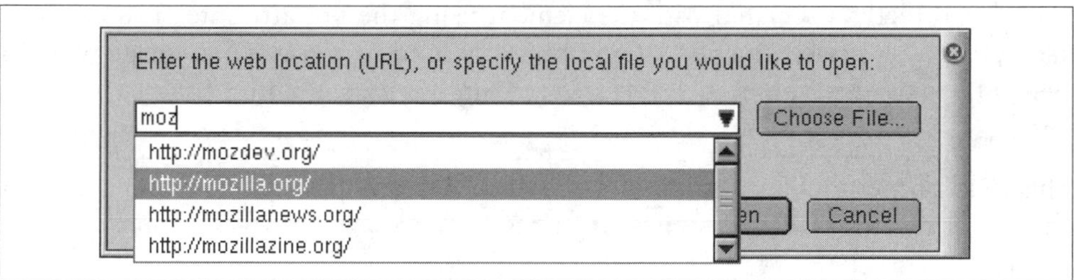

Figure 3-6. Autocomplete for Open Web Location

Text Display

Three tags available in XUL handle basic text display in the UI, and each has its own context for use. They include a `<caption>`, a `<label>`, and a `<description>` element.

The caption is designed specifically for the text that appears inline in the border of a group box. You can control where the caption appears by putting the caption element above or below the other content in the group box:

```
<groupbox id="textWidgetsBox">
    <caption id="textTitle" label="Text Widgets"/>
    <!-- content here -->
</groupbox>
```

`label` is more flexible than `caption` because it isn't tied to a particular widget and can even be used as a standalone.

For longer text, the `<description>` element is best. You can embed text in the description element and have it wrap to the maximum size of the containing element:

```
<decription>
The mozdev.org site provides free project hosting for the Mozilla community. You are
welcome to take a look at the more than 60 projects hosted on the site or to start
your own development project.
</decription>
```

Or you can use the value attribute when you're sure the text will not overflow. In this case, <description> is interchangeable with the <label> element for use in identifying other items in the UI:

```
<description value="Start a project today." />
```

Images

XUL supports the display of images in the native web formats of JPEG, PNG, and GIF. Most images you will find in the Mozilla UI are GIF files, which retain the best quality when compressed. Chapter 4 discusses theme issues and considerations in more detail. The basic syntax for displaying an image is:

```
<image src="myImage.png" />
```

The <image> element is analogous to the HTML <img> element. The image to be displayed is directly associated with the element using the src attribute. You can also use list-style-image, which is a CSS2 property used to associate an image with an element. To do this, you need a style *selector*—in this case, the id.

```
<image id="foo" />
```

The style property takes a value of src, which has one parameter, the image, or a chrome or resource URL pointing to the image.

```
#foo {
    list-style-image: url("myImage.png");
}
```

src is good for single images and for convenience, but in general, using the CSS property is recommended because it follows the principal of separating functionality from presentation and it better fits into a theme-swapping architecture, as used in the Mozilla suite.

Many in the open source community feel that PNG would have been a more natural choice for the project because it is a free format. Efforts to make this switch have been held up by a bug in gamma-corrected CSS color values and specified in both CSS1 and CSS2.

Images in other XUL elements

Image display is not the sole province of the image element. Using the list-style-image property, you can attach images to almost any element. For example, the tree widget has a couple of its own special associated CSS properties that allow you to define list-style-image values. -moz-tree-image defines images contained in a cell, and it takes input parameters that let you specify the id of the specific column and row to which the image should be applied:

```
treechildren:-moz-tree-image(col-id,row-id) {
     list-style-image: url("chrome://xfly/skin/images/outliner.gif");
}
```

Also, -moz-tree-twisty allows you define an image for the twisty that is used to open and close a level in a tree.

```
treechildren:-moz-tree-twisty {
    list-style-image: url("chrome://xfly/skin/images/twisty.gif");
}
```

The example above uses a parameter of open, but if no parameter is specified, the default is closed, so you can have a different image for both states.

The <tab> widget can also take a list-style-image property in CSS.

```
<tab id="TabOne" class="tabbies" selected="1" label="Click Me!"
oncommand="SelectTab(1);" />
```

In this case, the class attribute is used as a selector for associating the element with the style rule in which the image is referenced:

```
.tabbies {
    list-style-image: url("chrome://xfly/skin/images/tab.gif");
}
```

Form Controls

In the HTML world, the textbox is one of the most commonly used elements in a form control. While the XPFE toolkit has no concept of a form, it was originally designed to allow HTML in the UI when needed, but only on a limited scale. Although it's still possible to incorporate HTML when you use the correct namespace, the existence of XUL widgets such as the textbox, checkbox and radio group selector obviates the need for HTML elements.

Radio

Radio groups are useful UI controls that present the user with a choice of options in XUL. In HTML, radio choices are represented by the <INPUT> element with the type attribute set to the value of radio, all wrapped in a form element. Example 3-14 shows how to make radio group choices in XUL.

Example 3-14. A radio group choice of options

```
<radiogroup id="flyTypes" orient="vertical">
  <radio id="tachina" group="flyTypes" label="Tachinidae"
    oncommand="chooseType(this);"/>
  <radio id="primitive-crane" group="flyTypes" label="Tanyderidae"
    oncommand="chooseType(this);"/>
  <radio id="crane" group="flyTypes" label="Tipulidae"
    oncommand="chooseType(this);"/>
  <radio id="flower" group="flyTypes" label="Syrphidae"
    oncommand="chooseType(this);"/>
  <radio id="fruit" group="flyTypes" label="Tephritidae"
    oncommand="chooseType(this);"/>
</radiogroup>
```

The options must be enclosed in the <radiogroup> element, and each one is represented by a <radio> element. The important attributes are the id on the <radiogroup> and the group attribute on the <radio> elements. These attributes have to be identical to ensure that only one option at a time can be chosen. The this keyword in JavaScript lets you access the selected item in a straightforward way. In this case, it sends the node to the script every time an option is selected.

Checkbox

A checkbox is a simpler widget that needn't be part of a selection group. It is often used to indicate if some functionality should be turned on or off, as shown in Figure 3-7.

```
<checkbox id="closeWindow"
    label="Close this window when download is complete"
    checked="true" />
```

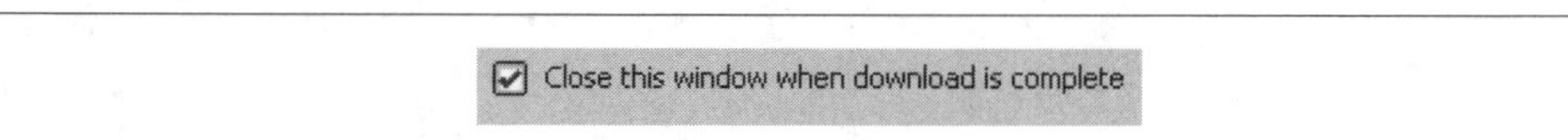

Figure 3-7. Checkbox widget

Clicking on the box sets the clicked attribute, for which the check indicates a positive value. You can set this attribute in script to give the checkbox an initial value.

Buttons

A button is a multipurpose widget that commonly lives in toolbars and dialog boxes. The two button elements, <button> and <toolbarbutton>, are essentially the same. Often only the class attribute values distinguish the two. You can use a <toolbarbutton> outside a toolbar or use a <button> inside a toolbar, though in practice, the two usually stay in their respective domains. This flexibility has the nice effect of letting you get the buttons in a particular area by using the getElementsByTagName method with, for example, the tag name "button."

A common form of the button contains text and an image, with image on the left and the text to the right by default. However, you may want to take advantage of some of the classes available in Mozilla to define a different orientation, or you can simply write your own style rules for your buttons.* The text that appears on the button is contained in the label attribute and shown in this example:

```
<button id="newfileBtn"
    tooltiptext="New File"
```

* Unfortunately, button skins and the class attributes that associate them with button widgets change too often to list here. Some classes like "toolbar-primary" tend to be reused often for buttons in Mozilla, but the best way to find and use classes is to consult the source code itself or to create your own.

```
        oncommand="doNew()"
        label="New"/>
```

You can associate the image with the button using the src attribute, but the more common way is to use the list-style-image style rule in CSS, as in the following snippet of code that uses the id style selector:

```
    #newfileBtn
    {
        list-style-image:    url("chrome://editor/skin/images/newfile.gif");
    }
```

Button types

Mozilla provides more than the standard "click" and "go" buttons in its toolkit. Table 3-3 describes the various button types in Mozilla.

Table 3-3. Button types

Type	Usage	Description
Menu	type="menu"	Menu integrated into the button with small arrow icon
Dual Menu	type="menu-button"	Menu appears distinct from the button, in separate clickable area
Checkbox	type="checkbox"	When selected, remains in a depressed state and toggles back to its natural state when selected again
Radio	type="radio"	Designed to be part of a group; only one button is selectable at a time
Disclosure	dlgtype="disclosure"	Shows/Hides a portion of a dialog window
Default	dlgtype="accept"	Performs the default action for a dialog
Cancel	dlgtype="cancel"	Closes the dialog and does not carry out the default action
Help	dlgtype="help"	Activates context-sensitive help

Taking one of the button types in Table 3-3 as a mini-case study, you could use a button with the type menu-button to display more than one option at a time. The default orientation for this type of button is for the menu to be to the right of the button. Mozilla uses buttons of type menu-button for its back and forward buttons, in which the menu items hold previously visited pages. Figure 3-8 shows the appearance of the browser's back button displaying the last several pages viewed.

Other possible uses include options for different variations of the same feature, such as a New button that displays New File, New Project, or New Template options. The button action is the default option and the menuitems contain the rest of the choices.

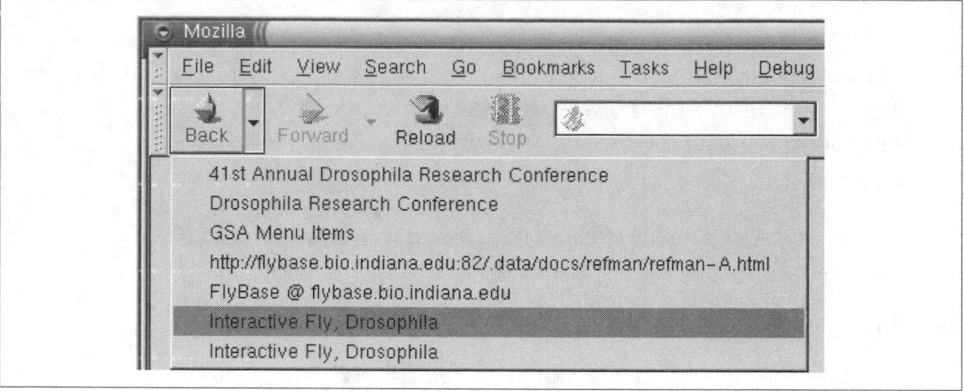

Figure 3-8. menu-button for browser's back functionality

Dialog buttons

The last four items in Table 3-3 are button types that make most sense in, and were designed especially for, dialog windows. The easiest way to include them in dialogs is to use the buttons attribute on the <dialog> element, which displays them automatically, as shown here:

```
<dialog
  xmlns="http://www.mozilla.org/keymaster/gatekeeper/there.is.only.xul"
    buttons="accept,cancel,help"
    buttonpack="center"
    ondialogaccept="return onAccept();"
    ondialogcancel="return onCancel();"
    ondialoghelp="return doHelpButton();">
```

The functions activated when these buttons are clicked on are defined in the ondialogaccept, ondialogcancel, and ondialoghelp event handler attributes. These event handler shortcuts are best if you simply want to inherit the default button text (Ok, Cancel, and Help). In cases when you want your own text, or want some extra control over the scripting, you can define your own button with the dlgtype attribute:

```
<button dlgtype="accept"
    label="Go For It!"
    oncommand="doExtraFunction()"/>
```

The buttonpack attribute determines whether the buttons appear on the right, left, or center of the window. If no value is given, the default platform orientation takes effect. On Windows, the default is the right, and on Unix, it's the center.

Widget Interaction

At a level above the use of widgets for different, singular functions in the application interface, Mozilla provides tools for hooking things together and creating application logic that can make your interfaces work more consistently and handle more complex tasks. If you have different elements in your application that execute the same function, for example, the command and observer system is the ideal way to facilitate reuse. Or you can use command sets to define command sets and key sets that can be overlaid and made available in different parts of your application, similar to how the cut and paste commands and others are spread over the Mozilla user interface but defined in a centralized file.

Broadcaster and Observers

Broadcasters and observers are a mechanism for making any number of elements aware of state and event information from a single, "broadcasting" element. That broadcasting element can be an actual `<broadcaster>` or a regular element that broadcasts its state with special attributes. A common example of broadcasting is the disabling of a group of elements—a menu item and a separate button for viewing source, for example—when the source for a web page is not available.

The state of a broadcaster has to be changed explicitly for its observers to be updated:

```
<broadcasterset>
  <broadcaster id="save_command" disabled="false"/>
</broadcasterset>
```

Once a broadcaster is defined, a XUL file may define elements that observe the broadcast command:

```
<button id="new" label="Save File" observes="save_command"/>
<key id="key_new" xulkey="true" key="s" observes="save_command" />
<menuitem id="new_menuitem" label="New" observes="save_command"/>
```

Observing elements can also be more specific about the attribute they want to mimic. This is done by using the `<observes>` element:

```
<menuitem id="new_menuitem" value="New" observes="open_new"/>
 <observes element="open_new" attribute="disabled"/>
</menu>
```

The `element` attribute associates the broadcaster and `attribute` tells the `<menuitem>` element to mimic the behavior of the broadcaster's "`disabled`" attribute.

Commands

Any number of commands can be contained in a `<commandset>`, and multiple sets can exist for different events in your application. It is also possible for sets to contain other command sets, mixed with commands or on their own. The idea is that there will be one base set that all other sets must inherit from; this base set can be defined in the top-level XUL file for your application. The following code has a command set that has its own commands and that pulls in a second set defined elsewhere (`moreEditItems`).

```
<commandset id="EditItems"
        oncommandupdate="updateCommandsetItems(this)"
        commandupdater="true" events="select">
    <commandset id="moreEditItems" />
    <command id="cmd_cut" oncommand="goDoCommand('cmd_cut');"/>
    <command id="cmd_copy" oncommand="goDoCommand('cmd_copy');"/>
    <command id="cmd_delete" oncommand="goDoCommand('cmd_delete');"/>
</commandset>
```

The command updater is the mechanism used to pass command events between widgets in the UI. When an event is carried out, the message filters through to the command sets. Thus in the example above, if the `select` event is activated, all UI elements in this `commandset` become active. For example, setting the `disabled` attribute on a command set for saving disables all functional elements depending on it—such as a menu item, a toolbar button, or a pop-up menu.

There are a number of ways to trigger the command updater. First, associate a widget with a particular command by using the `command` attribute:

```
<button id="cut-item" label="Cut" command="cmd_cut" enabled="true"/>
```

When this button is clicked, the command (`cmd_cut`) is located and carried out, firing the `goDoCommand` routine for that particular command.

Alternatively, your application might have a select event for a text element or an image. When the select event is fired, the message filters through to the command set, which, in turn, updates (by using `oncommandupdate`) the widgets-associated button with the commands.

The <keyset> element is a container for key elements. Key elements are used to execute commands from a keystroke combination. The keys Ctrl-Shift-s can be defined to execute a Save As command in your application (and that command can actually be defined in a `command` element):

```
<key id="key_saveas" key="s" modifiers="control,shift" command="cmd_saveas"/>
```

The key element has various special attributes like `key`, which is used to set an identifier shortcut key, or the `modifiers` attribute to set the trigger key. For example, `modifiers="accel"` would be the Ctrl key on Windows and GTK Unix platforms and the command button on Macintosh.

Example 3-15 shows a simple window that you can load up that has all element sets: commands, broadcasters, and keys.

Example 3-15. Shortcut keys with command observers

```
<?xml version="1.0"?>
<window id="hello-goodbye"
    title="Hello Goodbye"
    xmlns:html="http://www.w3.org/1999/xhtml"
    xmlns="http://www.mozilla.org/keymaster/gatekeeper/there.is.only.xul"
    style="min-width:100px;min-height:100px;background-color:white;">
```

Example 3-15. Shortcut keys with command observers (continued)

```
  <broadcasterset id="broadcasterset">
    <broadcaster id="cmd_hello"oncommand="alert('Hello There!');"/>
  </broadcasterset>
  <keyset id="keyset">
    <key id="key_h"key="H"observes="cmd_hello"modifiers="accel,shift"/>
    <key id="key_g"key="G"command="cmd_goodbye"modifiers="accel,shift"/>
  </keyset>
  <commandset id="commandset">
    <command id="cmd_goodbye"oncommand="alert('Goodbye!');"/>
  </commandset>
  <spacer flex="1"/>
  <label value="hello/goodbye"/>
  <textbox value="type ctl+shft+h"/>
  <textbox value="type ctl+shft+g"/>
  <spacer flex="1"/>
</window>
```

Content Panels

Content widgets allow you to load content into the UI for display. These widgets—`browser` and `editor`—provide a window into which you can load. In the standard browser, these documents can be written in HTML, XML, text, or other supported content types.

Browser and IFrame

The `<browser>` element displays online content and provides full browsing capabilities to your application, such as navigation features or maintaining a history.

```
<browser id="content" type="content-primary" src="ch3.html"/>
```

The behind-the-scenes implementation for `browser` gives you access to certain interfaces that can be used in your scripts. These interfaces include:

- nsIDocShell
- nsIWebNavigation
- nsIMarkupDocumentViewer
- nsIContentViewerEdit
- nsIContentViewerFile
- nsIWebBrowserFind
- nsIDocumentCharsetInfo

Without going into detail, these interfaces all provide sophisticated functionality for web browsing and other browser-like services, and are made available to JavaScript in the application interface. You can explore them further by looking at the interfaces themselves—at the IDL files of the same name in the Mozilla source tree.

If you would like to learn more about these available interfaces, the best place to look is the source code. The two recommended files to start with are *browser.xml*, which shows how the interfaces are exposed, and *navigator.js*, which shows how they are used. Both files can be browsed on the online Mozilla Cross Reference, at *http://lxr.mozilla.org*.

An alternative to `<browser>` is the `<iframe>`. It's similar to the browser widget in appearance, but better suited for simple or ephemeral content. It's often used as a preview window in HTML/XML editors and other WYSIWYG applications. iframes can also be good for dynamic document editing, as in the following example, in which the frame provides access to the document loaded as content. This can then be written to:

```
<iframe id="simple-content" />
```

The document's `open()`, `write()`, and `close()` methods, which are standard in the JavaScript engine, are used to write to the document:

```
var doc = window.frames[1].document;
doc.open();
doc.write("<html><body>Come fly with me ...</body></html>");
doc.close();
```

In this code snippet, you get a handle to the particular frame that you want by using `window.frames`, which returns an array of all frames contained in a document. There can be multiple frames in a document, which are indexed. Here it is assumed that we get the second (1 in a zero-based array) frame. The `doc` variable has a reference to the content area and uses the methods available on the `document` object to write content—in this case, HTML.

Ideas for using content panels include:*

- Create HTML or XML help pages for your application and upload them in a ready-made help browser.
- Create a previewer: test your XML, HTML, or CSS layout and styling in Gecko—one of the most standards-compliant layout engines around.
- A slight variation of the previous use, you could use mini-versions inline in dialogs to load up examples that change depending on the selection of the user from a number of choices (a font previewer, for example).
- Pop ups contained in a window for display of web content.

* Note that these examples are distinct from embedding the Gecko layout engine in your generic application. A separate toolkit and a set of APIs is available for doing this.

Editor

The <editor> element loads editable content and can handle text or HTML editing. A good example of its usage is in Mozilla Composer, the HTML editor that comes bundled with Mozilla.

The <editor> tag creates an instance of the *nsEditorBoxObject* interface when it's initialized. From that point, you can use JavaScript (via the `element.editorShell` property) to get to the `editorShell` methods for carrying out editing on the loaded document.

The editor is also used in the various XUL and HTML text widgets in Mozilla, such as `textbox` and HTML forms, and for composing HTML messages in Mail and News. The text widgets differ from the full-blown `editor` because they act on a subtree of the document. Also, text widgets have limited text-editing services.

Uses for the editor, both practical and speculative, include:

- Plain text editor
- Web forms editor
- An HTML-enabled bulletin board, a guestbook entry form, or a Wiki that is a web interface collaboration area for posting comments
- Instant Messaging

Keeping Track in Multiframe Documents

The content contained in a <browser>, <iframe>, and <editor> is treated as a separate document. At times, you may want to access that specific content, so how do you keep track of different content?

To return all the content frames in a document, you can use:

```
var contentAreas = content.frames;
```

There are two ways to access specific content in a script: through the index of the frame within the containing document or by using the `id` attribute.

By index, starting at 0:

```
var content = window.frames[ 1 ];
```

By `id`:

```
var content = window.frames[ contentId ];
```

This code returns the second frame.

To flag one as default, use the `type` attribute and give it a value.

```
<iframe id="print-panel" type="content-primary" src="about:blank" flex="1""/>
```

This code allows quick access to the default via the `window.content` property:

```
window.content.print();
```

The Box Model

The *box model* is the basic layout mechanism in XUL. Although it's possible to position your widgets in a window by using layout attributes of the `window` (a box-based container), using boxes allows you to arrange, nest, and position your widgets the way you want. The box model defines:

- How much space elements take up in relation to their siblings and containing elements
- The orientation of elements
- The relationship of elements to one another

Space can be determined in a number of ways. You can constrain size by putting fixed sizes on windows or the widgets contained therein. Or you can let the natural sizes take effect and let the elements size themselves according to their content. Applying boxes to your layout uses space efficiently and optimizes the layout of your XUL windows and dialogs.

Box Attributes

The XUL element `<box>` defines a number of attributes and some implicit behavior for layout. Boxes can be oriented within other boxes to define the general layout of the UI. Some boxes stretch to fit the space available within the top-level window or their containing element; others take only as much space as needed to display their own children.

Attributes on the box and its child elements determine the flexibility of the content contained within the box, the way that windows are resized, and the alignment of elements, as Table 3-4 describes.

Table 3-4. Common box attributes

Attribute	Values	Default value	Description
align	start | end | center | baseline | stretch | inherit	stretch	Determines how the children are aligned in conjunction with the box's orientation
flex	<number> | inherit	0.0	Determines the flexibility of the contained elements, which depends on their particular flex values
style	CSS property and value	N/A	Applies CSS style settings to the box
orient	horizontal | vertical | inline-axis | block-axis | inherit	inline-axis	Determines the layout of the children of the box

Table 3-4. Common box attributes (continued)

Attribute	Values	Default value	Description
pack	start | end | center | justify | inherit	start	Determines the use of remaining whitespace once all other objects are stretched to their full size
direction	normal | reverse | inherit	normal	Determines the direction of the children in the box
ordinal-group	<integer> | inherit	1	Controls the order in which widgets appear in a box

The attribute names in Table 3-4 (with the exception of `style`) are defined directly on the box. But there are also CSS versions of these properties that use the prefix `box-pack` becomes `box-pack` when it's defined in CSS, for example. These properties are not part of the CSS specification, so you may need to go one step further and use the format `-moz-box-pack`. These special extensions to CSS are described in the section "Special Mozilla Extensions" in Chapter 4.

The most commonly used attributes are `orient`, `align`, and `pack`. The orientation of the children of a box can be either vertical or horizontal. The default is horizontal for a plain `<box>`, but not for all box containers (`<groupbox>` is vertical). The `<vbox>` and `<hbox>` conveniences were created to bypass the use of this attribute and increase box layout efficiency in the rendering phase.

Here is a look at how the pack and align properties can effect the layout of widgets. First, here is a bit of code with no constraints:

```
<vbox style="width: 90px; height: 90px">
  <button label="Pack Me!" />
  <label value="This text is naturally aligned to the left" />
</vbox>
```

This XUL does not tell the button and text inside where to go, so they occupy the default positions shown in Figure 3-9.

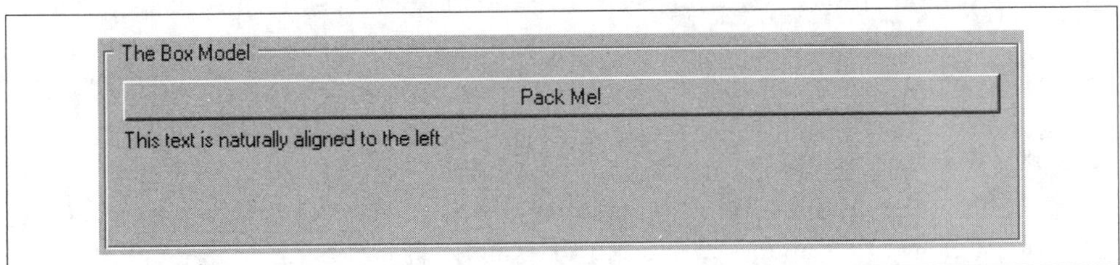

Figure 3-9. Default box positioning

Here is a changed box definition with the `align` and `pack` attributes set:

```
<vbox style="width: 90px; height: 90px" align="right" pack="center">
```

A noticeable visual difference can be seen in Figure 3-10.

Figure 3-10. Box packing and alignment effects

The `align` value moves the items to the right of the `box`, while simultaneously constraining the `button` to fit only the text `label`, making better use of space. `pack` centers both the items horizontally.

Box-Like Containers

The basic XUL box is represented by the `<box>`, `<vbox>`, and `<hbox>` elements, but several more XUL elements are designed as box-like containers. They include:

- `<radiogroup>`
- `<scrollbox>`
- `<tabbox>`
- `<groupbox>`
- `<toolbox>`
- `<stack>`
- `<deck>`
- `<listbox>`
- `<popup>`
- `<statusbar>`

Descriptions of the tabbed box and the group box follow. Additional information on other box widgets can be found in the XUL element reference in Appendix C.

Tab box

Tab boxes may contain only `<tabs>` and `<tabpanels>` elements, as shown in Example 3-16. Beyond this, there is no restriction on the content that can go into the panels themselves. For the panels to display content properly, there have to be the same number of children and tabs in the tab panels.

Example 3-16. Tabbed panels

```
<tabbox orient="vertical" flex="1">
  <tabs>
    <tab label="Fish" />
    <tab label="Birds" />
```

Example 3-16. Tabbed panels (continued)

```
    <tab label="Coders" />
  </tabs>
  <tabpanels flex="1">
    <button label="Swim"/>
    <button label="Fly"/>
    <button label="Hack"/>
  </tabpanels>
</tabbox>
```

Example 3-16 shows the main controls used to create a simple three-tab control with content elements on each panel. The tabs are associated with the appropriate panels by their order within the containing element.

Status bar

A status bar is a horizontal box that appears on the bottom of the screen in many Mozilla applications, including the Mozilla browser itself. It can be used for the same purpose in your application if you need it. The `<statusbar>` element typically contains icon images and text within one or more `<statusbarpanel>` elements:

```
<statusbar id="ch3-bar" persist="collapsed">
  <statusbarpanel class="statusbarpanel-iconic" id="book-icon"/>
  <statusbarpanel id="status-text" label="Thanks for reading chapter 3"
      flex="1" crop="right"/>
  <statusbarpanel class="statusbarpanel-iconic" id="book-icon-2"/>
</statusbar>
```

As a box, the statusbar behaves like any other box widget. The panels constrain to their natural sizing and layout attributes such as flex situate all elements within. In this example, the icons appear to the left and right of the bar, while the flexed text panel takes up the remaining space.

Additional Box Features

Boxes work in concert with a few other special elements, including the `<separator>` and `<spacer>`. These two elements create space between widgets in a box and can be horizontal or vertical depending on the orientation of the box. The separator is a visible divider and the spacer is invisible space. The default size for both of them is small, but they can be given `flex`, `width`, and `height` values like other elements. Used correctly, they can make all the difference in how your UI looks.

Visibility

You can control the visibility of a box by showing and hiding it in different circumstances—toggling the appearance of an advanced panel in a dialog, for example, or text that appears after a user selects something. One way to control visibility is to use the `collapsed` attribute to cede the space taken by the box to surrounding elements:

```
<box flex="1" collapsed="true" />
```

You can also set the CSS `display` property to `none`:

```
<box flex="1" style="display: none;" />
```

The document is rendered as though the element did not exist in the document tree. If you want the space to be maintained but the element to remain invisible, you can use the CSS `visibility` property:

```
<box flex="1" style="visibility: hidden;" />
```

Rendering the space but not the content avoids flicker and UI wobbles when content is being shown and hidden intermittently.

Overflow

A value of `scroll` or `auto` for the CSS `overflow` property ensures that a scrollbar appears and that the content can be accessed even when it can't be displayed. A value of `hidden` hides the content outside of the box. The content is not clipped if this value is set to `visible`, but it will be visible outside the box.

```
<vbox flex="1" style="height:39px;overflow: auto;">
```

This snippet constrains the height of the box but displays a scrollbar when the content exceeds the available space.

Stacks and Decks

A variant and special model of the `box` is available in the `stack` and `deck` elements. Both are boxes, but they lay their children out one on top of the other like a stack of crates or a deck of cards, rather than sequentially.

A `stack` shows all its levels at once. If you have transparency or extra space on one level, you can see underneath. Stacks are useful when you want to add shadows in your content or if you want to create transparent layering effects. If you have a bird's eye view of XUL content, you can see the elements on each layer flowing into each other, like the text on top of an image in Figure 3-11.

```
<stack>
  <image src="logo5.gif"/>
  <label value="BUZZ ..."
      style="font-weight:bold; font-size: large" top="70px" left="140px"/>
</stack>
```

Figure 3-11. Text stacked on an image

Decks show only one level at a time. In Example 3-17, *logo3.gif* is foremost because the selectedIndex attribute on the deck is set to 2 in a zero-based index.

Example 3-17. A deck with three image layers

```
<deck id="fly-deck" selectedIndex="2">
  <image src="logo1.gif" />
  <image src="logo2.gif" />
  <image src="logo3.gif" />
</deck>
```

As Example 3-18 shows, it is possible to switch pages using the DOM by changing the index on the deck. The setAttribute method changes the selectedIndex attribute of the deck element in script and can be executed, for example, when a user clicks a button or in other places in the interface.

Example 3-18. Deck layer switching

```
var deck = document.getElementById("fly-deck");
var selected = deck.getAttribute("selectedIndex");
if (!selected)
    selected = 0;
if (selected < 2)  {
    selected = parseInt(selected) + 1;
    deck.setAttribute("selectedIndex", selected);
}
else  {
    selected = 0;
    deck.setAttribute("selectedIndex", selected);
}
```

When applied to the deck in Example 3-17, the code in Example 3-18 continuously flips to the next image in the sequence and returns to the top of the deck when the last image is reached. In this case, there are only three images, so a maximum of 2 is put on the index check.

Moveable content

At one point in XUL toolkit development, an element called the bulletinboard allowed you to layer child elements one on top of another like its real-world namesake. You could change the coordinates of the child elements on the screen by using the top and left attributes. The order of the children in the XUL content determines the z-ordering on screen. As stack developed and took on much of this functionality, bulletinboard was officially deprecated and some of its properties were merged back into the stack element. As Example 3-19 demonstrates, this was a boon for the stack element, which can use coordinates to position children like its ancestor. The two boxes in the example are positioned at varying distances away from the stack's top left corner.

Example 3-19. Content positioning in a stack

```
<stack>
 <box id="box1" top="20px" left="40px">
  <image src="logo1.gif" />
 </box>
 <box id="box2" top="40px" left="50px">
  <image src="logo2.gif" />
 </box>
</stack>
```

You can position the two boxes, each containing an image, in any of the following ways:

- By placing the top and left attributes directly on the tags
- By setting them via stylesheets using the CSS properties top and left
- By using DOM calls in your script

Here is some script used to switch the position of the boxes from one location to another by changing the top and left attributes:

```
Box1=document.getElementById("box1")
Box1.setAttribute("top","40px")
Box1.setAttribute("left","50px")
Box2=document.getElementById("box2")
Box2.setAttribute("top","20px")
Box2.setAttribute("left","40px")
```

XUL Attributes

Each XUL element has an attributes property that contains an array of all its attributes. This section summarizes some of the general XUL attributes that developers find useful, including debug.

Stretchiness

An object becomes flexible when the flex attribute is placed on the element. Flexible objects can shrink or grow as the box shrinks and grows. Whenever extra space is left over in a box, the flexible objects are expanded to fill that space. Flex is specified as a numerical value, and all flex is relative. For example, a child with a flex of 2 is twice as flexible as a child with a flex of 1, as Example 3-20 shows. The flex attribute is invaluable for positioning elements in the box model.

Example 3-20. Flexible buttons

```
<?xml version="1.0"?>
<?xml-stylesheet href="chrome://global/skin" type="text/css"?>
<window
   xmlns="http://www.mozilla.org/keymaster/gatekeeper/there.is.only.xul">
```

Example 3-20. Flexible buttons (continued)

```
<box id="parent" style="margin: 50px;">
  <button flex="2" label="flex2" />
  <button flex="1" label="flex1" />
</box>
</window>
```

Style

The style attribute allows you to apply CSS style properties to your XUL element directly within the content. The attribute lets you access CSS properties (including width, height, min-width, min-height, max-width, and max-height), which give you more control over the size of your widget.

```
<button style="height: 20px; background-color: blue;" />
```

Don't use the style attribute too often, though, especially if you want to have more than one theme for your application. See the section "Inline styles" in Chapter 4 for information about how this attribute can make your application less modular and, for some, a better way to apply style to your XUL documents.

Persistence

The persist attribute preserves the state and appearance of a widget on an attribute-by-attribute basis. This feature is useful for properties that change or are set by users during a session, such as window size and positioning, splitter state, and the visibility of certain elements.

```
<splitter id="sidebar-splitter" collapse="before"
    persist="state hidden" align="center" orient="vertical">
```

When the state of the splitter changes—when a user handles the <grippy> and collapses the splitter, for example, and then quits—the persist attribute preserves the splitter state and its visibility for the next session.

The debug Attribute

Many of XUL elements, particularly container elements like box and toolbar, support the debug attribute as a useful tool for developers. If debug is set to true, extra borders are drawn around the element and all its children, with different color coding for each level. This setting can be used to check the orientation and the flexibility of elements. debug displays horizontal boxes with a blue border and vertical boxes with a red border, for example, making it easy to see subtle differences or layout bugs. The border above the element will be straight for nonflexible elements and grooved for flexible elements.

Overlays

An overlay is a separate file in which additional XUL content can be defined and loaded at runtime. Overlays are often used to define things like menus that appear in different components or parts of the application.

If you are creating a large application or a UI with many elements as a part of your design, the files can easily become large. The size in itself does not render it ineffective, but it does make the job of the developer a little difficult when tracking down and changing features. The best way to overcome this size problem is to use overlays. Another reason to use overlays is to extract information from a certain logical portion of the UI and contain it in a file of its own. This extraction and containment promotes modularization and reusability.

How to Use Overlays

The following declaration is the principal method for including reusable content in a XUL window.

```
<?xul-overlay href="chrome://global/content/globalOverlay.xul"?>
```

This declaration follows the same syntax as CSS processing instructions. Like other XML processing instructions, it uses a ? at the beginning and end, just inside the braces. The `href` attribute points to the overlay and uses Mozilla's *chrome://* type URL.

To insert content from an overlay, use the same `id` of an element in the "base file" for a similar element in your overlay content, and the overlay will replace the base file at runtime (or be merged with it, as described later in this chapter in the "Content Positioning" section).

When the base element is empty, it is replaced with the corresponding overlay element and any child subcontent. The following toolbar snippet shows a reference placed in a base file:

```
<toolbar id="main-toolbar" />
```

When an overlay is read with the content below, the previous line is replaced with that content:

```
<toolbar id="main-menubar" persist="collapsed">
  <toolbarbutton id="new-button" label="New" observes="cmd_new"/>
  <toolbarbutton id="open-button" label="Open" observes="cmd_open"/>
  <toolbarbutton id="save-button" label="Save" observes="cmd_save"/>
</toolbar>
```

Overlay files are XUL files with a *.xul* extension. The content within that file has to be contained in an `<overlay>` element, which is the root of the document. For example, the toolbar is a first level child of the root.

```
<overlay id="xflyOverlay">
  <toolbar id="main-toolbar" />
  <!-- more overlay content -->
</overlay>
```

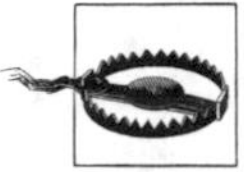

Styles from overlays override styles from base XUL files, so be careful not to load master styles in an overlay.

Dynamic loading

The usual method for loading overlays, as outlined previously, is to include the overlay processing instruction in your XUL file. The dynamic loading of content is more subtle, but just as effective. Mozilla has a registry of overlays, in the form of an RDF datasource that lives in the *chrome* directory. These overlays live in the tree in a directory called *overlayinfo* under the *chrome* root.* When a new package or component is registered, the overlays that come with it are loaded automatically.

Dynamic overlays are commonly used to extend certain parts of the Mozilla application itself when new packages are installed that need access points, as do new language packages and themes, for instance. Certain menus in the UI, for example, are open for third-party authors to add items. Adding the name of your package to Mozilla's Tasks menu, for example, provides a convenient launching point and is handled with dynamic overlays. Chapter 6 provides more information on this topic, in the section "Adding the xFly application to the Mozilla Tools menu."

Content Positioning

Content positioning is the order in which widgets appear in the UI. Usually content is laid out in the order elements are defined in the XUL file. However, there are a couple of ways to override this ordering in XUL.

Continuing with the example of the overlaid toolbar in the previous section, it is possible for both the base definition and the overlaid definition to have children. In this instance, the content is merged, with the original content appearing before the overlaid content by default:

```
<toolbar id="main-toolbar">
  <toolbarbutton id="print-button" label="Print" observes="cmd_print"/>
</toolbar>
```

If the `toolbarbutton` above is in the base XUL, then the ordering of the buttons would be Print, New, Open, and Save. It is possible to change this ordering by using `insertbefore`, however, as shown in Example 3-21.

* Chapter 9 has more information on RDF datasources. To delve deeper into the chrome layout and install issues, see Chapter 6.

Example 3-21. Positioning attributes

```
<toolbar id="main-toolbar" persist="collapsed">
  <toolbarbutton id="new-button" label="New" observes="cmd_new"
      insertbefore="print-button"/>
  <toolbarbutton id="open-button" label="Open" observes="cmd_open"/>
  <toolbarbutton id="save-button" label="Save" observes="cmd_save"
      position="2"/>
</toolbar>
```

The `insertbefore` attribute is placed on one of the child items to signify that it should go before a sibling in the base file. `insertbefore` takes an element `id` as a value and says, in this case, that the New button should go before Print. Conversely, you can move an item after it by using the `insertafter` attribute. For more precision, you can use `position` to position an item absolutely in the sequence of siblings. In Example 3-21, the position attribute puts the Save button in the second position, so the final order is New, Save, Print, and Open.

The Extras

Certain lesser-known elements and features are indispensable to the savvy XUL developer and can add that something extra to Mozilla applications, as shown here.

Tooltips

Tooltips are visual pop ups that appear when you place the cursor over a piece of the UI. The hovering behavior of a tooltip is useful for many things, including abbreviated help and the display of values that are otherwise obscured in the UI. In the Mozilla application, the most common places where they are used are on toolbar buttons and splitter grippies that divide panels in the window.

To invoke a tooltip, add a `tooltiptext` attribute to the widget that needs it:

```
<button id="printButton" label="Print" tooltiptext="Print this page" />
```

Defining this attribute is enough to ensure that the generic Mozilla tip box appears with the specified text when you place the cursor over the element.

Tooltips are actually implemented as an XBL binding. Underneath, a tooltip is essentially a pop up with a `description` element within that holds text. You can also create your own tooltips.

To create your own content and customized appearance for a tooltip:

1. Create the content.
2. Attach it to the pop-up element you will be using.
3. Give the pop up a unique ID.

The following snippet shows the kind of tooltip you can create and then reuse in your application code:

```
<popupset id="aTooltipSet">
    <popup id="myTooltip"
          class="tooltip"
          onpopupshowing="return FillInTooltip(document.tooltipNode);" >
      <description id="TOOLTIP-tooltipText"
          class="my-tooltip-label" flex="1"/>
    </popup>
</popupset>
```

Use your newly created widget by adding its `id` value to the `tooltip` attribute to the UI element that wants it:

```
<treeitem id="FlyDescription" tooltip="myTooltip" tooltiptext="" />
```

Note that this example assumes that the actual text will be applied dynamically to the `tooltiptext` attribute, which is initially empty. This is useful in many situations—for example, in tree cells that contain transient values.

The advantage of creating your own tooltip is that you can apply your own styles to it, giving the text and background whatever font and colors you want. A variation of the `tooltip` attribute named `contenttooltip` is used for content panels.

Progress Meter

Sometimes in your application you need to give the user feedback during a long operation. The classic example in the browser is the status bar that shows a visual representation of the time remaining when you load a big web page or download a file.

Of these two activities, loading pages and downloading files, downloading uses the determined mode, meaning that the time to complete the operation is calculable. In this case, an algorithm is written based on the file size and the bandwidth values to formulate the time remaining. The second of three modes of a progress meter is the undetermined mode, in which the time for the operation to complete is unknown. Commonly called the "barber pole," the progress meter shows a spinning pole when in undetermined mode. The third mode is normal, which shows an empty bar. You can get/set the mode by using the `mode` attribute.

Here is the XUL for a sample progress meter:

```
<progressmeter id="progressTask" mode="normal" value="0" onclick="alert(`Task is in
progress')"/>
```

Here is the accompanying script for activating the progress meter:

```
var meter = document.getElementById('progressTask');
meter.setAttribute('mode', 'undetermined');
sometask();
meter.setAttribute('mode', 'determined');
meter.setAttribute('value', '100%');
```

The mode is changed to undetermined just before carrying out the task, and is represented by the function `sometask()`. The JavaScript code is synchronous, so it will not hand back control until the operation is complete.

Links

Mozilla is a web application, and many programs and operating systems (e.g., Windows XP) are moving toward full web integration. Linking is fundamental in application programming, so Mozilla provides a couple of ways to do it in your XUL document.

Use of the <html:a> element

To use HTML in your XUL file, you must define the HTML namespace at the top of your document:

```
<window id="MyOverlay"
     xmlns:html="http://www.w3.org/1999/xhtml"
     xmlns="http://www.mozilla.org/keymaster/gatekeeper/there.is.only.xul">
```

Then you can use the HTML elements just as you would in a regular web page, but with the addition of the namespace you declared:

```
<vbox>
  <html:a href="myOverlay.html">Go to Help page</html:a>
</vbox>
```

When you use a page with code in your application, the user can click the link and open a Mozilla browser to the requested page or item.

Simple XLinks

You can also tap into the more sophisticated XML capabilities in Mozilla by trying a simple XLink. Again, the correct namespace is required:

```
<window xmlns:xlink=http://www.w3.org/1999/xlink ...>
```

Then you define your link as follows:

```
<xlink:link xlink:type="simple" xlink:href="c.xml">c.xml</xlink:link>
```

The element here is `link`, the `type` is simple, and the locator is `href`.

Building the Application Shell

Now that the main XUL widgets and some crucial concepts like the box model have been described, you can bring things together and create an *application shell*, a user interface that isn't (yet) hooked up to application code, but which can be re-used for different applications.

The XUL in Example 3-22 extends the xFly application work you've already done in Chapter 2. It defines the interface for a viewer that will let you browse the examples in this book, giving xFly a measure of introspection. Examine the code closely in Example 3-22 to give yourself a feel for how the elements in the UI interact with each other to form something that is greater than the sum of its parts. Look particularly at how box elements are used such as `vbox`, `hbox`, `tabbox`, and `statusbar`.

Example 3-22. xFly application main workspace

```
<?xml version="1.0"?>
<?xml-stylesheet href="chrome://global/skin" type="text/css"?>
<?xml-stylesheet href="chrome://xfly/skin" type="text/css"?>
<?xul-overlay href="chrome://xfly/content/xflyoverlay.xul"?>
<!DOCTYPE window SYSTEM "chrome://xfly/locale/xfly.dtd">
<window title="&window.title;"
  xmlns:html="http://www.w3.org/1999/xhtml"
  xmlns="http://www.mozilla.org/keymaster/gatekeeper/there.is.only.xul"
  type="xfly:main"
  width="800"
  height="600"
  onload="onLoad()">
<script type="application/x-javascript" src="chrome://xfly/content/xfly.js" />
<stringbundle id="bundle_xfly" src="chrome://xfly/locale/xfly.properties"/>
<toolbox>
  <menubar id="appbar">
    <menu label="xFly">
      <menupopup>
        <menuitem label="Close" oncommand="exitxFly()"/>
      </menupopup>
    </menu>
    <menu label="Examples">
      <menupopup>
        <!-- items to go here -->
      </menupopup>
    </menu>
    <menu label="Help">
      <menupopup>
        <menuitem label="About" oncommand="doAbout()"/>
      </menupopup>
    </menu>
  </menubar>
</toolbox>
<hbox flex="1">
  <vbox id="left-frame">
    <tree id="example-tree" />
    <hbox align="start">
      <image src="chrome://xfly/skin/images/logo5.gif" />
    </hbox>
  </vbox>
  <splitter collapse="before" resizeafter="grow" persist="state">
    <grippy />
  </splitter>
```

Example 3-22. xFly application main workspace (continued)

```
  <tabbox id="raven-main-tabcontent" flex="1" orient="vertical">
    <tabs orient="horizontal">
      <tab id="tab-view" label="View Example"/>
      <tab id="tab-source" label="View Example Source"/>
    </tabs>
    <tabpanels flex="1">
      <iframe id="right-frame" name="right-frame"
      flex="3" src="chrome://xfly/content/examples/2-1.xul"/>
      <iframe id="right-frame-source" name="right-frame-source"
          flex="3" src="view-source:chrome://xfly/content/examples/2-1.xul"/>
    </tabpanels>
  </tabbox>
</hbox>
<statusbar id="ch3-bar" persist="collapsed">
  <statusbarpanel class="statusbarpanel-iconic" id="book-icon"/>
  <statusbarpanel id="status-text" label="Thanks for reading the book!"
      flex="4" crop="right"/>
  <statusbarpanel class="statusbarpanel-iconic" id="example-status" flex="1"/>
</statusbar>
</window>
```

The main application windows consists of a menu bar, two frames, and a status bar. The menus provide access to application-level functions like closing the window, or launching an "About" window. At the bottom of the window, the status bar displays the book icon and some status messages for the application. Between the menu bar and the status bar are the two main panels: a vertical box (`<vbox>`) on the left that contains a tree for choosing examples with the xFly logo beneath it, and an `<iframe>` into which the examples are loaded on the right. There are two tabs in the example pane, one for showing the example rendered and one for looking at the source.

The code in Example 3-22 is not the final code for xFly, but it does show some important widgets used for the main layout of the application. But the layout in Example 3-22 (in which a `<toolbox>` holds the menus, a `<statusbar>` displays messages from the application, and the box model is used to layout the application display) is a very useful template for XUL applications.

What remains to define is the tree structure that actually holds the various examples. In Example 3-22, the `<tree>` has an ID attribute that is meant to pick up content defined in an overlay. Example 3-23 shows what such an overlay would look like, but if you'd rather, you can take the content of the `<tree id="example-tree">` element in this example, define it as direct content of the `<tree>` in Example 3-22, and end up with the application shell shown in Figure 3-12. See the section "Overlays" earlier in this chapter for more information about how to add content to your XUL using overlay files.

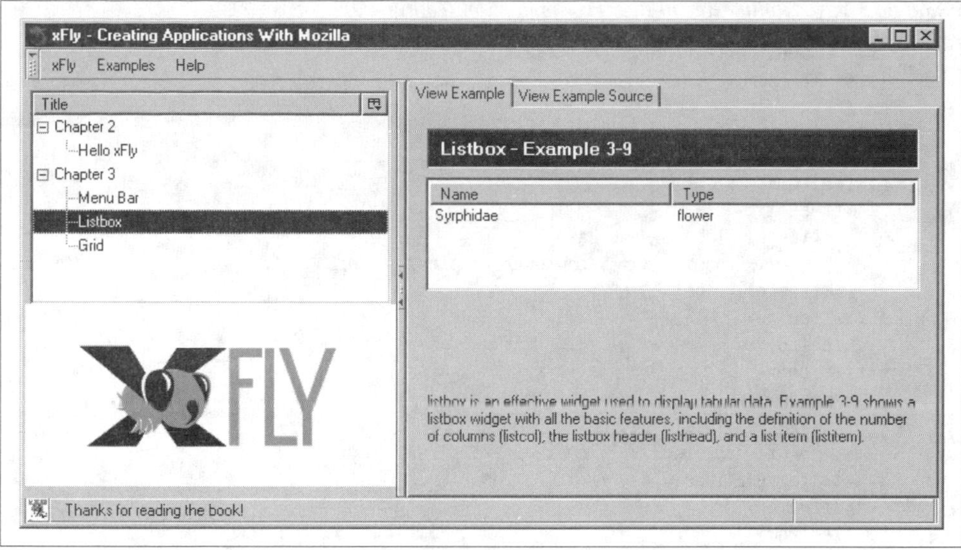

Figure 3-12. xFly example viewing application

Example 3-23. Example tree in the xFly application

```
<?xml version="1.0"?>
<overlay id="xflyOverlay"
    xmlns:html="http://www.w3.org/1999/xhtml"
    xmlns="http://www.mozilla.org/keymaster/gatekeeper/there.is.only.xul">
<tree id="example-tree" onselect="onExampleSelect();" seltype="single"
    hidecolumnpicker="false"
    enableColumnDrag="true" flex="1">
  <treecols>
    <treecol id="type" label="Title" flex="1" primary="true"
        persist="width ordinal hidden"/>
    <splitter class="tree-splitter"/>
    <treecol id="method" label="Example" flex="1"
        persist="width ordinal hidden"/>
  </treecols>
  <treechildren>
    <treeitem container="true" open="true">
      <treerow>
        <treecell label="Chapter 2"/>
      </treerow>
      <treechildren>  <!-- Second level row -->
        <treeitem>
          <treerow>
            <treecell label="Hello xFly"
                url="chrome://xfly/content/examples/2-1.xul"/>
            <treecell label="2-1"/>
          </treerow>
        </treeitem>
      </treechildren>
    </treeitem>
```

Example 3-23. Example tree in the xFly application (continued)

```
    <treeitem container="true" open="true">
      <treerow>
        <treecell label="Chapter 3"/>
      </treerow>
      <treechildren>  <!-- Second level row -->
        <treeitem>
          <treerow>
            <treecell label="Menu Bar"
                url="chrome://xfly/content/examples/3-5.xul"/>
            <treecell label="3-5"/>
          </treerow>
        </treeitem>
        <treeitem>
          <treerow>
            <treecell label="Listbox"
                url="chrome://xfly/content/examples/3-9.xul"/>
            <treecell label="3-9"/>
          </treerow>
        </treeitem>
        <treeitem>
          <treerow>
            <treecell label="Grid" url="chrome://xfly/content/examples/3-12.xul"/>
            <treecell label="3-12"/>
          </treerow>
        </treeitem>
      </treechildren>
    </treeitem>
  </treechildren>
</tree>
</overlay>
```

CHAPTER 4

CSS in Mozilla Applications

This chapter describes how Cascading Style Sheets (CSS) are used to create the look and feel of a Mozilla application's interface. Although XUL has a central role in creating a structure for an application's interface, defining widgets and their functionality, and creating the basic application code, it is CSS that creates the visible portion of an application. XUL and CSS often work so closely together that they seem inseparable, but XUL is generally responsible for the structure of an application's interface and CSS is responsible for the application's presentation. As described in the next sections, it is not until an XPFE application has been "skinned," or styled with stylesheets, that it has a usable interface.

The first few sections in this chapter provide basic information about using CSS and some examples of how the Mozilla interface is created. They include reference material you can refer back to as you learn more. Starting with the "Creating New Skins" section, you can dive in, have some fun with CSS, and begin to create your own skins. The xFly package example created earlier in the book shows how to add custom styles to the XUL files you created in Chapters 2 and 3.

Interface Basics

Before describing the practice of using CSS, let's get some basic theory out of the way. When we talk about the interface of an application, we mean all of the parts of the application that are displayed and allow the user to interact. Buttons, windows, pages, menus, sliders, and descriptive text are all parts of the interface. In Mozilla, XUL usually defines the basic structure of the interface and CSS defines its presentation. These two aspects of the interface—the way it's organized and the way it's presented—are kept as distinct from one another as possible in Mozilla and in many good programming environments. Indeed, this separation is what gives rise to the concept of skins—coherent, separate, and typically swappable "looks" for the same underlying structure. Mozilla uses Cascading Style Sheets, a quickly evolving series of standards already common in HTML web page presentation, to define the skin of XUL application interfaces.

Skins Versus Themes

When we say *skin* in this chapter, we refer to the look of the interface—to the CSS styles and its relationship to the XUL structure underneath. The term *theme* is also used often in conjunction with interfaces and skins. These words are used interchangeably, although there are some differences in their meaning.

A single, overall theme is made up of many skins. The Navigator component's skin described in *navigator.css*, for example, is part of the overall Modern theme of Mozilla. Following this definition, the Modern theme may be made up of as many as 20 or 30 different skins corresponding to the major components and major UI features within those components. In addition to *navigator.css*, for example, there are stylesheets for *toolbar.css*, *linkToolbar.css*, and others, which collectively make up the Navigator skin. The CSS files may also be described as skins, as when this book instructs you to "open the *messenger.css* skin in a text editor." All skins of a particular kind or look organized together comprise a single theme.

Themes are also often used to refer to the different looks that you can download and install for Mozilla and Netscape 6.x and 7.x. (To get new themes for the Mozilla browser go to View → Apply Themes → Get New Themes.) Any application created with Mozilla, though, can have different themes that users can install and select to customize the look of that application.

This distinction between a skin and a theme is not enforced—or even acknowledged—by many people in the Mozilla community, so you will see a profligate use of these terms in practice. Try to remain calm. The terminology differences aren't important. What is important is that you can create one (or many) looks for your application using CSS. This chapter will show you how.

Limitations of a Skin

Skins are used to style the structure of an interface that has been created with XUL. Once the interface has been defined in XUL, that structure is set and CSS can be used to change how that structure will look, but can't be used to change the structure itself. In practice, this means that you can use CSS to change the way a button looks—but to move a button from one toolbar to another within the interface, you need to edit your XUL code. Skins generally affect the usability or appearance, but not the functionality of an interface, though the use of XBL in CSS is an exciting exception to this rule, as you will see.

This separation of the style and the content of an application means that there are a number of things you can't change in an application using CSS. Here are some examples of the kinds of interface elements that cannot be manipulated with a skin.

- The position and contents of menus and menu items and the functionality they trigger.
- The overall layout and functionality of buttons.
- The general layout of the application (although you can use CSS to hide sections of an interface).

While the underlying structure of menus and buttons cannot be changed in the process of editing a theme, you can, of course, change the appearance of things quite radically. In fact, you can change whether an element—say, an item in a menu—has any visibility using the `visibility` or `display` CSS properties. One of the Mozilla extensions to CSS, `-moz-box-ordinal`, lets you set the order in which the elements in a container are displayed. We describe these extensions and others later in this chapter in the section "Special Mozilla Extensions."

Theme Abstraction (or Building Good Skins)

One of the most important parts of a well-written theme is that it be as separate as possible from the actual structure of the interface—that it be abstracted as a layer so it can be switched or updated without affecting or forcing you to edit the underlying XUL. Keeping an application's style separate is not mandatory, however, and you can have all presentation code in your XUL files, although we explain why this isn't a good idea.

As we have tried to stress, at the most basic level, abstraction means that the XUL should describe the structure and the CSS should describe the presentation, or look, of the interface. In reality, of course, the presentation layer is itself divided into different layers, where lower, more basic files like *xul.css* describe the look and feel of common UI elements such as buttons and menus, and higher-level CSS files consistently describe the layout and stylistic details of a component. When working on a theme or skin for your application, you should use as few inline style attributes as you can, as well as ensure that your themes are organized into component subdirectories and that one skin does not depend on another that is farther down in the "skin hierarchy." (This is discussed later in this chapter in the "CSS and Skin Hierarchies" section.).

Cross-Platform Interface Considerations

Often in traditional interface development, you try to make things look and work right on a single platform. Using something like MFC on Windows, for example, you can drop in the widget it provides and be reasonably assured that the interface will look like a Windows application interface whenever and wherever your application is run.

Planning Your Interface

Before you begin using CSS and images to style your XUL application code, it's important to have a sense of where your interface is heading. Begin by asking yourself some questions. What should the buttons look like? Do you want to give users the ability to switch skins in your application, as they can in the Mozilla browser? How will your application be affected when the user switches skins in Mozilla? What, if any, are the differences on the different platforms on which you expect users to run your application?

Although creating interfaces using XUL and CSS is fun and fast, it's best to do a mockup of your interface before you begin so you know where you are heading (both Adobe Photoshop and the GIMP are excellent tools for creating sophisticated images and mock-ups). The creators of the Modern and Classic themes do lots of visualization of the themes in image editing software and go through several iterations of testing and feedback.

One of the great advantages of using such an approach is that you will undoubtedly develop images and icons for your interface anyway, and you can slice and dice your mockup to get, for example, the icons for your buttons, the background images, and other real parts of the interface. You may find that you can actually use most of the mockup in your actual interface! See "Referencing Images in CSS" later in this chapter for an explanation of how this image slicing can work in an advanced way when you have XBL-based widgets that use GIF images that are stitched together.

Because the overall theme of an application will most likely consist of a large number of individual graphic elements and widgets, pay special attention to considerations of color palette, web-optimized file formats such as *.gif* and *.png*, and file size to make sure your interface looks good and loads quickly.

When you do cross-platform user interface development, you need to be aware of how your application will look on the platforms on which it will be used. One common difference, for example, is the layout of scrollbars in Windows applications and in Macintosh applications. On Windows, scrollbars typically have buttons at either end that advance the scrollbar button itself. On the classic Macintosh, the scrollbars are configured so that the buttons are clustered together. The difference is subtle, but it is a source of huge contention in the Mozilla world. Figure 4-1 shows the difference between the scrollbars on the two platforms. (This figure also shows a small notch in the lower righthand corner that is part of all classic Macintosh application windows and that shifts part of the Mozilla interface over to the left.)

When you use the XPFE, you use a single code base to deploy on any number of different platforms. In the Mozilla code, there are some tricks for making things work differently on different platforms. Like scrollbars, the layout of buttons in dialogs is another important area of platform difference. The layout code for the Open Web

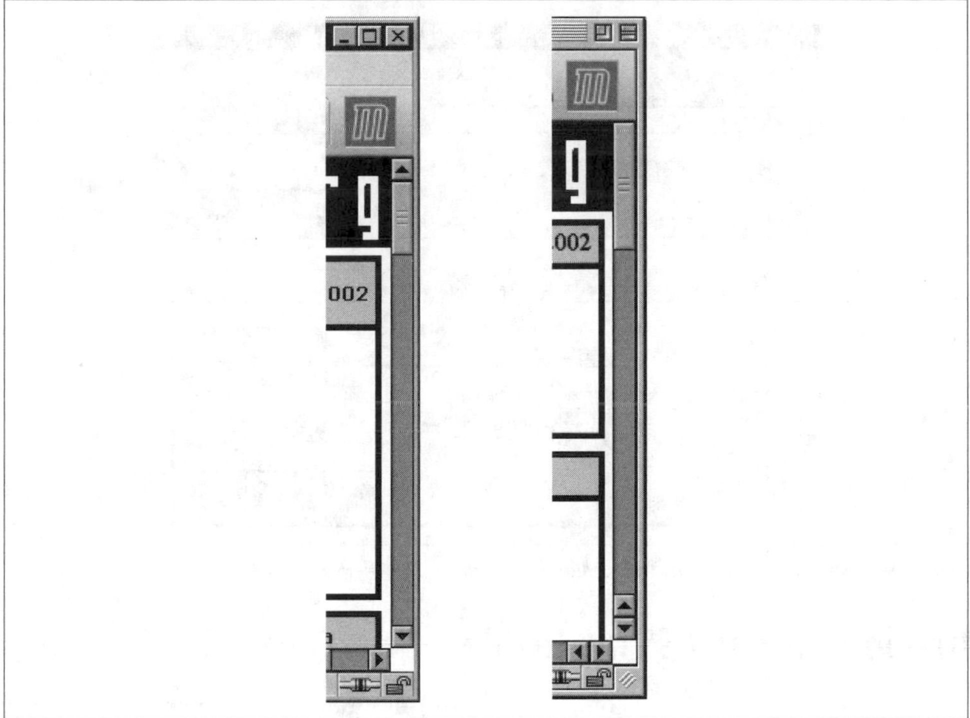

Figure 4-1. Scrollbars on Windows and on the Macintosh

Location dialog, for example, is defined in platform-specific files, and slightly different dialog layouts are deployed transparently to users (depending on their platform). Figure 4-2 illustrates the differing layouts of this dialog on different platforms (note the different positions of the Open and Cancel buttons in the two images).

If you look in the global resources area of the *xpfe* in the source code (using a tool like Mozilla's LXR), you can see the platform subdirectories where the buttons in the dialogs are arranged with `<spacer />` elements and different alignments:

```
mozilla/xpfe/global/resources/content/
  mac/
    platformDialogOverlay.xul
  os2/
    platformDialogOverlay.xul
  unix
    platformDialogOverlay.xul
  win
    platformDialogOverlay.xul
```

These platform-specific files allow the application developer to write XUL that works the same way on every platform, but preserves subtler aspects of an interface that users expect from their platform.

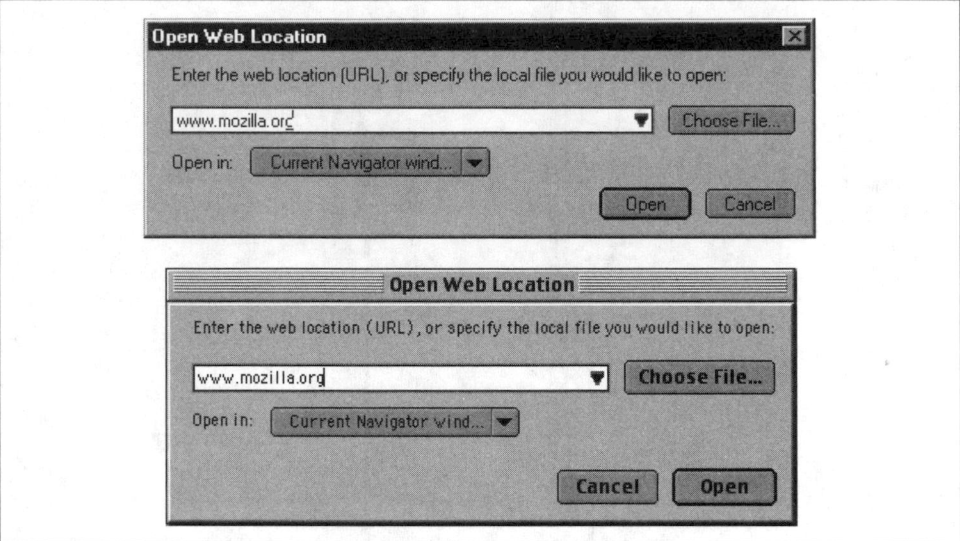

Figure 4-2. The Open Web Location dialog in Windows and the Macintosh

Introduction to CSS in Mozilla

Now that you have absorbed some of the most important basic aspects of interface design, we can begin to discuss how Mozilla uses CSS and images to make actual interfaces out of the structure defined in the XUL files. Though XUL contains the widgets and structure upon which the interface rests, it is not until at least some basic skin information has been loaded into the XUL that the interface becomes visible and editable by the user. In addition to this, CSS binds XBL widgets to the basic structure of the XUL code, allowing extended content to appear in your document. For more information about XBL, see Chapter 7.

Basic XUL + CSS Interaction

XUL and CSS interact at two basic levels in Mozilla. At the file level, XUL picks up CSS information by explicitly loading CSS stylesheets at runtime. At the element level, selectors bind CSS rules to specific XUL elements or groups of elements. For an XUL element to pick up a style defined in a CSS file, the XUL file must load the CSS file, and an element or group of elements in the XUL must match a selector in the CSS rule. We discuss these basic levels of interaction in the following two sections.

CSS and XUL file interaction

Like HTML, XUL loads style information by including a specific processing instruction somewhere at the top of the file. There are various ways to apply style to HTML pages, including the common example below, in which a `<link />` element with a URI loads an external stylesheet that holds the style information for the web page.

```
<link rel="stylesheet" href="../style.css" type="text/css">
```

In XUL, however, you must use one or more special processing instructions at the top of the XUL file to load the CSS stylesheet information, or skin, into the XUL.

```
<?xml-stylesheet href="chrome://global/skin" type="text/css"?>
```

Note that the XUL stylesheet loading supports the use of `http://` and `file://` type URLs, but most often, the `chrome://` type URL is used, which points to files that are available in the application's chrome subdirectory and that are registered with the chrome registry. The example above uses a special feature of this chrome type URL, which resolves directory pointers to files within those directories that have the same name as the directory itself (thus serving as a shorthand for main theme stylesheets). The chrome URL `chrome://global/skin`, in other words, loads a stylesheet found at `chrome://modern.jar:/global/skin/global.css`.

XUL also supports the use of *inline styles*, which is style information that is applied to individual elements with a style attribute. However, this practice is generally frowned upon, since it overrides the skin information and makes it very difficult for new skins to be applied correctly.

Actually, the chrome URL in the example does more than this. Another important function of the chrome registry is that it keeps track of which packages you have installed, which skin you have applied to your application, and resolves URLs like `chrome://global/skin` into the global skin information for the currently selected skin. If you apply the modern skin, for example, then this URL loads the global skin file from the *modern.jar*; if you apply the Classic skin, then the chrome URL actually resolves to `chrome://classic.jar:/global/skin/global.css` instead. This flexibility in the chrome registry abstracts the structure in the XUL files from the skin information and allows you to create and apply different skins.

Applying style rules to XUL

In CSS, *selector* refers to the element or group of elements to which a style rule is bound—to the thing that is selected for styling. In some cases, the selector is an actual XUL element. The following style rule, for example, says that all XUL `<menu/>` elements in the XUL file(s) into which this CSS is loaded will have a red background color:

```
menu {
  background-color: red;
}
```

In this case, the element selector names an element (menu) directly: all elements of that type match and are styled with the rule. In the next few sections, we describe the main types of selectors and the style rules that can be applied to them. With a couple of notable exceptions (see "Special Mozilla Extensions" later in this chapter), the CSS you use with XUL is the same one you use for HTML elements.

Inline styles

Another way to apply style to XUL elements is to use inline style rules. Use inline styles with caution. All XUL elements have a `style` attribute that can be used to define styles directly for that element. In the following example, the `style` attribute is used (in a common but somewhat deprecated manner) to hide the XUL element—to apply a style that suppresses rendering of the element (though it still takes up space in the UI):

```
<menuitem id="e_src"
  label="&editsrc.label;"
  style="visibility: none;" />
```

When you use inline styles, the syntax does not include the brackets, but you can still add multiple style rules by using the semicolon. The item before the colon is the property, and the item after it is its value. The format of inline styles is as follows:

```
style="style attribute1: value[; style attribute2: value; etc...]"
```

The reason why inline styles are frowned upon in XUL and skin development is that they can be extremely difficult to locate and work around when you design a new skin and want to change the appearance of an element that has an inline style. The style attribute takes precedence over styles applied from other sources—inline styles are the last rule in the cascade of style rules—so they cascade over styles defined in a skin and may "break" the overall look of that skin.

Besides this problem, many tricks for which application developers use the inline style can be done using XUL attributes. It's very common to use the CSS attribute-value pairs `display: none;` or `visibility: none;` to hide elements in order to change what's available from the interface. However, smart XUL developers use the `hidden` or the `collapse` attribute instead, thereby keeping structural matters as separate from style matters as possible.

Stylesheet Syntax

Cascading Style Sheets are the blueprints for Mozilla skins. In Cascading Style Sheets, style definitions take the following basic form:

```
element {
  style attribute1: value;
  style attribute2: value;
  style attribute3: value;
}
```

For example, the following definition makes all XUL menus appear with a one-pixel border, a light-blue background, and ten-point fonts:

```
menu {
  border: 1px;
  background-color: lightblue;
  font-size: 10pt;
}
```

This is an example of using the element itself—in this case, a "menu"—as a selector (the item to which the style definition is applied). In addition to the basic element selector and style rules, CSS provides the application of style information to classes of elements, element IDs, and elements with particular attributes or states. The following three sections demonstrate the basic format for these three common style selectors.

The element selector

The *element selector* is the most basic kind of selector. It is just the name of the element to be styled at the front of the style rule. In the previous example, the `<menuitem />` element, defined in a XUL file that loads this style rule, will have a light blue background color:

```
element { attribute: value; }
menuitem  { background-color: lightblue; }
```

The pseudoelement selector

The *pseudoelement selector* selects a piece of an element for styling. While a selector like `menuitem` picks up all menu items in a given XUL document, a pseudoelement selector like `menuitem:first-letter` binds the rule's styles to only the first letter in a `menuitem` value.

```
menuitem:first-letter { text-decoration: underline; }
description:first-line { margin-left: .25in; }
```

The first style rule above gives all menu items to which it applies the look of being `accesskey` enabled. The second creates an indentation in the first line of a XUL `description` element's text. Menu access keys let you open and choose items from a menu by using the underlined letters and modifiers (e.g., "F" and `<alt>` to open the File menu).

The class selector

The *class selector* applies the style rule to all XUL widgets of a given class. In the XUL files that define the structure of Netscape 7, the class is specified with the `class` attribute (e.g., `<menu class="baseline">`) and in CSS with the dot notation:

```
element.class { attribute: value;}
menu.baseline {   border: 0px;   font-size: 9pt; }
```

In this example, all menus with a XUL baseline class have no borders and a nine-point font size. Note that you can use the class without the preceding XUL element to skin all XUL elements with a given class. In Example 4-1, both the XUL box and the XUL menu pick up the style given in the "redbox" class style definition.

Example 4-1. Class selector in CSS

```
.redbox {
  border: 2px solid red;
  font-size: 9pt;
}
<box class="redbox">
    <menu class="redbox">
    <menu class="bluebox">
</box>
```

The ID selector

The CSS *ID selector* applies the style rule to a unique XUL element. As with `class`, the `ID` is specified in the XUL with an attribute (e.g., `<menu id="file_menu">`) and in the CSS with the pound sign preceding the `ID` itself. In this example, the menu with an ID of `edit` has a red color:

```
element#id { attribute: value;}
menu#edit { color: red;}
```

In the example above, both the element type and the element ID are given. You can also identify elements anonymously (though still uniquely) by using just the selector:

```
#whitey {
    background-color: white;
    margin: .25in;
}
```

In the case of IDs, these are selectors are identical, since IDs need to be unique across the whole XUL file. When you use classes, however, the typeless style rule is a good way to apply your style information to a range of elements.

The attribute selector

The *attribute selector* allows you to style XUL elements with particular attributes or with attributes of a particular value. In Example 4-2, all elements with a disabled attribute set to `true` will have a light-grey color.

Example 4-2. Attribute selector in CSS

```
element [attribute=value] { attribute: value; }
element [attribute~=value] { attribute: value; }
*[disabled="true"]
{
  color: lightgrey;
}
```

Example 4-2. Attribute selector in CSS (continued)

```
menu[value="File"] {
  font-weight: bold;
}
[id~="my"] { color: red; }
```

Note that Example 4-2 uses the * character for selecting all elements. This "wildcard" selector can be combined with attribute and other selectors to make a powerful filter in your CSS stylesheets—but of course, in an example like Example 4-2, it could be omitted and `[disabled=true]` would still apply to all elements with that attribute set to that value.

Example 4-2 also uses ~= to match attributes that contain the given fragment. In this case, any elements that have an ID with the fragment "my" have text colored red, as when you want to see all your customized elements for debugging purposes.

Pseudoclass selectors

Another feature of CSS-2 that Mozilla makes extensive use of is the *pseudoclass*. In CSS, pseudoclasses are used to represent different states for elements that are manipulated by the user, such as buttons. The states—represented by pseudoclasses such as `active`, `focus`, and `hover`—change when the user interacts with an element. The pseudoclasses actually correspond to events on the interface elements.

The : character is used to add these `pseudoclasses` in the CSS notation:

```
#forwardButton:hover
{
  list-style-image      : url("chrome://navigator/skin/forward-hover.gif");
}
```

The pseudoclass is often appended to another style. Since specific CSS style rules inherit from more general rules (see the section "CSS and Skin Hierarchies" later in this chapter for more information about this inheritance), the example above picks up any styles defined for the button with the `id` of `forwardButton` (and any class-based information, as well as the basic CSS for a button), but substitutes whatever image is used with this special GIF that represents a button being moused or hovered over.

In Mozilla's Modern skin, the pseudoclasses work collectively to give buttons their appearance and behavior. Each of the following button images in Figure 4-3 is associated with a different pseudoclass (or attribute, as we discuss in the next section). As soon as the pseudoclass is changed by user interaction (e.g., the user hovers the mouse over the button), the state changes and the effect is one of seamless transition.

Element relation selectors

Contextual subgroups—elements appearing within other elements, such as italicized text within a `<p>` element or a `<body>` in HTML—can be grouped in CSS, but this is

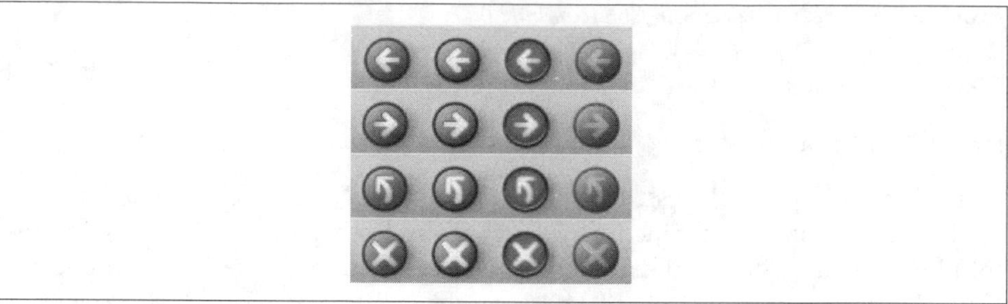

Figure 4-3. The different states for buttons in the Modern theme

an extremely inefficient way to style XUL. CSS2 also provides ways to group elements for styling based on their relationship in the object model. Table 4-1 lists these relational selectors.

Table 4-1. Relational selectors

Selector	Syntax	Example

Descendent	`ancestor descendent {`
	` attribute: value;`
	`}`
		`toolbar.primary menutitem#F {`
		`  border: 1px;`
		`}`

Parent-Child	`parent > child {`
	`  attribute: value;`
	`}`
		`menu#file > menuitem {`
		`  font-weight: bold;`
		`}`

Precedence	`elBefore + elAfter {`
	`  attribute: value;`
	`}`
		`menuitem#file + menuitem#edit {`
		`  background-color: black;`
		`}`

In the descendent example in Table 4-1, the "F" `menuitem` has a border only when it appears within the `toolbar` whose class is given as "primary." In the parent-child example, all menu items in a menu with the `id` "file" are made bold. Using +, the precedence selector says that the "edit" menu should have a black background only when it comes after the "file" menu. You can use these element relation selectors to create longer descensions (e.g., `toolbar.primary > menu#file > menuitem#new`), but remember that the processing gets more expensive with each new level, and that the descendent operation is particularly processor-intensive.

The !important keyword

As you might imagine, when you have a technology with such strong notions of precedence as Cascading Style Sheets (the ID-based style trumps the class-based style, inline style attributes trump those loaded from an external stylesheet, etc.), you may need to identify and set aside certain styles as the most important, regardless of where they are found in the cascade.

This is the role played by the `!important` keyword. Sitting to the right of a style value, it specifies that style rule should take precedence over all of its competitors and that it should be applied all the time. Example 4-3 demonstrates how no borders are rendered on *treecells* of the class *treecell-editor* because of the `!important` keyword.

Example 4-3. !important keyword in CSS

```
.treecell-editor,
.treecell-editor > box {
  margin: 0px !important;
  padding: 0px !important;
}
.treecell-editor {
  border: 0px !important;
}
```

You can search for the `!important` keyword in the LXR Mozilla source code tool and see its use in the Mozilla CSS.

The inherits value

CSS uses inheritance all over the place. Inheritance is implicit in the way style rules are applied, stylesheets are organized in the chrome, and skins borrow from one another in Mozilla. However, a special CSS value indicates that the selector explicitly inherits its value from the parent element.

When a CSS property has a value of `inherit`, that property's real value is pulled from the parent element:

```
.child {
  color: darkblue;
  height: inherit;
  background-color: inherit;
}
```

This block specifies a dark blue color for the font, but the values of the other two properties are inherited from the parent. In many cases, this has the same effect as not specifying any value at all for the child and letting the style rules above the current one in the document inheritance chain cascade down. However, not all style rules are inherited. Properties such as `!important`, `left`, and `height` are not inherited automatically by child elements, so you must use the `inherit` keyword to pick them up.

Box layout properties in CSS

People sometimes get confused about the various element spacing properties in CSS, such as `border`, `padding`, and `margin`. Though they work together a lot and often affect or overlap one another, these properties specify different things, as Table 4-2 shows.

Table 4-2. CSS spacing and layout properties

Property group	Description	Display

`padding`	Defines the space between the element's border and the content in the element.
	`td {padding-left: .25in;}`
	`td {padding-left: .0125in;}`
		padding-left
		padding-left

`margin`	Defines the space around elements. `td {margin-left: .25in;}`	left margin

`border`	Defines the border itself; it can control the thickness, color, style, and other aspects of an element's border.
	`td {border-style: inset;}`
	`td {border-color: blue;}`
	`td {border-left-width: 15px;}`
		inset
		blue
		fifteen

The position property

`position` is a special CSS property that specifies whether the given selector uses absolute or relative positioning. Unless you set the `position` property to absolute, you cannot use the related `top` and `left` properties to set the position of the current selector within its parent, as the example in Table 4-3 demonstrates. The `top` and `left` properties, when activated by the absolute position, specify the amount of distance from the top and left of the document, respectively. You can also set `position` to `fixed` to make it stay in one place as other content or UI is scrolled or moved.

Table 4-3. The position property

Example	Display

`<style>`
`#abdiv {`
` position: absolute;`
` top: 20px;`
` left: 70px;`
` background-color: lightblue;`
`}`
`#regdiv {`
` background-color: lightblue;`
`}`
`</style>`
`<div id="regdiv">other div</div>`
`<div id="abdiv">abdiv</div>`
	other div
	abdiv

Special Mozilla Extensions

Mozilla skins extend upon the CSS standards in just a few notable ways. These Mozilla CSS extensions take the form of special selectors and properties with the special `-moz-` prefix, indicating that they are not part of the actual CSS specifications.

You can find a complete list of these CSS keywords by searching for the file *nsCSSKeyWordList.h* in LXR.

Generally, these extensions are used to define CSS style and color values that are hardcoded into the C++ code and available for reuse in particular places in the Mozilla themes. You can use a few *-moz-* extensions, such as properties or special values or even, in some cases, style-related attributes in the XUL (e.g., `span[-moz-smiley="s1"]`, which grabs span elements in the HTML editor whose `-moz-smiley` attribute is set to `s1` and styles them accordingly). Actually, you can use any value in that CSS keyword list. Trial and error or a look in the C++ code will reveal what these values are. The values, like `-moz-fieldtext` and `-moz-mac-menushadow`, usually refer to actual color values. A list of some Mozilla CSS extensions appears in Table 4-4.

Table 4-4. Mozilla CSS extensions

Property	Description
`-moz-appearance`	Specifies that the element should appear, as much as possible, as an operating-system native.

`-moz-opacity`	Controls the opacity of any styleable element with a percentage value. The following example style rule creates a class of buttons that are only half visible above their backgrounds:
	`.op-butt {`
	`  -moz-opacity: 50%;`
	`}`

`-moz-binding`	The property for binding XBL to XUL. The value of `-moz-binding` is a URL pointing to the section in an XML bindings file where the XBL is defined:
	`new-widget {`
	`  -moz-binding:`
	`    chrome://xfly/bindings/extras.xml#super-button;`
	`}`

`-moz-border-radius`, `-moz-border-radius-bottomleft`, `-moz-border-radius-bottomright`, `-moz-border-radius-topleft`, `-moz-border-radius-topright`	Puts rounded corners on regular borders. The degree of rounding depends on the number of pixels you assign. For example, if you set this property to `2px`, you get a slightly rounded border, but if you set it to `8px`, you get a very round border.
`-moz-border-colors`, `-moz-border-colors-bottom`, `-moz-border-colors-left`, `-moz-border-colors-right`, `-moz-border-colors-top`	Sets the border colors on the various sides of an element.
`-moz-user-focus`	Indicates whether the given element can have focus. Possible values are `normal` and `ignore`.
`-moz-user-select`	Indicates whether the given element can be selected. Possible values are none and `normal`.

Table 4-4. Mozilla CSS extensions (continued)

<table>
<tr><th>Property</th><th>Description</th></tr>
<tr><td><code>-moz-smiley</code></td><td>This is typically given as an attribute to the span element in the HTML in a composer window and can be set to a value such as <code>s5</code> to pick up the laughing smiley image, to <code>s6</code> to pick up the embarrassed smiley image, and so on.

See the following source file for the values that can be set for this special property: http://lxr.mozilla.org/seamonkey/source/editor/ui/composer/content/EditorContent.css#77.</td></tr>
<tr><td><code>-moz-image-region</code></td><td>This was added to optimize the way image resources are used in the Mozilla skins. The value of the <code>-moz-image</code> region is a set of coordinates that designate an area within an "image sheet" that should be used as an icon in the user interface. The following CSS style definition specifies the top- and leftmost button in the btn1.gif image sheet used in Figure 4-3 to use as the default icon for the Back navigation button:
<pre>.toolbarbutton-1 {
 list-style-image: url("chrome://navigator/skin/icons/
btn1.gif");
 min-width: 0px;
}
#back-button {
 -moz-image-region: rect(0 41px 38px 0);
}</pre>
Of the two default skins, these image sheets are found only in the Modern skin. They are gradually making their way into the skins; as of this writing, there are three or four image sheets in the Modern skin—each corresponding to an area, toolbar, or set of buttons in the browser.</td></tr>
<tr><td><code>-moz-box-align</code></td><td>Sets the alignment for a XUL element from CSS. Possible values are <code>start</code>, <code>center</code>, <code>end</code>, <code>baseline</code>, and <code>stretch</code>.</td></tr>
<tr><td><code>-moz-box-direction</code></td><td>Sets the direction of a box's child elements. Possible values are <code>normal</code> and <code>reverse</code>.</td></tr>
<tr><td><code>-moz-box-flex</code></td><td>Sets the flexibility of an element relative to its siblings. The value is an integer.</td></tr>
<tr><td><code>-moz-box-flexgroup</code></td><td>Specifies that a group of elements have the same flex. The value is an integer.</td></tr>
<tr><td><code>-moz-box-ordinal</code></td><td>Specifies the order of an element relative to its peers in a container. By default, the value of this property is set to 1. When you set a new value, you can change the order, as in this example, which promotes the "View Source" menu item to the top of the menu by demoting the other two:
<pre><style>
#q { -moz-box-ordinal: 0; }
</style>
<menu>
  <menuitem id="e" label="e" />
  <menuitem id="v" label="v" />
  <menuitem id="q" label="q" />
</menu>
</window></pre>
You can also give elements the same ordinal value in CSS and group them, making sure they are not split by new, overlaid items.</td></tr>
<tr><td><code>-moz-box-orient</code></td><td>Sets the orientation of a container element. The value can be either <code>horizontal</code> or <code>vertical</code>.</td></tr>
<tr><td><code>-moz-box-pack</code></td><td>Packs the child elements of a container at the <code>start</code>, <code>center</code>, or <code>end</code>.</td></tr>
</table>

Referencing Images in CSS

Another basic function of the CSS in any Mozilla skin is to incorporate images into the user interface. A Mozilla skin can contain literally thousands of images, which are all referenced from particular style statements in the CSS. It's common for a single element to point to different versions of an image to reflect different states—as when a second image is used to give a button a pushed-down look as it is clicked—to create dynamism and provide feedback to the user. Example 4-4 shows the following two style statements handle the regular and active—or depressed—states, respectively.

Example 4-4. Image in CSS

```
button.regular {
    list-style-image: url(chrome://global/skin/arrow.gif);
    background-image: url(chrome://global/skin/regbutton.gif);
}
button.regular:active
{
    background-image: url(chrome://global/skin/button_pushed.gif);
}
```

In Example 4-4, the second of the two definitions inherits from the first, so it implicitly includes the *arrow.gif* as a foreground image. The second style definition says that when the XUL button of class `regular` is active, the image *button_pushed.gif* is used in place of *regbutton.gif* for the background.

Example 4-4 also illustrates the two common stylesheet properties that reference images: `list-style-image` and `background-image`. The `list-style-image` property specifies an image to go in the foreground of the selector; the `background-image` property specifies a separate image for the background. The availability of these two properties allows you to fine-tuning the images used to style the UI, as in this example, where the arrow icon is preserved and the wider, underlying button is swapped out.

In fact, the navigation buttons in the Modern skin are created by using both properties. In this case, the background is the basic round disk as seen in Figure 4-4, defined in the `toolbarbutton-1` class in *communicator\skin\button.css*, and the `list-style-image` is the arrow portion of the button, defined in the button ID and sliced out of a button image sheet with the special `-moz-image-region` property (see "Special Mozilla Extensions" later in this chapter for a description of image sheets).

Menu Skinning

As an example of using CSS in applications, Example 4-5 combines many common selectors described in this chapter in a set of rules for defining the look and basic behavior of menus. The CSS handles the basic look of the menus, their color and

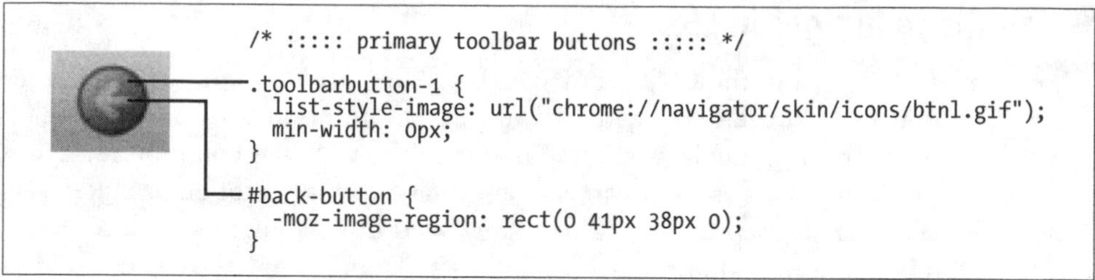

/* ::::: primary toolbar buttons ::::: */
.toolbarbutton-1 {
list-style-image: url("chrome://navigator/skin/icons/btnl.gif");
min-width: 0px;
}
#back-button {
-moz-image-region: rect(0 41px 38px 0);
}

Figure 4-4. Composite styles for the reload button

style, the look of the menu items when they are hovered over, and the look when they are selected.

Example 4-5. Mixing CSS and XUL

```
<menu id="sample">
  <menupopup>
    <menuitem class="m" label="File" />
    <menuitem class="m" label="Edit" />
    <menuitem class="m" id="q" label="Quit" />
  </menupopup>
</menu>
.m { background-color: lightgray; font-size: 9pt; }
.m:hover  { border: 1px; }
.m:active { background-color: gray; color: white; }
#q:active { background-color: black }
```

When you hover over any of the items in the menu generated by the code in Example 4-5, they display a border. When you select the item, it appears momentarily with a dark gray background and white lettering, like reverse video. The Quit menu item, unlike others, appears with a black background. Note that it also picks up the same white lettering as the other items of the `m` class, since this style information is inherited.

Mozilla Skins

At an earlier point in Mozilla's history, all interface files—the XUL, the CSS, and the images—were stored in directories named after the main Mozilla packages in the application chrome directory. The best way to look at a skin was just to poke around in those directories, change things in the CSS files you found, and reload to see what had changed in the browser. The CSS files are no longer stored in regular directories.

To organize things better and make a smaller footprint for Mozilla, all chrome is stored in special compressed archives in the *chrome* directory. These archives are Java Archive (JAR) files, whose subdirectory structure reflects the structure of Mozilla's major components, to some extent. There is one JAR archive for every theme. By default, Mozilla is distributed with the Classic and Modern themes, represented in the chrome as `classic.jar` and `modern.jar`. Figure 4-5 shows some of the contents of the `modern.jar` file in a zip utility.

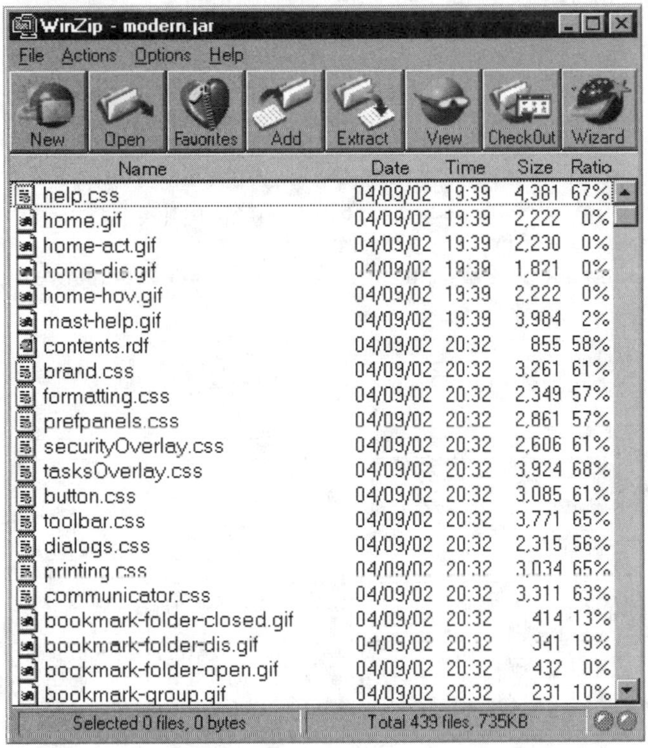

Figure 4-5. The contents of the modern.jar file

CSS and Skin Hierarchies

You have already seen some of the structure inherent to CSS in the previous examples. When an element has both a class-based and an id-based rule, for example (as well as a basic element "look and feel" defined in the global skin), the element style is applied. Then, the more specific class-based rule is applied and overwrites the properties of the general rule if they conflict. Finally, the ID-based rule is applied and overwrites whatever conflicting style values are in the more general selectors. In this way, the most specific style rules inherit from the most basic. This is the "cascade" in Cascading Style Sheets. In addition to this definition, the syntax of CSS allows you to specify selector relationships—such as when you create a parent-child selector and apply a style rule to only the selectors that have some other particular element as a parent in the XUL content model. However, there is also a strong inheritance mechanism in the way that the Mozilla browser uses CSS—in the way skin files are organized in the chrome and applied to the XUL. The strong hierarchical structure present in Mozilla's CSS and the XUL allow the chrome registry to maintain the skin and the various components that get skinned as different modules, but find and apply the right resources whenever they are called for. This structure is described in the "Basic Skin Structure" section later in this chapter.

Skin inheritance and skin modularization

For the sake of discussion, this book describes two kinds of inheritance: the more basic form, in which a specific skin like *navigator.css* inherits all style rules from *global.css*, and modularization, in which navigator skin rules specific to the toolbar are distributed into widget-specific CSS files (e.g., *toolbar.css* is part of the global skin). The global skin—once a large, unmodular set of style rules contained in *global.css*—is now spread out over several modularized CSS files, as Figure 4-6 shows.

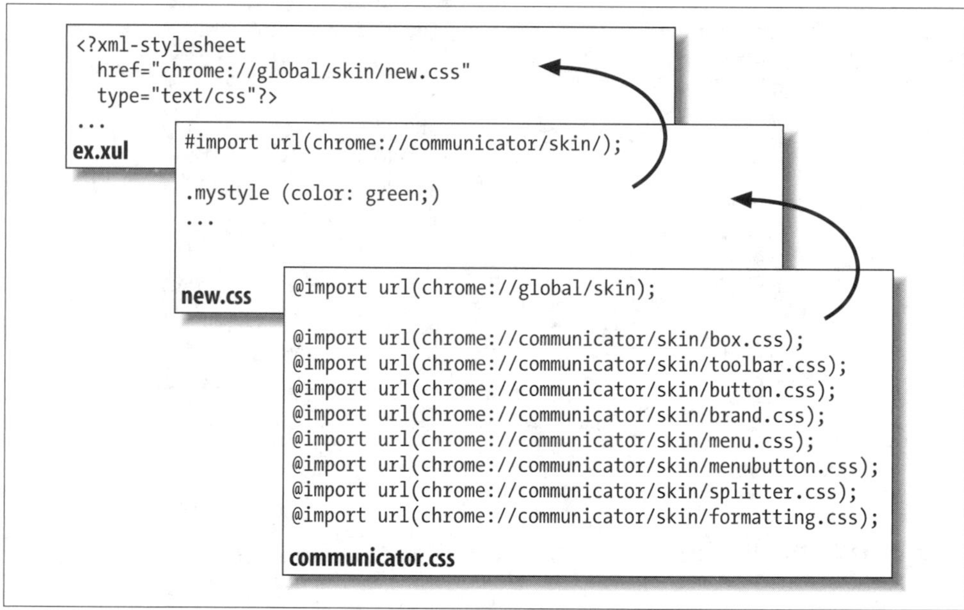

Figure 4-6. XUL file and skin loading

This modularization makes it possible for a XUL file to load the *global.css* file in a single statement and use any of the style rules defined in these skins. We will discuss the global skin in more detail in the section "Global skin" later in this chapter. Skin inheritance and skin modularization work together to give skins their structure and make it possible to create new skins or apply CSS only to particular parts of the application.

Figure 4-6 shows a very specific skin, *new.css*, inheriting the style information from *communicator.css* and then being loaded into the XUL file. In a situation like this, *ex.xul* can use any style rule defined in the *communicator.css* file (or in any CSS file that it imports).

Basic Skin Structure

Though they look very different, the Modern and Classic themes that are installed with Mozilla have similar structures. This is because the structure of a theme reflects, in many ways, the structure of the components to which it applies. So, for example, both themes have subdirectories (in the JAR files in which they are stored) where the CSS and image resources for each of the main components are stored. Modern, for example, has a *communicator* component subdirectory, and that subdirectory has subdirectories representing the various parts of the communicator interface: bookmarks, help, search, sidebar, and so on. Example 4-7 shows the Modern and Classically themed Navigation bars side by side.

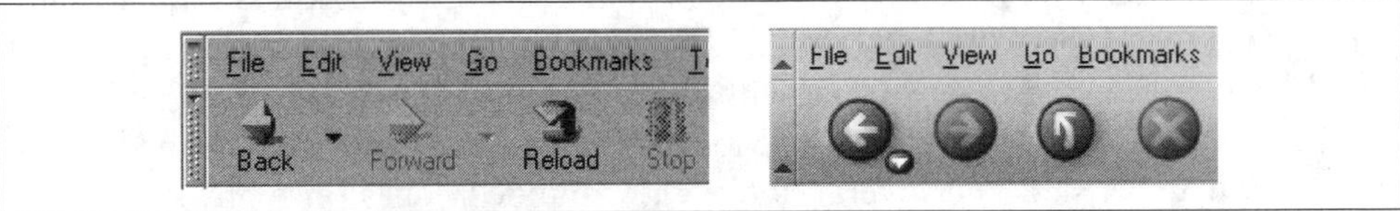

Figure 4-7. Classic and Modern Navigation toolbars

Both themes are complete. They each contain all skin resources for the major components of the application.* The resources themselves vary, but their structures are almost identical. This ability is what makes the skins dynamically changeable.

Skin developers can, for example, create a skin for a single component in Mozilla (e.g., messenger) and let the Modern theme continue to take care of the other components for which they have not created any new CSS information. Which components are skinned by which themes is specified in the *installed-chrome.txt* file, where a single entry represents the application of the appropriate theme resources to a single component, such as navigator. (See Chapter 6 for more information about this file and about how themes and other packages are registered and applied in Mozilla.) This situation does not apply to new applications like xFly, however, for which the XUL is typically a single package and the CSS that applies to it is another single package. Unlike the Mozilla browser, your application will probably have a single manifest and *content* subdirectory and a single manifest and *skin* subdirectory:

```
xfly.jar:
    content/
        contents.rdf
        <xul content here>
    skin/
        contents.rdf
        <css content here>
```

* There are just a couple of exceptions to this rule. The *content* directory of a package (typically the place where just the XUL and JS are stored) sometimes holds a file called *xul.css*. This file defines style information that is so fundamental to the way widgets are rendered—more fundamental, even, then *global.css* and its siblings—that it is set apart from the regular skin and put in with the content, where it is loaded automatically. It's not a good idea to edit this file.

An important difference here is that your skin requires a single manifest whereas the Mozilla themes use as many manifests as they have major components to skin. When the application that needs to be skinned is as large as the Mozilla browser, modularity is almost imperative—particularly if that application supports add-on applications (like xFly itself, which will be accessible from the Mozilla Tasks menu when you are done).

The Modern and Classic Themes

If you haven't already looked at it, using the skin-switching UI (View Menu → Apply Theme → Modern) in Mozilla will give you an idea about the differences between the two skins that come preinstalled with the browser. The Classic skin is modeled after earlier versions of the Mozilla UI and of the Netscape 4.x Communicator product. It has the familiar light grey box look, with the larger, primary-colored navigation button and a squared-off geometry. The Modern theme is a newer take on the browser interface. It has a smoother overall look, with rounded edges on many of the widgets, subtle color differentiations, gradients, and 3D icons.

However, both skins sit on top of the same XUL. With one notable exception—a powerful feature of CSS in Mozilla discussed later in this chapter in the "Binding New Widgets to the Interface Using XBL" section—the applications themselves are identical, and themes themselves provide all the differences in the browser's look and behavior.

Skin Files

Obviously, we cannot describe even a fraction of the CSS files that go into making up a single, overall theme. There are, however, some CSS files that help determine how the Mozilla browser looks. In this section, we will go over some of those files so you can see how they relate to one another, where the browser gets its look, and what strategies you might use to create your own complete skin.

The following sections provide a brief, representative sampling of the Modern theme. The global skin, the navigator skin, and the communicator skin are discussed as they pertain to the Modern theme in the Mozilla browser.

Navigator skin

One of the most specific and complex skin files in the Modern theme hierarchy is the *navigator.css* file, which contains style information for the browser itself. When you look through this skin, you will see rules for such things as the Print button. In Example 4-6, note how several selectors are grouped with a single style rule, and how the parent-child relationship between elements (see the earlier section "Element relation selectors" for an explanation of this selector) is used to style print buttons appearing in different places (i.e., under different element parents) in the UI.

Example 4-6. CSS for print button in navigator skin

```
#print-button
  {
    -moz-binding :
      url("chrome://communicator/skin/menubuttonBindings.xml#menubutton-dual-foo");
    list-style-image : url("chrome://global/skin/print.gif");
    margin           : 6px 6px 0px 6px;
  }
#print-button[disabled="true"],
#print-button[disabled="true"]:hover,
#print-button[disabled="true"]:hover:active,
#print-button[disabled="true"] > .menubutton-dual-stack > .menubutton-dual-button,
#print-button[disabled="true"] > .menubutton-dual-stack >
    .menubutton-dual-button:hover,
#print-button[disabled="true"] > .menubutton-dual-stack >
    .menubutton-dual-button:hover:active
  {
    list-style-image      : url("chrome://global/skin/print-disabled.gif");
  }
#print-button > .menubutton-dual-stack > .menubutton-dual-button:hover
  {
    list-style-image      : url("chrome://global/skin/print-hover.gif");
  }
#print-button > .menubutton-dual-stack > .menubutton-dual-button:hover:active
  {
    list-style-image      : url("chrome://global/skin/print-clicked.gif");
  }
#print-button > .menubutton-dual-stack > .menubutton-dual-dropmarker-box
  {
    margin-left        : 19px;
    margin-top         : 22px;
  }
```

Global skin

Almost all of the most specific skin files (e.g., *navigator.css*) inherit from the global skin, which includes but is not limited to the *global.css* file located in *chrome://modern.jar!/skin/global/skin/*.

The global skin includes other stylesheets that define localizable settings and general global formatting, which the *global.css* file loads at runtime. If you look at the top of the *global.css* file as shown in Example 4-7, you can see the stylesheet import statements that collect these skins into a single global skin:

Example 4-7. CSS Import statements in global skin

```
/* ===== global.css ==========================================================
   == Styles that apply everywhere.
   ======================================================================= */
/* all localizable skin settings shall live here */
@import url("chrome://global/locale/intl.css");
@import url("chrome://global/skin/formatting.css");
```

Example 4-7. CSS Import statements in global skin (continued)

```
@namespace url("http://www.mozilla.org/keymaster/gatekeeper/there.is.only.xul");
/* ::::: XBL bindings ::::: */
toolbarbutton[type="menu-button"] {
   -moz-binding: url("chrome://global/skin/globalBindings.xml#toolbar-menu-button");
}
.menulist-compact {
   -moz-binding:
      url("chrome://global/content/bindings/menulist.xml#menulist-compact");
}
...
```

The *global.css* serves as a base into which these other skins can be loaded. When you load *global.css* into your XUL file by means of a xul-stylesheet processing instruction, you in effect load these skins.

Also included in Example 4-7 are a couple of binding attachments, which attach content to elements that match certain style rules. On a related note, most global skins on a widget-per-widget basis are now included in the binding themselves, as opposed to being imported in a global skin, which used to be the case. Take this button stylesheet inclusion from the XBL file button.xml as a case in point:

```
<resources>
  <stylesheet src="chrome://global/skin/button.css"/>
</resources>
```

Here the XBL specific <stylesheet> element includes the stylesheet, which can be included in a binding and then inherited by other button bindings.

The communicator skin

Like *global.css*, the *communicator.css* file (Example 4-8) is another CSS file that does imports to build up the communicator skin. The CSS style rules in the file itself are minimal, but if you look at the top, you can see that many styles that the communicator component uses come from the CSS files also located in the *communicator* subdirectory of the current skin.

Example 4-8. CSS information from communicator.css

```
/* ==== communicator.css ====================================================
   == Styles shared everywhere throughout the Communicator suite.
   ========================================================================= */
@import url("chrome://global/skin/");
@import url("chrome://communicator/content/communicator.css");
@import url("chrome://communicator/skin/brand.css");
@import url("chrome://communicator/skin/button.css");
@import url("chrome://communicator/skin/formatting.css");

@namespace url("http://www.mozilla.org/keymaster/gatekeeper/there.is.only.xul");

/* ::::: online/offline icons ::::: */
```

Example 4-8. CSS information from communicator.css (continued)

```
#offline-status[offline="true"] {
  list-style-image: url("chrome://communicator/skin/icons/offline.gif");
}

#offline-status {
  list-style-image: url("chrome://communicator/skin/icons/online.gif");
}

/* ::::: directional button icons ::::: */

.up {
  min-width: 0px;
  list-style-image: url("chrome://global/skin/arrow/arrow-up.gif");
}

.up[disabled="true"] {
  list-style-image: url("chrome://global/skin/arrow/arrow-up-dis.gif");
}

.down {
  min-width: 0px;
  list-style-image: url("chrome://global/skin/arrow/arrow-dn.gif");
}

.down[disabled="true"] {
  list-style-image: url("chrome://global/skin/arrow/arrow-dn-dis.gif");
}

.up {
  list-style-image:url("chrome://global/skin/scroll-up.gif");
  min-width: 0px;
}
.up[disabled="true"] {
  list-style-image:url("chrome://global/skin/scroll-up-disabled.gif");
}
.down {
  min-width: 0px;
  list-style-image:url("chrome://global/skin/scroll-down.gif");
}
.down[disabled="true"] {
  list-style-image:url("chrome://global/skin/scroll-down-disabled.gif");
}
.sidebarTree {
  border: none;
  margin: 0px !important;
}
/* ::::: download manager ::::: */
#downloadView > treechildren:-moz-tree-image(Name) {
  margin-right: 2px;
}
```

Creating New Skins

You have already created the highest level of the directory structure you will need to create a skin for the xFly application (See "Creating the Hello xFly Package" in Chapter 2). So far, you have created three subdirectories corresponding to different parts of the package and you have added XUL to the *xfly/content* subdirectory. In the *xfly/skin* subdirectory, you will tell the xFly content where to expect to find its skin resources. As just mentioned, Mozilla applications outside of the browser itself typically restrict their skin to a single subdirectory and their skin manifest to a single RDF/XML file.

Since the *skin* subdirectory in your xFly package is already registered, you can create a new CSS file called *xfly.css*, save it in the *skins* subdirectory, and load it from your *xfly.xul* file by adding the following stylesheet loading instruction at the top:

```
<?xml-stylesheet href="chrome://xfly/skin" type="text/css" ?>
```

You will recall that the chrome pointer in the *href* resolves to a file named *xfly.css* (named after the directory) in the following *registered* directory in the chrome:

```
chrome/xfly/skin/
```

This CSS file will be the worksheet for all CSS for the xFly application. Any style rules you add here and associated with XUL elements in the xFly XUL code will affect the layout and presentation of that code on restart.

Importing the Global Skin

As you create a new skin for your application, the first step is to make sure that the application imports the global skin in which the most basic look and feel of the XUL widgets is defined. Even if you create a skin that looks completely different than the skins installed with Mozilla, you should import the global skin to avoid having to recreate so much of the basic presentation and behavior of the XUL widgets.

As much as possible, the global skin avoids providing theme-specific styles, and instead provides just enough information to make buttons, for example, look like buttons and menu items look like menu items. Increasingly, basic styles are also being defined in the XBL bindings for widgets. For instance, when you use a `toolbar` widget, you use a binding in which certain intrinsic looks and behaviors are defined in a way that's transparent to you and to the user of the application. The style for these bindings is located in the content subdirectories with the binding XML files. In this way, they "stay with" the widget and not with the selected skin. You can easily extend or overwrite any of the style information you pick up from the global skin, but loading the skin is a good place to start.

To do this, verify that you have the following line at the top of the *xfly.xul* file:

```
<?xml-stylesheet href="chrome://global/skin" type="text/css" ?>
```

If you do not have this line, add it now to the *xfly.xul* file and restart Mozilla. You ought to see a plain, UI-like collection of widgets in the XUL window. In the screenshots in Figure 4-8, you can see how loading the global skin affects the XUL file.

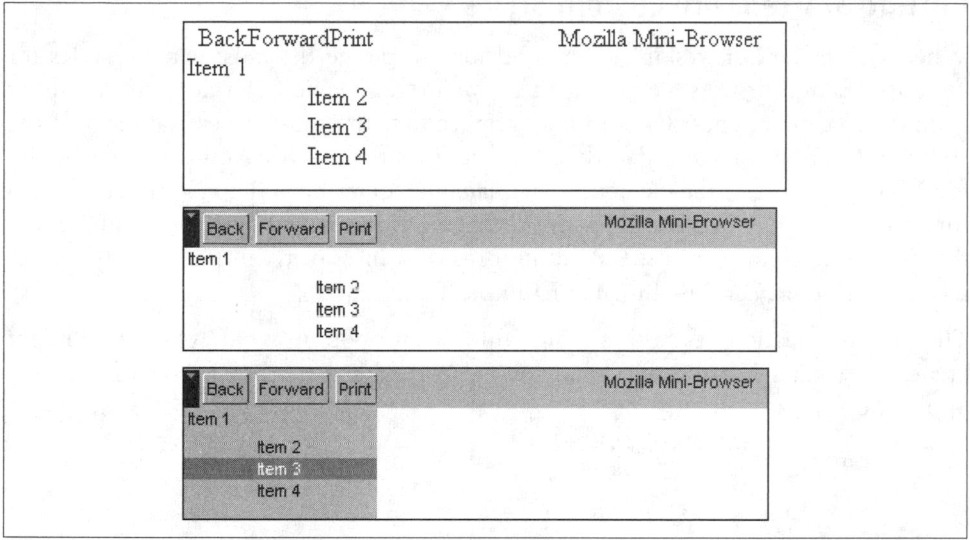

Figure 4-8. Stylesheet additions to a XUL file

The first screenshot in Figure 4-8 shows a XUL file loaded in Mozilla with no skin information. The second is the same XUL file with the global skin loading instruction at the top. The third is a screenshot of that XUL file with an instruction for loading your own stylesheet, which in turn imports the global skin:

```
<?xml-stylesheet href="chrome://xfly/skin/sample.css" type="text/css" ?>
```

The CSS information in the skin file *sample.css* loaded above looks like this:

```
@import url(chrome://global/skin/)
box#bbox { background-color: lightgrey; }
button#rd { background-color: red; color: white; }
```

Taking advantage of the modularity of Mozilla skins, you can design a decent interface (if the last screenshot above can count as that) with just a few lines of code.

Once you import the global skin and see what it buys you in terms of look and feel, you can begin to create your own skin for the xFly, overriding global styles where appropriate, extending them by "cascading" new, more specific style rules for your widgets, or adding new styles.

Before you begin to add styles to the *xfly.css* file, import it (as a blank skin) into *xfly.xul* so you can see your progress as you go. Add the following line to the top of the *xfly.xul* file to import the xFly skin from the proper subdirectory of the xFly package:

```
<?xml-stylesheet href="chrome://xfly/skin" type="text/css" ?>
```

You won't see anything extra when you quit and restart the application, but you now have the skin structure in place so you can see your work progress.

Getting Started with Custom Styles

When you make a new skin, it's a good idea to define the most general styles for your application first. As we described above, more specific CSS rules tend to inherit from more general ones. For the xFly application, the most general aspects of the style are the rules that apply to the xFly windows themselves. You can create styles for all windows using the element name, *window*, or you can define different classes for windows if your application supports them. In the *xfly.xul* file, for example, the root `<window>` element has the attribute `class="main"`, so it will pick up style rules given for *window.main*, as shown in Example 4-9.

The xFly application has both a main window and pop-up windows, so you might create style rules like the ones that follow to establish the basic look of the xFly application.

Example 4-9. CSS rules for xFly window

```
window.main {
   background-color:            #cccccc;
    display:                    block;
    overflow:                   hidden;
    font:                       small arial,helvetica,sans-serif,tahoma;
    padding:                    0px;
}
window.popup{

    background-color:           #cccccc;
    display:                    block;
    overflow:                   hidden;
    font:                       small arial,helvetica,sans-serif,tahoma;
    padding:                    2px;
    width:                      auto;
    height:                     auto;
}
```

Now, with the two stylesheets (*global.css* and the *xfly.css*) referenced at the top, you already have a window that is starting to look like an application.

Creating Styles for the xFly Buttons

Now that you have created a single custom style for the xFly application, you can see how easy it is to associate cascading style rules with any element in your interface. The next logical step is to style the buttons in the xFly sample application, since they make up such a large portion of the interface itself.

When you use the button widget without any extra style information, you already get a lot of the button-like presentation and behavior. The button has different looks, for example, when you hover over it and when you click it, and it has a basic three-dimensional shape as seen in Figure 4-9.

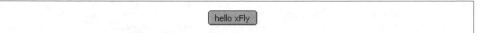

Figure 4-9. XUL button with no style

A common update to regular XUL buttons is to give them images, like the navigation buttons in the main Mozilla browser window. Adding the class-based style rule in Example 4-10 to the xFly stylesheet (and, of course, the GIF image itself to the *skin* subdirectory) will give all the "fly" buttons background images with flies in them.

Example 4-10. Custom styles for buttons

```
button.fly {
  list-style-image: url("chrome://xfly/skin/btnfly.gif");
}
button.fly[disabled="true"] {
  list-style-image: url("chrome://xfly/skin/btnfly-dis.gif ");
}
button.fly#hover {
  list-style-image: url("chrome://xfly/skin/btnfly-hov.gif ");
}
```

Describing the Skin in RDF

As described in Chapter 6, a manifest must accompany and describe the skin so it can be found and registered. The manifest is an RDF file called *contents.rdf* that sits at the highest level of the skin (i.e., at the top of the JAR or immediately under the *modern* directory when extracted to disk). Since the content, skin, and locale of an application are considered different packages, each must have its own manifest.

The listing in Example 4-11 shows the *contents.rdf* manifest that accompanies the xFly skin resources in the *xfly.jar!/skin/* directory.

Example 4-11. Skin manifest for the xFly sample

```
<?xml version="1.0"?>
<RDF:RDF xmlns:RDF="http://www.w3.org/1999/02/22-rdf-syntax-ns#
   xmlns:chrome="http://www.mozilla.org/rdf/chrome#">
  <RDF:Seq about="urn:mozilla:skin:root">
    <RDF:li resource="urn:mozilla:skin:classic/1.0" />
  </RDF:Seq>
  <RDF:Description about="urn:mozilla:skin:classic/1.0">
    <chrome:packages>
      <RDF:Seq about="urn:mozilla:skin:classic/1.0:packages">
```

Example 4-11. Skin manifest for the xFly sample (continued)

```
        <RDF:li resource="urn:mozilla:skin:classic/1.0:xfly"/>
      </RDF:Seq>
    </chrome:packages>
  </RDF:Description>
</RDF:RDF>
```

As you can see, the basic form of the manifest is something like, "This is the classic skin we have (given as a direct child of the RDF root element), which applies to the following packages: *xfly*." The second group of RDF in this manifest provides a list of packages to which the skin should apply. In the case of the xFly application, all XUL code is a single package. In Mozilla, a *contents.rdf* file in a package subdirectory of the *modern.jar*, for example, would describe the communicator package in a similar way, but it would be a composite of other package manifests in the theme to create a single, overarching manifest for the whole theme. Example 4-12 shows the manifest for just the Mozilla communicator package.

Example 4-12. Manifest for the communicator package of the modern skin in Mozilla

```
<?xml version="1.0"?>
<RDF:RDF xmlns:RDF="http://www.w3.org/1999/02/22-rdf-syntax-ns#"
         xmlns:chrome="http://www.mozilla.org/rdf/chrome#">
  <!-- List all the skins being supplied by this theme -->
  <RDF:Seq about="urn:mozilla:skin:root">
    <RDF:li resource="urn:mozilla:skin:modern/1.0" />
  </RDF:Seq>
  <!-- Modern Information -->
  <RDF:Description about="urn:mozilla:skin:modern/1.0">
    <chrome:packages>
      <RDF:Seq about="urn:mozilla:skin:modern/1.0:packages">
        <RDF:li resource="urn:mozilla:skin:modern/1.0:communicator"/>
      </RDF:Seq>
    </chrome:packages>
  </RDF:Description>
</RDF:RDF>
```

This RDF/XML file describes a skin to the chrome registry so it can be registered properly. All new packages must be accompanied by these sorts of RDF-based descriptions if they will be made available to users.

What Is Possible in a Skin?

In this final section, we describe a few things that make CSS in Mozilla particularly powerful and cases when this power is curtailed because of the security restrictions.

Binding New Widgets to the Interface Using XBL

A description of skins wouldn't be complete without a mention of binding widgets by using XBL, a very powerful feature of CSS in Mozilla. The `-moz-binding` keyword described in Table 4-4 is the key to binding special, prefabricated widgets to your XUL. The language in which these widgets are defined is another XML-based language called the Extensible Bindings Language. Chapter 7 describes this language in more detail.

To see how XBL works, go back and look at the first style rule for "print-button" in Example 4-6. The first style statement in that block has a property called `-moz-binding`. This property defines a *binding* for the XUL element styled by this style rule. The *chome URL* that the `-moz-binding` property points to is where an XBL-based definition of a print button is located.

Creating a style rule in which your XUL element (in this case, a button in which the ID is "print-button") and the use of the `-moz-binding` to point to the XBL defines new properties, behavior, or content for that XUL element, you can add to or totally recreate any widget in your interface. The binding itself is described in XBL, but XBL also provides structures (such as the `<content>` and `<handlers>` child elements) in which you can define new XUL content, new JavaScript, and new XPConnected interfaces. CSS glues the XUL together with the XBL.

In the first part of the snippet in Example 4-13, for example, the CSS rule binds the toolbar button to an XBL binding called *menu-button*, which adds a button and an image.

Example 4-13. CSS and XBL example

```
// In the CSS:
toolbarbutton[type="menu-button"] {
   -moz-binding: url("chrome://global/content/bindings/toolbarbutton.xml#menu-button");
}
// In the XBL file toolbarbutton.xml:
<binding id="menu-button" display="xul:menu"
    extends="chrome://global/content/bindings/button.xml#menu-button-base">
  <resources>
    <stylesheet src="chrome://global/skin/toolbarbutton.css"/>
  </resources>

  <content>
    <children includes="observes|template|menupopup|tooltip"/>
    <xul:toolbarbutton class="box-inherit toolbarbutton-menubutton-button"
                       anonid="button" flex="1" allowevents="true"
                       xbl:inherits="disabled,crop,image,label,accessKey,command,
                                     align,dir,pack,orient"/>
    <xul:dropmarker type="menu-button" class="toolbarbutton-menubutton-dropmarker"
                        xbl:inherits="align,dir,pack,orient,disabled"/>
  </content>
</binding>
```

When you use the Modern skin, you can see in Figure 4-10 that the menu button is a composite of the toolbar button, a dropmarker image resource, and a `menupopup` making the drop-down history available.

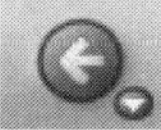

Figure 4-10. Modern menu button

You might also notice in Example 4-13 that this binding pulls in an external stylesheet (`toolbarbutton.css`), which is contained in the `<resources>` section of the binding. This stylesheet provides all the styles and theme information for a toolbar button, including the type of `menu-button`. More information on stylesheets in XBL can be found in Chapter 7.

User Stylesheets

In addition to the many CSS stylesheets that give the user interface its look, Mozilla also lets you create personal stylesheets that apply to all of the chrome and content you view in the browser. Two CSS files, *userChrome.css* and *userContent.css*, located in the *chrome* subdirectory of your user profile, can define rules that apply to all of the Mozilla application interfaces and all web pages you view, respectively. When these two files are present—sometimes they are installed in the user profile and sometimes you create them yourself—they come with example rules that are commented out. However, you can uncomment them and add your own rules to personalize the look of the browser and its content.

Example 4-14 shows the default commented rules in *userChrome.css*. Note the use of the `!important` keyword to specify that these rules should take precedence over rules that come from stylesheets in the current theme.

Example 4-14. userChrome.css style rules

```
/*
 * This file can be used to customize the look of Mozilla's user interface
 * You should consider using !important on rules which you want to
 * override default settings.
 */
/*
 * example: make the UI look a little more like Irix (nice readable
 *          slanted-helvetical menus, funny pink color on text fields)
 *
 * input {
 *   color: black !important;
 *   background-color: rgb(255, 225, 175) !important;
 * }
 *
 * menubar {
 *   font-family: helvetica !important;
 *   font-style: italic !important;
 *   font-weight: bold !important;
 *   font-size: 4mm !important;
```

Example 4-14. userChrome.css style rules (continued)

```
 * }
 */
/*
 * For more examples see http://www.mozilla.org/unix/customizing.html
 */
```

If you want to make the content in all your menu widgets white so you can read them better, get rid of these defaults and do something like this:

```
menu {
  background-color: white !important;
  color: darkblue !important;
  padding: 5px !important;
}
```

You can also use these stylesheets to change or do away with aspects of the user interface you don't like. The following rule, for example, shrinks the navigation buttons in the Modern theme:

```
.toolbarbutton-menubutton-button > .toolbarbutton-box,
.toolbarbutton-1 > .toolbarbutton-box
{
  max-width: 40px !important;
  text-align: center !important;
}
```

Or, if you can think of the appropriate selectors, you can use *userContent.css* to change the way banner images are displayed (or not displayed), how basic text is presented, or where certain elements of a web page are positioned.

Theme Security Restrictions

To prevent the wholesale overriding of the basic XUL application, various restrictions are placed on themes. In other words, you can do some things in XUL that you cannot do in CSS. The two preinstalled themes in Mozilla, Modern, and Classic use technologies like XBL, JavaScript, and XPConnect to provide additional behavior to the application. They are considered full-blown packages, like entirely separate interfaces (see Chapter 6 for a description the various types of packages and installations). When you install new themes, however, those themes do not have "script access" and have limited access to XBL bindings.

Code in the `<implementation>` and `<handler>` structures of an XBL binding are ignored, as are event handlers written in the `<content>` structures.

You can write these XBL goodies into your theme if you want (or develop a theme out of the Modern theme, where there is plenty of XBL, and see them disabled in your theme when they were working in that preinstalled version), but Mozilla will not read or execute them. You can use XBL to define new XUL content for a widget by way of CSS, but unless you create an "evil skin," that content has to be simple XUL to show up in your theme at all.

Evil Skins

In the Mozilla community, the term "evil skins" is sometimes used to describe skins with unlimited script access. An evil skin is a skin for which the security restrictions above do not apply. They can access the DOM of the web page and XUL content, use XPConnect to connect to the Mozilla services in XPCOM, or implement new application code in XBL widgets.

Remember that when you develop skins for Mozilla and package them for installation as skins, the script part of your skins will be disabled. However, if you create a skin and then install it as a new package, your skin will not be as limited, and you will have full access to XBL, XPConnect, and the script. To see how to install an evil skin and other new packages in Mozilla, see Chapter 6.

CHAPTER 5

Scripting Mozilla

In Mozilla, scripting plays important roles in the XPFE. Whether developers refer to script access and security, user interface logic, XPCOM object invocation, or script execution in element event handlers, scripting is so integral to application development that Mozilla, as a development platform, would be inconceivable without it.

The core scripting language used in Mozilla is JavaScript. Although it has had a reputation as an unsophisticated language used mostly in web pages, JavaScript is more like a first-tier programming language. Modularity, good exception handing, regular expression enhancement, and number formatting are just some features of the new JavaScript 1.5,* which is based on the ECMA-262 standard.† JavaScript 2.0, due sometime late in 2002, promises to be an even bigger promotion of the language.

Three distinct levels of JavaScript are identified in this chapter. A user interface level manipulates content through the DOM, a client layer calls on the services provided by XPCOM, and, finally, an application layer is available in which JavaScript can create an XPCOM component. The following section describes these levels in detail.

Faces of JavaScript in Mozilla

As you have already seen in some examples in this book, the user interface uses JavaScript extensively to create behavior and to glue various widgets together into a coherent whole. When you add code to the event handler of one element to manipulate another—for example, when you update the value of a textbox using a XUL button—you take advantage of this first "level" of scriptability. In this role, JavaScript uses the Document Object Model (DOM) to access parts of the user interface as a hierarchical collection of objects. The section "Adding Scripts to the UI," later in this chapter, discusses this highest level of scripting.

* This book does not pretend to give a complete overview of JavaScript. You can view the full JavaScript 1.5 reference online at *http://developer.netscape.com/docs/manuals/js/core/jsref15/contents.html.*

† The third edition of the EMCA-262 EMCAScript Language Specification can be found at *http://www.ecma.ch/ecma1/STAND/ECMA-262.HTM.*

At a second level, JavaScript glues the entire user interface to the XPCOM libraries beneath, which create the application core. At this level, XPConnect (see the section "What Is XPConnect?" later in this chapter) provides a bridge that makes these components "scriptable," which means that they can be invoked from JavaScript and used from the user interface layer. When JavaScript calls methods and gets data from scriptable components, it uses this second layer of scriptability.

Finally, at the third and ultimate level of Mozilla scripting, JavaScript can be used as a "first-order" language for creating the application core itself, for writing software components or libraries whose services are called. We discuss this third level of scripting and provide a long example in the section "Creating a JavaScript XPCOM Component" in Chapter 8.

When you use JavaScript in these contexts, the application architecture looks something like Figure 5-1, in which scripting binds the user interface to the application core through XPConnect and can reside as a software component using such technologies as XPIDL and XPCOM.

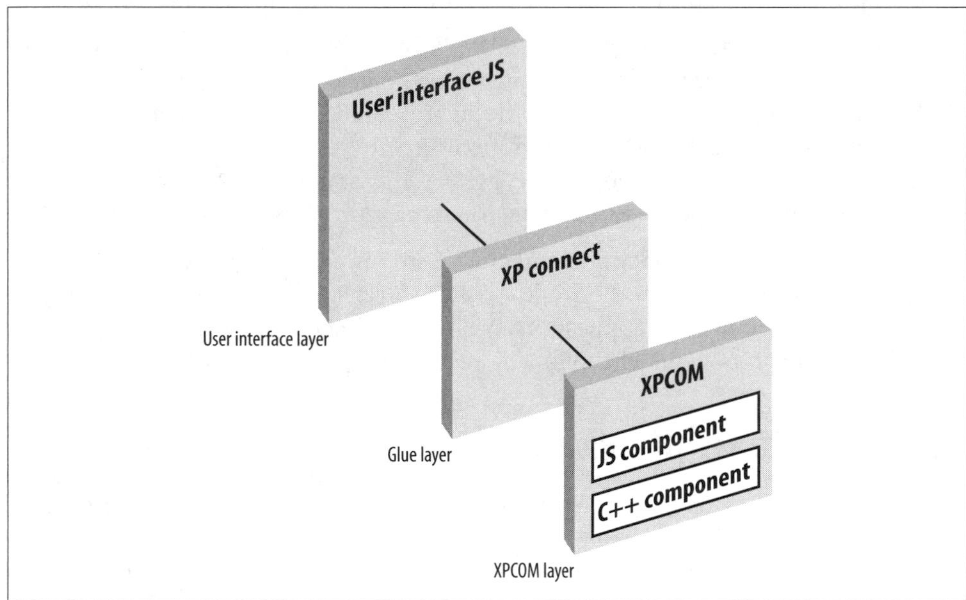

Figure 5-1. Scripting in Mozilla

JavaScript and the DOM

In the application layer of Mozilla, there is little distinction between a web page and the graphical user interface. Mozilla's implementation of the DOM is fundamentally the same for both XUL and HTML. In both cases, state changes and events are propagated through various DOM calls, meaning that the UI itself is content—not unlike that of a web page. In application development, where the difference between application "chrome" and rendered content is typically big, this uniformity is a significant step forward.

What Is the DOM?

The DOM is an API used to access HTML and XML documents. It does two things for web developers: provides a structural representation of the document and defines the way the structure should be accessed from script. In the Mozilla XPFE framework, this functionality allows you to manipulate the user interface as a structured group of nodes, create new UI and content, and remove elements as needed.

Because it is designed to access arbitrary HTML and XML, the DOM applies not only to XUL, but also to MathML, SVG, and other XML markup. By connecting web pages and XML documents to scripts or programming languages, the DOM is not a particular application, product, or proprietary ordering of web pages. Rather, it is an *API*—an interface that vendors must implement if their products are to conform to the W3C DOM standard. Mozilla's commitment to standards ensures that its applications and tools do just that.

When you use JavaScript to create new elements in an HTML file or change the attributes of a XUL `button`, you access an object model in which these structures are organized. This model is the DOM for that document or data. The DOM provides a context for the scripting language to operate in. The specific context for web and XML documents—the top-level `window` object, the elements that make up a web document, and the data stored in those elements as children—is standardized in several different specifications, the most recent of which is the upcoming DOM Level 3 standard.

The DOM Standards and Mozilla

The DOM specifications are split into different levels overseen by the W3C. Each level provides its own features and Mozilla has varying, but nearly complete, levels of support for each. Currently, Mozilla's support for the DOM can be summarized as follows:

- DOM Level 1: Excellent
- DOM Level 2: Good
- DOM Level 3: Poor; under construction

Mozilla strives to be standards-compliant, but typically reaches full support only when those standards have become recommendations rather than working drafts. Currently, Level 1 and Level 2 are recommendations and Level 3 is a working draft.

Standards like the DOM make Mozilla an especially attractive software development kit (SDK) for web developers. The same layout engine that renders web content also draws the GUI and pushes web development out of the web page into the application chrome. The DOM provides a consistent, unified interface for accessing all the documents you develop, making the content and chrome accessible for easy cross-platform development and deployment.

DOM Methods and Properties

Methods in the DOM allow you to access and manipulate any element in the user interface or in the content of a web page. Getting and setting attributes, creating elements, hiding elements, and appending children all involve direct manipulation of the DOM. The DOM mediates all interaction between scripts and the interface itself, so even when you do something as simple as changing an image when the user clicks a button, you use the DOM to register an event handler with the `button` and DOM attributes on the `image` element to change its source.

The DOM Level 1 and Level 2 Core specifications contain multiple interfaces, including *Node*, *NodeList*, *Element*, and *Document*. The following sections describe some interface methods used to manipulate the object model of application chrome, documents, or metadata in Mozilla. The *Document* and *Element* interfaces, in particular, contain useful methods for XUL developers.

Using dump() to print to STDOUT

The code samples in this chapter use a method called `dump()` to print data to STDOUT. This method is primarily used for debugging your code and is turned on using a `PREF`. You can turn this `PREF` on using the following code:

```
const PREFS_CID      = "@mozilla.org/preferences;1";
const PREFS_I_PREF   = "nsIPref";
const PREF_STRING    = "browser.dom.window.dump.enabled";
  try {
    var Pref        = new Components.Constructor(PREFS_CID, PREFS_I_PREF);
    var pref        = new Pref();
    pref.SetBoolPref(PREF_STRING, true);
  } catch(e) {}
```

This code is necessary only if you are doing development with a release distribution build of Mozilla. If you are using a debug or nightly build, this `PREF` can be set from the preferences panel by selecting Edit → Preferences → Debug → Enable JavaScript dump() output.

getElementById

`getElementById(aId)` is perhaps the most commonly used DOM method in any programming domain. This is a convenient way to get a reference to an element object by passing that element's `id` as an argument, where the `id` acts as a unique identifier for that element.

DOM calls like this are at the heart of Mozilla UI functionality. `getElementById` is the main programmatic entry point into the chrome and is essential for any dynamic manipulation of XUL elements. For example, to get a box element in script (i.e., to get a reference to it so you can call its methods or read data from it), you must refer to it by using the box `id`:

```
<box id="my-id" />
```

Since the return value of `getElementById` is a reference to the specified element object, you usually assign it to a variable like this:

```
var boxEl = document.getElementById('my-id');
dump("boxEl="+boxEl+"\n");
console output: boxEl=[object XULElement]
```

Once you have the box element available as `boxEl`, you can use other DOM methods like `getAttribute` and `setAttribute` to change its layout, its position, its state, or other features.

getAttribute

Attributes are properties that are defined directly on an element. XUL elements have attributes such as `disabled`, `height`, `style`, `orient`, and `label`.

```
<box id="my-id" foo="hello 1" bar="hello 2" />
```

In the snippet above, the strings "my-id," "hello 1," and "hello 2" are values of the box element attributes. Note that Gecko does not enforce a set of attributes for XUL elements. XUL documents must be well-formed, but they are not validated against any particular XUL DTD or schema. This lack of enforcement means that attributes can be placed on elements ad hoc. Although this placement can be confusing, particularly when you look at the source code for the Mozilla browser itself, it can be very helpful when you create your own applications and want to track the data that interests you.

Once you have an object assigned to a variable, you can use the DOM method `getAttribute` to get a reference to any attribute in that object. The `getAttribute` method takes the name of the desired attribute as a string. For example, if you add an attribute called `foo` to a box element, you can access that attribute's value and assign it to a variable:

```
<box id="my-id" foo="this is the foo attribute" />
<script>
  var boxEl = document.getElementById('my-id');
  var foo   = boxEl.getAttribute('foo');
  dump(foo+'\n');
</script>
```

The `dump` method outputs the string "this is the foo attribute," which is the value of the attribute `foo`. You can also add or change existing attributes with the `setAttribute` DOM method.

setAttribute

The setAttribute method changes an existing attribute value. This method is useful for changing the state of an element—its visibility, size, order within a parent, layout and position, style, etc. It takes two arguments: the attribute name and the new value.

```
<box id="my-id" foo="this is the foo attribute" />
<script>
  boxEl=document.getElementById('my-id');
  boxEl.setAttribute('foo', 'this is the foo attribute changed');
  var foo = boxEl.getAttribute('foo');
  dump(foo+'\n');
</script>
```

The script above outputs the string "this is the foo attribute changed" to the console. You can also use setAttribute to create a new attribute if it does not already exist:

```
<box id="my-id" />
<script>
  boxEl=document.getElementById('my-id');
  boxEl.setAttribute('bar', 'this is the new attribute bar');
</script>
```

By setting an attribute that doesn't already exist, you create it dynamically, adding a value to the hierarchical representation of nodes that form the current document object. After this code is executed, the boxEl element is the same as an element whose bar attribute was hardcoded into the XUL:

```
<box id="my-id" bar="this is the new attribute bar" />
```

These sorts of ad hoc changes give you complete control over the state of the application interface.

createElement

If you need to dynamically create an element that doesn't already exist—for example, to add a new row to a table displaying rows of information, you can use the method createElement. To create and add a text element to your box example, for example, you can use the following code:

```
<box id="my-id" />
<script>
  boxEl = document.getElementById('my-id');
  var textEl  = document.createElement('description');
  boxEl.appendChild(textEl);
</script>
```

Once you create the new element and assign it to the textEl variable, you can use appendChild to insert it into the object tree. In this case, it is appended to boxEl, which becomes the insertion point.

For mixed namespace documents like XUL and HTML, you can use a variation of createElement called createElementNS. To create a mixed namespace element, use this code:

```
var node = document.createElementNS('http://www.w3.org/1999.
xhtml', 'html:div');
```

Namespace variations for other functions include setAttributeNS, getElementsByTagNameNS, and hasAttributeNS.

createTextNode

In addition to setting the label attribute on an element, you can create new text in the interface by using the DOM method createTextNode, as shown in the following example:

```
<description id="explain" />
<script>
   var description = document.getElementById("explain");
   if (description) {
     if (!description.childNodes.length) {
       var textNode = document.createTextNode("Newly text");
       description.appendChild(textNode);
     }
     else if (description.childNodes.length == 1 ) {
      description.childNodes[0].nodeValue = "Replacement text";
    }
  }
</script>
```

Notice the use of appendChild. This method, discussed next, is used to insert the new element or text node into the DOM tree after it is created. Create-and-append is a common two-step process for adding new elements to the object model.

appendChild

To dynamically add an element to a document, you need to use the method appendChild(). This method adds a newly created element to an existing parent node by appending to it. If a visible widget is added, this change is visible in the interface immediately.

```
<groupbox id="my-id" />
<script>
  var existingEl  = document.getElementById('my-id');
  var captionEl   = document.createElement('caption');
  existingEl.appendChild(captionEl);
  captionEl.setAttribute('label', 'This is a new caption');
  captionEl.setAttribute('style', 'color: blue;');
</script>
```

This example creates a new element, gets an existing parent element from the document, and then uses appendChild() to insert that new element into the document. It also uses setAttribute to add an attribute value and some CSS style rules, which can highlight the new element in the existing interface.

cloneNode

For elements that already exist, a copy method allows you to duplicate elements to avoid having to recreate them from scratch. cloneNode, which is a method on the element object rather than the document, returns a copy of the given node.

```
<script>
  // this is untested --pete
  var element = document.getElementById('my-id');
  var clone = element.cloneNode(false);
  dump(`element='+element+'\n');
  dump(`clone='+clone+'\n');
</script>
```

The method takes a Boolean-optional parameter that specifies whether the copy is "deep." Deep copies duplicate all descendants of a node as well as the node itself.

getElementsByTagName

Another very useful method is getElementsByTagName. This method returns an array of elements of the specified type. The argument used is the string *element type*. "box," for example, could be used to obtain an array of all boxes in a document. The array is zero-based, so the elements start at 0 and end with the last occurrence of the element in the document. If you have three boxes in a document and want to reference each box, you can do it as follows:

```
<box id="box-one" />
<box id="box-two" />
<box id="box-three" />
<script>
  document.getElementsByTagName('box')[0];
  document.getElementsByTagName('box')[1];
  document.getElementsByTagName('box')[2];
</script.
```

Or you can get the array and index into it like this:

```
var box = document.getElementsByTagName('box');
```

box[0], the first object in the returned array, is a XUL box.

To see the number of boxes on a page, you can use the length property of an array:

```
var len = document.getElementsByTagName('box').length;
dump(l+'\n');
console output: 3
```

To output the id of the box:

```
<box id="box-one" />
<box id="box-two" />
<box id="box-three" />
<script>
  var el      = document.getElementsByTagName('box');
  var tagId   = el[0].id;
```

```
    dump(tagId+"\n");
  </script>
  console output: box-one
```

To get to an attribute of the second box:

```
  <box id="box-one" />
  <box id="box-two" foo="some attribute for the second box" />
  <box id="box-three" />
  <script>
    var el        = document.getElementsByTagName('box');
    var att       = el[1].getAttribute('foo');
    dump(att      +"\n");
  </script>
  console output: some attribute for the second box
```

`getElementsByTagName` is a handy way to obtain DOM elements without using `getElementById`. Not all elements have `id` attributes, so other means of getting at the elements must be used occasionally.*

Getting an element object and its properties

In addition to a basic set of attributes, an element may have many properties. These properties don't typically appear in the markup for the element, so they can be harder to learn and remember. To see the properties of an element object node, however, you can use a JavaScript `for in` loop to iterate through the list, as shown in Example 5-1.

Example 5-1. Printing element properties to the console

```
<box id="my-id" />
<script>
  var el = document.getElementById('my-id');
  for (var list in el)
    dump("property  = "+list+"\n");
</script>
console output(subset):
property = id
property = className
property = style
property = boxObject
property = tagName
property = nodeName
. . .
```

Note the implicit functionality in the `el` object itself: when you iterate over the object reference, you ask for all members of the class of which that object is an instance.

* You can use other DOM methods, but these methods are most commonly used in the XPFE. Mozilla's support for the DOM is so thorough that you can use the W3C specifications as a list of methods and properties available to you in the chrome and in the web content the browser displays. The full W3C activity pages, including links to the specifications implemented by Mozilla, can be found at *http://www.w3.org/DOM/*.

This simple example "spells" the object out to the console. Since the DOM recognizes the window as another element (albeit the root element) in the Document Object Model, you can use a similar script in Example 5-2 to get the properties of the window itself.

Example 5-2. Printing the window properties

```
<script>
  var el        = document.getElementById('test-win');
  for(var list in el)
    dump("property  = "+list+"\n");
</script>
console output(subset):
property = nodeName
property = nodeValue
property = nodeType
property = parentNode
property = childNodes
property = firstChild
. . .
```

The output in Example 5-2 is a small subset of all the DOM properties associated with a XUL window and the other XUL elements, but you can see all of them if you run the example. Analyzing output like this can familiarize you with the interfaces available from `window` and other DOM objects.

Retrieving elements by property

You can also use a DOM method to access elements with specific properties by using `getElementsByAttribute`. This method takes the name and value of the attribute as arguments and returns an array of nodes that contain these attribute values:

```
<checkbox id="box-one" />
<checkbox id="box-two" checked="true"/>
<checkbox id="box-three" checked="true"/>
<script>
  var chcks = document.getElementsByAttribute("checked", "true");
  var count = chcks.length;
  dump(count + " items checked \n");
</script>
```

One interesting use of this method is to toggle the state of elements in an interface, as when you get all menu items whose `disabled` attribute is set to true and set them to false. In the xFly sample, you can add this functionality with a few simple updates. In the *xfly.js* file in the xFly package, add the function defined in Example 5-3.

Example 5-3. Adding toggle functionality to xFly

```
function toggleCheck() {
  // get the elements before you make any changes
  var chex   = document.getElementsByAttribute("disabled", "true");
  var unchex = document.getElementsByAttribute("disabled", "false");
```

Example 5-3. Adding toggle functionality to xFly (continued)

```
  for (var i=0; i<chex.length; i++)
      chex[i].setAttributte("checked", "false");
  for (var i=0; i<unchex.length; i++)
      unchex[i].setAttributte("checked", "true");
}
```

Although this example doesn't update elements whose disabled attribute is not specified, you can call this function from a new menu item and have it update all menus whose checked state you do monitor, as shown in Example 5-4.

Example 5-4. Adding Toggle menus to xFly

```
<menubar id="appbar">
  <menu label="File">
     <menupopup>
       <menuitem label="New"/>
       <menuitem label="Open"/>
     </menupopup>
  </menu>
  <menu label="Edit">
     <menupopup>
       <menuitem label="Toggle" oncommand="toggleCheck();" />
     </menupopup>
  </menu>
  <menu label="Fly Types">
     <menupopup>
       <menuitem label="House" disabled="true" />
       <menuitem label="Horse" disabled="true" />
       <menuitem label="Fruit" disabled="false" />
     </menupopup>
  </menu>

</menubar>
```

When you add this to the xFly application window (from Example 2-10, for example, above the basic vbox structure), you get an application menu bar with a menu item, Toggle, that reverses the checked state of the three items in the "Fly Types" menu, as seen in Figure 5-2.

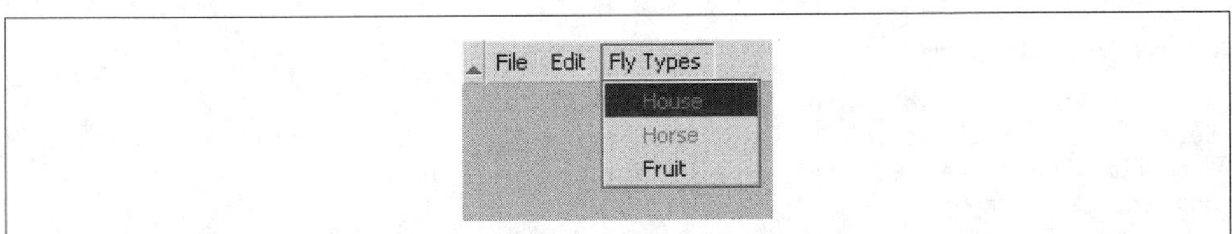

Figure 5-2. Toggling the state of menu items in xFly

The following section explains more about hooking scripts up to the interface. Needless to say, when you use a method like getElementsByAttribute that operates on all elements with a particular attribute value, you must be careful not to grab elements you didn't intend (like a button elsewhere in the application that gets disabled for other purpose).

Adding Scripts to the UI

Once you are comfortable with how JavaScript works in the context of the user interface layer and are familiar with some of the primary DOM methods used to manipulate the various elements and attributes, you can add your own scripts to your application. Though you can use other techniques to get scripts into the UI, one of the most common methods is to use Mozilla's event model, which is described in the next few sections.

Handling Events from a XUL Element

Events are input messages that pass information from the user interface to the application code. Capturing this information, or *event handling*, is how you usually tell scripts when to start and stop.

When the user clicks a XUL button, for instance, the button "listens" for the click event, and may also handle that event. If the button itself does not handle the event (e.g., by supplying executable JavaScript in an event handler attribute), then the event "bubbles," or travels further up into the hierarchy of elements above the button. The event handlers in Example 5-3 use simple inline JavaScript to show that the given event (e.g., the window loading in the first example, the button getting clicked in the second, and so on) was fired and handled.

As in HTML, predefined event handlers are available as attributes on a XUL element. These attributes are entry points where you can hook in your JavaScript code, as these examples show. Note that event handler attributes are technically a shortcut, for which the alternative is to register event listeners explicitly to specified elements. The value of these `on[event]` event handler attributes is the inline JavaScript that should be executed when that event is triggered. Example 5-5 shows some basic button activation events.

Example 5-5. Basic event handler attributes

```
<window onload="dump('this window has loaded\n');" />
<button label="onclick-test"
   onclick="dump('The event handler onclick has just been used\n');" />
<button label="oncommand-test"
   oncommand="dump('The event handler oncommand has just been used\n');" />
<menulist id="custom"
   onchange="doMyCustomFunction();" />
```

While the window and button events in Example 5-5 carry out some inline script, there is a variation with the onchange handler attached to the menulist element. onchange contains a JavaScript function call whose definition may live in the XUL document itself or in an external file that is included by using the src attribute on a script element:

```
<script type="application/x-javascript" src="chrome://mypackage/content/myfile.js" />
```

A large basic set of event handler attributes is available for use on XUL elements (and HTML elements). Appendix C has a full listing of these events along with explanations. The following subset shows the potential for script interaction when the UI uses event handlers:

```
onabort
onblur
onerror
onfocus
onchange
onclick
oncontextmenu
ondestroy
onload
onpaint
onkeydown
onkeypress
onkeyup
onunload
onmousemove
onmouseout
onmouseover
onmouseup
onmousedown
onrest
onresize
onscroll
onselect
onsubmit
```

Some of these event handlers work only on particular elements, such as window, which listens for the load event, the paint event, and other special events.

To see all event handler attributes on a particular element, you can execute the short script in Example 5-6, which uses the for in loop in JavaScript to iterate over the members of an object—in this case, a XUL element.

Example 5-6. Getting event handler attributes from an element

```
<script type="application/x-javascript">
  function listElementHandlers(aObj)
  {
    if(!aObj)
      return null;
    for(var list in aObj)
```

Example 5-6. Getting event handler attributes from an element (continued)

```
      if(list.match(/^on/))
        dump(list+'\n');
  }
</script>
<button label="oncommand" oncommand="listElementHandlers(this);" />
```

The function you added in Example 5-4 is also an example of event handler code in an application's interface.

Events and the Mozilla Event Model

The event model in Mozilla is the general framework for how events work and move around in the user interface. As you've already seen, events tend to rise up through the DOM hierarchy—a natural process referred to as event propagation or event bubbling. The next two sections describe event propagation and its complement, event capturing.

Event propagation and event bubbling

This availability of events in nodes above the element of origin is known as event propagation or event bubbling. Event bubbling means you can handle events anywhere above the event-raising element in the hierarchy. When events are handled by elements that did not initiate those events, you must determine which element below actually raised the event. For example, if an event handler in a menu element handles an event raised by one of the menu items, then the menu should be able to identify the raising element and take the appropriate action, as shown in Example 5-7. In this example, a JavaScript function determines which `menuitem` was selected and responds appropriately.

Example 5-7. Event propagation

```
<script type="application/x-javascript">
function doCMD(el) {
    v = el.getAttribute("label")
    switch (v) {
      case "New":
        alert('New clicked');
         break;
      case "Open":
        alert('Open clicked');
        break;
      case "Close":
        alert('Close clicked');
        break;
    }
}
</script>
...
<menu class="menu" label="File" oncommand="doCMD(event.target)">
```

Example 5-7. Event propagation (continued)

```
  <menupopup>
    <menuitem label="New" />
    <menuitem label="Open" />
    <menuitem label="Close" />
  </menupopup>
</menu>
```

The event handler in the parent node menu finds out which child `menuitem` was actually clicked by using `event.target` and takes action accordingly. Let's walk through another possible scenario. If a user of an application selects an item from a menu list, you could get the node of that item by using `event.target`. Your script could then abstract that item's value or other information, if necessary.

Trapping events. When an event is raised, it is typically handled by any node interested in it as it continues its way up the DOM hierarchy. In some cases, you may want to handle an event and then prevent it from bubbling further up, which is where the DOM Event method `stopPropagation()` comes in handy.

Example 5-8 demonstrates how event bubbling can be arrested very simply. When the XUL document in Example 5-8 loads, an event listener is registered with a `row` in the tree. The event listener handles the event by executing the function `stopEvent()`. This function calls an event object method, `stopPropagation`, which keeps the event from bubbling further up into the DOM. Note that the tree itself has an `onclick` event handler that should display a message when clicked. However, the `stopEvent()` method has stopped propagation, so after the data in the table is updated, the event phase is effectively ended. In this case, the function was used to trap the event and handle it only there.

Example 5-8. stopPropagation() event function

```
<?xml version="1.0"?>
<!DOCTYPE  window>
<window id="test-win"
  xmlns="http://www.mozilla.org/keymaster/gatekeeper/there.is.only.xul"
  orient="vertical"
  onload="load();">
<script type="application/x-javascript">
  function load() {
    el = document.getElementById("t");
    el.addEventListener("click", stopEvent, false);
  }
  function stopEvent(e) {
    // this ought to keep t-daddy from getting the click.
    e.stopPropagation();
  }
</script>
<tree>
  <!-- tree columns definition omitted -->
  <treechildren flex="1" >
    <treeitem id="t-daddy"
```

Example 5-8. stopPropagation() event function (continued)

```
      onclick="alert('t-daddy');"  // this event is never fired
      container="true" parent="true">
      <treerow id="t">
        <treecell label="O'Reilly" id="t1" />
        <treecell label="http://www.oreilly.com" id="t2" />
      </treerow>
    </treeitem>
  </treechildren>
</tree>
</window>
```

Capturing events

Event capturing is the complement of event bubbling. The DOM provides the `addEventListener` method for creating event listeners on nodes that do not otherwise supply them. When you register an event listener on an ancestor of the event target (i.e., any node above the event-raising element in the node hierarchy), you can use event capturing to handle the event in the ancestor before it is heard in the target itself or any intervening nodes.

To take advantage of event capturing (or event bubbling with elements that do not already have event listeners), you must add an event listener to the element that wants to capture events occurring below it. Any XUL element may use the DOM `addEventListener` method to register itself to capture events. The syntax for using this method in XUL is shown here:

```
XULelement = document.getElementById("id of XULelement");
XULelement.addEventListener("event name", "event handler code",
  useCapture bool);
```

The event handler code argument can be inline code or the name of a function. The `useCapture` parameter specifies whether the event listener wants to use event capturing or be registered to listen for events that bubble up the hierarchy normally. In Figure 5-3, the alert dialog invoked by the `menuitem` itself is not displayed, since the root `window` element used event capture to handle the event itself.

An `onload` event handler for a XUL window can also register a `box` element to capture all click events that are raised from its child elements:

```
var bbox = document.getElementById("bigbox");
if (bbox) {
  bbox.addEventListener("click", "alert('captured')", true);
}
...
<box id="bigbox">
  <menu label="File">
    <menupopup>
      <menuitem label="New" onclick="alert('not captured')" />
      ...
    <menupopup>
  </menu>
</box>
```

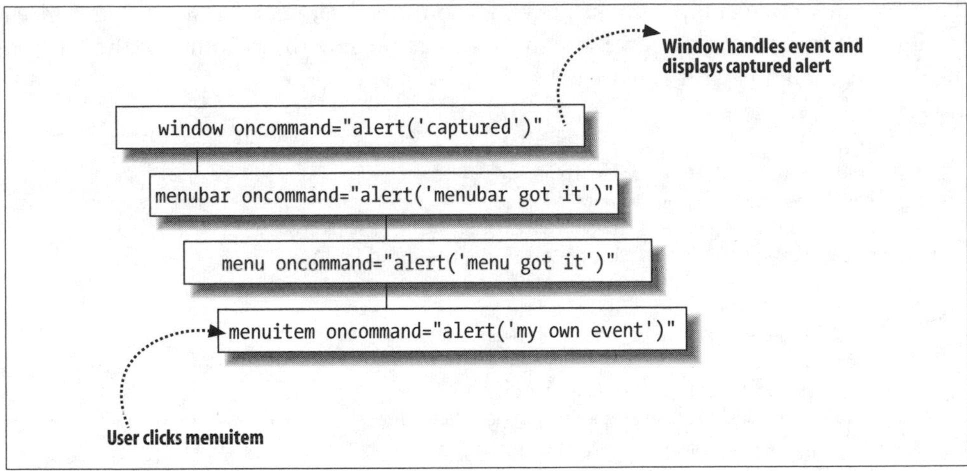

Figure 5-3. Event capturing

Changing an Element's CSS Style Using JavaScript

Much of what makes the Mozilla UI both flexible and programmable is its ability to dynamically alter the CSS style rules for elements at runtime. For example, if you have a button, you can toggle its visibility by using a simple combination of JavaScript and CSS. Given a basic set of buttons like this:

```
<button id="somebutton" class="testButton" label="foo" />
<spacer flex="1" />
<button id="ctlbutton"
  class="testButton"
  label="make disappear"
  oncommand="disappear();" />
```

as well as a stylesheet import statement at the top of the XUL like this:

```
<?xml-stylesheet href="test.css" type="text/css"?>
```

and a simple CSS file in your *chrome/xfly/content* directory called *test.css* that contains the following style rule:

```
#somebutton[hidden="true"]{ display: none; }
.testButton{
  border           : 1px outset #cccccc;
  background-color : #cccccc;
  padding          : 4px;
  margin           : 50px;
}
```

You can call `setAttribute` in your script to hide the button at runtime.

```
<script>
  function disappear(){
  return document.getElementById('somebutton').setAttribute('hidden', true);
  }
</script>
```

The previous code snippet makes a visible button disappear by setting its hidden attribute to true. Adding a few more lines, you can toggle the visibility of the button, also making it appear if it is hidden:

```
<script>
 function disappear(){
   const defaultLabel  = "make disappear";
   const newLabel      = "make reappear";
   var button          = document.getElementById('somebutton');
   var ctlButton       = document.getElementById('ctlbutton');
   if(!button.getAttribute('hidden')) {
     button.setAttribute('hidden', true);
     ctlButton.setAttribute('label', newLabel);
   } else  {
     button.removeAttribute('hidden');
     ctlButton.setAttribute('label', defaultLabel);
   }
  return;
 }
</script>
```

Another useful application of this functionality is to collapse elements such as toolbars, boxes, and iframes in your application.

The setAttribute method can also be used to update the element's class attribute with which style rules are so often associated. toolbarbutton-1 and button-toolbar are two different classes of button. You can change a button from a toolbarbutton-1—the large button used in the browser—to a standard toolbar button using the following DOM code:

```
// get the Back button in the browser
b1 = document.getElementById("back-button");\
b1.setAttribute("class", "button-toolbar");
```

This dynamically demotes the Back button to an ordinary toolbar button. Code such as this assumes, of course, that you know the classes that are used to style the various widgets in the interface.

You can also set the style attribute directly using the DOM:

```
el = document.getElementById("some-element");
el.setAttribute("style", "background-color:darkblue;");
```

Be aware, however, that when you set the style attribute in this way, you are overwriting whatever style properties may already have been defined in the style attribute. If the document referenced in the snippet above by the ID some-element has a style attribute in which the font size is set to 18pc, for example, that information is erased when the style attribute is manipulated in this way.

Creating Elements Dynamically

Using the `createElement` method in XUL lets you accomplish things similar to `document.write` in HTML, with which you can create new pages and parts of a web page. In Example 5-9, `createElement` is used to generate a menu dynamically.

Example 5-9. Dynamic menu generation

```
<?xml version="1.0"?>
<?xml-stylesheet href="test.css" type="text/css"?>
<!DOCTYPE  window>
<window id="test-win"
        xmlns="http://www.mozilla.org/keymaster/gatekeeper/there.is.only.xul"
        title="test"
        style="
        min-width : 200px;
        min-height: 200px;">
<script>
<![CDATA[
function generate(){
  var d            = document;
  var popup        = d.getElementById('menupopup');
  var menuitems    = new Array('menuitem_1',
                     'menuitem_2', 'menuitem_3',
                     'menuitem_4', 'menuitem_5');
  var l            = menuitems.length;
  var newElement;
  for(var i=0; i<l; i++)
  {
    newElement = d.createElement('menuitem');
    newElement.setAttribute('id', menuitems[i]);
    newElement.setAttribute('label', menuitems[i]);
    popup.appendChild(newElement);
  }
  return true;
}
]]>
</script>
<menu label="a menu">
  <menupopup id="menupopup">
  </menupopup>
</menu>
<spacer flex="1" />
<button id="ctlbutton" class="testButton" label="generate" oncommand="generate();" />
</window>
```

The JavaScript function `generate()` in Example 5-9 gets the `menupopup` as the parent element for the new elements, creates five `menuitems` in an array called `menuitems`, and stores five string ID names for those `menuitems`.

The variable *l* is the length of the array. The variable `newElement` is a placeholder for elements created by using the `createElement` method inside of the `for` loop.

generate() assigns newElement on each iteration of the loop and creates a new menuitem each time, providing a way to dynamically generate a list of menu choices based on input data or user feedback. Try this example and experiment with different sources of data, such as a menu of different auto manufacturers, different styles on group of boxes that come from user selection, or tabular data in a tree.

Sharing Data Between Documents

As the scale of your application development increases and your applications grow new windows and components, you may become interested in passing data around and ensuring that the data remains in scope. Misunderstanding that scope often leads to problems when beginning Mozilla applications.

Scope in Mozilla

The general rule is that all scripts pulled in by the base XUL document and scripts included in overlays of this document are in the same scope. Therefore, any global variables you declare in any of these scripts can be used by any other scripts in the same scope. The decision to put a class structure or more sophisticated design in place is up to you.

The relationship of a parent and child window indicates the importance of storing data in language constructs that can be passed around. This code shows a common way for a parent to pass data to a window it spawns:

```
var obj = new Object ();
obj.res = "";
window.openDialog("chrome://xfly/content/foo.xul", 'foo_main',
"chrome,resizable,scrollbars,dialog=yes,close,modal=yes",
obj);
```

Using the window.arguments array

The previous code snippet creates a new JavaScript object, obj, and assigns the value of an empty string to that object's res property. The object is then passed by reference to the new window as the last parameter of the openDialog() method so it can be manipulated in the scope of the child window:

```
function onOk() {
  window.arguments[0].res  = "ok";
  return;
}
function onCancel() {
  window.arguments[0].res  = "cancel";
  return;
}
```

In that child window, the object is available as an indexed item in the special window.arguments array. This array holds a list of the arguments passed to a window when it is created. `window.arguments[0]` is a reference to the first argument in the `openDialog()` parameter list that is not a part of the input parameters for that method, `window.arguments[1]` is the second argument, and so on. Using `window.arguments` is the most common way to pass objects and other data around between documents.

When the user clicks a button in the displayed dialog (i.e., the OK or Cancel button), one of the functions sets a value to the res property of the passed-in object. The object is in the scope of the newly created window. When control is passed back to the script that launched the window, the return value can be checked:

```
if (obj.res != "ok") {
  dump("User has cancelled the dialog");
  return;
}
```

In this case, a simple dump statement prints the result, but you can also test the result in your application code and fork accordingly.

XPConnect and Scriptable Components

At the second level of scripting, XPConnect binds JavaScript and the user interface to the application core. Here, JavaScript can access all XPCOM components that implement scriptable libraries and services through a special global object whose methods and properties can be used in JavaScript. Consider these JavaScript snippets from the Mozilla source code:

```
// add filters to the file picker
fp.appendFilters( nsIFilePicker.HTML );
// display a directory in the file picker
fp.displayDirectory ( dir );
// read a line from an open file
file.readLine(tmpBuf, 1024, didTruncate);
// create a new directory
this.fileInst.create( DIRECTORY, parseInt(permissions) );
retval=OK;
```

The `filepicker`, `file`, and `localfile` components that these JavaScript objects represent are a tiny fraction of the components available via XPConnect to programmers in Mozilla. This section describes how to find these components, create the corresponding JavaScript objects, and use them in your application programming.

What Is XPConnect?

Until now, scripting has referred to scripting the DOM, manipulating various elements in the interface, and using methods available in Mozilla JavaScript files. However, for real applications like the Mozilla browser itself, this may be only the beginning. The UI must be hooked up to the application code and services (i.e., the application's actual functionality) to be more than just a visual interface. This is where XPConnect and XPCOM come in.

Browsing the Web, reading email, and parsing XML files are examples of application-level services in Mozilla. They are part of Mozilla's lower-level functionality. This functionality is usually written and compiled in platform-native code and typically written in C++. This functionality is also most often organized into modules, which take advantage of Mozilla's cross-platform component object model (XPCOM), and are known as *XPCOM components*. The relationship of these components and the application services they provide to the interface is shown in Figure 5-4.

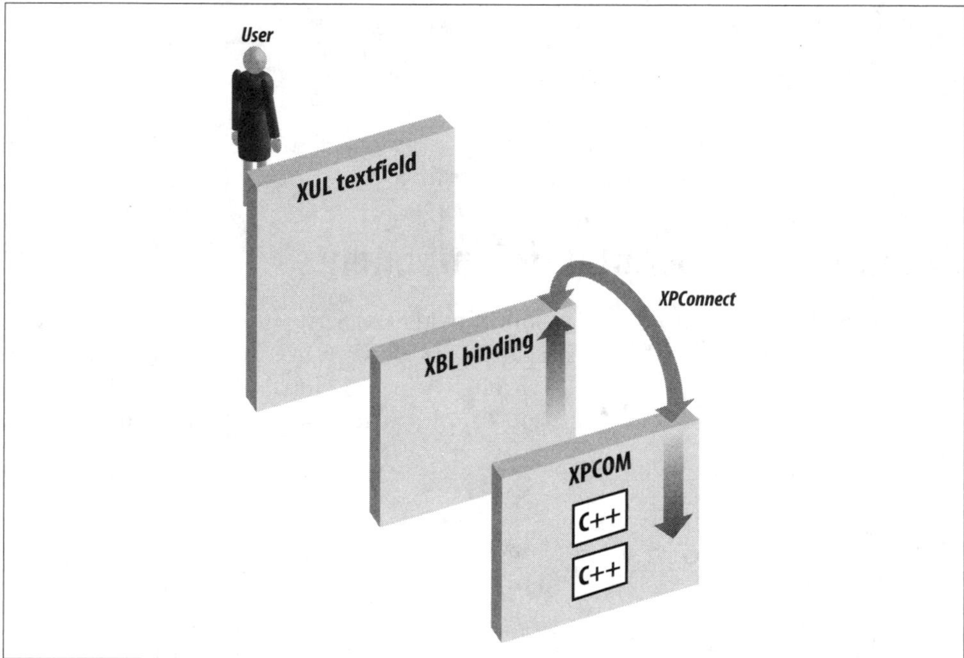

Figure 5-4. How XPConnect fits into the application model

In Mozilla, XPConnect is the bridge between JavaScript and XPCOM components. The XPConnect technology wraps natively compiled components with JavaScript objects. XPCOM, Mozilla's own cross-platform component technology, is the framework on top of which these scriptable components are built. Using JavaScript and XPConnect, you can create instances of these components and use their methods and properties as you do any regular JavaScript object, as described here. You can access any or all of the functionality in Mozilla in this way.

Chapter 8 describes more about the XPConnect technology and how it connects components to the interface. It also describes the components themselves and their interfaces, the XPCOM technology, and how you can create your own XPCOM components.

Creating XPCOM objects in script

Example 5-10 demonstrates the creation and use of an XPCOM component in JavaScript. In this example, the script instantiates the `filepicker` object and then uses it to display a file picker dialog with all of the file filters selected. To run this example, add the function to your *xfly.js* file and call it from an event handler on the "New" menu item you added in Example 3-5.

Example 5-10. Scriptable component example

```
// chooseApp:  Open file picker and prompt user for application.
chooseApp: function() {
  var nsIFilePicker = Components.interfaces.nsIFilePicker;
  var fp =
     Components.classes["@mozilla.org/filepicker;1"].
         createInstance( nsIFilePicker );
  fp.init( this.mDialog,
     this.getString( "chooseAppFilePickerTitle" ),
     nsIFilePicker.modeOpen );
  fp.appendFilters( nsIFilePicker.filterAll );
  if ( fp.show() == nsIFilePicker.returnOK && fp.file ) {
  this.choseApp   = true;
  this.chosenApp  = fp.file;
  // Update dialog.
  this.updateApplicationName(this.chosenApp.unicodePath);
}
```

Note the first two lines in the function and the way they work together to create the `fp` `filepicker` object. The first line in the function assigns the name of the *nsFilepicker* interface to the `nsIFilePicker` variable in JavaScript. This variable is used in the second line, where the instance is created from the component to specify which interface on that component should be used. Discovering and using library interfaces is an important aspect of XPCOM, where components always implement at least two interfaces.

In Example 5-11, an HTML file (stored locally, since it wouldn't have the required XPConnect access as a remote file because of security boundaries) loaded in Mozilla instantiates a Mozilla sound component and plays a sound with it. Go ahead and try it.

Example 5-11. Scripting components from HTML

```
<html>
<head>
<title>Sound Service Play Example</title>
</head>
<body>
<script>
  netscape.security.PrivilegeManager.enablePrivilege("UniversalXPConnect");
  var url = Components.classes["@mozilla.org/network/standard
      url;1"].createInstance();
  url = url.QueryInterface(Components.interfaces.nsIURL);
```

Example 5-11. Scripting components from HTML (continued)

```
  url.spec = "resource:/res/samples/test.wav";
  var sample = Components.classes["@mozilla.org/sound;1"].createInstance();
  sample = sample.QueryInterface(Components.interfaces.nsISound);
</script>
<form name="form">
  <input type="button" value="Play Sound" onclick="sample.play(url);">
<form>
</body>
</html>
```

As in Example 5-10, the `classes[]` array on the special Mozilla `Components` object refers to a particular component—in this case, the `sound` component—by contract ID. All XPCOM objects must have a contract ID that uniquely identifies them with the domain, the component name, and a version number `["@mozilla.org/sound;1"]`, respectively. See the "XPCOM Identifiers" section in Chapter 8 for more information about this.

Finding components and interfaces

Most components are scripted in Mozilla. In fact, the challenge is not to find cases when this scripting occurs (which you can learn by searching LXR for the `Components`), but to find Mozilla components that don't use scriptable components. Finding components and interfaces in Mozilla and seeing how they are used can be useful when writing your own application.

The Mozilla Component Viewer is a great tool for discovering components and provides a convenient UI for seeing components and looking at their interfaces from within Mozilla. The Component Viewer can be built as an extension to Mozilla (see "cview" in the extensions directory of the Mozilla source), or it can be downloaded and installed as a separate XPI from *http://www.hacksrus.com/~ginda/cview/*. Appendix B describes the Component Viewer in more detail.

Commonly used XPCOM objects in the browser and other Mozilla applications include file objects, RDF services, URL objects, and category managers.

Selecting the appropriate interface from the component

In all cases, the way to get the object into script is to instantiate it with the special `classes` object and use the `createInstance()` method on the class to select the interface you want to use. These two steps are often done together, as in the following example, which gets the component with the contract ID `ldap-connection;1`, instantiates an object from the *nsILDAPConnection* interface, and then calls a method on that object:

```
var connection = Components.classes
                ["@mozilla.org/network/ldap-connection;1"].
                createInstance(Components.interfaces.nsILDAPConnection);
    connection.init(queryURL.host, queryURL.port, null,
                    generateGetTargetsBoundCallback());
```

These two common processes—getting a component and selecting one of its interfaces to assign to an object—can also be separated into two different statements:

```
// get the ldap connection component
var connection = Components.classes
               ["@mozilla.org/network/ldap-connection;1";
// create an object from the nsILDAPConnection interface;
connection.createInstance(Components.interfaces.nsILDAPConnection);
// call the init() method on that object
connection.init(queryURL.host, queryURL.port, null,
               generateGetTargetsBoundCallback());
```

Mozilla constantly uses these processes. Wherever functionality is organized into XPCOM objects (and most of it is), these two statements bring that functionality into JavaScript as high-level and user-friendly JavaScript objects.

JavaScript Application Code

There are two ways to use JavaScript in the third, deepest level of application programming. The first is to organize your JavaScript into libraries so your functions can be reused, distributed, and perhaps collaborated upon.

The second way is to write a JavaScript component, create a separate interface for that component, and compile it as an XPCOM component whose methods and data can be accessed from XPConnect (using JavaScript). This kind of application programming is described in Chapter 8, which includes examples of creating new interfaces, implementing them in JavaScript or C++, and compiling, testing, and using the resulting component in the Mozilla interface.

This section introduces the library organization method of JavaScript application programming. The JSLib code discussed here is a group of JavaScript libraries currently being developed by Mozilla contributors and is especially useful for working with the XPFE and other aspects of the Mozilla application/package programming model. When you include the right source files at the top of your JavaScript and/or XUL file, you can use the functions defined in JSLib libraries as you would use any third-party library or built-in functions. You may even want to contribute to the JSLib project yourself if you think functionality is missing and as your Mozilla programming skills grow.

JavaScript Libraries

The open source JSLib project makes life easier for developers. The JSLib package implements some of the key XPCOM components just discussed and wraps them in simpler, JavaScript interfaces, which means that you can use the services of common XPCOM components without having to do any of the instantiation, interface selection, or glue code yourself. Collectively, these interfaces are intended to provide a general-purpose library for Mozilla application developers. To understand what

JSLib does, consider the following short snippet from the JSLib source file *jslib/io/file.js*, which implements a close() function for open file objects and provides a handy way to clean up things when you finish editing a file in the filesystem.

```
/********************* CLOSE ********************************
* void close()                                              *
*                                                           *
* void file close                                           *
* return type void(null)                                    *
* takes no arguments closes an open file stream and         *
* deletes member var instances of objects                   *
*   Ex:                                                     *
*     var p='/tmp/foo.dat';                                 *
*     var f=new File(p);                                    *
*     fopen();                                              *
*     f.close();                                            *
*                                                           *
*   outputs: void(null)                                     *
************************************************************/
File.prototype.close = function()
{
  /***************** Destroy Instances *********************/
  if(this.mFileChannel)   delete this.mFileChannel;
  if(this.mInputStream)   delete this.mInputStream;
  if(this.mTransport)     delete this.mTransport;
  if(this.mMode)          this.mMode=null;
  if(this.mOutStream) {
    this.mOutStream.close();
    delete this.mOutStream;
  }
  if(this.mLineBuffer)     this.mLineBuffer=null;
  this.mPosition           = 0;
  /***************** Destroy Instances *********************/
  return;
}
```

To use the close method as it's defined here, import the *file.js* source file into your JavaScript, create a file object (as shown in the examples below), and call its close() method.

The source files for JSLib are well annotated and easy to read. JSLib provide easy-to-use interfaces for creating instances of components (e.g., File objects), performing necessary error checking, and ensuring proper usage. To use a function like the one just shown, simply include the source file you need in your XUL:

```
<script type="application/x-JavaScript"
    src="chrome://jslib/content/jslib.js" />
```

Then you can include the specific library files you need in your JavaScript code by using the include method:

```
include("chrome://jslib/content/io/file.js");
include("chrome://jslib/content/zip/zip.js");
```

xpcshell

Most examples in this section are in *xpcshell*, but using these libraries in your user interface JavaScript is just as easy. You can access these libraries from a XUL file, as the section "Using the DirUtils class," later in this chapter, demonstrates.

xpcshell is the command-line interpreter to JavaScript and XPConnect. This shell that uses XPConnect to call and instantiate scriptable XPCOM interfaces. It is used primarily for debugging and testing scripts.

To run xpcshell, you need to go to the Mozilla *bin* directory or have that folder in your PATH. For each platform, enter:

Windows:

```
xpcshell.exe
```

Unix:

```
./run-mozilla.sh ./xpcshell
```

To run xpcshell on Unix, you need to supply environment variables that the interpreter needs. You can use the *run-mozilla.sh* shell script that resides in the Mozilla *bin* directory.

```
$ ./run-mozilla.sh ./xpcshell
```

To see the available options for xpcshell, type this:

```
$ ./run-mozilla.sh ./xpcshell --help
JavaScript-C 1.5 pre-release 4a 2002-03-21
usage: xpcshell [-s] [-w] [-W] [-v version] [-f scriptfile] [scriptfile]
[scriptarg...]
```

The two most important parameters here are -w, which enables warnings output, and -s, which turns on strict mode.

Installing JSLib

To use the JavaScript libraries, install the JSLib package in Mozilla. The package is available as a tarball, a zip file, or as CVS sources. The easiest way to obtain it is to install it from the Web using Mozilla's XPInstall technology, described in Chapter 6.

Using your Mozilla browser, go to *http://jslib.mozdev.org/installation.html* and click the installation hyperlink. The link uses XPInstall to install JSLIB and make it available to you in Mozilla. To test whether it is installed properly, type the following code in your shell:

```
./mozilla -chrome chrome://jslib/content/
```

You should see a simple window that says "welcome to jslib."

The JSLib libraries

Currently available JavaScript functions in the JSLib package are divided into different modules that, in turn, are divided into different classes defined in source files such as *file.js*, *dir.js*, and *fileUtils.js*. Table 5-1 describes the basic classes in the JSLib package's I/O module and describes how they are used.

Table 5-1. JSLib classes

Class / (filename)	Description
File / (*file.js*)	Contains most routines associated with the File object (implementing `nsIFile`). The library is part of the jslib I/O module.
FileUtils / (*fileUtils.js*)	The chrome registry to local file path conversion, file metadata, etc.
Dir / (*dir.js*)	Directory creation; variations of directory listings.
DirUtils / (*dirUtils.js*)	Paths to useful Mozilla directories and files such as *chrome*, *prefs*, *bookmarks*, *localstore*, etc.

Using the File class

The JSLib `File` class exposes most local file routines from the *nsIFile* interface. The `File` class is part of the JSLib I/O module, and is defined in *jslib/io/file.js*. Here is how you load the library from xpcshell:

```
$ ./run-mozilla.sh ./xpcshell -w -s
js> load(`chrome/jslib/jslib.js');
*********************
JS_LIB DEBUG IS ON
*********************
js>
```

Once JSLib is loaded, you can load the `File` module with an `include` statement:

```
js> include(`chrome://jslib/content/io/file.js');
*** Chrome Registration of package: Checking for contents.rdf at
resource:/chrome/jslib/
*** load: filesystem.js OK
*** load: file.js OK
true
js>
```

Note that *file.js* loads *filesystem.js* in turn. The class `FileSystem` in *filesystem.js* is the base class for the `File` object. You can also load *file.js* by using the top-level construct `JS_LIB_PATH`:

```
js> include(JS_LIB_PATH+'io/file.js');
```

Once you have the *file.js* module loaded, you can create an instance of a `File` object and call methods on it to manipulate the file and path it represents:

```
js> var f = new File('/tmp/foo');
js> f;
[object Object]
js> f.help; // listing of everything available to the object
. . .
js> f.path;
/tmp/foo
js> f.exists();   // see if /tmp/foo exists
```

```
false
js> f.create();    // it doesn't, so create it.
js> f.exists();
true
js> f.isFile();    // is it a file?
true
js> f.open('w');  // open the file for writing
true
js> f.write('this is line #1\n');
true
js> f.close();
js> f.open();      // open the file again and
js> f.read();      // read back the data
                   // you can also use default flag 'r' for reading
this is line #1
js> f.close();
```

You can also assign the contents of the file to a variable for later use, iterative loops through the file contents, or updates to the data:

```
js> f.open();
true
js> var contents = f.read();
js> f.close();
js> print(contents);
this is line #1
js>
// rename the file
js> f.move(`/tmp/foo.dat');
foo.dat
filesystem.js:move successful!
js> f.path;
/tmp/foo.dat
```

These examples show some ways the JSLib `File` object can manipulate local files. Using these interfaces can make life a lot easier by letting you focus on creating your Mozilla application without having to implement XPCOM `nsIFile` objects manually from your script.

Using the FileUtils class

To create an instance of the `FileUtils` class, use the `FileUtils` constructor:

```
js> var fu = new FileUtils();
js> fu;
[object Object]
```

Then look at the object by calling its `help` method:

```
js> fu.help;
```

The difference between using the *File* and *FileUtils* interfaces is that methods and properties on the latter are *singleton* and require a path argument, while the *FileUtils* utilities are general purpose and not bound to any particular file. The *FileUtils* interface has several handy I/O utilities for converting, testing, and using URLs, of which this example shows a few:

```
js> fu.exists('/tmp');
true
// convert a chrome path to a url
js> fu.chromeToPath('chrome://jslib/content/');
/usr/src/mozilla/dist/bin/chrome/jslib/jslib.xul
// convert a file URL path to a local file path
js> fu.urlToPath('file:///tmp/foo.dat');
/tmp/foo.dat
```

Most methods on the `FileUtils` objects are identical to the methods found in *file.js*, except they require a path argument. Another handy method in the `FileUtils` class is `spawn`, which spawns an external executable from the operating system. It's used as follows:

```
js> fu.spawn('/usr/X11R6/bin/Eterm');
```

This command spawns a new Eterm with no argument. To open an Eterm with vi, you could also use this code:

```
js> fu.spawn('/usr/X11R6/bin/Eterm', ['-e/usr/bin/vi']);
```

Checking to see if three different files exist would take several lines when using the File class, but the `FileUtils` class is optimized for this type of check, as the following listing shows:

```
js> var fu=new FileUtils();
js> fu.exists('/tmp');
true
js> fu.exists('/tmp/foo.dat');
true
js> fu.exists('/tmp/foo.baz');
false
```

You need to initialize the `FileUtils` class only once to use its members and handle local files robustly.

Using the Dir class

The `Dir` class is custom-made for working with directory structures on a local filesystem. To create an instance of the `Dir` class, call its constructor and then its `help` method to see the class properties:

```
js> var d = new Dir('/tmp');
js> d.help;
```

`Dir` inherits from the same base class as `File`, which is why it looks similar, but it implements methods used specifically for directory manipulation:

```
js> d.path;
/tmp
js> d.exists();
true
js> d.isDir();
true
```

The methods all work like those in the File and FileUtils classes, so you can append a new directory name to the object, see if it exists, and create it if (it does not) by entering:

```
js> d.append('newDir');
/tmp/newDir
js> d.path;
/tmp/newDir
js> d.exists();
false
js> d.create();
js> d.exists();
true
```

Using the DirUtils class

Note that some methods in the DirUtils class cannot be called from xpcshell and instead must be called from a XUL window into which the proper JSLib source file was imported. The following XUL file provides two buttons that display information in textboxes about the system directories:

```
<?xml version="1.0"?>
<?xml-stylesheet href="chrome://global/skin" type="text/css"?>
<window xmlns="http://www.mozilla.org/keymaster/gatekeeper/there.is.only.xul"
   xmlns:html="http://www.w3.org/1999/xhtml"
   id="dir-utils-window"
   orient="vertical"
   autostretch="never">
<script type="application/x-javascript" src="chrome://jslib/content/io/dirUtils.js"/>
<script>
var du = new DirUtils();
function getChromeDir() {
  cd = du.getChromeDir();
  textfield1 = document.getElementById("tf1");
  textfield1.setAttribute("value", cd);
}
function getMozDir() {
  md =   du.getMozHomeDir();
  textfield2 = document.getElementById("tf2");
  textfield2.setAttribute("value", md);
}
</script>
<box>
  <button id="chrome" onclick="getChromeDir();" label="chrome" />
  <textbox id="tf1" value="chrome dir" />
</box>
<box>
  <button id="moz" onclick="getMozDir();" label="mozdir" />
  <textbox id="tf2" value="moz dir" />
</box>
</window>
```

CHAPTER 6

Packaging and Installing Applications

The previous chapters covered the basic parts of building an application. Now that you've seen how to create an application with XUL, CSS, and JavaScript that can be used on your local computer, we will show you how to turn your program into something that can be installed by other users. This chapter discusses the technologies Mozilla provides for packaging and installing applications.

Until your project is packaged for distribution, it can't be fully considered a finished application (unless it was designed to work only on the computer where it was created). Making your application distributable, installable, and registrable allows others to use what you have created.

This chapter is divided into four main sections. It starts with a quick overview of the basics of packaging and installing applications. The second section provides details about how to get your application packaged and described so that Mozilla recognizes what it is. The next section specifies how to put your package into a cross-platform installation file that can be installed over the Web onto other machines. The last section provides tips for customizing how your application will look once it is installed.

Packaging and Installing Overview

Several different pieces comprise Mozilla's distribution technology. In fact, Mozilla may have a few more moving parts than other packaging systems because it needs a way to package and install new software uniformly across several different platforms. Figure 6-1 shows the major components of Mozilla's packaging system outlined in black.

As you can see in Figure 6-1, the Cross-Platform Installer (XPI), pronounced zippy or X-P-I, is the archive format used to distribute Mozilla applications. The XPI file contains a script that downloads and installs the application. The package inside the XPI has a manifest that is used to register the new Mozilla-based software with the Mozilla chrome registry.

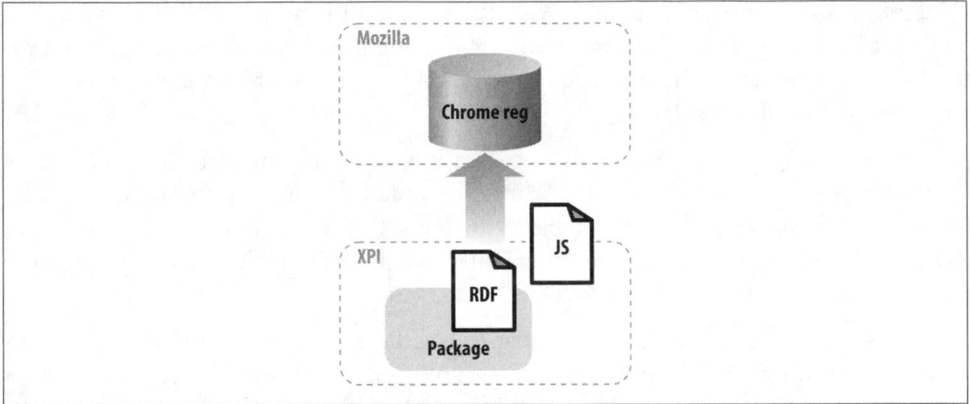

Figure 6-1. Mozilla packaging components

When a XPI contains a Mozilla-based package such as the xFly sample discussed in Chapter 2 and the following chapters, the installation script also takes care of the package registration process, described in the "Registering Packages" section later in this chapter. Example 6-1 shows a simple installation script and the kind of information it contains. The "Installation Scripts" section, also later in this chapter, discusses other scripts that may need to be used in the installation process, such as trigger scripts.

Example 6-1. Package installation script

```
var myFile = "xFly.jar";
initInstall(                          // initialize the installation
  "Install xFly",                     // display name of installation
  "xFly",                             // package name
  "0.0.1",                          // version of install
  1);                                 // flags
f = getFolder("Chrome"); // specify a target directory
setPackageFolder(f);
addFile(myFile);             // add software to the installation
registerChrome(
  PACKAGE | DELAYED_CHROME,           // chrome switch (i.e., type)
  getFolder("Chrome","xFly.jar"), // destination of package
  "content/xFly/");                   // location of manifest in package
if (0 == getLastError())    // if there have been no errors:
  performInstall();         // install "xfly.jar"
else                        // otherwise
  cancelInstall();          // cancel the installation.
```

The installation process requires a few different steps. First an installation must be initialized. Then the software to be installed is added to the specified target directory. Finally, packages in the installation are registered. At this point, the application is installed on a user's computer.

When you install new packages or Mozilla-based software, the chrome registry on the Mozilla side brokers the deal—reading the manifest, executing the installation script(s), and updating the package information that it maintains internally (storing this information using RDF).

The relationship of the packaging, installation, and registration—and all pieces involved—may seem a little complex and idiosyncratic at first, but bear with it. The upshot of this powerful but somewhat diffuse packaging technology is that you can bundle your software, put it on a server, and have users install it by simply clicking a link on a web page when using Mozilla.

It is possible to use this packaging system to bundle any sort of application or extension to an existing Mozilla application. You can install a XPI that adds functionality to the Mozilla browser, such as Mouse Gestures (*http://optimoz.mozdev.org/gestures/*), which enables the execution of common browser commands with mouse movements. You can package new Mozilla development tools and libraries like JSLib (see Chapter 5). You can also create installations for entirely new Mozilla applications.

Packaging Mozilla Applications

Packaging simply means organizing your files into a Mozilla application structure. Packaging your application is required to make it installable and to make it something that Mozilla recognizes as one of its own. Whether your Mozilla-based becomes a part of an existing Mozilla application, like Mouse Gestures, or will exist as a standalone application, like JabberZilla, you will need to package it.

When you are done with this packaging section, package your Mozilla-based applications in the same way that we packaged the xFly example in Chapter 2. This chapter describes the manifests and other necessary files. Then the Installation section shows how you can put your package in a XPI file and create installation script(s) so it can be distributed and installed.

Package Manifests

All new packages must have manifests describing their contents, skin information, and locale information. These manifests are formatted in RDF, which makes them easy to combine with the RDF data that makes up the chrome registry and makes it easy to fit the package into the Mozilla software. There is some flexibility about where in the package the manifest must appear, but the registration process must find and read it regardless of where it is.

The installation script points out the manifest locations so the package can be registered properly. Note that manifests appear in JARs, but they do not appear in XPIs, since the latter is a temporary file that gets deleted once the files it contains, including JARs, are installed (see the "Installing Mozilla Applications" section later in this chapter for more information about XPI install files).

Theme package manifests

Example 6-2 shows a manifest for a new theme to be installed in Mozilla. It is simple because it describes only one type of package, the "fly skin," and the existing component it interacts with, the communicator—the default Mozilla browser (the syntax and structure is the same for all manifests, however). The manifest says, in effect, this is what I have here (the metadata about the theme—its name, a description, etc.), and this is what it affects (the list of chrome:packages to which the theme should be applied).

Example 6-2. Simple theme package manifest

```
<?xml version="1.0"?>
<RDF:RDF xmlns:RDF="http://www.w3.org/1999/02/22-rdf-syntax-ns#"
  xmlns:chrome="http://www.mozilla.org/rdf/chrome#">
  <!-- List all the skins being supplied by this theme -->
  <RDF:Seq about="urn:mozilla:skin:root">
    <RDF:li resource="urn:mozilla:skin:flyskin/1.0" />
  </RDF:Seq>

  <!-- Fly Skin Information -->
  <RDF:Description about="urn:mozilla:skin:flyskin/1.0"
    chrome:displayName="Fly Skin"
    chrome:author="frillies"
    chrome:description="shimmering, purple/black, hairy">
   <chrome:packages>
     <RDF:Seq about="urn:mozilla:skin:classic/1.0:packages">
       <RDF:li resource="urn:mozilla:skin:classic/1.0:communicator"/>
     </RDF:Seq>
   </chrome:packages>
  </RDF:Description>
</RDF:RDF>
```

Language pack manifests

When you look at a package manifest that describes a new locale, as shown in Example 6-3 (which is for a German language pack in Mozilla), you see a similar structure. Again, the manifest describes the new package first and then lists the existing components to which this new package applies.

Example 6-3. Locale package manifest

```
<?xml version="1.0"?>
<RDF:RDF xmlns:RDF="http://www.w3.org/1999/02/22-rdf-syntax-ns#"
 xmlns:chrome="http://www.mozilla.org/rdf/chrome#">
 <!-- list all the skins being supplied by this package -->
 <RDF:Seq about="urn:mozilla:locale:root">
 <RDF:li resource="urn:mozilla:locale:en-DE"/>
 </RDF:Seq>
 <!-- locale information -->
 <RDF:Description about="urn:mozilla:locale:en-DE"
  chrome:displayName="English (German)"
  chrome:author="mozilla.org"
```

Example 6-3. Locale package manifest (continued)

```
  chrome:name="en-DE"
  chrome:previewURL="http://www.mozilla.org/locales/en-DE.gif">
  <chrome:packages>
   <RDF:Seq about="urn:mozilla:locale:en-DE:packages">
     <RDF:li resource="urn:mozilla:locale:en-DE:communicator"/>
     <RDF:li resource="urn:mozilla:locale:en-DE:editor"/>
     <RDF:li resource="urn:mozilla:locale:en-DE:global"/>
     <RDF:li resource="urn:mozilla:locale:en-DE:messenger"/>
     <RDF:li resource="urn:mozilla:locale:en-DE:navigator"/>
   </RDF:Seq>
  </chrome:packages>
 </RDF:Description>
</RDF:RDF>
```

Note that in Example 6-3's package manifest, all major components are affected by this new locale package. When the package is installed and the manifest is read, the chrome registry is made aware of a German language pack that it can use to display German in the interface of each Mozilla component.

contents.rdf Type Manifests

Package manifests are an area where Mozilla browser itself may not be the best model for learning about the best application development practice. Mozilla is such a large and modular application that it uses several manifests instead of one application-wide *manifest.rdf* file.

Although they have the same format, these distributed manifests are found in several *contents.rdf* files. In a single theme (e.g., the *modern.jar*), you can see as many as eight manifests (for major component to which the theme applies).

These two types of manifests—the *contents.rdf* file, which typically describes a single package-component relationship; and the *manifest.rdf* file, which describes the package's relationship to all affected components—are functionally equivalent. In both cases, the chrome registry reads all RDF/XML data and registers the package.

Because the manifest data format is RDF/XML, you can use either type of manifest in your own package development, although using a single *manifest.rdf* is generally much easier, especially if you want to change the list of affected components of any other metadata later.

The package manifests for content and new applications—which may include new content, skin, and locale information—have an identical syntax and a very similar structure, as you will see in the following sections. The manifest for a full Mozilla-based application like xFly describes the content, the skin, and the locale in a single file that sits at the top of that package.

Application manifests

When you create new applications on top of Mozilla, you will often create new content, new skins, and your own localizable language elements, such as DTDs. For applications, the manifest must describe these parts of your application if Mozilla is to find and register them properly.

Example 6-4, the package manifest from the XMLTerm Mozilla extension, describes the contents, skin, and locale in a single file, which is most common for Mozilla-based applications.

Example 6-4. manifest.rdf describing the XMLTerm extension

```
<?xml version="1.0"?>
<RDF:RDF xmlns:RDF="http://www.w3.org/1999/02/22-rdf-syntax-ns#"
         xmlns:chrome="http://www.mozilla.org/rdf/chrome#">
  <!-- list all the packages being supplied by this jar -->
  <RDF:Seq about="urn:mozilla:package:root">
    <RDF:li resource="urn:mozilla:package:xmlterm"/>
  </RDF:Seq>
  <RDF:Seq about="urn:mozilla:skin:root">
    <RDF:li resource="urn:mozilla:skin:modern/1.0" />
  </RDF:Seq>
  <RDF:Seq about="urn:mozilla:locale:root">
    <RDF:li resource="urn:mozilla:locale:en-US"/>
  </RDF:Seq>
  <!-- xmlterm package information -->
  <RDF:Description about="urn:mozilla:package:xmlterm"
        chrome:displayName="XMLterm"
        chrome:author="xmlterm.org"
        chrome:name="xmlterm">
  </RDF:Description>
  <!-- xmlterm overlay information -->
  <RDF:Seq about="urn:mozilla:overlays">
    <RDF:li resource="chrome://communicator/content/tasksOverlay.xul"/>
  </RDF:Seq>
  <RDF:Seq about="chrome://communicator/content/tasksOverlay.xul">
    <RDF:li>chrome://xmlterm/content/xmltermOverlay.xul</RDF:li>
  </RDF:Seq>
  <!-- locale information -->
  <RDF:Description about="urn:mozilla:locale:en-US"
        chrome:displayName="English(US)"
        chrome:author="mozilla.org"
        chrome:name="en-US"
        chrome:previewURL="http://www.mozilla.org/locales/en-US.gif">
    <chrome:packages>
      <RDF:Seq about="urn:mozilla:locale:en-US:packages">
        <RDF:li resource="urn:mozilla:locale:en-US:xmlterm"/>
      </RDF:Seq>
    </chrome:packages>
  </RDF:Description>
  <!-- xmlterm skin information -->
  <RDF:Description about="urn:mozilla:skin:modern/1.0"
        chrome:displayName="Modern"
```

Example 6-4. manifest.rdf describing the XMLTerm extension (continued)

```
        chrome:author="mozilla.org"
        chrome:name="modern/1.0">
    <chrome:packages>
      <RDF:Seq about="urn:mozilla:skin:modern/1.0:packages">
        <RDF:li resource="urn:mozilla:skin:modern/1.0:xmlterm"/>
      </RDF:Seq>
    </chrome:packages>
  </RDF:Description>
</RDF:RDF>
```

The structure in Example 6-4 is exactly the same as that in more focused manifests (Example 6-2 and Example 6-3), but all of the skin, content, and locale structures sit together in a single *manifest.rdf* file. This manifest follows the Mozilla convention of introducing the package contents at the top and then expanding upon the basic listing of each separate sections, providing the necessary metadata about the items in the middle, and then listing the components that are affected by the items at the end. However, the flexibility of the RDF format means you could just as easily order this information differently—which is why RDF is sometimes described as creating a "soup" of statements about resources.

Note that the overlay section in the middle of the example is part of the content description. It tells the chrome registry that the contents of the file *xmltermOverlay.xul* should be overlaid into the *tasksOverlay.xul* file in Mozilla, in which much of the Tools menu is defined. The package manifest for the xFly sample application that we discuss here, also a single file, is very similar to the manifest in Example 6-4.

Registering Packages

Typically, registration occurs during installation, which is why the "Installing Mozilla Applications" section of this chapter goes into more detail about the specific methods and objects available for package registration. The registration process deals with packages and package manifests, however, so the following two sections describe the two types of package registration that are possible in Mozilla. The first provides an overview of how to register a package on installation, as is typically done, and the second describes how to use a special file to register your work with Mozilla as you develop it so that you can view your work as it progresses.

Registering packages on installation

Generally, the registration process is a transaction that takes place between your installation scripts, the chrome registry, and the manifests that describe the package. Usually, registration happens upon installation. You can approach this transaction in many ways, but the general relationship is shown in Figure 6-2.

In this relationship, the install script is responsible for managing the transfer of files to a specified location on the local disk and alerting the chrome registry to the new

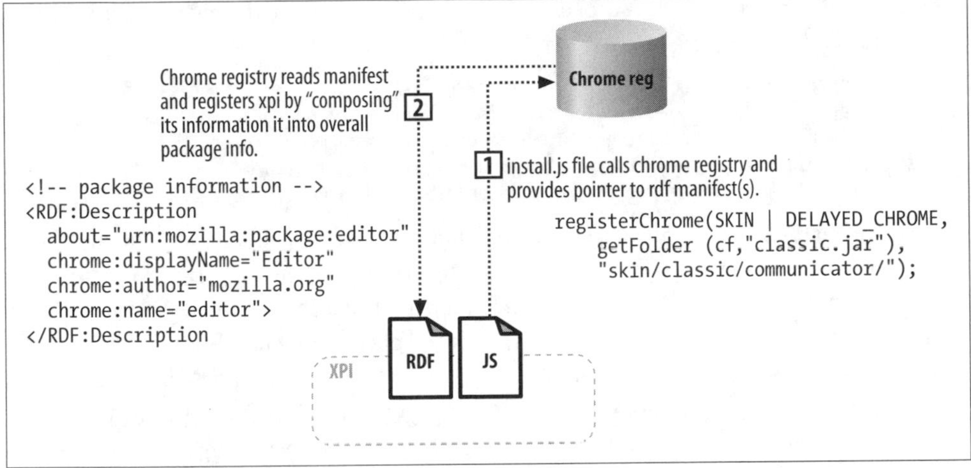

Figure 6-2. Package interaction overview

files and their manifests. The chrome registry then finds and reads those manifests. If the information there is formatted correctly, then that information is added to the sum of package information that the chrome registry manages—a single, overarching datasource of all packages in Mozilla, including skins, locales, overlays, and other software. In this way, the package is added to Mozilla. The major players in this interaction between the packages, the package descriptions, and the chrome registry are shown in the following list.

- Manifests in the archives themselves
- XPInstall, the technology that performs the downloading and resource installation
- The chrome registry, the database of packages, and user information that is read and written to when new software is installed

Registering packages as you develop them (installed-chrome.txt)

The file *installed-chrome.txt* is a convenience for developers who want to create and test new packages without having to install them with installation scripts and manifests. Some earlier xFly examples in this book already used this method. The *installed-chrome.txt* file is a list of entries that point to package manifests. Each line provides the chrome registry with a pointer to a manifest in which new software is described: new skin information, new packages, and new locales.

In the following snippet from the *installed-chrome.txt* file in the Mozilla *chrome* directory, five entries point to *contents.rdf* type manifests that describe the modern skin resources particular to the application's major components. The first line in this list, for example, tells the chrome registry to find a *contents.rdf* file in the subdirectory *skin/modern/communicator* contained in the *modern.jar* file, which describes the resources present there to skin the communicator component. When the chrome registry reads this line, it uses those resources to skin the communicator component, shown here:

```
skin,install,url,jar:resource:/chrome/modern.jar!/skin/modern/communicator/
skin,install,url,jar:resource:/chrome/modern.jar!/skin/modern/editor/
skin,install,url,jar:resource:/chrome/modern.jar!/skin/modern/global/
skin,install,url,jar:resource:/chrome/modern.jar!/skin/modern/messenger/
skin,install,url,jar:resource:/chrome/modern.jar!/skin/modern/navigator/
```

Instead of installing your package with installation scripts, you can add the appropriate entries to this file, as seen in the following examples. Adding these entries only registers local content on your machine. When you use the *installed-chrome.txt* file, you neither install a new package nor make that package installable by others. Editing the *installed-chrome.txt* file directly is a shortcut for making Mozilla aware of packages so that you can check your progress as you develop. You probably need to create an installer for packages you want to distribute and install on other systems.

To register a local copy of the xFly application with the Mozilla *chrome* directory, you would add the following three entries, where the *xFly* directory and the appropriate subdirectories sit directly under the *chrome* directory:

```
content,install,url,resource:/chrome/xfly/content/
skin,install,url,resource:/chrome/xfly/skin/
locale,install,url,resource:/chrome/xfly/locale/en-US/
```

The first line tells the chrome registry that the content is found in the directory *chrome/xfly/content*. The next line points to the skin resources at *chrome/xfly/skin*, and so on. Note that creating a single entry for the xFly skin and locating its resources underneath the xFly application directory (as opposed to a subdirectory in the modern and/or classic JARs) means that the xFly skin will not change when the user changes skins.

If we had the same structure archived in a JAR file called *xfly.jar* rather than in a directory, the *installed-chrome.txt* entries would look like this:

```
content,install,url,jar:resource:/chrome/xfly.jar!/content/
skin,install,url,jar:resource:/chrome/xfly.jar!/skin/
locale,install,url,jar:resource:/chrome/xfly.jar!/locale/en-US/
```

This code tells the chrome registry to look in the *content*, *skin*, and *locale/en-US* directories in the JAR file to locate the manifests.

This skin entry seems to indicate that only one set of skin information is available for the xFly sample, and that it always applies. If the xFly skin inherits, as many skins do, from one or another of the preinstalled theme (e.g., Modern), it may look very bad or even break when that theme is not selected. See the section "Skin inheritance and skin modularization" in Chapter 4 for a discussion of skin inheritance and tips on how to make sure your skin is structured to best take advantage of it.

When you make these additions to the *installed-chrome.txt* file and restart Mozilla, the chrome registry looks for manifests in the directories you specify and registers the packages described there. The *installed-chrome.txt* entries in this section do not necessarily need to be included on your final XPI resource, but you will see them in some XPIs bundled in their own *installed-chrome.txt* file separate form the main one. See the section "The Chrome Registry" for more information about this process.

Creating a Package

The xFly sample package is a relatively straightforward arrangement of content, skin, and locale. You have already seen how to set up most preliminaries you need to make it a package in Chapter 2, but this section will discuss the process in detail.

Setting up xFly

To start working immediately with tools like XUL and CSS, you can move some things around and hack one of the chrome registry files, as you have already seen. This section reviews those important preliminary application development steps in more detail.

Because it has its own interface and is not worried (for now) about being made available in languages other than English, the only one for which it has a language pack, the xFly package is self-contained:

```
chrome
   xfly
    content
    skin
    locale
```

All parts of the package can be held in a single JAR file or a single *chrome* subdirectory. Contrast this with a large component-like communicator that, when you include its content, skin, localized information, and the Mozilla services it uses via XPConnect, is spread out into all of the main JAR files that make up the distribution.

```
chrome/modern.jar!/skins/modern/communicator/
chrome/comm.jar!/content/communicator/
chrome/en-US.jar!/locale/en-US/communicator/
```

When you develop your application, it's typical to work within a regular directory. As you finish the application and make it available for distribution and installation, however, you may want to use one of the installation archive formats to package your work, such as a JAR file. See the section "The XPI File Format" later in this chapter for more details.

When your application is large and distributed in this way, the RDF-based manifests "compose" all of the metadata and treat all files as a single component.

Hacking the installed-chrome.txt file

The entries you made to the *installed-chrome.txt* in Chapter 2 tell the chrome registry that a new package must be registered:

```
content,install,url,resource:/chrome/xfly/content/
skin,install,url,resource:/chrome/xfly/skin/
locale,install,url,resource:/chrome/xfly/locale/en-US/
```

These entries tell the chrome registry that, in addition to all of the packages that make up the main Mozilla browser (e.g., the communicator skin in the Modern theme, the en-US locale, and the content that makes up the navigator), the xFly `content`, `skin`, and `locale` should be registered as components of a new package. When the chrome registry reads these entries, it tries to find the manifests for these parts of the xFly package. When it finds them, it registers the package, overlays any files it finds in that package (see the next section), and makes it accessible via the special *chrome://* URLs given in the manifests.

Adding the xFly application to the Mozilla Tools menu

Adding your application to one of the Mozilla browser menus (so users can easily launch your application once it is installed) makes your application feel official. Figure 6-3 shows the presence of the xFly item in the Tools menu. The Tools menu lists various extra components in Mozilla, including the DOM Inspector and the JavaScript Debugger (if they are installed).

Figure 6-3. xFly item in Tools menu

It is also possible to add an item to the Window menu that includes links to Navigator (the default browser), the Mail and Newsgroup client, the Chatzilla IRC client, Composer, and the Address Book (which only show up if they were added as part of the Mozilla installation process or if they were added separately afterwards).

Here we describe how you can use special constructions in your package's manifest to tell the chrome registry about files from your package that should be overlaid into the main browser. Overlaying these files lets you add interface items, such as this link to xFly, in an existing application. Example 6-5 shows the simple overlay file that puts xFly in the Tools menu.

The top-level element is an <overlay/> rather than a <window/>. Direct children of the overlay are associated with certain elements in the main browser (in this case, the <menupopup/> of the Tools menu) and their contents are interpolated into the list of children there. This file overlays an extra <menuitem/> into the Tools menu. In this case, the menuitem has an oncommand event handler that calls toOpenWindowByType—a function for opening new chrome defined in the *tasksOverlay.js* that much of the chrome in the Mozilla UI imports.

Example 6-5. The xFly overlay

```
<?xml version="1.0"?>
<overlay id="xflyTasksOverlay"
   xmlns="http://www.mozilla.org/keymaster/gatekeeper/there.is.only.xul">

  <menupopup id="taskPopup">
    <menuitem label="xFly"
        oncommand="toOpenWindowByType(`xfly:main', `chrome://xfly/content/');" />
  </menupopup>
</overlay>
```

But how does the overlay know where to overlay itself? The IDs of the overlay children and the original XUL are matched to find the target within the files, but the manifest that accompanies the overlay in your package tells Mozilla which overlays are associated with which XUL files. The part of the manifest that deals with an overlay looks like the code in Example 6-6. This code is put in the *contents.rdf* file in the *content* directory of the xFly package.

Example 6-6. Overlay information in the manifest

```
<!-- overlay information -->
  <RDF:Seq about="urn:mozilla:overlays">
    <RDF:li resource="chrome://communicator/content/tasksOverlay.xul" />
  </RDF:Seq>
  <RDF:Seq about="chrome://communicator/content/tasksOverlay.xul">
    <RDF:li>chrome://xfly/content/xflyOverlay.xul</RDF:li>
  </RDF:Seq>
```

The first RDF element in the manifest is a list of affected target files and the second is a list of files that should be overlayed into those targets. Do not be confused by the names of the files in this case: the *tasksOverlay.xul* file is a target—though it is an overlay, as described in the following section—and *xflyOverlay.xul* is the overlay with the xFly menu item.

Overlaying Mozilla files into your application

In the previous section, we described how to use the XUL overlay technology to put information from your application into the Mozilla browser. When developers use overlays in this way, they usually add a menuitem or a new UI to the browser that provides access to the application.

But overlays can also add interface elements and other data from Mozilla into the application itself. In fact, each component in Mozilla imports a lot of its own user interface from such XUL overlay mainstays as *globalOverlay.xul*, *tasksOverlay.xul* (the file into which the xFly `menuitem` is overlaid), and *navigatorOverlay.xul*. As you can see when you look at the main browser file, *navigator.xul*, shown in Example 6-7, most user interface is actually brought in from these reusable overlays. A relatively small percentage of all that appears in the browser is defined within that particular *navigator.xul* file.

Example 6-7. Overlays in navigator.xul

```
<?xul-overlay href="chrome://navigator/content/navigatorOverlay.xul"?>
<?xul-overlay href="chrome://navigator/content/navExtraOverlay.xul"?>
<?xul-overlay href="chrome://navigator/content/linkToolbarOverlay.xul"?>
<?xul-overlay href="chrome://communicator/content/sidebar/sidebarOverlay.xul"?>
<?xul-overlay href="chrome://communicator/content/securityOverlay.xul"?>
<?xul-overlay href="chrome://communicator/content/communicatorOverlay.xul"?>
<?xul-overlay href="chrome://communicator/content/bookmarks/bookmarksOverlay.xul"?>
```

Of these overlays, those with the most value for application developers are the *communicatorOverlay.xul*, which defines many of browser menus; the *tasksOverlay.xul*, which adds the Tools menu and brings in all of its application `menuitems` as well as a lot of important browser functions like `toOpenWindowByType` and `toNavigator` (for returning to the main browser window); and the `globalOverlay` (which is overlaid into *navigatorOverlay.xul*, so it gets loaded there), which defines even more general and low-level features like pop ups and functions for quitting the application or setting tooltip text.

Once files are divided into subdirectories and the manifests for each subdirectory, your application is technically a package—although until you compress it and create an install script, it's a package only for your computer and the environment in which it was created. See the section "Finishing Things Up" later in this chapter to see how you can use the file format and installation information to make the xFly something you can put on a web server and have users install with a single click on a web page.

The Chrome Registry

The chrome registry was briefly mentioned several times in this book. It plays an important (but sometimes invisible) role in the way Mozilla applications, including the Mozilla browser itself, deal with user information, new components, skins, and other resources.

At the beginning of the book, you had to create RDF files that would describe your application to Mozilla. Special entries also needed to be made to the *installed-chrome.txt* file in the *chrome* application directory. These entries are just two of the most common ways to address the chrome registry, which is what Mozilla uses to persist configurable aspects of the browser and its other applications.

Where is the chrome registry?

The chrome registry is not a single file and it's not stored in a single place. Rather, it is a distributed collection of data and interfaces for data manipulation. The data itself generally lives in RDF files, many of which are in the *chrome* application directory. The chrome registry APIs—principally `nsIChromeRegistry`—are used by installation scripts when they register new software, by the skin-switching UI, and by the language selection facility. The chrome registry is the means through which packages are registered.

In some cases, especially when you create and debug your Mozilla application, you may want to edit the RDF files that make up the chrome registry directly. But more often, you can use external scripts, inline JavaScript, or the *installed-chrome.txt* file to get what you need from the registry. Procedures for doing so are described in the section "Registering Packages" earlier in this chapter, and in the section "Installation Scripts" later in this chapter.

Accessing the chrome registry in installation scripts

An install script is a required part of a software package like the xFly. The two main functions of an installation script are the physical download and installation of files in the package and registration of that software with the chrome registry. Install scripts use functions from the XPInstall API to install the files and functions from the chrome registry interface to handle the latter, as seen in this snippet:

```
registerChrome(PACKAGE | DELAYED_CHROME, getFolder("Chrome", "help"), "content/");
```

The registration process is typically something that happens between the install initialization and the actual execution of the install:

```
initInstall() // initialize the overall installation
// add items to installed using:
// addFolder, addDirectory, getFolder, and others
registerChrome(TYPE, dir, subdir)
performInstall();
```

Scripts and the installation process, including the registration of installed packages, are detailed in the next section.

Installing Mozilla Applications

Once your application is packaged, the next step is to create a cross-platform installation, or XPI. A XPI is a special file archive that contains your Mozilla package(s) and its own installation instructions. The relationship of the various parts of the installation process—the XPI itself, the internal installation script, the trigger script that begins the installation, and the Mozilla browser—can be visualized in Figure 6-4.

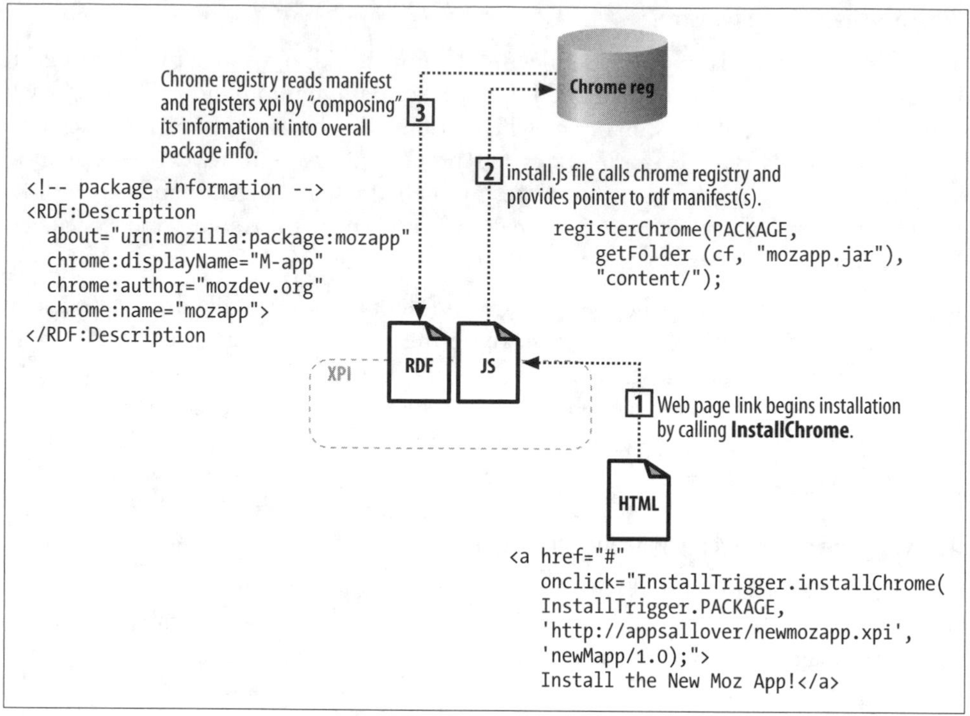

Figure 6-4. Installation process overview

The XPI File Format

Mozilla cross-platform installations use XPIs as the file format in which to organize, compress, and automate software installations and software updates. A XPI is a PKZIP-compressed archive (like ZIP and JAR files) with a special script at the highest level that manages the installation. A quick scan of the contents of a XPI file (which you can open using with any unzip utility) reveals the high-level directory structure shown in Example 6-8.

Example 6-8. Top level of the browser.xpi archive

```
install.js
bin\
  chrome\
  components
  defaults\
  icons\
  plugins\
  res\
```

Note that the high-level structure in Example 6-8 parallels the installed browser's directory structure very closely. The *bin* directory at the highest level of the archive corresponds to the Mozilla application directory. On Unix, this directory is actually called bin, where all of the resources are stored. On other platforms, the installation puts these resources in the application directory itself.

In the case of the Mozilla browser, the XPIs manage the transfer and registry of all components—the chrome files in the JARs, the executables, the default user information, and the libraries. As you will see in the installation script, the contents of the archive are installed onto the filesystem in much the same way as they are stored in the archive itself, although it's possible to rearrange things arbitrarily upon installation—to create new directories, install files in system folders and other areas, or execute software that handles other aspects of the installation, such as third-party installers.

XPI example

When the items to be installed are very simple, XPIs may contain nothing more than a single executable and the install script itself, as shown in Figure 6-5. In this figure, the WinZip utility has been used to display the contents of a XPI that installs a text editor on a Win32 system.

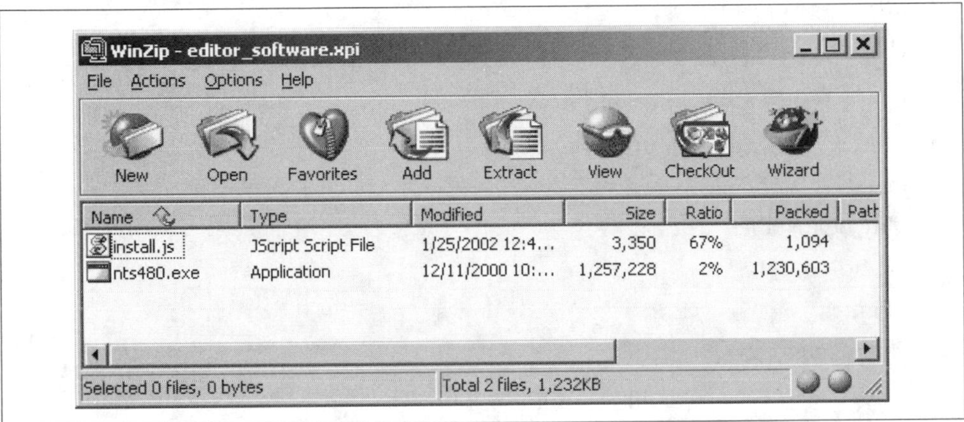

Figure 6-5. Simplest XPI archive

This example uses XPInstall technology to install something that may or may not be a Mozilla application. The *install.js* script in Example 6-8 would look like this. In Mozilla application development, however, XPIs often contain JAR files that are installed as new packages in the Mozilla distribution. To make a XPI for your package, use any zip software (applications or extensions that will be part of the main Mozilla distribution are required to use the free *zip* utility from InfoTools so that they can be run as part of the build process) to archive your files.

JARs versus XPIs

Technically, only the internal installation script distinguishes JARs and XPIs. However, Mozilla treats them differently. Since JARs do not include this installation script, they cannot install full content or applications by themselves. In this case, "content" means XUL, XBL, or JavaScript files that have script access to XPCOM. Files of this kind that are in JARs are denied access to XPConnect and are not registered as content in the chrome registry. JARs are used primarily to install locales, or language packs, and skins.

Skins that contain scripts and bindings (see the section "Theme Security Restrictions" and the "Evil Skins" sidebar, both in Chapter 4) are seen more as chrome content and must be installed in XPIs if they are to be fully functional. Like executables that are fetched from the Web, XPIs can cause trouble when downloaded by unprepared users since the software in XPIs are given the same privileges on the Mozilla platform that the browser chrome itself has.

The characteristics and usage of an XPI are:

- Has an *install.js* file
- Can install anything via XPInstall API
- PKZip-compressed
- May contain one or more JAR packages
- Mozilla installation
- Used for new packages

The characteristics and usage of a JAR are:

- Contains only the resources themselves
- Installed with an external script
- May be installed inside a XPI
- PKZip-compressed
- Themes
- Languages packs
- Storage archive for installed components

Mozilla uses the presence of this internal installation script and not the file suffix (which can be changed easily enough) to determine what type of archive it is. Accordingly, JARs are most often used to install new themes and new language packs, which can be done by using just a brief trigger script on a web page loaded into Mozilla. When they contain new chrome—new XUL and JavaScript that will access the Mozilla objects via XPConnect—JAR files must be put within a XPI that can register them properly.

Installation Scripts

Most new packages in Mozilla are installed by means of installation scripts. These scripts are written in JavaScript. Unlike regular web page JavaScript, however, which uses `window` as the top-level object, installation scripts have a special install object context. As you will see in the following examples, the `Install` object—even when it's implicit and not prefixed to the object methods—is the top-level object upon which most methods are called.

Script examples

At their very simplest, installation scripts look something like Example 6-9.

Example 6-9. Simple install script

```
// initialize the installation first
initInstall("My Package Install", "package_name", "1.0", 1);
// add files to the installation
f = getFolder("Program");
setPackageFolder(f);
addFile("package.xpi")
// perform the installation
performInstall();
```

These methods are being called on the Install object, which is implicit in an installation script. Example 6-10 is an equivalent (and still very compact) installation script. The Install object is prefixed explicitly to the install functions.

Example 6-10. Script that explicitly prefixes the Install object

```
Install.initInstall("My Package Install", "package_name", "1.0", 1);
f = Install.getFolder("Program");
Install.setPackageFolder(f);
Install.addFile("package.xpi")
Install.performInstall();
```

As they become more complicated, install scripts may set up and arrange target directories in more specific ways, do more error checking, and include variables to make the code more readable and reusable, as seen in the longer install script in Example 6-11.

Example 6-11. A more complicated install script

```
var vi = "10.10.10.10";
var xpiSrc = "adddir1";
initInstall("addFileNoVers1", "adddir_1", vi, 1);
f = getFolder("Program");
setPackageFolder(f);
err = addDirectory(xpiSrc);
logComment("the error = " + err);
if (0 == getLastError())
  performInstall();
else
  cancelInstall();
```

Web page installations

XPInstall technology makes software installation from a web page very easy. When a link on a web page kicks off the installation of new software, "trigger" code on the web page starts the process and gets the XPI onto the local system. Once this is done, the *install.js* file in the XPI can take up the full installation and registration of new files.

In Example 6-12, the trigger script—placed in an `onclick` event handler on the page—starts the installation of a new theme on the local machine, where the XPI can be unpacked and its installation script executed in full.

Example 6-12. Trigger script on a web page

```
<a href="#"
   onclick="InstallTrigger.installChrome(
   InstallTrigger.SKIN,
   'http://wildskins/newblue.xpi',
   'newblue/1.0');">
   Install the New Blue theme</a>
```

Later, we discuss in more detail the `Install` object, whose methods are typically called in installation scripts.

Scriptless installations

When you have a simple Mozilla package like a theme, which does not need special security privileges and which is always installed in a particular location, you can leave out the XPI and its internal installation script altogether and use a trigger script like Example 6-13 and a regular JAR file to download and register the new package.

Example 6-13. Scriptless install of a JAR

```
<a href="#"
   onclick="InstallTrigger.installChrome(
   InstallTrigger.SKIN,
   'http://wildskins/newblue.jar',
   'newblue/1.0');">
   Install the New Blue theme</a>
```

The only difference here is that the item to be installed is a JAR and not a XPI file. Also, no internal installation script is present (since of the two, only XPIs carry their own *install.js* file). When the `InstallTrigger` object gets a JAR with a package manifest it can read and a package type that doesn't break the security boundary for applications (i.e., a new theme, a new language pack, or new content that doesn't use XPConnect), it can download and register that package with the chrome registry and make it available to users. The JAR and a trigger script like the one just shown are all you need in this case. See the earlier section, "JARs versus XPIs" for more detail on the limitations of scriptless installs.

The xFly application accesses XPCOM objects in Mozilla, which makes it a full-blown XPConnected application. Thus, it needs to be installed in a XPI file that has its own internal installation script.

Platform-dependent installation

Though the XPI format is by definition cross-platform, the files you distribute within it may need to be installed on a per-platform basis. The platform can be retrieved using the `platform` property of the `Install` object or the `getFolder` function. Example 6-14 shows a JavaScript function for *install.js* for returning the platform that the script is running on.

Example 6-14. Getting the operating system in an install script

```
function getPlatform()
{
    var platformStr;
    var platformNode;
    if('platform' in Install)
    {
        platformStr = new String(Install.platform);
        if (!platformStr.search(/^Macintosh/))
            platformNode = 'mac';
        else if (!platformStr.search(/^Win/))
            platformNode = 'win';
        else
            platformNode = 'unix';
    }
    else
    {
        var fOSMac  = getFolder("Mac System");
        var fOSWin  = getFolder("Win System");
        logComment("fOSMac: "  + fOSMac);
        logComment("fOSWin: "  + fOSWin);
        if(fOSMac != null)
            platformNode = 'mac';
        else if(fOSWin != null)
            platformNode = 'win';
        else
            platformNode = 'unix';
    }
    return platformNode;
}
```

It's often necessary to check the platform when you install new language packs. At the time of this writing, issues related to write access to the chrome folder on Unix systems require some forking in the install script. There are also certain JAR files that are installed on a per-platform basis in language packs. Example 6-14 covers the three major platforms (Windows, Mac, and *nix). Here is how you use it:

```
platformNode = getPlatform();
if (platformNode != 'unix') {
  // do Unix script and files
}
```

```
else if (platformNode != 'win') {
  // do Windows script and files
}
else {  // mac
  // do Mac script and files
}
```

The install log

When you are testing your XPI or need a way to troubleshoot installation problems, one of the best methods is to consult the installation log file. This file is called *install.log* and lives in the *bin* directory.

The *install.log* file is generated the first time you try to install software in Mozilla and appended to for each subsequent installation. The format of the file—in which the URL and date of the installation appear as a heading—makes it easy to find the installation you are checking on in the install log.

Example 6-15 shows the output in *install.log* after a single successful installation.

Example 6-15. install.log

```
-------------------------------------------------------------------------------
http://books.mozdev.org/examples/xfly.xpi  --  06/28/2002 19:12:59
-------------------------------------------------------------------------------
     Install xFly (version 0.0.1)
     ------------
     [1/4]    Installing: C:\MOZILLA\BIN\chrome\xfly.jar
     [2/4]    Register Content: jar:resource:/chrome/xfly.jar!/content/
     [3/4]    Register Skin: jar:resource:/chrome/xfly.jar!/skin/
     [4/4]    Register Locale: jar:resource:/chrome/xfly.jar!/locale/en-US/
     Install completed successfully  --  06/28/2002 19:13:03
```

In your *install.js* file, you can use the method `logComment` to create output other than these standard logging messages. This can be very useful for debugging your install scripts or providing extra feedback:

```
logComment( "Installation started ..." );
```

The output for this call will appear in *install.log* formatted like this:

```
** Installation started ...
```

When installation is not smooth, Mozilla outputs an error code to track down what is happening. For example, if you declare a constant variable twice in your install script, you will receive notification of an script error in the UI, and this error will be logged in *install.log*:

```
** Line: 4    redeclaration of const X_JAR_FILE
Install **FAILED** with error -229  --  07/01/2002 11:47:53
```

A full list of error codes can be found at *http://lxr.mozilla.org/seamonkey/source/xpinstall/src/nsInstall.h* or in the *XPInstall API Reference* at *http://developer.netscape.com/docs/manuals/xpinstall/err.html*.

Though XPInstall is enabled by default, there is preference to turn it on and off in the user profile preferences file (*prefs.js*). To disable XPInstall, set the preference like this:

```
user_pref("xpinstall.enabled", false);
```

And be aware that target installation platforms may have this preference turned off, which prevents you from installing any new software in Mozilla.

XPInstall

XPInstall is a technology used for cross-platform installation. Mozilla uses it extensively to install new packages, but as a general-purpose technology, it can be used to install anything on your computer. The XPI file format we described in the section "The XPI File Format" earlier in this chapter is the basic unit of exchange in an XPInstall and the installation script manages the installation.

Installation scripts—whether they appear within the XPI, on a web page as an external "trigger script," or elsewhere in JavaScript—use the XPInstall API to do all the heavy lifting. The XPInstall API includes installation functions (Example 6-16) organized into such high-level objects as the `Install` object, the `InstallTrigger` object, and the `File` object, which you can use to install new Mozilla packages.

Example 6-16. Common XPInstall functions

```
initInstall()      // initializes every installation
getFolder()        // creates a new folder on the target system
addFile()          // adds files and directories to the install
performInstall()   // executes the installation
cancelInstall()    // cancels installation if there are errors
```

In addition to the XPInstall API installation functions, installation scripts often call methods on the chrome registry itself. As described earlier in this chapter in the "The Chrome Registry" section, the chrome registry handles the registration of new files and packages on the local system, the maintenance of user configurable data (such as what skin or theme you currently selected), and several utility functions used to make installations easier and more successful.

The Install object

The `Install` object is the main object in the XPInstall API. It provides most of the methods and properties used in installation scripts.

```
initInstall(displayName, name, version, flags)
```

The `initInstall()` method that initializes the installation process takes the following parameters: *displayName* is the name you give to the installation itself; *name* is the name of the package to be installed (which must match the name given to the package in the manifests); *version* is the version of the package being installed (also specified in the manifest); and *flags* is an optional parameter reserved for future use (which is set to "0" by default and about which you don't have to worry).

```
Example: initInstall("Example Installation", "xfly", "0.9", 0);
addFile(file)
```

The `addFile()` method adds a single file to the initialized installation. `file` is a pointer to the file in the XPI that will be installed.

```
Example: addFile("simple.exe");
err = performInstall()
```

The `performInstall()` method starts the installation that you set up.

```
Example: performInstall();
```

The `Install` object exposes the methods listed in Table 6-1.

Table 6-1. Install object methods

Method	Description
`AddDirectory`	Unpacks an entire subdirectory.
`AddFile`	Unpacks a single file.
`Alert`	Displays an Alert dialog box with a message and an OK button.
`CancelInstall`	Aborts the installation of the software.
`Confirm`	Displays a Confirm dialog box with the specified message and OK and Cancel buttons.
`deleteRegisteredFile`	Deletes the specified file and its entry in the Client Version Registry.
`Execute`	Extracts a file from the XPI file to a temporary location and schedules it for later execution.
`Gestalt`	Retrieves information about the operating environment (Mac OS only).
`GetComponentFolder`	Returns an object representing the directory in which a component is installed.
`GetFolder`	Returns an object representing a directory, for use with the `addFile` method.
`GetLastError`	Returns the most recent nonzero error code.
`getWinProfile`	Constructs an object for working with a Windows *.ini* file.
`getWinRegistry`	Constructs an object for working with the Windows registry.
`InitInstall`	Initializes installation for the given software and version.
`LoadResources`	Returns an object whose properties are localized strings loaded from the specified property file.
`LogComment`	Adds a comment line to the install log.
`Patch`	Applies a set of differences between two versions.
`PerformInstall`	Finalizes the installation of software.

Table 6-1. Install object methods (continued)

Method	Description
RegisterChrome	Registers chrome with the chrome registry.
ResetError	Resets a saved error code to zero.
setPackageFolder	Sets the default package folder that is saved with the root node.

The InstallTrigger object

When you have very simple installations—such as when you want to install a new skin—you may not need to use the services from the `Install` object. Besides providing the services necessary for "triggering" the downloading of a package from a web site, the `InstallTrigger` object offers some simple methods for installing when you do not need to rearrange of the disk, register complications, or do other install-type preparation (see Table 6-2).

Table 6-2. InstallTrigger interface showing the role of the InstallTrigger object in the overall installation process

Method	Description
compareVersion	Compares the version of a file or package with the version of an existing file or package.
Enabled	Indicates whether the Software Installation is enabled for this client machine.
getVersionInfo	Returns an `InstallVersion` object representing the version number from the Client Version Registry for the specified software or component.
Install	Installs one or more XPI files on the local machine.
installChrome	Installs new skin or locale packages in Netscape 6 and Mozilla.
startSoftwareUpdate	Initiates the download and installation of specified software. Note: deprecated in favor of install.

This web page installation script defines its own `install` method in which a callback parameter on the `InstallTrigger`'s own `install()` method checks the success of the installation and displays a relevant alert for the user (as shown in Example 6-17).

Example 6-17. Install script callback

```
function doneFn (name, result)
{
   if (result != 0 && result != 999)
     alert("The install didn't seem to work, you could maybe try " +
           "a manual install instead.\nFailure code was " + result + ".");
   else
     alert("Installation complete, please restart your browser.");
}
function install(packageName, fileName)
{
   var xpi = new Object();
   xpi[packageName] = fileName;
```

Example 6-17. Install script callback (continued)

```
    InstallTrigger.install(xpi, doneFn);
}
<a href="javascript:install('xFly','xfly.xpi');">install</a>
```

Installing non-Mozilla software

The XPInstall technology downloads and installs any software on any machine using Mozilla or Netscape 6/7. The same `Install` object methods that download, register, and install new Mozilla packages (e.g., new themes or new Mozilla applications like xFly) can be used to download other executables and software into any location on the local machine.

As with Mozilla application installs, you use an installation script within a XPI to initialize the installation, add the files you want to the installation, and then perform the install and put the software in the designated locations. Note that non-Mozilla software installations do not include a registration step, since the chrome registry does not track non-Mozilla software or any more general additions to the operating system. Example 6-18 shows a simple and typical non-Mozilla installation.

Example 6-18. Non-Mozilla software installation script

```
var xpiSrc = "file.txt";
initInstall(
  "Adding A File",
  "testFile",
  "1.0.1.7",
  1);
f = getFolder("Program"); // keyword for the main program
                          // directory on the target platform
                          // (e.g., the "Program Files" dir on win32)
setPackageFolder(f);
addFile(xpiSrc);
if (0 == getLastError())
    performInstall();
else
    cancelInstall();
```

Refer to the "XPInstall API Reference" on *http://developer.netscape.com* for more detailed information about the XPInstall API and how it can be used in more complex installations.

Uninstalling Applications

You may have noticed an `uninstall()` method on the `Install` object in the XPInstall API. This method does some of the work you need to do to uninstall packages from Mozilla, but it's a buggy process and doesn't finish the job.* Beyond the physical

* Currently, some open bugs in Bugzilla are tracking the progress of this method and its improvement.

removal of the package resources during the uninstall, several RDF files in the chrome registry need to be updated, and the XPInstall `uninstall()` does not get to some of these files.

Fortunately, the JSLib JavaScript developer's library has a well-implemented uninstall function, which you can use by importing the *uninstall.js* file and calling uninstall on the package you want uninstalled. *uninstall.js* is one of the JS file collections that comprise the JSLib.

Once you install JSLib, using the uninstall method is simple:

```
include("chrome://jslib/install/uninstall.js");
var p = new Uninstall('myPackageName');
p.removePkg();
```

You might want to put this uninstall routine in a function so you can reuse it.

```
function unInstall(pkg) {
   var p = new Uninstall(pkg);
   p.removePkg();
}
```

This method removes the resources themselves and deletes all references to the package in the chrome registry. The `pkg` parameter is the name of the package as defined in the manifest for that package. The xFly package manifest, for example, defines "xfly" as the name of the package, as shown in Example 6-19.

Example 6-19. Package metadata in the xFly manifest

```
<!-- xFly package information -->
  <RDF:Description about="urn:mozilla:package:xfly"
        chrome:displayName="xFly"
        chrome:author="frillies"
        chrome:name="xfly">
  </RDF:Description>
```

Example 6-9 comes from the content package manifest for xFly, which is similar to the full content manifest for the XMLTerm application you saw in Example 6-4.

To uninstall the xFly package, then—as you should do to the working version you have as you develop before installing the final version—hook up a menuitem to call the uninstall routine:

```
<menuitem id="uninstall-item" label="Uninstall xFly" oncommand="unInstall("xfly")" />
```

This menuitem should have access to a JavaScript file and contains the following code:

```
include("chrome://jslib/install/uninstall.js");
function unInstall(pkg) {
   var p = new Uninstall(pkg);
   p.removePkg();
}
```

Finishing Things Up

We dealt with the xFly example earlier in this chapter and then discussed general information about file formats, installation scripts, and xpinstall. You now have everything you need to make the xFly package an installable application. Borrowing liberally from the examples in the earlier sections "The XPI File Format" and "Installation Scripts," you can bundle a JAR file or the entire subdirectory structure you already created for xFly in the *chrome* directory:

```
chrome
    xfly      content
      skin
      locale
```

Bundle the JAR file into a ZIP file, add an installation script to that ZIP file (and a web trigger script to the application's web page), and make your application available to Mozilla users everywhere.

Creating the xFly XPI

An XPI file is nothing more than a ZIP file with its own installation script. Using a ZIP utility, you can archive the *xfly* directory and preserve the subdirectory structure so it's installed in the user's *chrome* directory as it is in your own. Make sure that the ZIP file, whatever it's called, contains the top-level *xfly* subdirectory as part of this structure. If it is a JAR file you are distributing for your package, make the JAR file (*xfly.jar*) the top level, with the *content*, *skin*, and *locale* directories contained within:

```
xfly.jar
  content
  skin
  locale
```

The URLs you used to refer to various parts of your xFly application (e.g., *chrome://xfly/content/xfly.js* as part of the command that imports the external script file into the main XUL file) will be registered during the installation process with that *xfly* directory or JAR file directly underneath the Mozilla *chrome* directory.

Adding the Installation Script

Once you understand the "Installation Scripts" section (earlier in this chapter), creating an installation script for the xFly application is straightforward, as Example 6-20 shows. In this case, we bundled all the xFly subdirectories in a single JAR file, *xfly.jar*.

Example 6-20. xFly installation script

```
const X_MSG             = "Install xFly";
const X_NAME            = "xFly";
const X_VER             = "0.0.1";
```

Example 6-20. xFly installation script (continued)

```
const X_JAR_FILE        = "xfly.jar";
const X_CONTENT         = "content/";
const X_SKIN            = "skin/";
const X_LOCALE          = "locale/en-US/";
const X_CHROME          = "chrome";
var err = initInstall(X_MSG, X_NAME, X_VER);
logComment("initInstall: " + err);
logComment( "Installation started ..." );
addFile("We're on our way ...", X_JAR_FILE, getFolder(X_CHROME), "");
registerChrome(CONTENT|DELAYED_CHROME, getFolder(X_CHROME, X_JAR_FILE), X_CONTENT);
registerChrome(SKIN|DELAYED_CHROME, getFolder(X_CHROME, X_JAR_FILE), X_SKIN);
registerChrome(LOCALE|DELAYED_CHROME, getFolder(X_CHROME, X_JAR_FILE), X_LOCALE);
err = getLastError();
if ( err == SUCCESS )  {        // if there have been no errors:
  performInstall();             // install "xfly.jar"
  alert("Please restart Mozilla");
}
else  {                         // otherwise
  cancelInstall();              // cancel the installation.
}
```

Save the installation code in Example 6-20 as *install.js* and add it to the ZIP file you created out of the *xfly* subdirectory. Name this zip file *xfly.xpi*. The installation script should be archived at the top level of the XPI file and appear next to the *xfly* subdirectory or JAR file. Another feature of this script is the declaration of constant variables at the top, for various values used in the script. This feature is good for re-use and organizing your script.

Web Page Installer

The XPI file you created in the last two sections, with its internal *install.js* file, is all you need to make your Mozilla application portable and installable. The final step creates a link on a regular web page that tells Mozilla where this file is, as shown in Example 6-21.

Example 6-21. Web page trigger

```
<a href="#"
   onclick="InstallTrigger.install(
   {`xfly' :
   'xfly.xpi'});">
   Install my cool xFly Application</a>
```

When the user browses the application web page and clicks the "Install my cool xFly Application" link shown above, Mozilla finds and downloads *xfly.xpi* in the same directory. It then opens the archive, reads the install script, creates the *xfly* subdirectory on the local machine or moves the JAR file onto the local machine, and registers it with the chrome registry. When the user restarts the browser, the xFly application is integrated into Mozilla and ready for use. The user can access it with any overlays that put it into the browser's interface (e.g., as an item in the Tools menu) or invoke it directly by using the special chrome option for pointing to a registered chrome:

```
mozilla -chrome chrome://xfly/content
```

You don't need to have an install page to install a XPI in Mozilla. If, instead of a web page, you provide a URL that points directly to a XPI, Mozilla displays a dialog that asks the user whether they want to initiate the installation of that XPI. As with any new software installation, however, a page that describes the package and what it does can help allay fears and promote use.

Extra Tricks for Customizing an Application

If the Mozilla application you are working on is more autonomous than a package that sits up on a Mozilla installation, you may want to add extra customization. Here are two common features: the program icon and the splash screen. Some features require that you build the source code yourself, even just a particular module instead of the whole tree. Refer to Appendix A for more details on obtaining and building the source code.

Icons

Program icons are important for several reasons. Primarily, however, they are a visual representation of your application on the system that it runs on, whether it runs in a file explorer, a taskbar, or an application selector. This section tells you where to locate the current icons in the Mozilla application and what files or resources need to be changed to make your icon the default for Mozilla.

Windows

In Windows, create your own icon and then follow these steps:

1. Go to the *mozilla/xpfe/bootstrap* folder in the source tree.
2. Open the *splash.rc* resource file. This can be done in the text editor of your choice or in any program with special handling for Windows resource files.
3. Change the icon resource to the file of your choice.

   ```
   // Program icon.
   IDI_APPLICATION ICON
   "mozdev.ico"
   ```

4. Recompile the bootstrap module. This recompilation regenerates the *mozilla.exe* executable file.

   ```
   C:\mozilla\src>cd mozilla\xpfe\bootstrap
   C:\mozilla\src\mozilla\xpfe\bootstrap>nmake -f makefile.win
   ```

An alternative to Steps 2 and 3 is to give your icon the same name as the Mozilla icon (*mozilla.ico*) and just drop it into the tree, replacing the existing one shown in Figure 6-6.

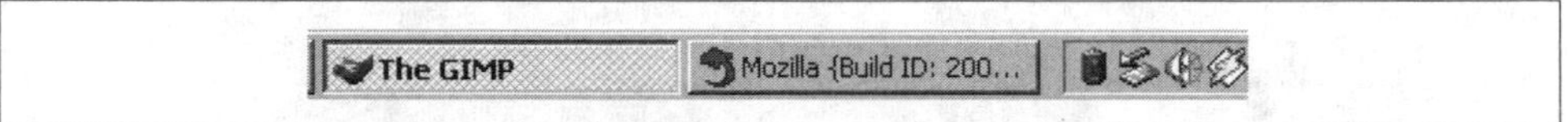

Figure 6-6. Windows taskbar with Mozilla icon

Unix

X Windows uses the common X Pixmap (XPM) format for icons. XPM files are C source code files, with each pixmap defined as a static character array. The window manager expects to find two XPM files for each icon specified in the configuration files as *ICON*. Mozilla has two files for icons located in *mozilla/src/gtk*: *mozicon16.xpm* and *mozicon50.xpm*. Many utilities, such as the GIMP, PaintShopPro, and Xview, can transform images from other common formats.

Macintosh

The Macintosh BNDL resource (OS icons for files and applications) and related resource types (4bit, 8bit, large, small icons, masks, and FREF) are contained in *nsMacBundle.rsrc,* located at *mozilla/xpfe/bootstrap*. It also contains a `MOZZ` resource that references the Mozilla software license. All Macintosh software have this set of resources.

If you want to change icons on a window-by-window basis, do it only in Mozilla on the Windows platform. In the chrome root, there exists a directory *\icons\default*. Within this directory, you can place any number of icons for windows in your application. The filename has to be the same as the XUL window ID: `<window_id>.ico`. One example of an icon being used in this way is the DOM Inspector window in Mozilla. In the *\icons\default* directory you will find the file *winInspectorMain.ico* on Windows. This option is good for package authors who add windows to the Mozilla application and do not want to hijack this resource completely. Icons can be installed as part of an XPI.

Splash Screen

Are splash screens a necessary startup feature for a program or a shameless plug? The answer is probably somewhere in between, leaning toward the necessary in the case of Mozilla (Figure 6-7 shows Mozilla's splash screen).

Because Mozilla is a large application and needs to process so much (including profiles, initialization code, and theme/locale selection from the chrome registry) before you actually see the first window appear, users need a visual clue that something is happening when Mozilla starts up.

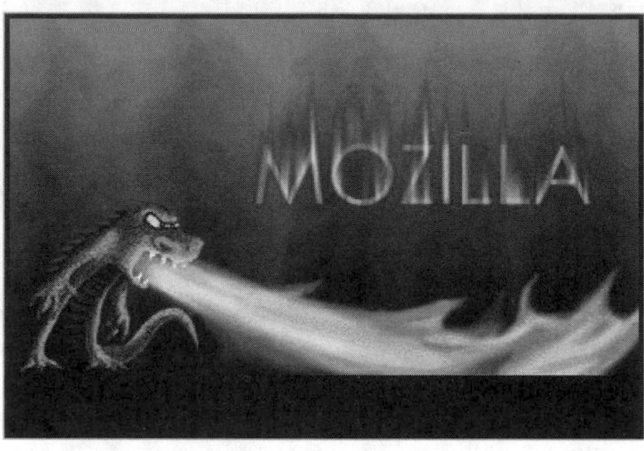

Figure 6-7. Mozilla's splash screen

If your application also requires a lot of processing at startup or if you would like to customize your application, then creating and using your own unique splash screen is essential.

Windows

The splash screen file is a bitmap image that also lives in the same *splash.rc* file that houses the icon file, perhaps more appropriately named in this case.

```
// Splash screen bitmap.
IDB_SPLASH BITMAP
    "splash.bmp"
```

Again, you have the option of changing the resource file or calling the image file the same name as the Mozilla splash (*splash.bmp*) and dropping it into the tree. Both of options require recompilation of the bootstrap module.

Unix

The splash screen uses the same XPM format as is used for the icons. The file is called *splash.xpm* and is located in *mozilla/xpfe/bootstrap*. Note that the splash display is turned off by default on this platform and can be displayed by using the -splash switch in a command shell.

```
/mozilla -splash
```

Macintosh

The file *Splash.rsrc* (located in the source tree at *mozilla/xpfe/bootstrap*) contains Macintosh resources to display the splash screen (native DLOG, DITL, PICT) during startup while the shared libraries are loaded and before the profile manager is shown.

CHAPTER 7

Extending the UI with XBL

You now know that XUL is the basic tool set for creating your application interface, but even it has limitations. It is just a finite set of widgets that your programming needs may transcend. If you find that you reimplement many of the same groups of widgets in different applications, or if you want to extend your application's interface in some other way, you will find the eXtensible Binding Language (XBL) an invaluable tool.

This chapter describes what XBL is and how it is used. Basically, XBL provides a way to attach new content or behavior to your application by using XBL bindings. XBL can extend, add to, and reorganize user interfaces. XBL can also help you organize scattered XUL code into a set of self-contained widgets that make building and maintaining your Mozilla application much easier. Appendix C provides a reference for the XBL element set, with which new elements can be created.

What Is XBL?

XBL is an XML markup language invented specifically for creating widgets. XBL looks similar to XUL, and may even contain XUL or HTML and other markup (see the "Namespaces and XBL" section later in this chapter for more information about how other markup is used in XBL bindings), but its purpose is different. Flexibility and interoperability are the point of XBL.

If the XUL `textbox` is inadequate, for example, you can use XBL to create and attach a new widget called `<datafield/>`, possibly based on `textbox`, that provides special attributes and functionality for validating input data against a database.

A *binding* is a single XBL language entity that can contain content as other markup (such as XUL) behavior that is represented as methods and properties, and event-handling capabilities. Bindings can be anything from small widget objects to large, complex blocks of code with extensive functionality. Figure 7-1 shows the different components that make up a binding: fields, properties, functions, event handlers, and content. The section "Anatomy of a Binding," later in this chapter, provides more detail about a binding's structure.

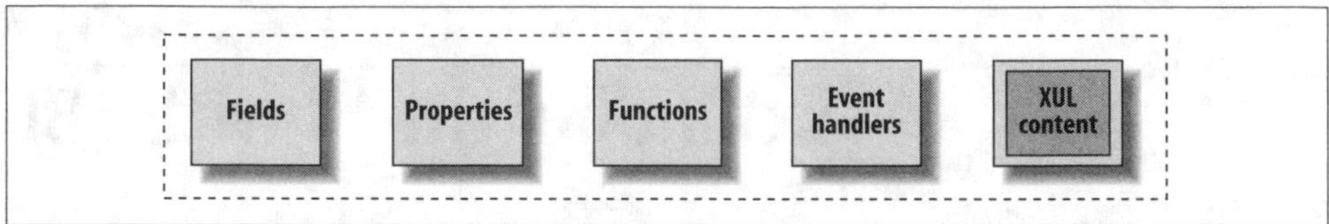

Figure 7-1. Mozilla XBL binding structure

Bindings differ from XUL overlays because they are fully self-contained, reusable, and generally have no dependencies outside of the binding itself. Although XUL is used most often as content in an XBL binding, XBL can also bind to and from HTML and XML. If you have worked with Java or C#, you may recognize some parallels between XBL bindings and Java objects.

XBL Terminology

The following terms are used to describe XBL and its use in the XPFE:

XBL
: An acronym for the eXtensible Binding Language. In some contexts, the term XBL refers to actual code (e.g., "the XBL in this example..."). XBL is an XML syntax.

Binding
: A single unit of the XBL language, one or more of which is contained in a binding document. Most bindings are made up of content and implementation, although each are mutually exclusive; if you add event handlers to that list, each one can appear on its own in a binding.

Binding document
: An XBL file with an *.xml* extension that contains one or more bindings.

Bound document
: A XUL (or HTML) document that has one or more bindings attached to it as content.

Bound element
: A bound element is a widget or element that uses a particular binding. It can be an existing element in the XUL or HTML set or a newly invented one.

Anonymous content
: Content (e.g., XUL elements) contained in a binding that is hidden from the document object (DOM). Refer to the section "XBL and the DOM," later in this chapter, for a more detailed discussion of its characteristics and how to programmatically gain access to the content.

Attachment and detachment
: Attachment is the process through which a binding is associated with a bound element. It is essentially a way of telling the element which binding to use. Detachment is the process of removing that link and with it, the binding display.

Insertion point

The point in anonymous content at which children of the bound element are inserted. The section "Extra Binding Content and Insertion Points," later in this chapter, details the insertion process.

Inheritance

During inheritance, characteristics of one object are passed on to another object. In XBL, this process is multifaceted. Bindings can inherit from other bindings, anonymous content can inherit attributes from the bound element, and a binding implementation can inherit the behavior of another widget. All concepts are explained in the section "Inheritance," later in this chapter.

An XBL Document

XBL documents are files saved with an *.xml* filename extension. Most bindings implement XUL content and behavior with script, so XBL files reside in your XUL application's chrome content area and have full access to XPConnect-wrapped XPCOM objects.

Several bindings often reside inside the same XBL file. Performance benefits from this arrangement, if you have multiple related bindings, because only one XBL document needs to be loaded, rather than multiple documents. Organization is another factor. Mozilla has dozens of bindings that are interrelated by either inheritance or filename identifiers. Individual pieces to a menu widget reside in a file called *menu.xml*, button bindings are in *button.xml*, and so forth. Keeping these bindings together is wise.

The XBL document's root container is the `<bindings>` tag. Inside this element is one or more individual child bindings, defined by the `<binding>` tag. A simple XBL document is as follows:

```
<?xml version="1.0"?>
<bindings id="dataBindings" ...>
  <binding />
  <binding />
</bindings>
```

An XBL document is a valid XML document. The XML preamble you are used to seeing in XUL files is present. It also contains the single root element (in this case, `<bindings>`) and the child nodes that define the bindings (empty).

Bindings are the atomic units of an XBL document. An XBL document may define any number of individual bindings, each of which is bound (i.e., associated with other XML/XUL elements by way of CSS class definitions) somewhere in the interface. In other words, an XBL document may be a set of unrelated or barely related bindings that are picked up by the XUL interface.

Namespaces and XBL

Because XBL is a binding language for other markup, remember to distinguish between the XBL markup (such as `<binding>` and `<handler>`) and markup from another language (such as XUL). Namespaces are a feature of the XML language that was invented to handle this separation of intermingled markup, and XBL uses namespaces. For more information on namespaces, refer to the W3C at *http://www.w3.org/TR/REC-xml-names/*.

Namespaces are declared in the root element of an XML document. The most common implementation is the declaration of two namespaces: a default namespace for XBL and a namespace for the other markup. This code shows the root of a bindings document in which the XUL namespace declaration (`xmlns:xul`) and the XBL default namespace are declared:

```
<bindings id="dataBindings"
  xmlns=http://www.mozilla.org/xbl
  xmlns:xul=
    http://www.mozilla.org/keymaster/gatekeeper/there.is.only.xul>
```

An *NCName* is the part of a namespace declaration that qualifies the markup type for that particular namespace. It is placed after a colon, and in many XPFE documents, is the markup language name (`xul`, `xbl`, or `rdf`). The XBL namespace is the default in this instance because it does not declare a namespace prefix (`NCName`).

You can choose to namespace your document in a different way. For example, if you have a large mass of XUL code in your binding and do not wish to use the `xul:` prefix repeatedly, you can declare the XBL namespace as `xmlns:xbl`; you won't need to use prefixes on the XUL content since it is set as the default. Another option is to namespace a parent element:

```
<box xmlns="http://www.mozilla.org/keymaster/gatekeeper/there.is.only.xul">
```

This code enables all children inside the `<box>` to be in the scope of the XUL namespace; therefore the explicit `xul:` tag prefix declaration is not necessary.

XBL and HTML

Although XUL usually makes up the content of an XBL binding in Mozilla, HTML is another valid and popular binding format. Using the XBL with HTML combination can be advantageous. With it, web pages (rendered in Mozilla) can be more feature-rich and move beyond the limitations of the HTML specification's finite element set. It means a possible mingling of one or many markup languages, including HTML, XUL, and RDF.

The following snippet, in which a simple binding defines the name of the browser in an HTML `div`, gives you a feel for its potential:

```
<binding id="browser">
  <content>
    <html:div>Mozilla 1.0</html:div>
    <children />
  </content>
</binding>
```

The bound element in HTML is called browser_name and is attached to the anonymous content in the HTML document's inline style.

```
<head>
  <title>Browser Information</title>
  <style>
  browser_name  {
   -moz-binding: url("brand.xml#browser");
  }
  </style>
</head>
<body>
<h1><browser_name /> Guide</h1>
...
```

Although the <browser_name/> element is not a valid HTML element, one of XBL's great capabilities is that Mozilla finds the binding, reads the content there, and makes the substitution. The browser name can be included in several places in the HTML document. Like a poor man's DTD, the binding lets you change the definition of browser_name in one place and propagate that change to every instance of its use. This feature is useful because it requires the touching of fewer files during code maintenance.

Anatomy of a Binding

The best way to understand a binding is to watch one evolve from start to finish. This section examines a binding from its inception, into the construction of the binding, and through its use in a XUL document. At the end of the section, you should be able to take the pieces and construct your own binding, so try to follow it like a step-by-step guide.

Design is important in XBL. The implementation can sometimes be tricky; for example, when you intend to reuse the binding elsewhere or when others use it in a way you don't foresee. Ideally, a binding should be as small as possible to facilitate reuse. And it's a good idea to separate your binding into smaller pieces—perhaps smaller "subbindings"—so you can recombine when necessary. You could design the <datafield/> widget mentioned in the introduction—for example, as a combination of the XUL <textfield/> widget and your own new binding, <validator/>, which you could then use elsewhere.

The widget constructed in this section is a good example of a small, reusable binding. It is a special text input widget called inputfield—a self-contained extension to a XUL textbox that can be used on its own or as part of another binding. The binding combines a <label> and a <textbox>, allows child elements, and offers functions that work with the data and style of the <textbox>.

CSS Attachment

Attachment is the process through which the binding is connected to the bound document that uses it. This process is most commonly achieved through CSS, but can also be done by using the DOM. The section "XBL and the DOM," later in this chapter, details the interaction between XBL and the document object model. The CSS connection begins where the bound element is placed in the XUL file:

```
<inputfield/>
```

Remember that XML ignores elements it doesn't recognize, so this new element won't be rendered until you add information to the stylesheet; a binding is attached with the special `-moz-binding` attribute. The style selector must be associated with the bound element in the XUL file. In the following example, the binding is attached to every `<inputfield>` tag because the element name itself is used as the style selector. However, `-moz-binding` can also be inside a class selector, an ID selector, or any other CSS selector you wish to use:

```
inputfield {
  -moz-binding: url("inputfield.xml#inputfield");
}
```

It also can be from an inline style:

```
<inputfield
  id="ifd"
  style="-moz-binding: url("inputfield.xml#inputfield")"/>
```

The constituent parts of this style rule are the `-moz-binding` property, the `url` binding locator that takes the bindings file (and possibly the path to it) as a parameter, and the `id` of the binding denoted with the # notation. For the binding to take, the XBL file must contain a binding with the same `id`.

```
<binding id="inputfield">
  <!-- binding content / behavior / handlers -->
</binding>
```

The ID of `inputfield` matches the value specified in the URL after the # symbol. When the UI is drawn in Mozilla, the binding content, behavior, and handlers are applied to the bound document at the point where the `<inputfield>` element appears in the document. Figure 7-2 shows a visual representation of the constituent parts of a binding attachment occurring via CSS.

In this example, we use our own new element name called `<inputfield>`, but you can also extend existing XUL widgets by including:

```
<box id="inputfield" flex="1"/>
```

Because they are bound through CSS, bindings cannot be guaranteed to be loaded until the whole document is loaded, which means that any inline scripts accessing bindings should be considered incorrect because you cannot guarantee that the binding is loaded.

```
<inputfield id="ifd" klabel="Input Field">
   <label value="Eric's"/>
</inputfield>
```

XUL

```
inputfield {
  _moz-binding: url("inputfield.xml#inputfield");
}
```

CSS

```
<binding id+"inputfield">
  <content>
    <children/>
    <xul:label xbl:inherits="value+label"?>
    <xul:textbox anonid="input" flex="1"/>
  </content>
  <implementation>
    <property name+"uppercase" readonly="true"
       onget="return this.value.to.UpperCase();"/>
    <method name="setValue">
       <parameter name="newValue"/>
       <body>
         this.input.value=newValue;
       </body>
    </method>
  </implementation>
</binding>
```

XBL

Figure 7-2. CSS binding attachment components

XBL content is considered "invisible" in the context of the document object because it is not contained directly in the XUL document. Refer to the later section "XBL and the DOM" for more information on this concept.

Because a document binding can have multiple instances, something must happen to make the content unique in each one. When a binding is attached to a document, its content is automatically cloned in memory. Every instance of a binding shares the same fields, properties, methods, and event handlers because separate copies of those are simply not necessary. These elements cannot be changed dynamically, but the content document model can.

The XBL Content Element

The `<binding>` element requires an `id` attribute to make the binding unique within the entire document. In the general XML specification, there can only be one element in a document that has a certain ID string. As in XUL, if you use an ID twice, the last one parsed is the only one seen. This situation can lead to unexpected behavior. Figure 7-3 shows the appearance of an `inputfield` binding.

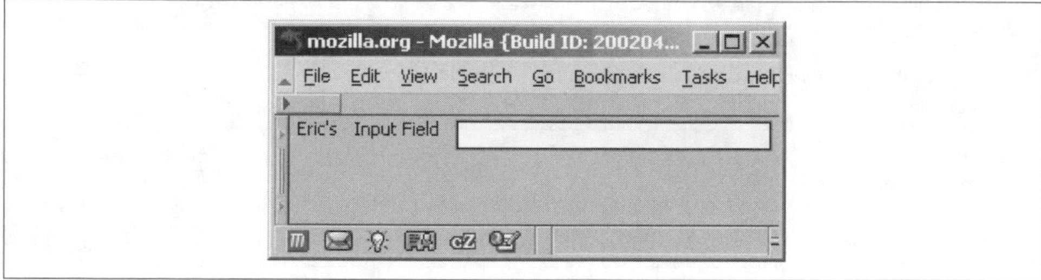

Figure 7-3. The inputfield alone in the XUL document

An <inputfield> has a <label> attached to it, shown here as "Input Field." It also has a regular <textbox>. The "Eric's" label is not part of the binding, but is still displayed inside of it as a child. Child content is discussed later in the section "Extra Binding Content and Insertion Points." The binding content is defined as:

```
<content>
  <children/>
  <xul:label xbl:inherits="value=label"/>
  <xul:textbox anonid="input" flex="1"/>
</content>
```

<children/>, the first element in the binding, lets any elements that existed in the original XUL document pass through the binding's display if it exists inside the <inputfield> tag.

```
<inputfield id="ifd" label="Input Field">
  <label value="Eric's"/>
</inputfield>
```

In this case, the XUL label is inserted into the anonymous content at the point of the <children/> element when the binding is rendered. This ability is useful for changing the ordering of content and adding extra content within a binding.

You can limit which tags are displayed as child content by using something like:

```
<children includes="treehead|treechildren"/>
```

These filtering capabilities open the possibility of multiple <children/> in your binding.

The next content element is <xul:label/>. Notice how the XML namespace of xul is used in the content. Using this notation is the most common way to apply namespace XUL elements in bindings.

The label element has an XBL-namespaced inherits attribute. This code translates an attribute used on the original bounded tag into something usable by a content element:

```
<inputfield id="ifd" label="Input Field">
```

The final element in the content is a typical XUL textbox that has a namespace like the label. The anonid attribute on the textbox is fabricated and used here to avoid bugs and scope issues with the id attribute in content. The id attribute should be used only on the <binding> and <bindings> tags, but anonid works well as direct DOM access to this element and is shown in the next section.

The Implementation Element

The next part of the binding, and also the most complex, is the behavior. The <implementation> element contains the <constructor>, <destructor>, <field>, <property>, and <method>—all of which handle the binding's implementation features.

All elements can contain JavaScript, which changes the binding into a dynamic widget that does more than display content on the screen. The binding implementation accepts user input, dynamically changes the UI, interacts with remote sites through web protocols, and surfaces Mozilla library functions in widgets.

Constructor

In the example binding, some variables and style rules are set up for access by the rest of the binding to make the code cleaner. These rules are set up by using the constructor:

```
<constructor><![CDATA[
   this.input=document.getAnonymousElementByAttribute
     (this,"anonid","input");
// Initialize color and backgroundColor to something besides a "" value
   this.input.inputField.style.backgroundColor="white";
   this.input.inputField.style.color="black";
   this.input.inputField.setAttribute("onchange","");
]]></constructor>
```

The first JavaScript command accesses the <textbox> with the anonid label and puts it into the *this.input* variable. getAnonymousElementByAttribute is a custom DOM method used to access anonymous content. The section "The XBL DOM Interfaces," later in this chapter, talks more about the XBL DOM methods.

The use of the this keyword and the "dot notation" comes from Java. If you have programmed in Java, these bindings can be considered similar to Java classes. They are self-contained and can be extended. Using this is not necessary but it's common practice and clarifies that the variable or property is a member of the binding, especially if you define elements in the binding's constructor.

In the next two commands, an object called inputField contains the style object property. You may be familiar with this structure in HTML elements, and in fact, this inputField is a version of the HTML <input> textbox. The <textbox> in XUL derives from that HTML element.

The color and backgroundColor are set here manually to return something other than the initial value of a blank string when they are accessed. The last line in the <constructor> sets up the onchange event handler for the textbox. This event handler is also used in a property for this binding.

Destructor

This section of a binding executes anything that needs to be done immediately before a binding is unloaded. Here is an example:

```
<destructor>
  this.input=null;
</destructor>
```

The code you see here is not necessary in this binding, but it shows you the format for executing code in the destructor. Destructors are great to use when you have loaded a component in the binding and want to set the variable representing the component to null to avoid memory leaks. If you have a lot of bindings that load and then unload components while a Mozilla session is still running, a significant amount of memory can be eaten up unless you take this kind of step.

Properties

Like Java properties, an XBL <property> has getters and setters, so they can behave differently when you read or write data. Here is a subset of properties used in this binding:

```
<property name="value" readonly="true">
  <getter>
    return this.input.value;
  </getter>
</property>
<property name="uppercase" readonly="true"
          onget="return this.value.toUpperCase();"/>
<property name="backgroundColor">
  <getter>
    return this.input.inputField.style.backgroundColor;
  </getter>
  <setter>
    this.input.inputField.style.backgroundColor=val;
    return val;
  </setter>
</property>
```

At this point, the characteristics of properties to watch out for include the readonly attribute, the getter and setter elements, and the existence of a val keyword that is used internally for accessing a property's current value. For your reference, this binding's property extracts are used for getting the value of the input field, returning an uppercase version of the inputted text, and getting or setting the input field's background color.

Methods

Methods in XBL are self-contained functions represented by the <method> tag and encapsulated within the <implementation> element. They usually provide a binding object with a specific function like copying and saving some data or showing and hiding widget controls. Like properties, they can be called from within the binding, from another binding that subclasses that binding, and directly from the bound element.

```
<method name="clear">
  <body>
    this.input.value='';
  </body>
</method>
<method name="setValue">
  <parameter name="newValue"/>
  <body>
    this.input.value=newValue;
  </body>
</method>
```

The method code is contained in a <body> tag, and each method can have 0 or more parameters, which gather the values passed into the method when called.

Handlers

Handlers in XBL mimic regular document events like onclick and onmousedown, and provide a means for trapping them within your binding and carrying out tasks associated with them.

```
<handlers>
  <handler event="mouseover">
    this.input.focus();
  </handler>
</handlers>
```

Each handler is contained in a <handler> tag and the event name is placed in the event attribute—minus the "on" prefix. The handler in the code shown above places the focus in the inputfield when the mouse goes over it. See the section "Event Handling," later in this chapter, for more details.

Style

The sample binding's last piece of the puzzle is style. Any XUL elements used in the content inherit the default styles for those widgets, but if you want to add more, you can include your own stylesheet like this:

```
<resources>
  <stylesheet src="inputfield.css"/>
</resources>
```

Notice the <resources> container element, which is a prerequisite for this feature. The use of stylesheets in bindings is covered more thoroughly at the end of the chapter in the section "Resources for Bindings."

At this point, you should be familiar with the pieces that make up a binding, which, at the top level, are the content, implementation, event handlers, and extra resources. The binding that you have constructed is small, yet it shows all the main concepts involved in structuring a binding. With some personalizing, it could be included in potentially any application.

Adding Behavior to Bindings

Like XUL widgets, XBL uses JavaScript to provide functionality to bindings by accessing XPCOM methods via XPConnect. Like binding content, behavior is optional in a binding. Each can exist without the other. At times, you might want only implementations, such as a base binding that contains certain properties that are inherited by other bindings.

The <implementation> element is the container for all other elements that make up a binding's behavioral portion. Example 7-1 shows an empty implementation shell that highlights the element's contained hierarchy.

Example 7-1. XBL implementation element

```
<implementation>
  <constructor />
  <destructor />
  <method name="">
    <parameter name="" />
    <body />
  </method>
  <property>
    <getter />
    <setter />
  </property>
  <field />
</implementation>
```

The code in Example 7-1 shows the <implementation> element having a constructor, destructor, method, property, and field as possible children. Each component can exist in quantities of zero or more, with the exception of the constructor and destructor, of which there can be only zero or one. The rest of this section describes each binding implementation component in more detail.

Binding Methods

Bindings can exist solely as content generators, acting passively when they are drawn. But you can also create bindings that provide new capabilities and more interactive functions or that execute routines in your application.

In the spirit of self-containment, functions can be added to a binding that carry out functionality related to that binding. These functions are the behavior of a binding. The ideal way to add behavior is to add methods to your binding with the <method> element. Each parameter for a method defined in the <method> element is contained within its own <parameter> tag.

```
<method name="dumpString">
  <parameter name="aString1"/>
  <parameter name="aString2"/>
  <body>
    <![CDATA[
      if (!aString1 && aString2)
        return;
      return dump(aString1+" "+aString2+"\n");
    ]]>
  </body>
</method>
```

To use the method to print text to the command shell, call the name that is specified in the name attribute. All methods created in a binding are added to the binding element object and called as members of that object, as shown here:

```
<mybinding id="myNewWidget">
  <image src="http://www.mozdev.org/sharedimages/header.gif" />
</mybinding>
<button label="test method"
    oncommand="document.getElementById('myNewWidget')
        .dumpString('hello', 'there!');"/>
```

Using the `<![CDATA` XML entity is also important. The purpose of `<![CDATA` is to escape JavaScript that may otherwise cause conflicts with the XML parser. Having characters like quotes and slashes in XML is problematic when they are not escaped. Using `<!CDATA` with large portions of JavaScript in a binding can improve performance and minimize bugs.

Methods were designed for language neutrality with the type attribute and getter and setter elements. Currently, bindings support only JavaScript, which is the default when no type is specified. However, this may change as other scripting engines are plugged into Gecko.

Attachment and detachment

Two special methods exist in XBL that allow you to manipulate what happens when a binding is added or removed from a document. These methods use the native <constructor> and <destructor> tags. A constructor is valuable, for example, when you need to initialize a binding object or prefill the UI based on stored values. Destructors can clean up when a binding is discarded.

When bindings are attached, their content is inserted into the document at the point you specify. After insertion—or, more specifically, after the attachment occurs—the code in the <constructor> executes. Similarly, you can use the <destructor> element to execute functions when a binding is destroyed.

```
<implementation>
  <constructor>
    <![CDATA[ dump("\n********\nCreate\n********\n");]]>
  </constructor>
  <destructor>
    <![CDATA[ dump("\n********\nDestroy\n********\n");]]>
  </destructor>
</implementation>
```

This example prints some text to output, but you can include code that carries out variable initialization or anything else you want to occur at these stages of the binding's life. Bound elements constructed before the document `load` event execute this script before the document `load` event fires. In the case of extended bindings, base handlers are fired first, followed by derived handlers.

Binding Properties

Properties on a binding are included by using the `<property>` element. Fundamentally, properties are used to hold and manipulate values that are used elsewhere in the binding, such as when a text widget has its displayed value changed periodically by the application. Currently, there are two classifications for properties, one of which gets a raw value directly on the element.

```
<property name="someAttribute">
  false;
</property>
```

This example always sets the attribute named `someAttribute` to false. Though still supported, this use of the `<property>` element was replaced by a new element called `<field>`. Although it is not in the XBL 1.0 specification, the `<field>` element is implemented and used in the Mozilla code base. It has the same syntax but a different name. We recommend using the `<field>` element.

```
<field name="someAttribute">
  false;
</field>
```

The second property usage defines functions that are carried out when getting and setting a property's value. Take this anonymous content with a `label` child:

```
<xul:box align="left" flex="1">
  <xul:label xbl:inherits="value=title"/>
  <xul:spacer flex="1"/>
</xul:box>
```

This content simply shows some text on the screen. The bound element that uses this content looks like this:

```
<mybinding id="my-binding" title="For Those Who Love to Use XBL" />
```

The XUL `label` used in the binding inherits the `title` attribute value that is set on the bound element. Example 7-2 shows how to set this title and its retrieval. Both access the bound element, and any changes filter down to the label.

Example 7-2. An XBL property setting and getting a value

```
<property name="title">
  <setter>
    <![CDATA[
      this.setAttribute('title',val); return val;
    ]]>
  </setter>
  <getter>
    <![CDATA[
      return this.getAttribute('title');
    ]]>
  </getter>
</property>
```

The script keyword `val` is used internally to represent the latest property value. The request to change the property or retrieve its value can come from another property in the same binding (`this.<propertyName>`), from a binding method, or from a method in the bound document that accesses the binding object directly. This JavaScript sets the value of a property named `title` on the binding object:

```
var titleElement = document.getElementById("my-binding");
titleElement.title = "The Adventures of an XBL hacker";
```

You can use the `onget` and `onset` attribute as an alternative to `<getter>` and `<setter>` elements. Properties are initialized after the content is generated but before the binding attached event is set off. This ensures that all properties are available once that event occurs.

Although it is most commonly used just for getting and setting values on the property, nothing stops you from putting more code in the `<properties>` element that carries out other actions on the binding. One scenario shown in Example 7-3 is if you have a property that holds a search value, you can send that text to the Google[*] API, and fill another widget in the UI with the results every time the value is updated.[†]

Example 7-3. Performing a Google search when setting a property

```
<property name="searchString">
  <setter>
    <![CDATA[
      var s = new SOAPCall();
```

[*] This example is modified code taken from *http://www.segment7.net/mozilla/GoogleAPI/GoogleAPI.html*, and is covered by a three-clause BSD license. More on SOAP and the SOAP API in Mozilla can be found at *http://lxr.mozilla.org/mozilla/source/extensions/xmlextras/docs/Soap_Scripts_in_Mozilla.html*.

[†] The Google API requires a Google Key, and more information can be found at *http://www.google.com/apis/*.

Example 7-3. Performing a Google search when setting a property (continued)

```
        var q = val;
        if (!s)
          return "Error creating SOAPCall object";
        var soapversion = 0;
        var method = "doGoogleSearch";
        var object = "urn:GoogleSearch";
        var headers = [ ];
        var params = [
          new SOAPParameter(this.googleKey, "key"),
          new SOAPParameter(q, "q"),
          new SOAPParameter(this.start, "start"),
          new SOAPParameter(this.maxResults, "maxResults"),
          new SOAPParameter(this.filter, "filter"),
          new SOAPParameter(this.restrict, "restrict"),
          new SOAPParameter(this.safeSearch, "safeSearch"),
          new SOAPParameter(this.lr, "lr"),
          new SOAPParameter("utf8", "ie"),
          new SOAPParameter("utf8", "oe")
        ];
        s.encode(soapversion, method, object, headers.length, headers,
          params.length, params);
        s.transportURI = "http://api.google.com/search/beta2"
        var response = s.invoke();
        if (response.fault)
          return { msg : "SOAP call error", fault : response.fault };
        // At this point you would pass the results back to the UI
        return response.message;
      ]]>
    </setter>
</property>
```

The value of the search string is set to the value that has been given to the property: `var q = val`. This value is then added to the parameter list (`SOAPParameter`) for the SOAP call, along with other parameters that are obtained from other properties in the binding (e.g., `this.maxResults`).

XBL and the DOM

This section introduces the DOM interfaces in XBL, illustrates how they work, and explains the core concepts involved in XBL interaction with the DOM, such as scope characteristics and insertion points.

The XBL DOM Interfaces

XBL has two core DOM interfaces, `DocumentXBL` and `ElementXBL`. These extensions to the *Document* and *Element* interfaces are not part of the formal DOM specifications. All methods can be accessed and used from JavaScript. Here is a list of these interface methods.

DocumentXBL methods

The *DocumentXBL* interface gains access to and interacts with an XBL document. The methods of this interface are as follows:

loadBindingDocument(URL)
: XBL documents are loaded only the first time a bound document uses a binding from it. You can get around this problem and load the binding documents synchronously by using this method. It returns an XBL document for use within a bound document. If your document is large and you need to optimize performance, this method may provide better performance.

```
document.loadBindingDocument('chrome://package/content/myBindings.xml');
```

getBindingParent(element)
: For use only within a binding, this method returns the bound element—i.e., the top-level node of the binding, when passed an element within a binding.

```
var listbox = document.getBindingParent(this);
var cellValue = listbox.childNodes[3].firstChild.label;
```

getAnonymousNodes(element)
: Returns an array with the input binding's top-level content nodes. Refer to the section "Accessing Anonymous Nodes," later in this chapter, for more details.

getAnonymousElementByAttribute(element, attribute, value)
: Returns a single anonymous element when passed an element, an attribute from that element, and its value. Refer to the section "Accessing Anonymous Nodes" for more details.

ElementXBL methods

The *ElementXBL* interface adds and removes bindings from a bound element. The methods of this interface are as follows:

addBinding(element, URL)
: Dynamically attaches a binding, given as a parameter, to an element. Refer to the following sections for more details.

removeBinding(element, URL)
: Dynamically removes the given binding. Refer to the following sections for more details.

Dynamically adding a binding

The section "Anatomy of a Binding" covered the attachment of a binding to a bound element using CSS. This technique is the most common method, but you can also attach bindings with the `addBinding` method.

Using this method as an alternative to CSS attachment is useful when you do not want to attach a binding in all circumstances. In an application based on user input, you may not want to load a binding until certain values are entered. For example, in a membership database, the information that appears on screen may depend on the user's level of membership. The following snippets show how it is used.

```
<mybinding id="myNewWidget" class="attached" />
```

To load a binding, add these two lines in your script.

```
var binding = document.getElementById("myNewWidget");
document.addBinding(binding, "chrome://mypackage/content/myBindings.xml#super");
```

Notice that the URL used to access the binding takes the same format as in the CSS property—i.e., the path to the file and the `id` of the binding qualified by `#`.

Neither `addBinding` nor `removeBinding` are implemented at the time of writing. They are covered because they are part of the XBL 1.0 specification. When implemented, they offer crucial alternatives for attaching and detaching bindings, making XBL a more interactive technology.

Removing bindings

The best way to remove a binding attached via CSS is to change the style rule for that element. You can change the `class` to one that does not have a different or null binding reference, for example. Then a stylesheet can be set up to provide binding references for both an attached and unattached element.

This example shows how to remove a reference to a binding by resetting it to an empty reference:

```
mybinding.attached {
  -moz-binding : url("mybindings.xml#my-binding");
}
mybinding.unattached {
  -moz-binding : url("");
}
```

When you want to detach the binding from an element, you can do this:

```
var mywidget = document.getElementById("binding1");
mywidget.setAttribute("class","unattached");
```

An element can have only one binding attached at a time, so this is a programmatic trick for knocking the "real" binding out of its place with an empty one, rather than actually removing it.

`-moz-binding:url("")` can be used at this time as a hack around the `-moz-binding:none` binding. The later binding does not currently work in Mozilla.

The other method used to detach a binding, which is more intuitive from a DOM perspective, uses the `removeBinding` method:

```
var binding = document.getElementById("myNewWidget");
document.removeBinding(binding, "chrome://mypackage/content/myBindings.xml#super");
```

This method ensures that other style information is not lost if you have it attached to a particular class.

When a binding is removed, the anonymous content is destroyed and the methods, properties, and event handlers no longer apply.

In the case of an inheritance chain (see the "Inheritance" section later in this chapter for more details), the bindings are destroyed from the bottom upwards. This means that if there is tear-down code in the form of a destructor, it is executed last on the base binding.

Binding Parents

Although a document cannot access the content of bindings attached to it, a binding can access the document it is attached to (bound document). This gives bindings the ability to provide more than just additional content to the document. It also means that you can find information about the context of bound element in a document and provide information about it from within the binding.

From the perspective of nodes inside the anonymous content, you can use DOM properties to find a higher-level node and then in turn use that to get to other nodes:

`parentNode`
: This property is the bound element for the top-most element in the anonymous content. This bound element resides in the document that the binding is attached to.

`ownerDocument`
: For all elements in the anonymous content, this is the document the bound element resides in.

While higher-level nodes can be accessed from anonymous content, parents do not have explicit access to their anonymous children using the DOM `childNodes` property. Using `firstChild` or `nextSibling` will also not work.

Example 7-4 illustrates both properties in use.

Example 7-4. Accessing a bound document from a binding

```
<binding id="my-binding">
  <content>
    <xul:vbox>
      <xul:button label="A" id="button1"
        oncommand="alert(this.parentNode.parentNode.nodeName)"/>
      <xul:button label="B" id="button2"
        oncommand="alert(this.ownerDocument.firstChild.nodeName)"/>
    </xul:vbox>
  </content>
</binding>
```

Example 7-4 is a binding with two buttons, each of which brings up an alert when activated. The alert simply shows the name of an element that is accessed in the code attached to the button. In Button A, the parent node is the containing box. One level further is the bound element, `<mybinding>`—the parent node of the `box` parent. The alert dialog raised by the alert shows "mybinding." Once a binding is applied, the binding's owner (`ownerDocument`) is the bound document. Assuming that Button B is a XUL window, the alert, when activated, shows "window." This property can be used to access properties of the document object.

Accessing Anonymous Nodes

Content bound to a document can introduce different levels of scope. Some of the scope is available at the document level, and some is at the binding level. With content in different scopes, there are limits to which standard DOM methods can be used to access other elements and objects in and above a binding. XBL contains some special methods to help work around some of the limitations caused by these barriers, such as not being able to change binding content dynamically or access certain property values.

The two XBL-specific interfaces that exist on the document to get a handle on this content are *getAnonymousNodes* and *getAnonymousElementByAttribute*. The advantage of using these interfaces is that they provide a bridge between behavior and content. Use them when you want to dynamically manipulate content or get a value—for example, when accessing a particular textbox contained in binding, reminiscent of the one used earlier in the chapter when you were introduced to the `<inputfield />` binding.

getAnonymousNodes

The method `getAnonymousNodes(element)` takes a node as a parameter and returns a list of nodes that are in the anonymous content. The following code uses script in the `<getter>` to access the anonymous node and return a value contained in it.

```
<getter>
  <![CDATA[
    var list = document.getAnonymousNodes(this)[0];
    return list.selectedItem.getAttribute('label');
  ]]>
</getter>
```

If we assume that this binding's content is a XUL menu list, then this code gets the `label` attribute of the menu item that is currently selected in that list (`list.selectedItem`). The list variable contains the value returned by the `getAnonymousNodes` function, which is passed the binding node (`this`). The method returns an array, so the item is accessed via the first index of 0.

getAnonymousElementByAttribute

The method `getAnonymousElementByAttribute(element, attr, value)` returns a single anonymous node rather than a list. This node is qualified by an element name, a particular attribute, and the value of that attribute, and returns this specific node. This retrieval provides faster access to anonymous content elements when you know an attribute's value.

```
<property name="emailID" onget="return document.getAnonymousElementByAttribute(this,
'id', 'emailAddressNode');" readonly="true"/>
```

This example uses an id attribute to retrieve a specific node. You can use this method when multiple elements of the same type exist and you need to get access to a particular one—for example, a particular field on a database entry submission form like an email address or a telephone number.

Although these two functions (getAnonymousNodes and getAnonymousElements-ByAttribute) were probably designed to be used within a binding scope, they can be used both inside and outside a binding to access anonymous content. Bindings are meant to be self-contained, and getting anonymous nodes outside a binding breaks this philosophy. However, these functions can act as a bridge between scopes if you are careful.

Extra Binding Content and Insertion Points

All examples in the chapter have so far dealt with standard binding content rendering within a bound document. The processes outlined in this section can, in one sense, be seen as abnormal because they allow ordering of the content to change based on insertion points defined in the binding. This process is done with the XBL <children> element

Working with children of the bound element

Zero or more children can be contained in anonymous content. These children are marked up with the XBL-specific <children> tag. They can be either the content of the element using the binding or anonymous content generated by the base binding. If the <children> tag contains its own elements, then it will be used as the default content. If the element the binding is attached to contains children, the default content will be ignored.

The location of the <children> tags determines the content's insertion point. Insertion points play an important role in the generation of content within a template because they affect how the content is displayed and accessed by the DOM.

```
<binding id="my-binding">
  <content>
    <xul:vbox>
      <children />
    </xul:vbox>
  </content>
</binding>
```

This stripped-down binding has only a vertical box as its own content and looks to the children of the bound element for more content by using the <children> element. Here is the XUL content that uses the binding:

```
<mybinding id="myNewWidget" flex="1" class="attached">
  <label value="this is child 1" />
  <label value="this is child 2" />
</mybinding>
```

When the binding is attached and the content is drawn, the insertion point for the two labels is inside the container vertical box inside the binding. This scenario could be used when a binding is used multiple times. Each time, it needs to be rendered differently with extra content that can be provided this way.

Selective inclusion

Sometimes multiple siblings are located within a box in the XUL, but you want to use only some of them in the binding, such as when a user logs into a system and content is displayed depending on its level of membership. In these cases, you can be selective about which children should be included in the binding. Example 7-5 shows how to use the includes attribute on the <children> element.

Example 7-5. Selective inclusion of child content in a binding

```
<binding id="my-binding">
  <content>
    <xul:vbox class="insideBox">
      <xul:description value="Top" />
      <xul:box>
        <children includes="image" />
      </xul:box>
      <xul:description value="Bottom" />
    </xul:vbox>
  </content>
</binding>
```

The children element in Example 7-5 essentially tells, "Of all the content contained in the bound element, insert only the image element at this particular insertion point." Here is the XUL code that goes with this example:

```
<mybinding id="myNewWidget" flex="1">
  <image src="http://www.mozdev.org/sharedimages/header.gif" />
  <label value="a non includes element" />
</mybinding>
```

The image is the only child taken from the XUL content and the label is ignored.

If you have children that are not defined in the includes attribute, then the binding is discarded and not used. If the bound element uses another element in addition to an image element, the binding is discarded and only the explicit content is used. If the image element isn't used at all, the binding is discarded.

```
<mybinding id="myNewWidget" flex="1">
  <image src="http://www.mozdev.org/sharedimages/header.gif" />
```

```
    <label value="an element" />
  </mybinding>
```

This example renders the image and the label and discards the binding. The anonymous content does not appear because the binding is discarded and only the explicit content is used.

Inheritance

In XBL, inheritance is the process in which one object included in another object is allowed to use properties from that parent object. These properties can be many things, depending on the implementation, ranging from methods to attribute property values. Inheritance is a concept familiar in programming languages, most notably object-oriented ones. It's not something alien to markup, however, and it is deployed effectively in XBL. This section examines three forms of XBL inheritance: binding, attribute, and implementation. As you will see, inheritance promotes self-contained (modular) and flexible bindings that permit shared content across and within XBL documents.

Binding Inheritance

Binding inheritance occurs when one binding is linked to another binding or XUL element and uses some or all properties of it, whether they are content or behavior. A binding can inherit from another binding that exists in the same or different file. In one way, this useful feature makes a binding like a class, with content and methods that can be used elsewhere. Bindings become modules, which prevents code duplication, makes maintenance easier, and gets slotted in and out of documents.

Linkage or inheritance is enabled by the `extends` attribute on the `<binding>` element. This attribute contains the URL of the binding that you inherit from. This URL is made up of the location and name of the file that contains the binding (the # symbol), and the `id` of the specific binding being used. In this way, it is similar to the access method used in CSS attachment.

Although it is in the XBL 1.0 specification, Mozilla hasn't fully implemented `type="inherits"` on the children tag yet, so the best way to work with binding inheritance is to use the `extends` attribute. Example 7-6 shows a few bindings used in the implementation of the `listbox` cell in the Mozilla tree. It illustrates how `extends` is used to inherit from another binding.

Example 7-6. Binding inheritance

```
<binding id="listbox-base">
  <resources>
    <stylesheet src="chrome://global/skin/listbox.css"/>
  </resources>
```

Example 7-6. Binding inheritance (continued)

```
</binding>
<binding id="listcell"
    extends="chrome://global/content/bindings/listbox.xml#listbox-base">
  <content>
    <children>
      <xul:label class="listcell-label"
          xbl:inherits="value=label,flex=flexlabel,crop,disabled"
          flex="1" crop="right"/>
    </children>
  </content>
</binding>
<binding id="listcell-iconic"
    extends="chrome://global/content/bindings/listbox.xml#listcell">
  <content>
    <children>
      <xul:image class="listcell-icon" xbl:inherits="src=image"/>
      <xul:label class="listcell-label"
          xbl:inherits="value=label,flex=flexlabel,crop,disabled"
          flex="1" crop="right"/>
    </children>
   </content>
</binding>
```

In Example 7-6, `listcell-iconic` inherits `listcell`. In turn, `listcell` inherits `listbox-base`, which holds resources. The `listcell` binding is a cell with text only and the `listcell-iconic` binding has text and an image. Thus, the user has a choice of using a list cell binding with an icon or no icon. Yet both of these bindings have access to the stylesheet resource declared in the base binding. If `listcell-iconic` is used, the duplicate `xul:label` is ignored in the inherited binding and the stylesheet inherited from the base binding via the inherited binding is used. We've used this technique to illustrate how resources in multiple bindings are shared.

With binding extensions that use the `extends` attribute, you can also extend a XUL element as a model, using extensions as a proxy to mimic that XUL element. The element may not be included directly in the anonymous content, but its characteristics are still present on the bound element. If you use the XUL namespace `xul:` in the same way you use it for XUL content in a binding, you can inherit the XUL element properties as illustrated in Example 7-7.

Example 7-7. Inheriting XUL widget characteristics using extends

```
<binding id="Widget1" extends="xul:vbox">
  <content>
    <xul:description value="Top" />
    <children includes="image" />
    <xul:description value="Bottom" />
  </content>
</binding>
```

In Example 7-7, the binding has all of the attributes and behavior of a XUL box. Because you extend a box element, the base widget `<mybinding>` is now a vertical box. The anonymous content is laid out according to the box model, and all attributes that are recognized on the bound element are applied to the box.

Attribute Inheritance

Also known as "attribute forwarding," *attribute inheritance* is a way for anonymous content to link to the attributes from the bound element. When the bound element attribute is changed, this modification filters down to the binding attribute list. The code in Example 7-8 shows anonymous content where multiple attributes are picked up by the `xbl:inherits` attribute, with each one separated by a comma.

Example 7-8. XBL attribute inheritance

```
<xul:box class="insideBox" xbl:inherits="orient, flex, align">
  <xul:description value="Top" />
    <xul:box>
      <children includes="image" />
    </xul:box>
    <xul:description value="Bottom" />
  </xul:box>
</xul:box>
```

The element that inherits the attributes can be anywhere in the chain of anonymous content. In this case, it is on the top-level box. It assumes the value given to these attributes in the bound element. Here is the XUL that uses the binding content from Example 7-8:

```
<mywidget orient="vertical" flex="1" align="center" />
```

The `xul:box` element inherits the attribute values `vertical`, `1`, and `middle`, respectively, from the bound element (`mywidget`). The box in the anonymous content contains three children: two text (description) elements and an image contained in another box. The default orientation for a box is horizontal, but these child elements are now positioned vertically.

You may notice that the `inherits` attribute is preceded with the `xbl:` prefix, unlike other attributes in the XBL element set. Why is this unique? It guarantees that the effect is on the binding and not directly on the element that uses it. This ensures that the element can have an `inherits` attribute of its own if needed. This scenerio is unlikely and you might wonder why this rule does not apply to other attributes used on XBL elements. To achieve correct binding, the XBL namespace must be declared on an element at a higher level than the element using it, most commonly the `<bindings>` container, as explained earlier. Here is what the code will look like:

```
<binding id="my-bindings"
    xmlns="http://www.mozilla.org/xbl"
    xmlns:html="http://www.w3.org/1999/xhtsml"
    xmlns:xbl="http://www.mozilla.org/xbl">
```

Implementation Inheritance

The third type of inheritance, inheritance of behavior, is also achieved by using the `extends` attribute and is useful when you want to use methods or properties in another binding. Example 7-9 shows how one binding inherits implementation from another in the same file.

Example 7-9. Inheritance of behavior between bindings

```
<binding id="Widget1" extends="test.xml#Widget2">
  <content>
    <xul:box class="insideBox">
      <xul:description value="Top" />
      <xul:box>
        <children includes="image" />
      </xul:box>
      <xul:description value="Bottom" />
    </xul:box>
  </content>
</binding>
<binding id="Widget2">
  <implementation>
    <constructor>
      this.init();
    </constructor>
    <method name="init">
      <body>
      <![CDATA[ dump("This is Widget2");]]>
      </body>
    </method>
  </implementation>
</binding>
```

The `Widget1` binding in Example 7-9 pulls in `Widget2` using `extends`. `Widget2` has implemented a constructor that dumps some text to output. When `Widget1` is bound and it does not find any implementation to initiate, it looks to the inherited binding and, in this case, dumps "This is Widget2" to output.

In a bindings inheritance tree, more than one implementation could have a method with the same name. In this case, the most derived binding—the one nested deepest in the inheritance chain—is the one used. It is even possible for some common DOM functions used on the bound element outside of the anonymous content to find imitators when implementing the attached bindings.

```
<method name="getElementById">
  <parameter name="id" />
  <body>
    <!-- implementation here -->
  </body>
</method>
```

If you glance through the source code for the Mozilla chrome, you may notice that many of the standard XUL widgets used were extended by using XBL. The button is a good example.

On its own, the button can display text with the value attribute and an image with the src attribute. Usually, this is sufficient, and you can color the button and change the text font with CSS. But you may want to take advantage of inherent behaviors in other elements or inherit from other bindings. Mozilla buttons are a mix of <box>, <text>, and <image> elements, and they take on the characteristics of each.

Event Handling

Event handlers are attributes that listen for events. They intercept events raised by certain user actions, such as button clicks. When intercepted, control is given to the application to carry out some functionality.

Mouse and keyboard actions are included in these events. XBL uses all events that are available on an element in XUL and calls them by their name, minus the on prefix. Thus, for example, the onmouseclick event handler becomes mouseclick in XBL. Refer to Appendix C for a full list of these events, which also describes the difference between XUL and XBL event handling.

The <handler> element contains a single event. Sets of individual <handler> elements need to be included in a <handlers> element. The event that sets off the action is contained in the event attribute.

```
<handlers>
  <handler event="mousedown" action="dumpString('hello', 'there!')" />
</handlers>
```

This code uses the action attribute to point to script that is executed when the event is triggered. The alternative way to set up the actions is to put the executable script between the handler tags, like you can with the XUL <script> element. If you use this "embedded" syntax, wrap your script in a CDATA section so it gets interpreted and executed properly:

```
<handlers>
  <handler event="mousedown">
    <![CDATA[
      var list = document.getElementById('someElement');
      list.setAttribute('style', 'display:block;');
    ]]>
  </handler>
</handlers>
```

You cannot use both inline and external scripts in an XBL event handler. If this instance does occur, the action attribute is used. Like code decisions in other contexts, which one you use depends on whether you want to reuse the code. In our experience, using inline scripts is best in most circumstances unless useful code libraries can be accessed in external scripts.

The Time and Venue

Event handlers in XBL allow for fine-tuning, using built-in attributes that control when, where, and how they are executed. Events are not limited to bindings. They can be registered with other UI elements that pre-empt behavior when, for example, a `create` or `load` event occurs. This registration occurs when using the `attachto` attribute.

```
<handler event="create" attachto="window" action="returnNode()">
```

The handler is designed to update the list in the binding when the application is loaded up and the window shows. Other possible values for `attachto` are `document` and `element`.

The `attachto` feature is disabled for Mozilla 1.0, but it is included here for completeness and to highlight XBL's full capabilities.

Another nice feature of event handlers in XBL is the existence of extra modifiers on mouse and key events using the `modifiers` and the `key` or `keycode` attributes. The value is a list of one or more modifier keys separated by a comma. The most common combination is the use of the `alt`, `control`, or `shift` modifiers. The key codes have special identifiers like `VK_INSERT` and `VK_UP`.

```
<handler event="keypress" modifiers="control, alt" keycode="VK_UP" action="goUp()">
```

Finally, when talking about event handlers, the `phase` attribute allows you to control the point in the event's lifecycle when the code is to be executed.

```
<handler event="mouseup" phase="capturing" action="goUp()">
```

The possible values are `bubbling` (the default), `targeting`, and `capturing`.

Here is an example of a handler implementation that fills a tooltip when the `popup` element displaying it is shown:

```
<handler event="popupshowing">
  <![CDATA[
    var label = "";
    var tipNode = document.tooltipNode;
    if (tipNode && tipNode.hasAttribute("tooltiptext"))
      this.label = tipNode.getAttribute("tooltiptext");
  ]]>
</handler>
```

This event handler first checks that the current `popup` is in fact a tooltip via the document's `tooltipNode` property and then extracts the text from it. This text is assigned to the binding's label, which will propagate via inheritance to the text display content widget used in the binding, which could be a `label` or `description` element.

Resources for Bindings

This chapter stresses that bindings used in XUL documents are designed to be modular, self-contained widgets that have a certain appearance and carry out a specific set of functionality. This final section extends the notion of XBL as an organization of content, behavior, and event handling by describing extra resources (such as stylesheets and pictures) that are available in the XBL framework for use in your bindings. If you are creating templates, for example, you should consider using these approaches to application development.

Stylesheets in XBL

You can include stylesheets in an XBL document by using the XBL-specific element `<stylesheet>`. The example below shows the color-picker stylesheet as it would be included in a `<resources>`-containing element, allowing styles contained therein to be used by the bindings that referenced it.

```
<stylesheet src="chrome://xfly/skin/color-picker.css" />
```

The `<stylesheet>` element is intended for the styling of bound elements and anonymous content. It can be used on anonymous content generated by the binding and in explicit children in documents that use the bindings. Typically, you would include this element in a binding and inherit it to style other bindings when there are many bindings that have a similar appearance.

```
<binding id="popup-base">
  <resources>
    <stylesheet src="chrome://global/skin/popup.css" />
  </resources>
</binding>
```

Then you can access the stylesheet in your binding by using the extends attribute:

```
<binding id="popup" extends="chrome://global/content/bindings/popup.xml#popup-base">
```

Beyond this static usage of stylesheets, two attributes, `applyauthorstyles` and `styleexplicitcontent`, can affect the appearance of a binding element if a stylesheet is applied to it. Although they are part of the XBL 1.0 specification, these attributes were not implemented at the time of writing. They are attributes of the `<binding>` element.

`applyauthorstyles`
: A Boolean value that determines the use of stylesheets from the document that contains the bound element. The default is false.

`styleexplicitcontent`
: A Boolean value that indicates whether the stylesheets loaded in the XBL document can be applied to a bound element's explicit children and not just the bound element itself. The default is false.

Stylesheets take effect from the inside scope and move outwards. This means that styles on a binding can be overridden easily by styles attached to elements contained in anonymous content.

The <image> XBL element works much like a XUL element and pulls in the image by using the src attribute.

```
<binding id="images">
  <resources>
    <image src="plane.png"/>
    <image src="boat.png"/>
    <image src="bicycle.png"/>
  </resources>
</binding>
```

If an element calls this binding, the pictures would lay out side-by-side horizontally in the bound document.

CHAPTER 8

XPCOM

This chapter provides a high-level introduction to XPCOM component technology. XPCOM can be difficult to master, but after reading this chapter, you should have a good sense of what it is and the important part it plays as Mozilla's core technology. You should be able to find and use existing scriptable components in your own applications and create a simple XPCOM component by using JavaScript or C++.

XPCOM permits a reusable code module to be globally accessible to a Mozilla-based application. You do not need to worry about including external source files in your application distribution and you can distribute components by using XPInstall. This type of architecture makes the development of core application services flexible and entirely modular.

The section "Creating a JavaScript XPCOM Component" lets you create an interface from start to finish—writing the implementation for that interface, compiling it into a type library, registering it with Mozilla, and then testing the new component. One advantage of using XPCOM is that you can create multiple implementations for a single interface; following the JavaScript component section, we will take the same `nsISimple` interface and implement it in C++ as well.

The section "C++ Implementation of nsISimple" includes some techniques and programming tasks that are particular to C++ components, such as handling return values and generating header files and useful macros. The section "Other Languages for XPCOM" introduces the XPCOM bindings for the Python language (pyXPCOM). First, it provides an overview of XPCOM and how it relates to other technologies used in Mozilla.

What Is XPCOM?

XPCOM is Mozilla's cross-platform component object model. Although it is similar to Microsoft's COM technology, this chapter points out some important differences.

Essentially, when you program in a component-based environment, you do one of three things: you create a new component using existing components, write a component that implements other components, and establish interdependencies and a service network.

What Is a Component?

You've already seen components used in this book. In some cases, you may have used the services of Mozilla components without knowing it—for example, when you created a XUL tree widget in the section "High Performance Trees" in Chapter 3, and used its built-in layout and view capabilities. Some of this functionality is defined in an interface called *nsITreeView*, which provides specific methods and properties for a XUL tree, persisting its state, row, cell, and column properties, navigation, and other object metadata used in a tree object. Behind the scenes, you'll find an XPCOM-instantiated tree view object where methods and properties associated with the XUL element are accessed via DOM → JavaScript → XPConnect → XPCOM layers.

A component is a reusable or modular piece of code that implements a clearly defined interface. In Mozilla, this code can exist as a singleton service or an object instance. A singleton service is an object instance that is created only once and then used by other code (usually called "callers," "clients," or "consumers"). An object instance is an object that is instantiated once or many times. Components are written as classes that typically have member variables and methods. The basic purpose of a component is to implement a clearly defined set of APIs that exist in a public interface. The interface exists separately so that the implementation is abstracted away, and it can be changed without affecting the interface or breaking binary compatibility. When interfaces are deployed in a production environment, they are frozen, which means they are held in an immutable state—theoretically for as long as the application exists. While MSCOM provides a component-based programming model on Microsoft platforms, XPCOM provides it on all platforms where Mozilla is available.

Example 8-1 shows how simple using XPCOM components can be. In two lines, an XPConnect-wrapped `nsIBookmarksService` object is instantiated, and one of its methods is called, providing easy access to this XPCOM component from JavaScript.

Example 8-1. Using an XPCOM object in script

```
// create a bookmark service object in JS
var bmks =
  Components.classes["@mozilla.org/browser/bookmarks-service;1"].
      getService(Components.interfaces.nsIBookmarksService);
// call one of the object's methods:
// flush the bookmarks to disk if they've been touched.
bmks.Flush();
```

As you can see, the assignment of an XPCOM object to the variable *bmks* takes only a single line. Once you are comfortable using XPCOM from JavaScript, you can use any of Mozilla's scriptable interfaces in your application. Once an object like `bmks` is created, as in Example 8-1, it can be used to call any method in the *nsIBookmarksService* interface, of which `Flush()` is an example.

XPConnect and the Component Object

As shown the previous example, the XPCOM object is called and instantiated from script. For an interpreted language like JavaScript to call and instantiate it, a bridge must bind JavaScript types to XPCOM types. These type bindings are part of a technology called XPConnect.

In XPConnect, XPCOM interfaces, `classIDs`, and `progIDs` are stored as global JavaScript objects and properties that can be manipulated directly through a top-level object called `Components`. This object accesses any component that is declared "scriptable" in an XPCOM IDL interface. Through the `Components` object, you can access and use the services that these interfaces provide. The `Component` object's top-level properties and methods include:

QueryInterface
: A method used to match an interface with a desired implementation. The implementation can be in C, C++, JavaScript, Python, and other languages for which appropriate bindings are created. You can have multiple implementations for an interface. Through `QueryInterface`, you can ask for and assign the desired interface to its implementation. Each XPCOM object needs to implement `QueryInterface` in order to return an instance of that object's class:

```
js> var clz  = Components.classes['@mozilla.org/file/local;1'];
js> var inst = clz.getService();
js> inst.QueryInterface(C.interfaces.nsILocalFile);
[xpconnect wrapped nsILocalFile @ 0x81b7040]
```

interfaces
: A read-only object array containing all the interfaces declared scriptable in the IDL file. The object name has the same name as the interface it represents.

```
Components.interfaces.nsILocalFile
```

The source file for this particular interface, for example, is *nsILocalFile.idl*. This XPIDL compiler compiles this file to produce a cross-platform binary type library, *nsILocalFile.xpt*, which contains tokenized IDL in an efficiently parsed form.

classes
: A read-only array of all the XPCOM component classes indexed by the `ProgID` (or human-readable name) of the component class. The `classes` object has these properties associated with it:

```
toString       Returns the string progID.
QueryInterface Used to QI this interface.
```

```
name           Returns the string progid name.
number         Returns the string components uuid
               number.
valid          Boolean verifies if the instance is
               valid.
equals         The Boolean used to match identical
               instances.
initialize     I don't know what this does.
createInstance Will create an instance of the
               component; you can have many
               instances.
getService     Will instantiate the component as a
               service; you can have only one
               instance of a service.
```

classesByID

The same as classes, except this time the array is indexed by the "canonical" or "well-established" form of their CLSID:

```
Components.classesByID['{dea98e50-1dd1-11b2-9344-8902b4805a2e}'];
```

The `classesByID` object has the same properties object associated with it as the `class` object. The properties are also used in the same way:

```
toString
QueryInterface
name
number
valid
equals
initialize
createInstance
getService
```

stack

A read-only property that represents a snapshot of the current JavaScript call stack. JavaScript handles each code interpretation one call at a time and then places that code onto a call stack. This property can be used for recondite diagnostic purposes:

```
js> var C=Components;
js> C.stack;
JS frame :: typein :: <TOP_LEVEL> :: line 2
js>  C.stack;
JS frame :: typein :: <TOP_LEVEL> :: line 3
```

results

An object array of `nserror` results:

```
Components.results.NS_ERROR_FILE_ACCESS_DENIED;
 2152857621
```

manager

A reflection of the XPCOM global native component manager service. Using the component manager is the only way for a component to actually be created. It uses the components factory to create an instance of the `class` object.

ID

A constructor used for a component written in JavaScript This component needs to register itself with the component manager by using its own `nsID` (an ID that is not already registered and thus does not appear in *Components.classes*).

Exception

A JavaScript constructor used to create exception objects. When implementing XPCOM interfaces in JavaScript, these exception objects are the preferred types of exceptions. When an XPCOM exception is thrown in your JS code, it takes the form of an `Exception` object that has properties associated with this object. Exceptions are usually caught in a "catch" block.

Constructor

A JavaScript constructor object that constructs new instances of XPCOM components:

```
js> var File=new Components.Constructor(
  "@mozilla.org/file/local;1", "nsILocalFile", "initWithPath");
```

The interface *nsILocalFile* and the method `initWithPath` are optional. This example creates and initializes the *nsILocalFile* component.

isSucessCode

A function that determines if the results code argument is successful. It takes an argument of `nsresult` and returns the Boolean values true or false:

```
js> Components.isSuccessCode(Components.results.NS_OK);
  true
js> Components.isSuccessCode(Components.results.NS_ERROR_FAILURE);
  false
```

The methods and properties of the `Components` object listed above provide the only means to instantiate and access XPCOM objects from JavaScript. They are found often in the Mozilla codebase. In the sections that follow, they will be used frequently.

XPCOM Interfaces and the IDL

All XPCOM interfaces are defined with the Interface Definition Language (IDL). IDL provides a language-neutral way to describe the public methods and properties of a component. Mozilla actually uses a modified, cross-platform version of IDL called XPIDL to compile interface source files.

The separation of interface and implementation is a key distinction of COM programming. If the application programming interface (API) is abstracted from the implementation language and then frozen, consumers of that API will receive a guaranteed, established contract with the interface that ensures it will not be changed. This is perhaps the main reason why COM was invented: to maintain compatibility on a binary level so the client code can find and use the library it needs without worrying about linking to it. To make this sort of modularity possible at runtime, IDL interfaces are compiled into binary files called type libraries, which are described later in the section "XPCOM Type Libraries."

Interfaces versus components

It is important to understand that most XPCOM components implement at least two interfaces. Like COM, each component needs the `QueryInterface`, `AddRef`, and Release functions to be available as an XPCOM object. These methods are derived from a basic interface called *nsISupports*, which is the XPCOM equivalent to Microsoft COM's `IUnknown`, shown in Table 8-1.

Table 8-1. The IUnknown interface

Name	Type	Description	Parameters / return value
AddRef	`ULONG AddRef(void)`	Increments the reference count on the COM object.	Returns: int, which is the new incremented reference count on the object. This value may be useful for diagnostics or testing.
QueryInterface	`HRESULT QueryInterface(/* [in] */ REFIID riid, /* [iid_is][out] */ void **ppvObject)`	Retrieves a pointer to the requested interface.	Parameters: iid, which is an [in] identifier of the requested interface. ppvObject, which is an [out] pointer to the interface pointer identified by iid. If the object does not support this interface, ppvObject is set to NULL. Returns: HRESULT, which is the standard HRESULT value.
Release	`ULONG Release(void)`	Decrements the reference count on the COM object.	Returns: int, which is the new decremented reference count on the object. This value may be useful for diagnostics or testing.

Tables 8-1 and 8-2 illustrate the minor differences between Microsoft's *nsIUnknown* and Mozilla's *nsISupports* root interfaces. The usage is covered in detail throughout this chapter.

Table 8-2. The nsISupports interface

Name	Type	Description	Parameters / return value
AddRef	*NS_IMETHOD_(nsrefcnt)* AddRef(void)	Increases the reference count for this interface. The associated instance will not be deleted unless the reference count is returned to zero.	Returns: The resulting reference count.
QueryInterface	*NS_IMETHOD QueryInterface(REFNSIID aIID,* void** aInstancePtr)	A runtime mechanism for interface discovery.	Parameters: param aIID [in], which is a requested interface IID. param aInstancePtr [out], which is a pointer to an interface pointer that receives the result. Returns: NS_OK if the interface is supported by the associated instance; NS_NOINTERFACE if it is not; and NS_ERROR_INVALID_POINTER if aInstancePtr is NULL.
Release	*NS_IMETHOD_(nsrefcnt) Release*(void) = 0;	Decreases the reference count for this interface. Generally, if the reference count returns to zero, the associated instance is deleted.	Returns: The resulting reference count.

Root interfaces

`QueryInterface`, `Addref`, and `Release` are required methods that are implemented by every component. `QueryInterace` matches a specific interface with its implementation class module. `Addref` and `Release` are methods used for reference counting. When an instance of a component is created, one or more pointers may reference that object. For each reference, a count is incremented by one. When a reference is no longer used, `Release` is called to decrement the count. You must hold a reference count to ensure that no pointers reference an object after it is deleted. When pointers try to access objects that are deleted, the application core dumps. Reference counting can get tricky, which is why smart pointers manage `Addref` and `Release` for you, as described in the later section "Useful C++ Macros and Types."

Defining `QueryInterface`, `Addref`, and `Release` every time an interface is created is clearly not very efficient. Instead, these methods are defined in the base interface called *nsISupports*. All interfaces inherit from this mother of all interfaces and don't need to redefine these three basic functions.

XPIDL supports the C style syntax preparser directive *#include* to include other IDL files—not unlike MSCOM, which uses the import statement. At the top of any IDL file that you create, you need to include *nsISupports*:

```
#include "nsISupports.idl"
interface nsISimple : nsISupports {
  readonly attribute string value;
};
```

Core IDL Types

The core types used in IDL interface files are listed in the file *xpcom/base/nsrootidl.idl*. This file is included in *nsISupports*. (This means it is included in every interface file, since all interfaces inherit from *nsISupports*.) All interfaces used in a system are valid IDL types. For example, *nsISimple* is a valid type to use as a method parameter or a method return type. Some of the main types listed in this interface are:

```
typedef boolean              PRBool;
typedef octet                PRUint8;
typedef unsigned short       PRUint16;
typedef unsigned short       PRUnichar;
typedef unsigned long        PRUint32;
typedef unsigned long long   PRUint64;
typedef unsigned long long   PRTime;
typedef short                PRInt16;
typedef long                 PRInt32;
typedef long long            PRInt64;
typedef unsigned long        nsrefcnt;
typedef unsigned long        nsresult;
typedef unsigned long        size_t;
```

The XPIDL compiler

An IDL compiler is a tool that creates a binary distribution file called a *type library* from an interface description source file. Since support for many different platforms is a requirement for Mozilla, a modified version of the libIDL compiler from the Gnome project is used. This variant is called the XPIDL compiler and is primarily used to compile Mozilla's own dialect of IDL, conveniently called XPIDL. The XPIDL compiler generates XPCOM interface information, headers for XPCOM objects, and XPT type libraries from which objects may be accessed dynamically through XPConnect. It can also generate HTML files for documentation and Java class stubs. Another feature of the XPIDL compiler is the option to generate C++ code stubs. This feature creates nearly all the declaratory C++ code you need when you start a new project, which makes XPIDL useful as a coding wizard that helps you get started. Code generation is covered later in this chapter in the section "C++ Implementation of nsISimple."

The XPIDL compiler is located in *xpcom/typelib/xpidl/* in the Mozilla sources. If you built Mozilla, you can add this directory to your PATH:

```
$ PATH=$PATH:/usr/src/mozilla/xpcom/typelib/xpidl
```

Using the compiler is fairly easy. If you use the help command, you can see the usage syntax and other basic information about the compiler:

```
$ ./xpidl --help
Usage: xpidl [-m mode] [-w] [-v] [-I path] [-o basename] filename.idl
       -a emit annotations to typelib
       -w turn on warnings (recommended)
       -v verbose mode (NYI)
       -I add entry to start of include path for ``#include "nsIThing.idl"''
       -o use basename (e.g. ``/tmp/nsIThing'') for output
       -m specify output mode:
          header         Generate C++ header             (.h)
          typelib        Generate XPConnect typelib      (.xpt)
          doc            Generate HTML documentation     (.html)
          java           Generate Java interface         (.java)
```

XPCOM Type Libraries

The key to the component architecture of XPCOM is the presence of binary-independent interface files that are used uniformly across platforms, languages, and programming environments. These interface files are compiled into *.xpt* files by the XPIDL compiler. The Mozilla *components* subdirectory is where type libraries and modules are typically stored. If you create a cross-platform type library for your component, you must place it in this directory for it to be accessible to XPCOM.

Creating a type library file from an IDL interface

To create a (*.xpt*) typelib file, use the flag `-m typelib` with warning (`-w`) and verbose (`-v`) modes turned on. `-o` is used for the name of the output file and `-I` is used to specify paths to other IDL files you want to include. To successfully compile your interface, you must always point to the directory where *nsISupports* is located.

```
# include path to nsISupports.idl
$ $XPIDL_INC = /usr/src/mozilla/xpcom/base
#compile nsISimple.idl
$ xpidl -m typelib -w -v -I $XPIDL_INC \
> -o nsISimple nsISimple.idl
```

The file created after compilation is *nsISimple.xpt*. It provides the necessary type information about your interface at runtime. Typelib files enumerate the methods of interfaces and provide detailed type information for each method parameter.

XPCOM Identifiers

To simplify the process of dynamically finding, loading, and binding interfaces, all classes and interfaces are assigned IDs. An ID is a unique 128-bit number that is based on universally unique identifiers (UUIDs) generated by various tools such as *uuidgen* (which we will cover later in this chapter). They are stored in the structure format defined below:

```
struct nsID {
  PRUint32 m0;
  PRUint16 m1, m2;
  PRUint8 m3[8];
};
```

To initialize an ID struct, declare it like this:

```
ID = {0x221ffe10, 0xae3c, 0x11d1,
       {0xb6, 0x6c, 0x00, 0x80, 0x5f, 0x8a, 0x26, 0x76}};
```

One thing that gives XPCOM its modularity is the dynamic allocation of objects through the use of unique identifiers at runtime. This system of canonical identifiers is used for interface querying and component instantiation. Having an interface is important because it ensures that an immutable binary holds a semantic contract defined for a specific interface class.

The two types of identifiers used in XPCOM are the contract ID and the class identifier. These identifiers are shuttled to the Component Manager's `createInstance()` or the Service Manager's `getService()` methods in order to instantiate a component.

The Contract ID

The program ID (`progID`), also known as the Contract ID, is a unique human-readable string. Example 8-2 shows various `progIDs` for different components. This example can be used to instantiate an XPCOM component through the use of a Contract ID.

Example 8-2. progIDs

```
// progID: @mozilla.org/file/local;1
var f = Components.classes[`@mozilla.org/file/local;1'];
// progID: @mozilla.org/browser/bookmarks-service;1
var bmks =
  Components.classes["@mozilla.org/browser/bookmarks-service;1"].
      getService(Components.interfaces.nsIBookmarksService);
```

The class identifier

The other type of identifier is the `classID`, or CLSID. The interface and implementation are identified by this 128-bit numerical identifier string:

```
// clsid: {2e23e220-60be-11d3-8c4a-000064657374}
var f = Components.classesByID["{2e23e220-60be-11d3-8c4a-000064657374}"];
```

Using XPConnect, XPCOM interfaces, `classIDs`, and `progIDs` are stored as global JavaScript objects and properties and can be manipulated directly through the top-level `Components` object discussed earlier.

Generating identifiers

To obtain a UUID on Unix, you can use a command-line program called *uuidgen* that generates a unique number for you:

```
$ uuidgen
ce32e3ff-36f8-425f-94be-d85b26e634ee
```

On Windows, a program called *guidgen.exe* does the same thing and also provides a graphical user interface if you'd rather point and click.

Or you can use one of the special "bots" on IRC at the *irc.mozilla.org* server.

```
irc irc.mozilla.org
/join #mozilla
/msg mozbot uuid
```

This command makes the bot generate and return a uuid, which you can then copy into your component source code. The information can then be used to uniquely identify your component.

Component Manager

One major goal of XPCOM modularization is the removal of link-time dependencies, or dependencies that arise when you link libraries during compilation. The achievement of this goal allows you to access and use modules at runtime. The trouble then becomes finding those modules and figuring out which of their interfaces you want to use. This problem is solved through the use of the Component Manager.

The Component Manager is a special set of component management classes and implementation classes that reside in object libraries (*.dll*, *.so*, *.js*, *.py*, etc.). These classes also include factories, which let you create objects without having access to their class declarations. When you bind to objects at runtime, as you do in XPCOM, you need functionality like this to help you discover and use objects without looking at their code. The Component Manager also includes the Component Manager class itself, known as `nsComponentManager`, which is a mapping of class IDs to factories for the libraries they contain. The Component Manager is responsible for the autoregistration of all new or add-on modules located in the *components* directory. This autoregistration happens behind the scenes and allows you to use new components as they become available without having to register them yourself.

A component author first creates an interface file that defines all APIs that will be publicly available for a component. The component author then creates an implementation for the methods and attributes in a separate implementation class. For example, an *nsILocalFile* interface may have an `nsLocalFile` implementation class. Then a factory or module is needed to abstract the implementation class, and reduce compile and link-time dependencies. It then creates instances of the implementation class through its own implementation of `QueryInterface`. For example:

```
// create an instance of the implementation class
var f = Components.classes[`@mozilla.org/file/local;1'].createInstance();
```

The variable *f* is assigned an instance of a *nsLocalFile* implementation class using the *nsIFactory* method `createInstance()`. To match the correct interface (*nsILocalFile* in this case) to the implementation, you need a class instance to be created before you can call on its member method `QueryInterface()`:

```
// QI for nsILocalFile interface
var f = f.QueryInterface(Components.interfaces.nsILocalFile);
```

Once you do this, the variable *f* is ready to use the *nsILocalFile* interface to access the newly created instance of the `nsLocalFile` class from script.

Simply put, a factory or module is a set of classes used by the Component Manager to register and create an instance of the component's implementation class. A factory can make its way into the Mozilla component repository in several ways. The most direct is through using the Component Manager method `RegisterFactory()`, which supports two different registration mechanisms. The first mechanism, which takes a class ID and a pointer to a factory, can be used on factories that are actually linked into the executable. The second, which takes a class ID and the path to a dynamically loadable library, can be used both inside an executable at runtime and externally by using the `aPersist` flag to tell the repository to store the class ID/library relationship in its permanent store. The Component Manager discovers new factories or modules placed in the *components* directory and queries those modules for the XPCOM components they provide. The name, contract IDs, and class IDs are placed into a small component registry database for quick retrieval. The factory provides this information through a simple set of APIs required by every XPCOM module. Module creation, covered later in this chapter, describes the process through which all components contain an implementation of a module or factory.

Getting and Using XPCOM

Mozilla is a client application that implements XPCOM, so everything you need to use or build new XPCOM components is already included in the source code and/or the binaries. Whenever you use the JavaScript `Components` object, as described earlier, you use XPCOM.

If you'd rather not build the entire Mozilla browser and you have no interest in existing Mozilla components or the large footprint that comes with an entire distribution, then standalone XPCOM is for you. To pull the XPCOM source on Unix using Mac OS X or *cygwin* on Windows, invoke the following commands:

```
cvs -z 3 co mozilla/client.mk
cd mozilla
gmake -f client.mk pull_all BUILD_MODULES=xpcom
```

To build the XPCOM Stand Alone version, type:

```
configure --enable-modules=xpcom
gmake
```

When you build standalone XPCOM, the directory *xpcom/sample* contains the source code for a sample application and a nsTestSample component. The sample application built from these sources, also called nsTestSample, is installed in the Mozilla *bin* directory. *libsample.so* (Unix), which is the component that the sample application tries to instantiate, should have been installed in *bin/components*. To run the test that indicates whether standalone XPCOM is installed successfully, change to the *mozilla/dist/bin* directory and run the following commands:

```
./run-mozilla.sh ./nsTestSample
```

You should see the following output. If you do not, there is a problem with the installation of standalone XPCOM:

```
Type Manifest File: /D/STAND_ALONE_XPCOM/mozilla/dist/bin/components/xpti.dat
nsNativeComponentLoader: autoregistering begins.
nsNativeComponentLoader: autoregistering succeeded
nNCL: registering deferred (0)
Inital print: initial value
Set value to: XPCOM defies gravity
Final print : XPCOM defies gravity
Test passed.
```

Using standalone XPCOM is a powerful way to use the Mozilla framework of cross-platform COM. Even if you're just hacking on Mozilla, standalone XPCOM is a great way to learn about and use XPCOM for application development.

Creating XPCOM Components

As we mentioned, one advantage of using XPCOM is that it separates the implementation from the interface so you can write a component in a language-agnostic manner. The services your component provides are available to all other components despite the language used to implement it. This means, for example, that you can use JavaScript not only to access the services of an XPCOM component, but also to create those services. As described in Chapter 5, using JavaScript as a modularized application programming language provides the deepest level of scripting in Mozilla.

In your Mozilla build or distribution, you will find a subdirectory named *components*. Inside this directory, you will see many compiled components. You will also see a number of JavaScript components. If you look at the source of these components, you can get an idea of how a JavaScript component is created. For example, look at the files *nsFilePicker.js* and *nsSidebar.js*. These JavaScript components are used in the Mozilla distribution.

JavaScript XPCOM components have the advantage over regular scripts of being fast, reusable, and globally accessible to any caller. They also have the advantage over C++-based XPCOM components of being easier to write and maintain. The next few sections describe the creation of a JavaScript-based XPCOM component. If you would rather do your work in C++, then skip to the C++ implementation section in this chapter.

Creating a JavaScript XPCOM Component

To create a JavaScript component, you need to create an IDL interface source file and a JavaScript implementation source file. In the Mozilla sources, naming source files with an *ns* prefix is common practice, so the implementation file should be called something like *nsSimple.js*. The interface source file, or IDL file, uses a similar convention: it is typical for interfaces to begin with *nsI*, using an *I* to distinguish them as interfaces rather than implementations. Call the IDL source file *nsISimple.idl*.

In addition to these two source files (*nsSimple.js* and *nsISimple.idl*), you will compile a cross platform binary interface file, or type library, with the XPIDL compiler, calling it *nsISimple.xpt*. This *.xpt* file tells Mozilla that the interface is available and scriptable. You can use it on any platform that Mozilla supports. In other words, you can pick up *nsISimple.xpt*, which may have been compiled on Unix, drop it into Windows or Mac OS, and use it.

All *.xpt* interface files for Mozilla live in the *components* directory located in *mozilla/dist/bin* if you are developing with the Mozilla source code. Otherwise, for binary distributions of Mozilla, they are located in *mozilla/components*. Mozilla checks this directory upon start up, looking for any new components to register automatically.

The XPIDL interface source file

Usually, the first step in creating a new component is writing the interface. To begin, open up your favorite text editor and create a new file called *nsISimple.idl*.

The complete source code for the *nsISimple.idl* interface file is:

```
#include "nsISupports.idl"
[scriptable, uuid(ce32e3ff-36f8-425f-94be-d85b26e634ee)]
interface nsISimple : nsISupports
{
    attribute string yourName;
    void write();
    void change(in string aValue);
};
```

The `#include` line above includes the file *nsISupports.idl*, which defines this interface's base class. The `[scriptable, uuid..]` line declares the interface scriptable and assigns a UUID to the interface. You can use the UUID provided, but creating your own using one of the UUID generation tools described earlier is usually better. The third line, next to the `interface` keyword, declares the interface's name, *nsISimple*, and says that it derives from *nsISupports*.

Various attributes and methods are defined within the definition of the `nsISimple` interface. Attributes are properties of interface objects. They may be read-only or read/write variables. In *nsISimple*, an attribute called `yourName` is of the type `string`. In this implementation, you may get and set this attribute's value. Of the methods defined in this interface, the write() method takes no arguments and the change() method takes an argument of type string called aValue. The parameter aValue will be a new value that replaces the current value held by yourName. The complete interface IDL is:

```
#include "nsISupports.idl"
[scriptable, uuid(ce32e3ff-36f8-425f-94be-d85b26e634ee)]
interface nsISimple : nsISupports
{
    attribute string yourName;
    void write();
    void change(in string aValue);
};
```

JavaScript implementation file

Once you have created an interface file that publicly defines the component's methods and attributes, the next step is to implement those methods and attributes in a separate source file. The listings below walk through the implementation of nsISimple step by step.

First, you must declare an empty function called SimpleComponent, which is a standard constructor for a JavaScript object prototype. It's a good idea to name the component in a way that clearly describes both the component and the interface, as SimpleComponent does (i.e., SimpleComponent is an implementation of the nsISimple interface):

```
function SimpleComponent() {}
```

With the function declared, we start defining the JavaScript class prototype.

```
SimpleComponent.prototype = {
    mName : "a default value",
```

In the prototype, we first create a member variable called *mName* that will be the string placeholder for the IDL attribute yourName. The variable assigns the string a default value. Remember to place commas after all definitions in a prototype. IDL attributes are always implemented as getter functions. Methods marked with [noscript] will not be available for use with scripting languages.

Next we implement the functions below for our definition of attribute string yourName in our file *nsISimple.idl*.

```
    get yourName()      { return this.mName; },
    set yourName(aName) { return this.mName = aName; },
```

When someone calls an IDL attribute in an interface, getters and setters are used to get or set values for the attribute:

```
simple.yourName='foo';
```

Or similarly read values from the attribute:

```
var foo = simple.yourName;
```

We first call on the setter function to set a value to the attribute yourName and then use the getter function to obtain the currently set value of yourName.

The first function defined in nsISimple is called void write(). For this method, the implementation can be as simple as the following code:

```
write : function () { dump("Hello " + this.mName + "\n"); },
```

This example implements the declaration void write() by dumping the current value of the variable *mName* to stdout. The code uses the this keyword to indicate that you are calling to the component's own member variable *mName*.

The void change() method is then implemented as follows:

```
change : function (aValue) { this.mName = aValue; },
```

change() is a method used to change the value variable.

Implementing the required XPCOM methods in JavaScript

Once the definitions in the *nsISimple* interface are implemented, you need to implement required methods and factories that make this JavaScript implementation class an XPCOM component. Recall that all XPCOM components must implement the nsISupports interface.

Example 8-3 shows an implementation of QueryInterface specific to our new component. QueryInterface ensures that the correct interface (nsISimple) is used by matching the iid with the nsISimple interface that this component implements. If the interface doesn't match, then the argument is invalid. In this case, the exception *Components.results.NS_ERROR_NO_INTERFACE* is thrown, which maps to the error code number 2147500034, and code execution is stopped. If the interface identifier parameter matches the interface, then an instance of the implementation class object SimpleComponent with its interface is returned as a ready-to-use XPCOM component. In XPCOM, every component you implement must have a QueryInterface method.

Example 8-3. QueryInterface method for nsISimple interface

```
QueryInterface: function (iid)
{
 if(!iid.equals(Components.interfaces.nsISimple)
      && !iid.equals(Components.interfaces.nsISupports))
     throw Components.results.NS_ERROR_NO_INTERFACE;
 return this;
}
```

The next requirement is to create a JavaScript object called Module. This module implements the methods needed for autoregistration and component return type objects.

```
var Module = {
    firstTime  : true,
```

The Boolean firstTime is a flag used only when the component is initially registered:

```
registerSelf: function (compMgr, fileSpec, location, type) {
  if (this.firstTime) {
    dump("*** first time registration of Simple JS component\n");
    this.firstTime = false;
    throw Components.results.NS_ERROR_FACTORY_REGISTER_AGAIN;
  }
```

The Component Manager can do a lot in the registration process, but you have to add some logic for first time registration so the Component Manager has the information it needs. RegisterSelf is called at registration time (component installation) and is responsible for notifying the component manager of all components implemented in this module. The fileSpec, location, and type parameters can be passed on to the registerComponent method unmolested. Next, register the component with the Component Manager using code like the following example. The parameters include the CID, a description, a progID, and the other parameters you can pass without changing:

```
  dump(" ***** Registering: Simple JS component! ****\n");
  compMgr.registerComponentWithType(this.myCID,
            "My JS Component",
            this.myProgID, fileSpec,
            location, true, true,
            type);
    },
```

The GetClassObject method produces Factory and SingletonFactory objects. Singleton objects are specialized for services that allow only one instance of the object. Upon success, the method returns an instance of the components factory, which is the implementation class less its interface:

```
getClassObject : function (compMgr, cid, iid) {
  if (!cid.equals(this.myCID))
      throw Components.results.NS_ERROR_NO_INTERFACE;
  if (!iid.equals(Components.interfaces.nsIFactory))
      throw Components.results.NS_ERROR_NOT_IMPLEMENTED;
  return this.myFactory;
  },
```

In the previous list, the member variables *myCID* and *myProgID* are the class ID and the human-readable canonical program ID, respectively:

```
myCID: Components.ID("{98aa9afd-8b08-415b-91ed-01916a130d16}"),
myProgID: "@mozilla.org/js_simple_component;1",
```

The member object myFactory is the components factory, which through its own member function, createInstance(), constructs and returns an instance of the complete component (if the iid parameter is specified and is the correct interface). Otherwise, if no iid parameter is used, the iid of *nsISupports* is used and an instance of the module is created that will then need a subsequent call to QueryInterface to instantiate the object as a component.

```
        myFactory: {
          createInstance: function (outer, iid) {
            dump("CI: " + iid + "\n");
            if (outer != null)
            throw Components.results.NS_ERROR_NO_AGGREGATION;
            return (new SimpleComponent()).QueryInterface(iid);
      }
    },
```

The method canUnload unloads the module when shutdown occurs and is the last function in the module. The componentManager calls the method NSGetModule to initialize these required XPCOM methods and objects:

```
    canUnload: function(compMgr) {
      dump("****** Unloading: Simple JS component! ****** \n");
      return true;
    }
    function NSGetModule(compMgr, fileSpec) { return Module; }
```

The code in Example 8-4 shows the implementation for the *nsISimple* interface in its entirety.

Example 8-4. JavaScript implementation of nsISimple

```
SimpleComponent.prototype = {
   mName: "a default value"
   get yourName()        { return this.mName; },
   set yourName(aName)   { return this.mName = aName; },
   write: function () { dump("Hello " + this.mName + "\n"); },
   change: function (aValue) { this.mName = aValue; },
   QueryInterface: function (iid) {
     if (!iid.equals(Components.interfaces.nsISimple)
         && !iid.equals(Components.interfaces.nsISupports))
       throw Components.results.NS_ERROR_NO_INTERFACE;
     return this;
   }
}
var Module = {
  firstTime: true,
  registerSelf: function (compMgr, fileSpec, location, type) {
  if (this.firstTime) {
    dump("*** first time registration of Simple JS component\n");
    this.firstTime = false;
    throw Components.results.NS_ERROR_FACTORY_REGISTER_AGAIN;
  }
  dump(" ***** Registering: Simple JS component! ****\n");
  dump(" ***** Registering: Simple JS component! ****\n");
           this.myCID,
           "My JS Component",
           this.myProgID, fileSpec,
           location, true, true,
           type);
  },
```

Example 8-4. JavaScript implementation of nsISimple (continued)

```
  getClassObject : function (compMgr, cid, iid) {
    if (!cid.equals(this.myCID))
      throw Components.results.NS_ERROR_NO_INTERFACE
    if (!iid.equals(Components.interfaces.nsIFactory))
      throw Components.results.NS_ERROR_NOT_IMPLEMENTED;
    return this.myFactory;
  },
  myCID: Components.ID("{98aa9afd-8b08-415b-91ed-01916a130d16}"),
  myProgID: "@mozilla.org/js_simple_component;1",
  myFactory: {
    createInstance: function (outer, iid) {
      dump("CI: " + iid + "\n");
      if (outer != null)
      if (outer != null)
      return (new SimpleComponent()).QueryInterface(iid);
    }
  },
  canUnload: function(compMgr) {
    dump("****** Unloading: Simple JS component! ****** \n");
    return true;
  }
}; // END Module

function NSGetModule(compMgr, fileSpec) { return Module; }
```

Compiling the Component

Once you create an IDL source file and a JavaScript implementation file, you need to compile `nsISimple.idl` into a *.xpt* type library.

Compiling the type library

To compile the XPIDL interface file *nsISimple.idl*, you need to add the path of the XPIDL compiler to your environment. As mentioned earlier, the XPIDL compiler is located at *mozilla/xpcom/typelib/xpidl*. Here is the output of a *Unix/cygwin/OSX* session showing the compilation starting with the source file (*nsISimple.idl*) created earlier in the chapter. Afterwards, *nsISimple.xpt* and *nsSimple.js* are copied to the *components* directory:

```
$ ls
nsISimple.idl  nsSimple.js
$ PATH=$PATH:/usr/src/mozilla/xpcom/typelib/xpidl
$ echo $PATH
/sbin:/bin:/usr/sbin:/usr/bin:/usr/games:/usr/local/bin:/usr/X11R6/bin:/root/bin:/
usr/src/mozilla/xpcom/typelib/xpidl
$ export XPIDL_INC=/usr/src/mozilla/xpcom/base
$ echo $XPIDL_INC
/usr/src/mozilla/xpcom/base
$ xpidl -m typelib -w -v -I $XPIDL_INC \
> -o nsISimple nsISimple.idl
```

```
$ ls
nsISimple.idl  nsISimple.xpt  nsSimple.js
$ cp nsISimple.xpt nsSimple.js \
> /usr/src/mozilla/dist/bin/components/
```

This output illustrates the compilation of the *nsISimple.idl* source file into the *nsISimple.xpt* typelib file. The newly compiled *typelib* file and the JavaScript implementation file are then copied to the Mozilla distribution components directory where component registration will occur automatically when Mozilla is launched.

Creating a Makefile for your component project

All previous steps were done manually. You can also create a Makefile to automate this process by using GNU make, in which case you would create a Makefile with the following variables and targets defined:

```
TOP_SRC=/usr/src/mozilla
INST_DIR=$(TOP_SRC)/dist/bin/components
XPIDL=$(TOP_SRC)/xpcom/typelib/xpidl
XPIDL_INC=$(TOP_SRC)/xpcom/base
FLAGS=-m typelib -w -v -I $(XPIDL_INC) -o
all:
  $(XPIDL)/xpidl $(FLAGS) \
  nsISimple nsISimple.idl
install:
  cp nsISimple.xpt nsSimple.js $(INST_DIR)
clean:
  rm -rf *.xpt
uninstall:
  rm -f $(INST_DIR)/nsISimple.xpt
  rm -f $(INST_DIR)/nsSimple.js
```

Remember that you must indent after your targets with a `<tab>`.

In this file, which can be used on Unix, Windows using *cygwin*, or Mac OS X, the `TOP_SRC` environment variable points to the Mozilla source tree's top-level directory, the `INST_DIR` points to the directory where the component should be installed, and the XPIDL variables drive the XPIDL executable and its environment and compiler flags. The "all" Makefile target compiles and creates the type library *nsISimple.xpt*.

Note that in addition to the type libraries, the XPIDL compiler compiles header files, Java class files, and special HTML documentation, if necessary.

Testing the Component

When you start up *xpcshell*, the Component Manager finds the new `nsISimple` component and registers it. The result of your test should look similar to Example 8-5.

Example 8-5. Scripting the "simple" component in xpcshell

```
$ cd /usr/src/mozilla/dist/bin/
$ ./run-mozilla.sh ./xpcshell
```

Example 8-5. Scripting the "simple" component in xpcshell (continued)

```
Type Manifest File: /home/petejc/MOZILLA/mozilla/dist/bin/components/xpti.dat
nsNativeComponentLoader: autoregistering begins.
nsNativeComponentLoader: autoregistering succeeded
*** first time registration of Simple JS component
nNCL: registering deferred (0)
 ***** Registering: Simple JS component! ****
nNCL: registering deferred (0)
js>const Simple=new Components.Constructor("@mozilla.org/js_simple_component;1",
"nsISimple");
js> var simple=new Simple();
CI: {ce32e3ff-36f8-425f-94be-d85b26e634ee}
js> for(var list in simple)
print(list);
QueryInterface
yourName
write
change
js> simple.yourName;
a default value
js> simple.yourName="Pete";
Pete
js> simple.write();
Hello Pete
null
js> simple.change("Brian");
null
js> simple.write();
Hello Brian
null
js> simple.yourName;
Brian
js> quit();
CanUnload_enumerate: skipping native
****** Unloading: Simple JS component! ******
```

Once the component is tested and registered as an XPCOM object, you can use JavaScript from a local web page or from the chrome to create an `nsISimple` object and use it as you would any ordinary JavaScript object:

```
<script type="application/x-JavaScript">
netscape.security.PrivilegeManager.enablePrivilege("UniversalXPConnect");
var Simple=new Components.Constructor("@mozilla.org/js_simple_component;1",
"nsISimple");
var s = new Simple();
for(var list in s)
document.write(list+"<br>\n");
</script>
```

In addition to creating a component in JavaScript, you can implement XPCOM components in C++ and Python. The next sections cover the C++ implementation of the `nsISimple` interface.

Useful C++ Macros and Types

Before you begin working on an actual implementation of a C++ component, familiarize yourself with some of the tools that make C++ programming for XPCOM a little easier. Templates, special types, and macros can ease some of the extra housekeeping that programming XPCOM requires.

More tools than we can cover in this introduction are available, but this section reviews some of the most common, including a macro that implements the `nsISupports` methods `QueryInterface`, `AddRef`, and `Release`, macros for testing `nsresults`, `smart pointers`, and special types.

The NS_IMPL_ISUPPORTS1_CI macro

Rather than having to implement `QueryInterface`, `AddRef`, and the `Release` methods like we did in our JavaScript component, the `NS_IMPL_ISUPPORTS` macro inserts the implementation code for you.

To use this macro for the `nsISimple` interface, type:

```
NS_IMPL_ISUPPORTS1_CI(nsSimpleImpl, nsISimple)
```

The following lines define this macro:

```
#define NS_IMPL_ISUPPORTS1(_class, _interface) \
NS_IMPL_ADDREF(_class)                         \
NS_IMPL_RELEASE(_class)                        \
NS_IMPL_QUERY_INTERFACE1(_class, _interface)
```

As you can see, the macro is made up of other macros that implement basic methods of the `nsISupports` interface. Unless you need to modify these macros, they should be left as is. This macro is used later on when we create our C++ component.

Example 8-6 shows a reference implementation of the `QueryInterface` method in C++.

Example 8-6. Reference implementation of QueryInterface

```
NS_IMETHODIMP
nsMyImplementation::QueryInterface( REFNSIID aIID, void** aInstancePtr )
{
  NS_ASSERTION(aInstancePtr, "QueryInterface requires a non-NULL destination!");
  if ( !aInstancePtr )
    return NS_ERROR_NULL_POINTER;
  nsISupports* foundInterface;
  if ( aIID.Equals(nsCOMTypeInfo<nsIX>::GetIID()) )
    foundInterface = NS_STATIC_CAST(nsIX*, this);
  else if ( aIID.Equals(nsCOMTypeInfo<nsIY>::GetIID()) )
    foundInterface = NS_STATIC_CAST(nsIY*, this);
  else if ( aIID.Equals(nsCOMTypeInfo<nsISupports>::GetIID()) )
    foundInterface = NS_STATIC_CAST(nsISupports*, NS_STATIC_CAST(nsIX*, this));
  else
    foundInterface = 0;
```

Example 8-6. Reference implementation of QueryInterface (continued)

```
  nsresult status;
  if ( !foundInterface ) {
    status = NS_NOINTERFACE;
  } else {
    NS_ADDREF(foundInterface);
    status = NS_OK;
  }
  *aInstancePtr = foundInterface;
  return status;
}
```

The results macros

Since all XPCOM methods return result codes called *nsresults*, another useful macro is the NS_SUCCEEDED macro. This indicates whether an XPCOM accessor has returned a successful result. It is defined in *nsError.h*:

```
#define NS_SUCCEEDED(_nsresult) (!((_nsresult) & 0x80000000))
```

A related macro, NS_FAILED, is indicates whether an XPCOM accessor returned a failure code result. It too is defined in *nsError.h*. The following code demonstrates the typical use of these two macros:

```
nsresult rv;
nsCOMPtr<nsILocalFile> file(do_CreateInstance("@mozilla.org/file/local;1", &rv));
  if (NS_FAILED(rv)) {
    printf("FAILED\n");
    return rv;
  }
  if (NS_SUCCEEDED(rv)) {
    printf(" SUCCEEDED \n");
    return rv;
  }
```

You may have noticed that the declaration of the identifier rv as the type nsresult. nsresult is a 32-bit unsigned integer declared in *nscore.h*:

```
typedef PRUint32 nsresult;
```

We assign an *nsCOMPtr* or smart pointer named file to a newly created instance of the nsILocalFile component. Using the NS_FAILED and NS_SUCCEEDED macros, we test for the nsresult to see if our attempt to create an instance of the component failed. If it did, rv would be assigned an integer with a specific error return code. Return codes are defined in *nsError.h*. Alternatively, you can test your results for the success code:

```
nsresult rv = nsComponentManager::CreateInstance("@mozilla.org/file/local;1",
                                    nsnull,
                                    NS_GET_IID(nsILocalFile),
                                    (void **)&refp);
```

If a result is successful, the value of rv returns NS_OK, which is 0.

Return codes are used in XPCOM instead of exceptions. Exceptions are not allowed because of their inconsistent implementation across different compilers. All error code numbers equate to a specific type of error. For example NS_ERROR_FAILURE and NS_ERROR_NULL_POINTER are common types of error code return values used throughout the Mozilla code base. If a value returned to rv was NS_ERROR_NULL_POINTER, the test for failure would be true and the code would return the numerical result code for NS_ERROR_NULL_POINTER.

The nsnull type

Another widely use type is nsnull, defined in *nscore.h*. Here is the definition:

```
#define nsnull 0
```

This definition, nsnull, is the most common way to use null. The following code shows how to use nsnull:

```
nsresult rv;
nsCOMPtr<nsILocalFile> file =
do_CreateInstance("@mozilla.org/file/local;1", &rv);
if (NS_SUCCEEDED(rv)) {
  char* msg = "we successfully created an instance of file\n";
  *_retval = (char*) nsMemory::Alloc(PL_strlen(msg) + 1);
  if (!*_retval)
    return NS_ERROR_OUT_OF_MEMORY;
  PL_strcpy(*_retval, msg);
} else {
  *_retval = nsnull;
}
```

The NS_IMETHODIMP macro

If you look in the Mozilla C++ source code, you will see the macro NS_IMETHODIMP used frequently. This macro identifies the type of your interface implementation method. It is also defined in *nscore.h*, as shown in Example 8-7.

Example 8-7. Platform macros in xpcom/base/nscore.h

```
#define NS_IMETHODIMP NS_IMETHODIMP_(nsresult)
#ifdef NS_WIN32
  #define NS_IMETHODIMP_(type) type __stdcall
#elif defined(XP_MAC)
  #define NS_IMETHODIMP_(type) type
#elif defined(XP_OS2)
  #define NS_IMETHODIMP_(type) type
#else
  #define NS_IMETHODIMP_(type) type
#endif
```

Example 8-8 shows a typical use of the NS_IMETHODIMP macro. All methods that implement an interface are of the type NS_IMETHODIMP.

Example 8-8. NS_IMETHOD macro

```
NS_IMETHODIMP
nsMyImpl::GetSomeString(char** _retval)
{
  nsresult rv;
  nsCOMPtr<nsILocalFile> file =
  do_CreateInstance("@mozilla.org/file/local;1", &rv);
  if (NS_SUCCEEDED(rv)) {
    char* msg = "we successfully created an instance of file\n";
    *_retval = (char*) nsMemory::Alloc(PL_strlen(msg) + 1);
    if (!*_retval)
      return NS_ERROR_OUT_OF_MEMORY;
    PL_strcpy(*_retval, msg);
  } else {
    *_retval = nsnull;
  }
  return NS_OK;
}
```

The macro in Example 8-8 declares the method `GetSomeString` as an XPCOM implementation.

nsCOMPtr smart pointer

As described earlier, XPCOM provides a C++ tool called a smart pointer to manage reference counting. A smart pointer is a template class that acts syntactically, just like an ordinary pointer in C or C++. You can apply * to dereference the pointer, ->, or access what the pointer refers to. Unlike a raw COM interface pointer, however, `nsCOMPtr` manages `AddRef`, `Release`, and `QueryInterface` for you, thereby preventing memory leaks.

Here is how to create a raw pointer:

```
nsILocalFile *refp(nsnull);
nsresult rv = nsComponentManager::CreateInstance("@mozilla.org/file/local;1",
   nsnull,
  NS_GET_IID(nsILocalFile),
  (void **)&refp);
if (refp)
  printf("%p\n", (void*)refp);
```

After you create a new object that `refp` points to, `refp` is considered an owning reference, and any other pointers that point to it must be "refcounted." Example 8-9 uses `anotherPtr` and `oneMorePtr` to point to `refp`, and manually manages `AddRef` and `Release`.

Example 8-9. Manual reference counting using raw pointers

```
nsILocalFile *refp(nsnull);
nsresult rv = nsComponentManager::CreateInstance("@mozilla.org/file/local;1",
   nsnull,
   NS_GET_IID(nsILocalFile),
   (void **)&refp);
```

Example 8-9. Manual reference counting using raw pointers (continued)

```
nsILocalFile *anotherPtr = refp;
NS_IF_ADDREF(anotherPtr); // increment refcount
nsILocalFile *oneMorePtr = refp;
NS_IF_ADDREF(oneMorePtr); // increment refcount
if (!someCondition) {
  NS_RELEASE(anotherPtr); // decrement refcount
  return NS_OK;
}
. . .
NS_RELEASE(anotherPtr); // decrement refcount
NS_RELEASE(oneMorePtr); // decrement refcount
return NS_OK;
}
```

In Example 8-9, if `someCondition` is false, `anotherPtr` is released and the function then returns (`NS_OK`). But what about `oneMorePtr`? In this instance, it is never released; if you remember, an object cannot be released from memory until our `refcount` is at zero. The `refcount` is out of sync, `oneMorePtr` is never decremented before the return, and the object is thus left dangling in memory. With the `refcount` off, the object leaks. Remember that `Release()` calls the C++ `delete` operator to free up the allocated XPCOM object only when the count is decremented to 0. If `Release` thinks there are still references to the object because the `refcount` hasn't been properly decremented, `delete` is never called. The correct code is shown below:

```
if (!someCondition) {
  NS_RELEASE(anotherPtr); // decrement refcount
  NS_RELEASE(oneMorePtr); // decrement refcount
  return NS_OK;
}
```

As you can see, manual management of reference counting is prone to error. To alleviate this burden and extra code bloat, `nsCOMPtr` implements `AddRef` and `Release` for you and makes life much easier. Before the `nsCOMPtr` class is removed from the stack, it calls `Release` in its destructor. After all references are properly released, `delete` is called and the object is freed from memory. Example 8-10 shows a typical use of `nsCOMPtr`.

Example 8-10. Using nsCOMPtr in your code

```
nsCOMPtr<nsILocalFile> refp = do_CreateInstance("@mozilla.org/file/local;1");
nsCOMPtr<nsILocalFile> anotherPtr = refp;
nsCOMPtr<nsILocalFile> oneMorePtr = refp;
nsresult rv;
if (!someCondition)
  return NS_OK;
. . .
//no need to release here because nsCOMPtr smart pointer's destructor
// will call release automatically and the above references will be
// properly decremented.
return NS_OK;
```

Wherever the code returns, all pointers holding references to the nsLocalFile XPCOM object are released automatically in the nsCOMPtr class destructor before the instructions are removed from the stack. By letting nsCOMPtr manage AddRef and Release for you, you remove a margin for error, code complexity, and bloat.

C++ Implementation of nsISimple

Now that you have seen some of the C++ tools you need for XPCOM, you can turn to an actual implementation.

Earlier in this chapter, the section "Creating a JavaScript XPCOM Component" showed you how to create an interface and implement it in JavaScript. However, you may need a C++ implementation to benefit from the better performance offered by a compiled language.

Most components used in Mozilla are written in C++. This section discusses how to create a C++ implementation for the nsISimple interface. A few more steps are involved, but as you will see, they are generally similar to the processes described in the JavaScript component section, facilitated to some extent by the available tools and templates discussed previously.

Creating a C++ component

First, you must find a good place to put the source file you create for the component. In your local Mozilla source tree, *mozilla/xpcom/sample/* is a great place to start because it's the directory in which the sample XPCOM interface and implementations already reside.

First, create a new directory and call it *simple*:

```
$ mkdir simple
$ cd simple
```

You can place the nsISimple interface you created earlier in this new directory as a file called *nsISimple.idl*:

```
#include "nsISupports.idl"
[scriptable, uuid(ce32e3ff-36f8-425f-94be-d85b26e634ee)]
interface nsISimple : nsISupports
{
    attribute string yourName;
    void write();
    void change(in string aName);
};
```

Once you have the interface source file in which the attribute yourName and the methods write() and change() are defined, you can create a header file for the implementation source file.

nsISimple C++ header file

Earlier, you created the type library *nsISimple.xpt* for the JavaScript component and installed it in the components subdirectory. Since we've already covered those steps, we can move forward to generating a C++ header file. To create a C++ header file from your original IDL, run your IDL file through the *xpidl* compiler:

```
$ xpidl -m header -w -v -I $XPIDL_INC \
> -o nsISimple nsISimple.idl
```

The generated file is *nsISimple.h* and is shown in Example 8-11.

Example 8-11. nsISimple header file generated by xpidl compiler

```
/*
 * DO NOT EDIT.  THIS FILE IS GENERATED FROM nsISimple.idl
 */
#ifndef __gen_nsISimple_h__
#define __gen_nsISimple_h__
#ifndef __gen_nsISupports_h__
#include "nsISupports.h"
#endif
/* For IDL files that don't want to include root IDL files. */
#ifndef NS_NO_VTABLE
#define NS_NO_VTABLE
#endif
/* starting interface:    nsISimple */
#define NS_ISIMPLE_IID_STR "ce32e3ff-36f8-425f-94be-d85b26e634ee"
#define NS_ISIMPLE_IID \
  {0xce32e3ff, 0x36f8, 0x425f, \
    { 0x94, 0xbe, 0xd8, 0x5b, 0x26, 0xe6, 0x34, 0xee }}
class NS_NO_VTABLE nsISimple : public nsISupports {
 public:
  NS_DEFINE_STATIC_IID_ACCESSOR(NS_ISIMPLE_IID)
  /* attribute string yourName; */
  NS_IMETHOD GetYourName(char * *aYourName) = 0;
  NS_IMETHOD SetYourName(const char * aYourName) = 0;
  /* void write (); */
  NS_IMETHOD Write(void) = 0;
  /* void change (in string aName); */
  NS_IMETHOD Change(const char *aName) = 0;
};
/* Use this macro when declaring classes that implement this interface. */
#define NS_DECL_NSISIMPLE \
  NS_IMETHOD GetYourName(char * *aYourName); \
  NS_IMETHOD SetYourName(const char * aYourName); \
  NS_IMETHOD Write(void); \
  NS_IMETHOD Change(const char *aName);
/* Use this macro to declare functions that forward the behavior of this interface to
another object. */
#define NS_FORWARD_NSISIMPLE(_to) \
  NS_IMETHOD GetYourName(char * *aYourName) { return _to ## GetYourName(aYourName); } \
  NS_IMETHOD SetYourName(const char * aYourName) { return _to ## SetYourName(aYourName); }
\
```

Example 8-11. nsISimple header file generated by xpidl compiler (continued)

```
  NS_IMETHOD Write(void) { return _to ## Write(); } \
  NS_IMETHOD Change(const char *aName) { return _to ## Change(aName); }
/* Use this macro to declare functions that forward the behavior of this interface to
another object in a safe way. */
#define NS_FORWARD_SAFE_NSISIMPLE(_to) \
  NS_IMETHOD GetYourName(char * *aYourName) { return !_to ## ? NS_ERROR_NULL_POINTER : _to
##->GetYourName(aYourName); } \
  NS_IMETHOD SetYourName(const char * aYourName) { return !_to ## ? NS_ERROR_NULL_POINTER
: _to ##->SetYourName(aYourName); } \
  NS_IMETHOD Write(void) { return !_to ## ? NS_ERROR_NULL_POINTER : _to ##-> Write(); } \
  NS_IMETHOD Change(const char *aName) { return !_to ## ? NS_ERROR_NULL_POINTER : _to ##->
Change(aName); }
#if 0
/* Use the code below as a template for the implementation class for this interface. */
/* Header file */
class nsSimple : public nsISimple
{
public:
  NS_DECL_ISUPPORTS
  NS_DECL_NSISIMPLE
  nsSimple();
  virtual ~nsSimple();
  /* additional members */
};
/* Implementation file */
NS_IMPL_ISUPPORTS1(nsSimple, nsISimple)
nsSimple::nsSimple()
{
  NS_INIT_ISUPPORTS();
  /* member initializers and constructor code */
}
nsSimple::~nsSimple()
{
  /* destructor code */
}
/* attribute string yourName; */
NS_IMETHODIMP nsSimple::GetYourName(char * *aYourName)
{
    return NS_ERROR_NOT_IMPLEMENTED;
}
NS_IMETHODIMP nsSimple::SetYourName(const char * aYourName)
{
    return NS_ERROR_NOT_IMPLEMENTED;
}
/* void write (); */
NS_IMETHODIMP nsSimple::Write()
{
    return NS_ERROR_NOT_IMPLEMENTED;
}
/* void change (in string aName); */
NS_IMETHODIMP nsSimple::Change(const char *aName)
{
```

Example 8-11. nsISimple header file generated by xpidl compiler (continued)

```
    return NS_ERROR_NOT_IMPLEMENTED;
}
/* End of implementation class template. */
#endif
#endif /* __gen_nsISimple_h__ */
```

As you can see, the *xpidl* compiler can do a lot of work for you. The code generated in Example 8-11 is a C++ header file that declares the methods of `nsISimple`. It provides the class definition, macros for using the interface, and a template for the class implementation, which contains stubbed-out declaratory code that you can paste into your implementation file to quickly get started.

Creating the implementation file

The implementation file actually contains the C++ code that implements the member functions and properties declared in your interface. For `nsISimple`, these members are the `yourName` attribute and the `write()` and `change()` methods.

First you need to generate a new UUID for the new implementation class you'll write. Every XPCOM implementation class must have its own UUID:

```
$ uuidgen
79e9424f-2c4d-4cae-a762-31b334079252
```

As part of the generated file *nsISimple.h*, all the code stubs you need to get started are ready to be copied and pasted into the C++ source files. You can use those stubs as a guide to implement the component. In a text editor, create a new file called *nsSimple.h* and enter the code shown in Example 8-12.

To maintain clarity, the C++ implementation class is named `nsSimpleImpl`, where the default class name generated by the *xpidl* compiler is `nsSimple` and the header file, *nsSimple.h*, is shown in Example 8-12.

Example 8-12. The component header file nsSimple.h

```
#include "nsISimple.h"
// 79e9424f-2c4d-4cae-a762-31b334079252
#define NS_SIMPLE_CID \
{ 0x79e9424f, 0x2c4d, 0x4cae, { 0xa7, 0x62, 0x31, 0xb3, 0x34, 0x07, 0x92, 0x52 } }
#define NS_SIMPLE_CONTRACTID "@mozilla.org/cpp_simple;1"
class nsSimpleImpl : public nsISimple
{
public:
    nsSimpleImpl();
    virtual ~nsSimpleImpl();
    // nsISupports interface
    NS_DECL_ISUPPORTS
    NS_DECL_NSISIMPLE
private:
    char* mName;
};
```

Example 8-12 includes the ID-generated header file *nsISimple.h*, which holds the C++ declarations for the interface class nsISimple. It then takes the new UUID and breaks it into a class ID struct defined as NS_SIMPLE_CID. Next, it defines the contract ID for this implementation class.

The example uses a completely different class ID and contract ID than the one used for the JavaScript component because it's a different implementation class and needs to have it's own unique identification (even though it implements the same interface).

Now the example makes the class declaration of the implementation, called nsSimpleImpl, which inherits from nsISimple, defining the class constructor and virtual destructor. NS_DECL_ISUPPORTS is a macro that holds the declaration of our required QueryInterface, AddRef, and Release methods. NS_DECL_NSISIMPLE is created in the generated header file *nsISimple.h*. It expands to the used interface method declarations. Finally Example 8-12 shows the addition of the char* member variable identified as *mName*. This variable is used to hold the value of the interface attribute yourName, just as it did earlier in the JavaScript class implementation.

Once you have the header file, you are ready to start the implementation source file. With a text editor, create a new file called *nsSimple.cpp*. As in any C++ source file, you should add the header files required by the implementation:

```
#include "plstr.h"
#include "stdio.h"
#include "nsCOMPtr.h"
#include "nsMemory.h"
#include "nsSimple.h"
```

Start by adding the implementation of our class constructor and destructor:

```
// c++ constructor
nsSimpleImpl::nsSimpleImpl() : mName(nsnull)
{
    NS_INIT_REFCNT();
    mName = PL_strdup("default value");
}
// c++ destructor
nsSimpleImpl::~nsSimpleImpl()
{
    if (mName)
        PL_strfree(mName);
}
```

Then add the macro NS_IMPL_ISUPPORTS1_CI. As discussed earlier, this macro conveniently implements QueryInterface, AddRef, and Release:

```
NS_IMPL_ISUPPORTS1_CI(nsSimpleImpl, nsISimple);
```

Next you are ready to implement the actual nsISimple interface methods:

```
NS_IMETHODIMP
nsSimpleImpl::GetYourName(char** aName)
```

```
{
    NS_PRECONDITION(aName != nsnull, "null ptr");
    if (!aName)
        return NS_ERROR_NULL_POINTER;
    if (mName) {
        *aName = (char*) nsMemory::Alloc(PL_strlen(mName) + 1);
        if (! *aName)
            return NS_ERROR_NULL_POINTER;
        PL_strcpy(*aName, mName);
    }
    else {
        *aName = nsnull;
    }
    return NS_OK;
}
```

A C++ implementation of an IDL method is declared as the type `NS_IMETHODIMP`. The implementation starts with the getter method `GetYourName`, which takes a `char**` parameter for the method's return value. Return values in C++ XPCOM components are marshaled via method arguments because interface implementations must always return a numerical `nsresult`, as described earlier. To ensure that the `aName` parameter is a pointer, use the macro `NS_PRECONDITION` to warn if null, follow with a null test in the line below, and return the error result code `NS_ERROR_NULL_POINTER`. Then test whether the member variable *mName* holds a value. If it does, allocate the necessary memory to accommodate the size of the copy. Then by using `PL_strcpy`, you can assign the value to the parameter `aName`. Otherwise, *mName* is null and you can assign null into `aName` and return:

```
NS_IMETHODIMP
nsSimpleImpl::SetYourName(const char* aName)
{
   NS_PRECONDITION(aName != nsnull, "null ptr");
    if (!aName)
        return NS_ERROR_NULL_POINTER;
    if (mName) {
        PL_strfree(mName);
    }
    mName = PL_strdup(aName);
    return NS_OK;
}
```

After implementing the getter, implement the setter. Again, use `NS_PRECONDITION` and then a null test on the `aName`. If that parameter holds data, you can free it by using `PL_strfree` and calling `PL_strdup`. Then assign the new value to class member `mName`:

```
NS_IMETHODIMP
nsSimpleImpl::Write()
{
  printf("%s\n", mName);
  return NS_OK;
}
NS_IMETHODIMP
```

```
nsSimpleImpl::Change(const char* aName)
{
  return SetYourName(aName);
}
```

Finally, implement the Write and Change methods by using printf to write the value of mName to stdout and set a new value to mName. Example 8-13 shows the C++ source code in its entirety.

Example 8-13. nsSimple.cpp

```
#include "plstr.h"
#include "stdio.h"
#include "nsSimple.h"
#include "nsCOMPtr.h"
#include "nsMemory.h"
// c++ constructor
nsSimpleImpl::nsSimpleImpl() : mName(nsnull)
{
    NS_INIT_REFCNT();
     = PL_strdup("default value");
}
// c++ destructor
nsSimpleImpl::~nsSimpleImpl()
{
    if ()
        PL_strfree();
}
// This macro implements the nsISupports interface methods
// QueryInterface, AddRef and Release
NS_IMPL_ISUPPORTS1_CI(nsSimpleImpl, nsISimple);
NS_IMETHODIMP
nsSimpleImpl::GetYourName(char** aName)
{
    NS_PRECONDITION(aName != nsnull, "null ptr");
    if (!aName)
        return NS_ERROR_NULL_POINTER;
    if () {
        *aName = (char*) nsMemory::Alloc(PL_strlen() + 1);
        if (! *aName)
            return NS_ERROR_NULL_POINTER;
        PL_strcpy(*aName, );
    }
    else {
        *aName = nsnull;
    }
    return NS_OK;
}
NS_IMETHODIMP
nsSimpleImpl::SetYourName(const char* aName)
{
   NS_PRECONDITION(aName != nsnull, "null ptr");
    if (!aName)
        return NS_ERROR_NULL_POINTER;
```

Example 8-13. nsSimple.cpp (continued)

```
    if () {
        PL_strfree();
    }
     = PL_strdup(aName);
    return NS_OK;
}
NS_IMETHODIMP
nsSimpleImpl::Write()
{
  printf("%s\n", );
  return NS_OK;
}
NS_IMETHODIMP
nsSimpleImpl::Change(const char* aName)
{
  return SetYourName(aName);
}
```

The nsSimple module code

As you needed to do with the JavaScript implementation, you must create the code for the module. The module code abstracts the implementation class and makes the implementation a component library. In your text editor, create a file called *nsSimpleModule.cpp* and enter the code shown in Example 8-14.

Example 8-14. nsSimpleModule.cpp

```
#include "nsIGenericFactory.h"
#include "nsSimple.h"
NS_GENERIC_FACTORY_CONSTRUCTOR(nsSimpleImpl)
static NS_METHOD nsSimpleRegistrationProc(nsIComponentManager *aCompMgr,
                                          nsIFile *aPath,
                                          const char *registryLocation,
                                          const char *componentType,
                                          const nsModuleComponentInfo *info)
{
    return NS_OK;
}
static NS_METHOD nsSimpleUnregistrationProc(nsIComponentManager *aCompMgr,
                                            nsIFile *aPath,
                                            const char *registryLocation,
                                            const nsModuleComponentInfo *info)
{
    return NS_OK;
}
// For each class that wishes to support nsIClassInfo, add a line like this
NS_DECL_CLASSINFO(nsSimpleImpl)
static nsModuleComponentInfo components[] =
{
  { "A Simple Component",    // a message to display when component is loaded
    NS_SIMPLE_CID,           // our UUID
```

Example 8-14. nsSimpleModule.cpp (continued)

```
    NS_SIMPLE_CONTRACTID,     // our human readable PROGID or CLSID
    nsSimpleImplConstructor,
    nsSimpleRegistrationProc       /* NULL if you dont need one */,
    nsSimpleUnregistrationProc     /* NULL if you dont need one */,
    NULL /* no factory destructor */,
    NS_CI_INTERFACE_GETTER_NAME(nsSimpleImpl),
    NULL /* no language helper */,
    &NS_CLASSINFO_NAME(nsSimpleImpl)
  }
};
NS_IMPL_NSGETMODULE(nsSimpleModule, components)
```

The final steps for a C++ component

Once you have an interface file *nsISimple.idl*, a C++ source file *nsSimple.cpp* with its header file *nsSimple.h*, and a module file *nsSimpleModule.cpp*, you can create a Makefile like the one shown in Example 8-15. This Makefile can compile the sources into an XPCOM component.

A Makefile directs the Mozilla build system to build the sources and install them into the Mozilla *dist/bin/components* directory. To use the Makefile, run gmake to compile and install the component library file.

Example 8-15. Sample Makefile

```
topsrcdir        = ../../..
srcdir           = .
VPATH            = .
include $(DEPTH)/config/autoconf.mk
MODULE           = xpcom
XPIDL_MODULE     = simple
LIBRARY_NAME     = simple
IS_COMPONENT     = 1
MODULE_NAME      = nsSimpleModule
REQUIRES         = string \
                   xpcom  \
                   $(NULL)
CPPSRCS          =
                 nsSimple.cpp \
                 nsSimpleModule.cpp
                 $(NULL)
XPIDLSRCS        = nsISimple.idl
include $(topsrcdir)/config/config.mk
LIBS             +=              \
                 $(XPCOM_LIBS) \
                 $(NSPR_LIBS)  \
                 $(NULL)
include $(topsrcdir)/config/rules.mk
EXTRA_DSO_LDOPTS += $(MOZ_COMPONENT_LIBS)
install:: $(TARGETS
```

To test the newly compiled component, you can use *xpcshell* like you did for the JavaScript component. Example 8-16 shows a session with *xpcshell* that tests the new component.

Example 8-16. Sample use of component in xpcshell

```
$ ./run-mozilla.sh ./xpcshell
Type Manifest File: /usr/src/commit_mozilla/mozilla/dist/bin/components/xpti.dat
nsNativeComponentLoader: autoregistering begins.
*** Registering nsSimpleModule components (all right -- a generic module!)
nsNativeComponentLoader: autoregistering succeeded
nNCL: registering deferred (0)
js> var Simple = new Components.Constructor("@mozilla.org/cpp_simple;1", "nsISimple");
js> var s = new Simple();
js> s.yourName;
default value
js> s.write();
default value
js> s.change('pete');
js> s.yourName;
pete
js> s.yourName = 'brian';
brian
js>
```

Creating an instance of an existing Mozilla component

Creating an instance of a component and accessing methods and attributes is different in C++ than it is in JavaScript. Using the *nsILocalFile* interface lets you walk through the code to create an instance of this component from C++:

```
nsCOMPtr<nsILocalFile>
file(do_CreateInstance("@mozilla.org/file/local;1"));
```

You can also instantiate the object as follows:

```
nsresult rv;
nsCOMPtr<nsILocalFile> file =
    do_CreateInstance("@mozilla.org/file/local;1", &rv);
if (NS_FAILED(rv))
  return rv;
```

Both techniques assign an `nsCOMPtr` to a newly allocated instance of an `nsLocalFile` object.

Example 8-17 accesses the public methods available from this component by using the pointer identifier `file`.

Example 8-17. Example 8-17: Testing for nsresults from component methods

```
if (file) {
  nsresult rv;
  rv = file->InitWithPath(NS_LITERAL_STRING("/tmp"));
  if (NS_FAILED(rv))
    return rv;
```

Example 8-17. Example 8-17: Testing for nsresults from component methods (continued)

```
  PRBool exists;
  rv = file->Exists(&exists);
  if (NS_FAILED(rv))
    return rv;
  if (exists)
    print("yep it exists!\n");
  nsAutoString leafName;
  rv = file->GetLeafName(leafName);
  if (NS_FAILED(rv))
    return rv;
  if (!leafName.IsEmpty())
    printf("leaf name is %s\n", NS_ConvertUCS2toUTF8(leafName).get());
}
```

Always test accessors of all XPCOM public methods, getters, and setters. Failures can appear at any time, so be sure to use result checking in your implementations.

Other Languages for XPCOM

Although most components available from XPCOM are written in C++, the XPConnect/XPCOM pairing can also accommodate other languages. Language independence is a goal of the XPCOM architecture. Currently, implementations for Python (PyXPCOM) and Ruby (rbXPCOM) exist, with other language bindings being developed. In this respect, the Mozilla framework dovetails with one of the main trends in application development, which is to mix different languages in the development environment.

PyXPCOM: the Python binding for XPCOM

Python has emerged as a very popular programming language in the last couple of years. It even does some of the application work and other heavy lifting that were the province of C++. Mozilla now offers a Python "binding" similar to the XPConnect binding for JavaScript that allows you to write application code in Python, compile it in XPCOM, and make it available like you would any C++ component in the Mozilla application framework. As with other XPCOM programming languages, you must create an implementation file (in Python) and an interface file (in IDL), as shown in Examples 8-18 and 8-19, respectively.

The terms and constructs for Python components are similar to those of C++. In the implementation, you need to import components from the XPCOM module to access the standard public members. The syntax is the same as that for importing any regular Python library:

```
from xpcom import components
```

The IDL for a Python implementation of an XPCOM component can be identical to one for a JavaScript- or C++-based component (which is the point of XPCOM, after all). As in any component, your IDL needs to include *nsISupports.idl* and declare itself as scriptable with a unique UUID:

```
[scriptable, uuid(6D9F47DE-ADC1-4a8e-8E7D-2F7B037239BF)]
```

JavaScript accesses the component in the same way, using classes and interface members of the component's interfaces to set up an instance of the component:

```
Components.classes["@foo.com/appSysUtils;1"].
    getService(Components.interfaces.appISysUtils);
```

With these foundations, and assuming that you have to have a Python distribution on your system that Mozilla can access, you are ready to go! Example 8-18 shows a complete implementation of a PyXPCOM component. This file needs to be saved with a *.py* extension and put in the *components* directory and registered like any other component.

Example 8-18. Sample Python component implementation

```
import sys, os
from xpcom import components, nsError, ServerException
class appSysUtils:
    _com_interfaces_ = [components.interfaces.appISysUtils]
    _reg_clsid_ = "{56F686E0-A989-4714-A5D6-D77BC850C5C0}"
    _reg_contractid_ = "@foo.com/appSysUtils;1"
    _reg_desc_ = "System Utilities Service"
    def __init__(self):
        self.F_OK = os.F_OK
        self.R_OK = os.R_OK
        self.W_OK = os.W_OK
        self.X_OK = os.X_OK
    # ...
    def Access(self, filename, mode):
        return os.access(filename, mode)
```

The special attributes defined in the appSysUtils class correspond to the special identifiers you must use in XPCOM to make your code a reusable component (see "XPCOM Identifiers," earlier in this chapter). Table 8-3 describes these attributes.

Table 8-3. Special XPCOM attributes in Python

Attribute	Description
_com_interfaces_	The interface IDs supported by this component. This attribute is required. It can be a single IID or a list, but you do not have to list base interfaces such as *nsISupports*.
_reg_contractid_	The component's contract ID. Required.
_reg_clsid_	The Class ID (CLSID) or progID of the component in the form: @domain/component;version. Required.
_reg_desc_	A description of the component. Optional.

Example 8-19 is the IDL file you also need to create a Python component.

Example 8-19. IDL for the Python component

```
#include "nsISupports.idl"
// some useful system utilities
[scriptable, uuid(6D9F47DE-ADC1-4a8e-8E7D-2F7B037239BF)]
interface appSysUtils : nsISupports {
    boolean IsFile(in string filename);
    boolean IsDir(in string dirname);
    void Stat(in string filename,
              out PRUint32 st_mode,
              out PRUint32 st_ino,
              out PRUint32 st_dev,
              out PRUint32 st_nlink,
              out PRUint32 st_uid,
              out PRUint32 st_gid,
              out PRUint32 st size,
              out PRUint32 st_atime,
              out PRUint32 st_mtime,
              out PRUint32 st_ctime);
    boolean Access(in string filename, in PRUint32 mode);
    readonly attribute PRUint32 F_OK;
    readonly attribute PRUint32 R_OK;
    readonly attribute PRUint32 W_OK;
    readonly attribute PRUint32 X_OK;
};
```

Finally, Example 8-20 shows how this component might be used in script—for example, in a function you define for an event handler in the XUL interface.

Example 8-20. Using the Python component in script

```
var appSysUtils = Components.classes["@foo.com/appSysUtils;1"].getService(Components
        interfaces.appISysUtils);
// Read-write status
var write = appSysUtils.Access(url, appSysUtils.W_OK);
var read = appSysUtils.Access(url, appSysUtils.R_OK);
var rwcheck = document.getElementById('rwCheckbox');
if (read)  {
    if (write && read)
        ro = false;
    else
        ro = true;
    rwcheck.setAttribute('checked', ro);
}
```

The component is a small system utility that checks the read/write permissions status of a file on the local filesystem. The JavaScript uses it to display a visual notifier of the status in the UI. In this case, the DOM's `rwcheck` node refers to a checkbox. It's easy to imagine this component being extended to do other things, such as getting information about a file (the `Stat` stub is in the IDL). The source code, samples, and documentation for PyXPCOM are located in the Mozilla tree at *mozilla/extensions/python*.

XPCOM as an Open Cross-Platform Solution

XPCOM can be an entire book in itself. This chapter has merely touched upon the role it plays in Mozilla application development. Understanding the basics of this framework is vital to understanding the very foundation of Mozilla's componentized architecture.

Although other component-based systems exist on various platforms—MSCOM for Microsoft or a CORBA system for GNOME, for example—if you want to write truly cross-platform component-based applications, then XPCOM is the best tool for the job. It can be deployed on any platform Mozilla is ported to, and can be scripted by using JavaScript or Python.

Above all, XPCOM is entirely open source, so there are no costs associated with it, no proprietary secrets in how it's put together, and you have various software licenses to choose from. Although XPCOM has become a solid framework, its developers are still making improvements and uncovering and fixing bugs. However, XPCOM offers tremendous flexibility as a software development framework and the Mozilla community is an excellent technical support resource for all technologies covered in this book.

CHAPTER 9

XUL Templates

XUL templates are dynamically generated XUL elements and groups of XUL elements. They are often used to render lists and tables that display mutable, frequently updated data, such as your Inbox, your list of bookmarks, and user profiles. A XUL template can be used to create something as simple as a list of menu items, as you will see here, but it can also be used in much more exciting ways, as shown at the end of this chapter. You should consider using a XUL template instead of XUL when you want to create an interface that displays data, such as a roster of names, when the set of data is very large, when the data may change frequently, or when you create a display that you want to use for different sets of data.

RDF, the format for data that goes into templates, is described in detail in Chapter 10. The actual data used to build the template examples is displayed in Examples 10-1 and 10-4. However, this chapter precedes the RDF chapter because templates are much easier to understand than RDF. Extending on the XUL programming done in Chapters 2 and 3, templates are a practical application of RDF data. They can also help you understand the abstract concepts introduced in Chapter 10.

Understanding XUL Templates

By defining special rules and applying them to data stored in RDF files, XUL templates build user interfaces dynamically. A XUL template consists of a set of special tags inside a XUL element—often `<listbox>`, `<menu>`, or `<tree>` elements that match data in an RDF datasource. A XUL template is defined in a regular XUL file and may appear anywhere regular XUL content can be placed.

The template defines rules for filling out the parent elements with the associated RDF data. Example 9-1 shows how to get a `<listbox>` in XUL to display RDF file contents. A template like this could display data stored in a RDF file that, because it's so long, complex, or ephemeral, shouldn't be hardcoded into XUL list elements. The data that comes from RDF and goes into a template should be anything that doesn't directly relate to the user interface.

Example 9-1. Simple XUL template in a listbox element

```
<?xml version="1.0"?>
<?xml-stylesheet href="chrome://global/skin" type="text/css"?>
<window
  xmlns="http://www.mozilla.org/keymaster/gatekeeper/there.is.only.xul">
  <listbox datasources="10-1.rdf" ref="urn:root" flex="1">
    <template>
      <rule>
        <conditions>
          <content uri="?jar"/>
          <triple subject="?jar"
                  predicate="http://xfly.mozdev.org/fly-rdf#types"
                  object="?types"/>
          <member container="?types" child="?type"/>
          <triple subject="?type"
                  predicate="http://xfly.mozdev.org/fly-rdf#name"
                  object="?name"/>
        </conditions>
        <action>
          <listitem uri="?type">
            <listcell label="?name"/>
          </listitem>
        </action>
      </rule>
    </template>
  </listbox>
</window>
```

Because the template is built to match the RDF data, different parts of the template in Example 9-1 correspond to parts of the RDF file used as the datasource. Obviously, you need to know about the data's organization—the "graph" created by the data—to build effective templates for it. However, once you create the rules, you can apply them to very large sets of data, which is one of the benefits of using templates in the interface.

As you can see in Example 9-1, rules typically comprise most of a template's definition. The next several sections break down Example 9-1 to help you understand the parts of a XUL template.

Basic template structure

Example 9-2 shows the template's basic structure. In this case, the data that meets the conditions defined in the `conditions` element is rendered by the XUL elements defined in the actions element, allowing the translation of RDF data into XUL elements.

Example 9-2. Basic structure of a XUL template

```
<listbox datasources="10-1.rdf" ref="urn:root">
  <template>
    <rule>
      <conditions>
```

Example 9-2. Basic structure of a XUL template (continued)

```
        ...
      </conditions>
      <action>
        ...
      </action>
    </rule>
  </template>
</listbox>
```

In the first lines of the XUL template, a <template> is defined within a <listbox> element, which is a simple container for templates in XUL:

```
XUL:
  <listbox datasources="10-1.rdf" ref="urn:root" flex="1">
RDF:
  <rdf:Description about="urn:root">
```

When it appears inside the <template>, the <listbox> tag has two special attributes. The datasources attribute specifies the RDF file's location. The ref attribute is the starting point in that RDF-based data for the template processing, which is equivalent to the about attribute of the root node in the actual RDF file. The ref attribute tells the template where to begin reading the data in the RDF file, and the about attribute in the RDF data file specifies where its own beginning is. In this case, the RDF and XUL starting point is the root of the data. Note that you do not need to define a template at the base of an RDF data file: an RDF file may have several avenues of information (e.g., different groups of bookmarks) and your template may render only one group or some portion of all of the RDF file data.

Template rule conditions

```
XUL:
  <template>
    <rule>
      <conditions>
RDF:
  <!-- no equivalent -->
```

The <template> and <rule> tags set up the template. The template's rule element defines conditions that must be met for the template to render the referenced data. A common condition in a template, for example, is that an element be of a particular type or have an attribute set to a certain value. The conditions in Example 9-2 render this content (*10-1.rdf*) if it defines a types property and gives individual child elements as types.

Applying template rules to a datasource drives the dynamic creation of the template-based UI. You can imagine a template going through data and selecting only the bits of data that match, based on matching rules, and then rendering that selected data into XUL (again based on rules defined in the template itself).

Generated values from the RDF are stored in variables that can be used throughout the template. They are represented by the values inside the attributes beginning with a ?. When you create variables in a template once, you can use them wherever you need them in the template. In Example 9-1, the *?type* variable is created as a child of types in the conditions block, is used again, and is then used a third time in the action block to describe the element that should be rendered in the template:

```
XUL:
  <content uri="?jar"/>
  <triple subject="?jar"
          predicate="http://xfly.mozdev.org/fly-rdf#types"
          object="?types"/>
RDF:
  ... about="urn:root" ...
  ... xmlns:fly="http://xfly.mozdev.org/fly-rdf#" ...
  </fly:types>
```

The `<content>` tag signifies the root of the template rule. The `uri` attribute value is automatically filled with `urn:root` from the listbox `ref` attribute, which originates from the RDF `about` attribute on the first resource. This value is now stored in the *?jar* variable. Assigning variables in a template for use elsewhere in the template is an essential part of template-building in XUL, as it is in programming languages that work with data.

A `<triple>` is a test on a subject and predicate. When triples match the subject and predicate in the RDF, their object value is produced. In this case, the container is the object result `?types`, which holds individual `?type` nodes. Each one of these is drawn as a `<listitem>`.

The `<member>` element initiates a loop-like effect. When the template builds, this effect exposes the container so it can read through all the objects and add them to the template. In essence, `?type` holds three different values throughout the template generation:*

```
XUL:
  <member container="?types" child="?type"/>
RDF:
  <fly:types>
    <rdf:Bag>
      <rdf:li>
        <rdf:Description ...
```

To finish the template conditions, one more `<triple>` correlates with the literal's value.

* An `rdf:Bag` is a type of RDF container, but when you use the `<member>` tag, you do not have to specify whether the container is of the type Alt, Bag, or Sequence (see "nsIRDFContainer" in Chapter 10 for more details on working with containers in RDF). A template can only build the values sequentially out of a container, no matter what type it is. Thus, using an `rdf:Seq` or `rdf:Alt` element produces the same visual output in these Mozilla templates.

```
XUL:
  <triple subject="?type"
          predicate="http://xfly.mozdev.org/fly-rdf#name"
          object="?name"/>
RDF:
  ... xmlns:fly="http://xfly.mozdev.org/fly-rdf#" ...
  <rdf:li>
    <rdf:Description fly:name="Horse"/>
```

Like ?type, ?name holds three different values during its lifetime, and "Horse" will be the first value generated from the RDF.

The <conditions> part of the template extracts the data from the RDF graph, as in our graphical examples. It makes the data available in variable-like objects; those objects can be used in the template's <action>, demonstrated in the next section.

Template rule actions

XUL elements that are used to build content from data matched by the template conditions are placed in the <action> element in a template rule. The <listbox> is the most popular way to display this data because all of its child elements fall neatly into place inside the template. However, you can use any XUL element that supports the type of tabular display required by the data (e.g., <tree>, <groupbox>, and <menu>).

```
<action>
  <listitem uri="?type">
    <listcell label="?name"/>
  </listitem>
</action>
```

For the RDF content to be displayed, it needs a parent/children team to define and fill in the values where needed. The parent, ?type, is used as a point of reference three times during its lifetime by objects directly in the container. The template generates ?name into the three literal children, as shown in Table 9-1.

Table 9-1. Output of each template iteration

Iteration	First child	Second child	Third child
?type	rdf:#$LtOki1	rdf:#$MtOki1	rdf:#$NtOki1
?name	"horse"	"house"	"fruit"

Directly inside the <action> element is the first XUL element that gets repeated, the <listitem>. This element must have the uri attribute with the container's object variable, which in Example 9-2 is *?type*. This variable establishes the root of the content—a point of reference in the template for any children below that point.

Once the container elements are matched to the <listitem>, ?name can be used in any attribute on any tag below it. In the previous example code, the <listcell> label shows the value of ?name. Interesting implementations can result from the use of variables to hold values for attributes like class, which is often used to define style rules for elements. This implementation is demonstrated in the section "Using Data for Style," later in this chapter

Example 9-3 shows what a generated template looks like as hardcoded XUL.

Example 9-3. Hardcoded representation of generated XUL

```
<?xml version="1.0"?>
<?xml-stylesheet href="chrome://global/skin" type="text/css"?>
<window
   xmlns="http://www.mozilla.org/keymaster/gatekeeper/there.is.only.xul">
  <listbox datasources="10-1.rdf" ref="urn:root" flex="1">
    <listitem id="rdf:#$mPgLw2">
      <listcell label="Horse"/>
    </listitem>
    <listitem id="rdf:#$nPgLw2">
      <listcell label="House"/>
    </listitem>
    <listitem id="rdf:#$oPgLw2">
      <listcell label="Fruit"/>
    </listitem>
  </listbox>
</window>
```

It's beneficial to see how this document is translated into a DOM tree using Mozilla's DOM Inspector tool, with which the structure is presented in a view that makes it easy to follow. Figure 9-1 shows how the template tree nodes are generated into an actual tree. To use this tool, select "DOM Inspector" from the Tools → Web Development menu in Mozilla. If you have the template displayed in an open browser window, you can load it in the DOM Inspector by selecting File → Inspect a Window and choosing it from the list.

In Figure 9-1, you can see how the <listitem> was generated three times from the template. Interestingly, the generated code doesn't replace the original template, but is appended to the <tree> as another tree row.

Finally, Figure 9-2 shows what the actual XUL file looks like when loaded. If you save the template in Example 9-1 to a file called *9-1.xul*, save the RDF data in Example 10-1 to a file called *10-1.rdf* (which the template looks for by name in the same directory), and then load the template into the browser, you ought to see something very similar.

Enhancing XUL Templates

Creating simple XUL templates can help familiarize you with the flexibility and complex design issues of a template. The RDF file created in Example 9-4 introduces the concept of nested content. A <listbox> can generate nested content from multiple containers in the RDF datasource. These multiple containers must have the same basic design to work properly, so the design must be abstracted to apply to all datasources. Example 9-5 uses the <fly:list> design to accomplish this task.

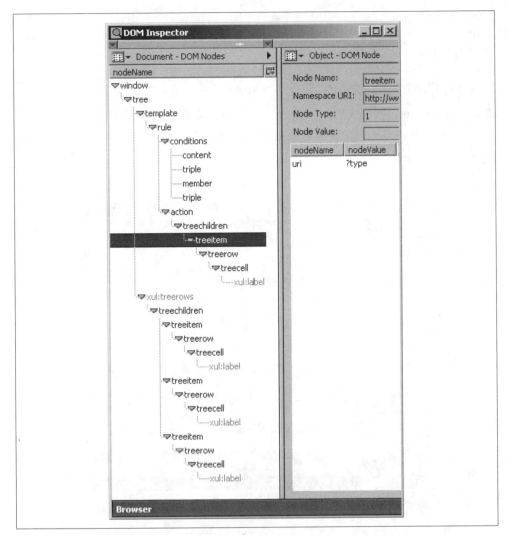

Figure 9-1. DOM representation of XUL template generation

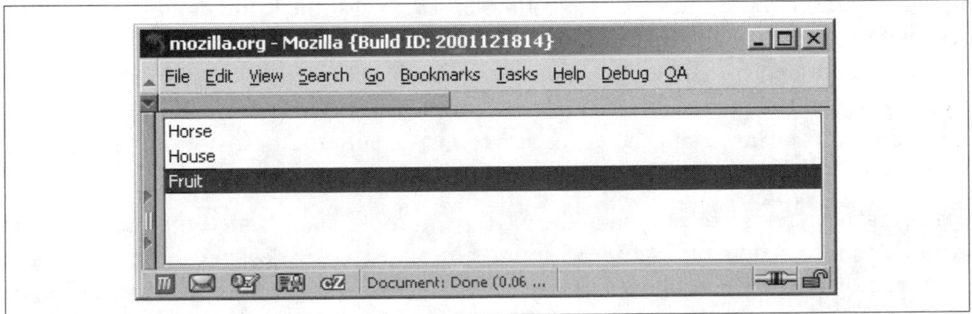

Figure 9-2. View of XUL tree in Mozilla

The advantage of having nested content in XUL templates is that you can organize items visually, even when those things come from different sources. Nested content allows you to form subtrees and submenus rather than long monolithic lists.

Nested Content Sample

The window in Figure 9-3 represents a template with nested data and styled elements. Note that the top of the content area has a standard <listbox> and a color-styled <tree> is on the bottom. The next several sections describe the creation of the XUL file in Figure 9-3.

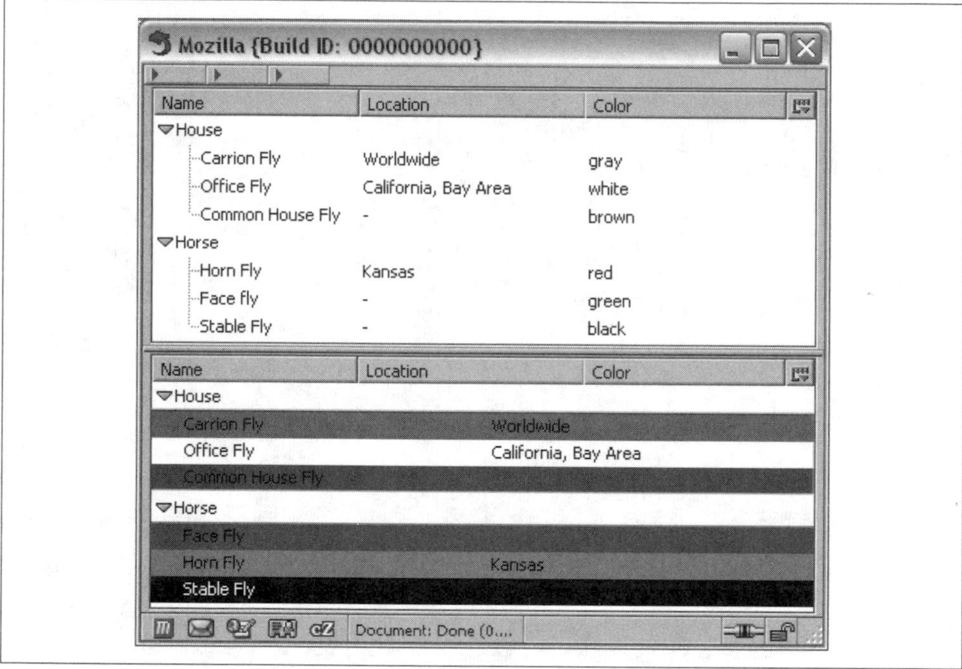

Figure 9-3. Listbox and tree template

In this example, both the <tree> and the <listbox> use the same data, but different template formats. Only two columns appear in the <listbox>, for example, and the rows were created to display the color of the data's color attribute. You could as easily have styled the <tree> this way and left the <listbox> as a regular list. To display large amounts of raw data, however, <tree> is usually the best option because it's faster with big datasets, offers built-in sorting, and looks cleaner.

The <listbox> template can make the XUL seem more complicated than the content would seem to require in Figure 9-3, but a template's basic design can be similar for all types of data, which allows you to write once and apply templates to different datasets. In this case, you gain more efficiency because the RDF contributes more to the template generation than does the XUL, making template-based applications data-driven.

Example 9-4 contains the XUL for producing the tree shown in Figure 9-3. The difference between the code in Examples 9-2 and 9-9 is minimal, but the latter produces a much more impressive visual result. Remember that a XUL template and RDF produce the content you see when loading these listbox examples. No stylesheets or other enhancements are needed.

Example 9-4. XUL tree template in Figure 9-3

```
<listbox datasources="10-4.rdf" ref="urn:root" flex="1"
      containment="http://xfly.mozdev.org/fly-rdf#list">
  <template>
    <rule>
      <conditions>
        <content uri="?uri"/>
        <triple subject="?uri"
                predicate="http://xfly.mozdev.org/fly-rdf#list"
                  object="?list"/>
        <member container="?list" child="?listitem"/>
        <triple subject="?listitem"
                predicate="http://xfly.mozdev.org/fly-rdf#label"
                  object="?label"/>
      </conditions>
      <bindings>
        <binding subject="?listitem"
                predicate="http://xfly.mozdev.org/fly-rdf#color"
                 object="?color"/>
        <binding subject="?listitem"
                predicate="fly-location#location"
                object="?location"/>
      </bindings>
      <action>
        <listitem uri="?listitem" class="?color">
          <listcell label="?label" class="treecell-indent"/>
          <listcell label="?location" class="treecell-indent"/>
        </listitem>
      </action>
    </rule>
  </template>
  <listcols>
    <listcol flex="1"/>
    <listcol flex="1"/>
  </listcols>
</listbox>
```

The biggest difference between Example 9-4 and earlier examples is the `<bindings>` section. All matching in a binding element is optional, unlike the condition content. The elements in the bindings are simply optional triples. Placing these triples in a binding affords you some flexibility when data is missing from the RDF file or when you are not certain about its contents—such as when you create a roster but don't have all the people's addresses.

The `containment` attribute on the tree specifies the URI of all the containers. In this case, the container is the `<fly:list>` tag in the RDF. To see how such a complex-looking `<listbox>` can be generated from so little XUL, look at how the containers are set up in the RDF. The RDF file appears (in a reformatted and somewhat simplified form) in Example 9-5. This simplified form can help you see the structure underlying the data and how it is reused to order the data efficiently.

Example 9-5. Simplified version of 10-4 RDF data

```
<rdf:Description about="urn:root">
  <fly:list>
    <rdf:Seq>
      <rdf:li>
        <rdf:Description ID="House">
          <fly:label>House</fly:label>
          <fly:list>
            <rdf:Seq>
              <rdf:li>
                <rdf:Description about="musca_autumnalis"
                                 fly:label="Face Fly"/>
              </rdf:li>
            <rdf:Seq>
          </fly:list>
      </rdf:li>
    </rdf:Seq>
  </fly:list>
</rdf:Description>
```

The RDF data in Example 9-5 demonstrates a two-level pattern of recursion: `fly:list/fly:label` are both reused at different levels in the RDF data. The template in Example 9-4 generates the data into a tree showing two levels, as shown in Figure 9-3.

Example 9-5 clearly shows that only `fly:list` and `fly:label` are needed to generate the template. The other data, such as color, are not mandatory because they are defined in a `<binding>` rather than a `<triple>`.

Using Data for Style

RDF data are used for more than containers and labels. It's possible to use RDF to define CSS classes, XUL attributes, and other arbitrary bits of XUL content. In Example 9-4, the `<listitem>` has a `class` attribute that is filled by `?color`:

```
<listitem uri="?listitem" class="?color">
  <treecell label="?label"/>
  <treecell label="?location"/>
</listitem>
```

If a stylesheet has class definitions for the same values located in the RDF, then every generated row can have its own style. Here is a simple class showing style rules defined for items of the "green" class.

```
.green
{
  background-color: green;
}
```

As shown in the earlier examples of this chapter, using `<listbox>` with templates generally yields flexible and simpler implementations. Trees, covered next, are not as flexible, but they can be better for raw data display, as when you have spreadsheet-like information, many columns, or other data that can be sorted.

Tree Template

`<tree>` is the best choice for displaying simple data with better visual speed, automatic sorting, and column selection capabilities. In contrast to listboxes, trees do not create a full DOM representation data when the template generates. Instead, a tree keeps data in its own database and updates its display more quickly than a listbox when the user scrolls or sorts.

The XUL tree in Example 9-6 can be compared to the `listbox` XUL in Example 9-4. The template design is almost exactly the same in both examples, but the elements surrounding the template in the tree—`treebody`, `treecol`, and `treecells`—are more complex and allow a precise layout by giving you more granular control over the parts of the layout. These parts include the header, the columns, and the parent-child relationships. XUL's parent element affects the presentation of the template-based data.

Example 9-6. Tree template code of Figure 9-3

```
<tree datasources="10-4.rdf" flex="1" ref="urn:root"
      containment="http://xfly.mozdev.org/fly-rdf#list">
  <treecols>
    <treecol id="LabelCol" flex="1" sort="?label" label="Name"
             primary="true" />
    <treecol id="LoCol" flex="1" sort="?location" label="Location"/>
    <treecol id="ColCol" flex="1" sort="?color" label="Color"/>
  </treecols>
  <template>
    <rule>
      <conditions>
        <content uri="?uri"/>
        <triple subject="?uri"
                predicate="http://xfly.mozdev.org/fly-rdf#list"
                object="?list"/>
        <member container="?list" child="?listitem"/>
        <triple subject="?listitem"
                predicate="http://xfly.mozdev.org/fly-rdf#label"
                object="?label"/>
      </conditions>
      <bindings>
        <binding subject="?listitem"
```

Example 9-6. Tree template code of Figure 9-3 (continued)

```
                    predicate="http://xfly.mozdev.org/fly-rdf#color"
                    object="?color"/>
          <binding subject="?listitem"
                    predicate=" http://xfly.mozdev.org/fly-rdf#location"
                    object="?location"/>
        </bindings>
        <action>
          <treechildren>
            <treeitem uri="?listitem">
              <treerow>
                <treecell ref="LabelCol"  label="?label"/>
                <treecell ref="LoCol" label="?location"/>
                <treecell ref="ColCol" label="?color"/>
              </treerow>
            </treeitem>
          </treechildren>
        </action>
      </rule>
    </template>
  </tree>
```

One major difference between this example and earlier ones is that Example 9-6 has three columns. The color data cannot be used for style in this tree scenario because trees do not support CSS data styling.

All generated data can be sorted automatically by clicking on the column headers. Besides the tree parent element in the XUL, the other main difference between this template and the one used with a listbox in Example 9-4 is the structure directly beneath `<conditions>`, where `<content>` is replaced by `<treerow>`.

Multiple Rules Tree

In Example 9-6, empty cells were left blank. Sometimes situations demand that missing data be represented by something other than whitespace, such as a special character or marker. Fortunately, multiple `<rule>` tags can exist in a template, as shown in Example 9-7. Alternate rule tags allow the display of missing data with other, more general rules. Using alternate tags, you can set up templates that look like conditional blocks; if the first rule is not satisfied, then the second rule is tried, followed by the third, and so on. Example 9-7 shows this structure of multiple rules.

Example 9-7. Tree template with rules

```
<tree datasources="10-4.rdf" flex="1" ref="urn:root"
      containment="http://xfly.mozdev.org/fly-rdf#list">
  <treecols>
    <treecol id="LabelCol" flex="1" sort="?label" label="Name"
             primary="true" />
    <treecol id="LoCol" flex="1" sort="?location" label="Location"/>
    <treecol id="ColCol" flex="1" sort="?color" label="Color"/>
```

Example 9-7. Tree template with rules (continued)

```
</treecols>
<template>
  <!-- RULE 1: Row contains both a color and location. -->
  <rule>
    <conditions>
      <content uri="?uri"/>
      <triple subject="?uri"
              predicate="http://xfly.mozdev.org/fly-rdf#list"
              object="?list"/>
      <member container="?list" child="?listitem"/>
      <triple subject="?listitem"
              predicate="http://xfly.mozdev.org/fly-rdf#label"
              object="?label"/>
      <triple subject="?listitem"
              predicate="http://xfly.mozdev.org/fly-rdf#color"
              object="?color"/>
      <triple subject="?listitem"
              predicate=" http://xfly.mozdev.org/fly-rdf#location"
              object="?location"/>
    </conditions>
    <action>
      <treechildren>
        <treeitem uri="?listitem">
          <treerow>
            <treecell ref="LabelCol" label="?label"/>
            <treecell ref="LoCol" label="?location"/>
            <treecell ref="ColCol" label="?color"/>
          </treerow>
        </treeitem>
      </treechildren>
    </action>
  </rule>
  <!-- RULE 2: Row contains a color and no location. -->
  <rule>
    <conditions>
      <content uri="?uri"/>
      <triple subject="?uri"
              predicate="http://xfly.mozdev.org/fly-rdf#list"
              object="?list"/>
      <member container="?list" child="?listitem"/>
      <triple subject="?listitem"
              predicate="http://xfly.mozdev.org/fly-rdf#label"
              object="?label"/>
      <triple subject="?listitem"
              predicate="http://xfly.mozdev.org/fly-rdf#color"
              object="?color"/>
    </conditions>
    <action>
      <treechildren>
        <treeitem uri="?listitem">
          <treerow>
            <treecell ref="LabelCol" label="?label"/>
```

Example 9-7. Tree template with rules (continued)

```
              <treecell ref="LoCol" label="-"/>
              <treecell ref="ColCol" label="?color"/>
            </treerow>
          </treeitem>
        </treechildren>
      </action>
    </rule>
    <!-- RULE 3: Row contains neither a color or location. -->
    <rule>
      <conditions>
        <content uri="?uri"/>
        <triple subject="?uri"
                predicate="http://xfly.mozdev.org/fly-rdf#list"
                object="?list"/>
        <member container="?list" child="?listitem"/>
        <triple subject="?listitem"
                predicate="http://xfly.mozdev.org/fly-rdf#label"
                object="?label"/>
      </conditions>
      <action>
        <treechildren>
          <treeitem uri="?listitem">
            <treerow>
              <treecell ref="LabelCol" label="?label"/>
              <treecell ref="LoCol" label=" "/>
              <treecell ref="ColCol" label=" "/>
            </treerow>
          </treeitem>
        </treechildren>
      </action>
    </rule>
  </template>
</tree>
```

In contrast to Example 9-6, Example 9-7 moves `?location` from `<bindings>` to `<conditions>` in the first `<rule>` in the template, making it a required match. To avoid breaking the template—because not all objects in the RDF file have a `?location` value—you need to make a backup plan for generating this template when it encounters an object without a `?location`. This backup can be a second set of more broadly defined conditions, so that objects that "fall out" of the first condition are picked up by the next. See the next section for an example of using different sets of rules.

The most important additions to Example 9-7 are the `container="?uri" member="?listitem"` attributes on the `<template>`. These attributes specify which container you should apply multiple rules to, and the `member` is for the objects in a container that must be checked. Adding these attributes keeps the template from dying when the data doesn't meet the first rule. The second rule, which doesn't have a `<triple>` or `<binding>` to identify it, is used only when a `?location` isn't present. Instead, it automatically fills in that cell with a hyphen (Figure 9-4).

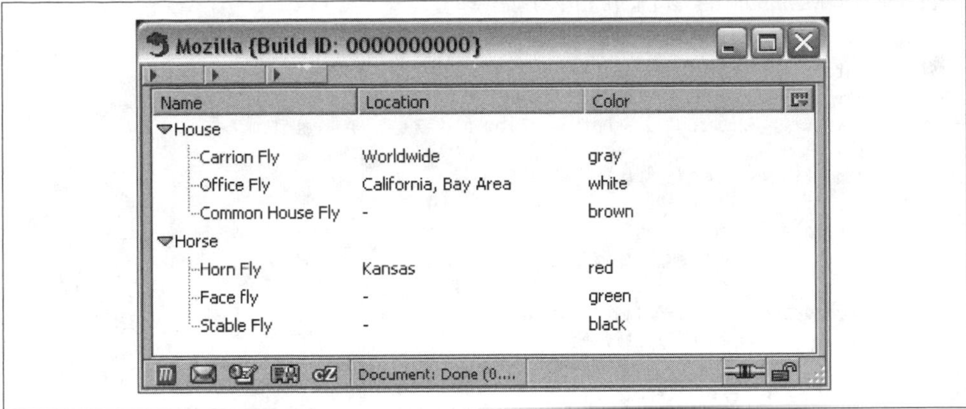

Figure 9-4. Tree template with hyphen rule

As you can see at the top of Example 9-7, the template datasource is a file called *10-4.rdf*, which contains all the data listed in Example 10-4 (in the next chapter). If you save the template listed in Example 9-7 and the RDF listed in Example 10-4, you can display the tree shown in Figure 9-4.

Multiple Rules Menubar

Example 9-7 is a `<tree>` template that contains three rules. In Example 9-8, where a `<menubar>` is shown with three rules, all possible menu scenarios must be covered. Table 9-2 provides a list of these scenarios. Use scenarios like this to make sure you have content that can be created for all the data you need represented.

Table 9-2. Scenarios used for building template rules

Scenario	Description
Scenario 1	A `<menu>` has a `label` and contains a `<menupopup>`. Inside it are two `<menuitem>`s: `?location` and `?color`. The Horn Fly, Carrion Fly, and Office Fly fall into this category.
Scenario 2	A `<menu>` has a `label` and contains a `<menupopup>`. Inside it is one `<menuitem>`: `?color`. The Common House Fly, Stable Fly, and Face Fly fall into this category.
Scenario 3	A `<menu>` has a `label` and contains a `<menupopup>`. Inside there is no `<menuitem>` (only `<menus>`). Horse and House fall into this category.

The scenarios in Table 9-2 can be translated directly into three template rules. Scenario 1 would be the first rule because it uses the most content. Scenario 2 would be the second rule because it's missing only the location. Scenario 3 will be the final rule because it doesn't have a location or color.

Example 9-8. Menubar template with three rules

```
<menubar datasources="10-4.rdf" ref="urn:root"
    containment="http://xfly.mozdev.org/fly-rdf#list">
<template>
  <!-- RULE 1: Menu contains both a color and location menuitem. -->
  <rule>
    <conditions>
      <content uri="?uri"/>
      <triple subject="?uri"
              predicate="http://xfly.mozdev.org/fly-rdf#list"
              object="?list"/>
      <member container="?list" child="?listitem"/>
      <triple subject="?listitem"
              predicate="http://xfly.mozdev.org/fly-rdf#label"
              object="?label"/>
      <triple subject="?listitem"
              predicate="http://xfly.mozdev.org/fly-rdf#color"
              object="?color"/>
      <triple subject="?listitem"
              predicate="fly-location#location"
              object="?location"/>
    </conditions>
    <action>
      <menu label="?label" uri="?listitem">
        <menupopup uri="?listitem">
          <menuitem label="?color"/>
          <menuitem label="?location"/>
        </menupopup>
      </menu>
    </action>
  </rule>
  <!-- RULE 2: Menu contains only a color menuitem. -->
  <rule>
    <conditions>
      <content uri="?uri"/>
      <triple subject="?uri"
              predicate="http://xfly.mozdev.org/fly-rdf#list"
              object="?list"/>
      <member container="?list" child="?listitem"/>
      <triple subject="?listitem"
              predicate="http://xfly.mozdev.org/fly-rdf#label"
              object="?label"/>
      <triple subject="?listitem"
              predicate="http://xfly.mozdev.org/fly-rdf#color"
              object="?color"/>
    </conditions>
    <action>
      <menu label="?label" uri="?listitem">
        <menupopup uri="?listitem">
          <menuitem label="?color"/>
        </menupopup>
      </menu>
    </action>
```

Example 9-8. Menubar template with three rules (continued)

```
    </rule>
    <!-- RULE 3: Menu contains no color or location menuitems. -->
    <!-- This applies to the main menus, shown on the menubar. -->
    <rule>
      <conditions>
        <content uri="?uri"/>
        <triple subject="?uri"
                predicate="http://xfly.mozdev.org/fly-rdf#list"
                object="?list"/>
        <member container="?list" child="?listitem"/>
        <triple subject="?listitem"
                predicate="http://xfly.mozdev.org/fly-rdf#label"
                object="?label"/>
      </conditions>
      <action>
        <!-- Create the menus across the menubar -->
        <menu label="?label" uri="?listitem">
          <!-- Give the menu the ability to popup content -->
          <menupopup uri="?listitem"/>
        </menu>
      </action>
    </rule>
  </template>
</menubar>
```

As you can see, Example 9-8 is a long XUL section. When you create the first rule, it becomes easier, though, because the subsequent rules are just versions of the rules above them. Figure 9-5 shows how this `<menubar>` template draws the data in the *9-5.rdf* datasource.

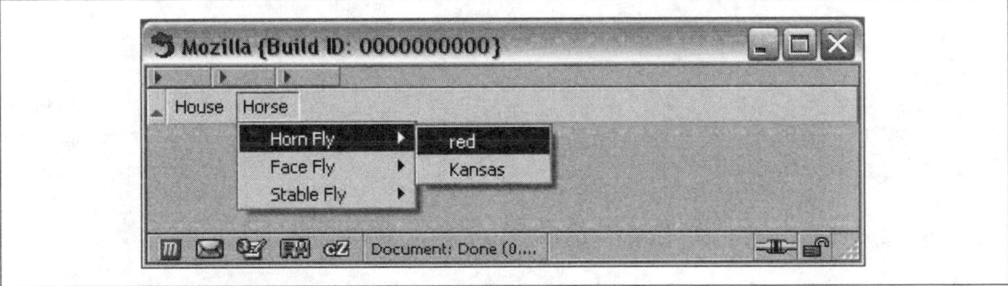

Figure 9-5. Menubar template with menus

Using Other XUL Tags for Templates

Almost any XUL element that can be used as a container can use a template to define its inner content. Example 9-9 shows a `<box>` used as the start for a XUL template. Templates like this can create content that doesn't look as tabular or ordered.

Example 9-9. Template implemented in a box with buttons as content

```
<box datasources="10-4.rdf" ref="urn:root"          containment="http://xfly.mozdev.org/
     fly-rdf#list">
  <template>
    <rule>
      <conditions>
        <content uri="?uri"/>
        <triple subject="?uri"
                  predicate="http://xfly.mozdev.org/fly-rdf#list"
                    object="?list"/>
        <member container="?list" child="?listitem"/>
        <triple subject="?listitem"
                  predicate="http://xfly.mozdev.org/fly-rdf#label"
                    object="?label"/>
      </conditions>
      <bindings>
        <binding subject="?listitem"
                   predicate="http://xfly.mozdev.org/fly-rdf#color"
                     object="?color"/>
        <binding subject="?listitem"
                   predicate="fly-location#location"
                     object="?location"/>
      </bindings>
      <action>
          <vbox uri="?listitem">
            <button label="?label"/>
            <button label="?location"/>
            <button label="?color"/>
            <splitter/>
          </vbox>
      </action>
    </rule>
  </template>
</box>
```

The content generated in Example 9-9 includes three `<button>`s and a `<splitter>` inside a vertical `<box>`. The template building process is repeated for every object in the RDF graph, and some buttons are left blank. The result is a window full of buttons for each piece of data, which may get you started making heads-up displays or panel-like applications for templates, such as flight simulators.

Once you understand the basics of templates, it is fun to see what kind of XUL you can generate from it, such as games that need to render content on the fly, spreadsheets, database front ends, or other data-driven application user interfaces.

CHAPTER 10

RDF, RDF Tools, and the Content Model

Chapter 9 introduced the Resource Description Framework (RDF) as the basis for building display data in the interface, where XUL templates take RDF-based data and transform it into regular widgets. But RDF is used in many other more subtle ways in Mozilla. In fact, it is the technology Mozilla uses for much of its own internal data handling and manipulation.

RDF is, as its name suggests, a framework for integrating many types of data that go into the browser, including bookmarks, mail messages, user profiles, IRC channels, new Mozilla applications, and your collection of sidebar tabs. All these items are sets of data that RDF represents and incorporates into the browser consistently. RDF is used prolifically in Mozilla, which is why this chapter is so dense.

This chapter introduces RDF, provides some detail about how Mozilla uses RDF for its own purposes, and describes the RDF tools that are available on the Mozilla platform. The chapter includes information on special JavaScript libraries that make RDF processing much easier, and on the use of RDF in manifests to represent JAR file contents and cross-platform installation archives to Mozilla.

Once you understand the concepts in this chapter, you can make better use of data and metadata in your own application development.

RDF Basics

RDF has two parts: the *RDF Data Model* and the *RDF Syntax* (or Grammar). The RDF Data Model is a graph with nodes and arcs, much like other data graphs. More specifically, it's a *labeled-directed* graph. All nodes and arcs have some type of label (i.e., an identifier) on them, and arcs point only in one direction.

The RDF Syntax determines how the RDF Data Model is represented, typically as a special kind of XML. Most XML specifications define data in a tree-like model, such as XUL and XBL. But the RDF Data Model cannot be represented in a true tree-like structure, so the RDF/XML syntax includes properties that allow you to represent the same data in more than one way: elements can appear in different orders but mean the same thing, the same data can be represented as a child element or as a parent attribute, and data have indirect meanings. The meaning is not inherent in the structure of the RDF/XML itself; only the relationships are inherent. Thus, an RDF processor must make sense of the represented RDF data. Fortunately, an excellent RDF processor is integrated into Mozilla.

RDF Data Model

Three different types of RDF objects are the basis for all other RDF concepts: *resources*, *properties*, and *statements*. Resources are any type of data described by RDF. Just as an English sentence is comprised of subjects and objects, the resources described in RDF are typically subjects and objects of RDF statements. Consider this example:

> Eric wrote a book.

Eric is the subject of this statement, and would probably be an RDF resource in an RDF statement. *A book*, the object, might also be a resource because it represents something about which we might want to say more in RDF—for example, the book is a computer book or the book sells for twenty dollars. A property is a characteristic of a resource and might have a relationship to other resources. In the example, the book was written by Eric. In the context of RDF, *wrote* is a property of the *Eric* resource. An RDF statement is a resource, a property, and another resource grouped together. Our example, made into an RDF statement, might look like this:

> (Eric) wrote (a book)

Joining RDF statements makes an entire RDF graph.

We are describing the RDF data model here, not the RDF syntax. The RDF syntax uses XML to describe RDF statements and the relationship of resources.

As mentioned in the introduction, the RDF content model is a *labeled-directed* graph, which means that all relationships expressed in the graph are unidirectional, as displayed in Figure 10-1.

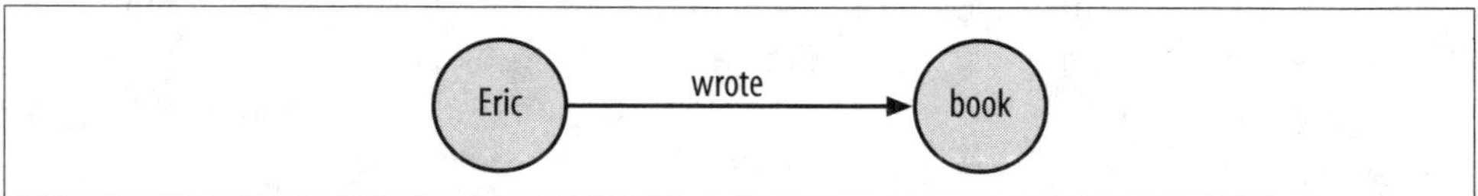

Figure 10-1. Simple labeled-directed graph

A resource can contain either a URI or a literal. The root resource might have a URI, for example, from which all other resources in the graph descend. The RDF processor continues from the root resource along its properties to other resources in the graph until it runs out of properties to traverse. RDF processing terminates at a literal, which is just what it sounds like: something that stands only for itself, generally represented by a string (e.g., "book," if there were no more information about the book in the graph). A literal resource contains only non-RDF data. A literal is a terminal point in the RDF graph.

For a resource to be labeled, it must be addressed through a universal resource identifier (URI). This address must be a unique string that designates what the resource is. In practice, most resources don't have identifiers because they are not nodes on the RDF graph that are meant to be accessed through a URI. Figure 10-2 is a modified version of Figure 10-1 that shows *Eric* as a resource identifier and *book* as a literal.

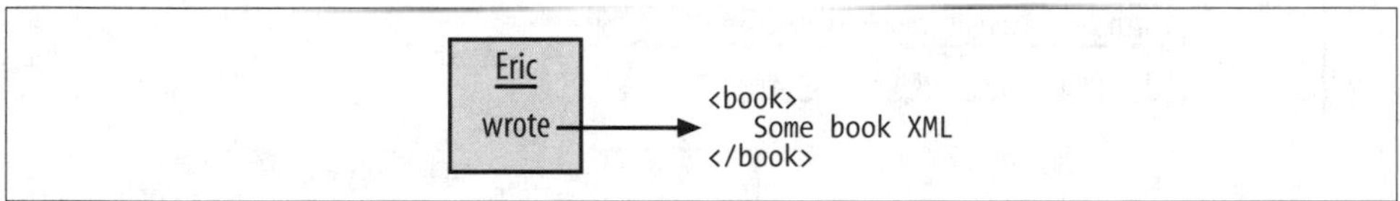

Figure 10-2. Resource to literal relationship

Resources can have any number of properties, which themselves differ. In Figure 10-2, *wrote* is a property of *Eric*. However, resources can also have multiple properties, as shown in Figure 10-3.

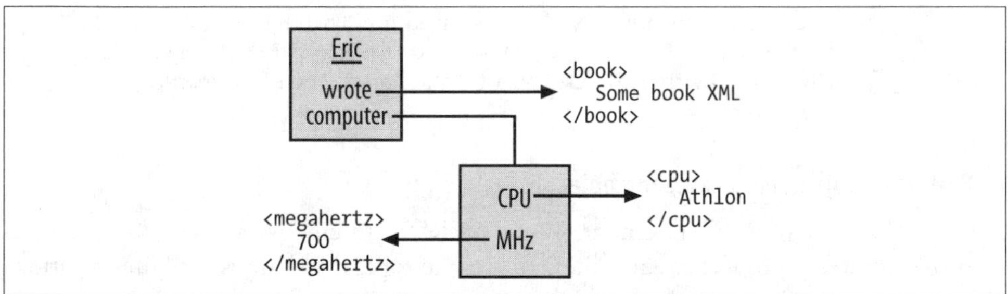

Figure 10-3. RDF Graph with five nodes

The RDF graph in Figure 10-3 has five nodes, two resources, and three literals. If this graph were represented in XML, it would probably have three different XML namespaces inside of it: RDF/XML, a *book* XML specification, and a *computer* XML specification. In English, the graph in Figure 10-3 might be expressed as follows:

> Eric wrote a book of unknown information. Eric's computer is 700 MHz and has an Athlon CPU.

Note that if Eric wrote a poem and a book, it would be possible to have two *wrote* properties for the same resource. Using the same property to point to separate resources is confusing, however. Instead, RDF containers (see the section "RDF containers," later in this chapter) are the best way to organize data that would otherwise need a single property to branch in this way.

RDF URIs relating to namespaces

The URIs used in RDF can be part of the element namespace. (See "The XUL Namespace" in Chapter 2 and in "Namespaces and XBL" in Chapter 7 for more information about XML namespaces.) This use is especially true for properties. Some namespaces can be created from previous examples:

```
xmlns:rdf="http://www.w3.org/1999/02/22-rdf-syntax-ns#"
xmlns:book="http://www.oreilly.com/rdf#"
xmlns:comp="my.computer.hardware#"
```

When you use namespaces, the graph looks much different, as shown in Figure 10-4.

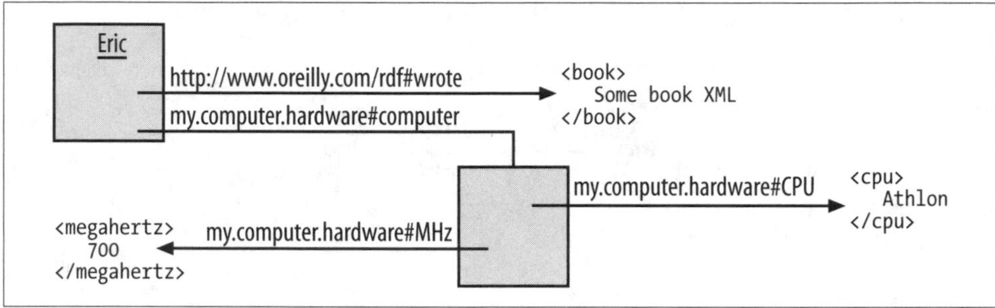

Figure 10-4. Namespaces applied to Figure 10-3

The resource identifier is often displayed in a URL format too, but it shouldn't use the same namespace URL as the RDF/XML file. The URL typically tries to describe a unique object, such as *http://my.jar-of-flies.com*.

RDF triples: subject, predicate, and object

A triple is a type of RDF statement. While an RDF statement can be a loose collection of resources, properties, and literals, a triple typically defines a tighter relationship between such elements.

The first part of a triple is the *subject*. This part is the resource described by the triple. The second part of the triple is the *predicate*. This part is a subject's property, a thing that joins it with something else. The third part is the *object*, which is either a resource or a literal.

RDF triples are significant because their stricter semantics guarantee the relationship between parts. A triple is a more formal version of the RDF statement, which is used more broadly. In Figure 10-4, all statements are formally subject → predicate → object, so those statements are triples.

RDF data model terminology

When reading RDF specifications, documentation, examples, and other related material on the Internet, you can encounter a dizzying array of terms that mean the same thing. Table 10-1 should help clarify these different terms. The italicized versions of the synonyms all do not technically mean the same thing, but are loose synonyms whose meanings depend on the context in which they are used.

Table 10-1. Synonyms in RDF

Common term	Synonyms
Resource	Subject, object
Resource identifier	Name, (resource) URI, ID, identifier, URL, label
Properties	Attributes
Statement	Triple, tuple, binding, assertion
Subject	Source, resource, node, root
Predicate	Arc, (statement) URI, property, atom
Object	Value, resource, node, literal

RDF Syntax

Mozilla uses XML to represent RDF data. In 1999, the W3C defined the RDF/XML specification syntax to make it the most common way RDF is used. The RDF/XML format is sometimes called the RDF serialization syntax because it allows RDF models to be sent easily from one computer application to another in a common XML format.

When an application reads an RDF file, the Mozilla RDF processor builds a graphical interpretation in-memory. In this section, you learn how to build an RDF file from scratch and see what the graph looks like after running through Mozilla's RDF processor.

RDF:RDF is a common namespace representation of RDF/XML data and is the one most frequently used in Mozilla files. However, it can be hard to read, so this chapter uses `rdf:RDF`. The W3C also used `rdf:RDF` in the RDF recommendation document.

Examining a simple RDF file

We begin with an example of an RDF file whose basic layout and simple syntax can be a model for the more advanced data introduced later. The RDF file shown in Example 10-1 is a list of three types of "flies," with the context of those "flies" inside a "jar." Example 10-1 also contains a namespace that defines these types of flies and shows the `rdf` and `fly` XML intertwined.

Example 10-1. Simple RDF file with "fly" namespace

```
<?xml version="1.0"?>
<rdf:RDF
   xmlns:rdf="http://www.w3.org/1999/02/22-rdf-syntax-ns#"
```

Example 10-1. Simple RDF file with "fly" namespace (continued)

```
    xmlns:fly="http://xfly.mozdev.org/fly-rdf#">
  <rdf:Description about="http://my.jar-of-flies.com">
    <fly:types>
      <rdf:Bag>
        <rdf:li>
          <rdf:Description fly:name="Horse"/>
        </rdf:li>
        <rdf:li>
          <rdf:Description fly:name="House"/>
        </rdf:li>
        <rdf:li>
          <rdf:Description fly:name="Fruit"/>
        </rdf:li>
      </rdf:Bag>
    </fly:types>
  </rdf:Description>
</rdf:RDF>
```

`<rdf:Description>` is the tag used to outline a resource. Example 10-1 shows how the `about` attribute references the resource identifier and makes this resource unique in the document. Two resources cannot have the same `about` value in a document, just as tags cannot share an `id` in an XML document. Both attributes guarantee the unique nature of each element and relationship.

```
<rdf:Description about="http://my.jar-of-flies.com">
  <fly:types>
    <rdf:Bag>
```

`http://my.jar-of-flies.com`, is the subject shown in the previous code snippet. *My jar of flies* is a resource definition and defines only what *flies* are inside of the statement. The predicate, which addresses a property in the resource, is defined by the tag `<types>` (of the `http://xfly.mozdev.org/fly-rdf#` namespace).

The final part of the statement, the object, is the actual data of the predicate and a container of type bag. The container is an RDF resource that "holds," or points to, a collection of other resources. In the next section, container types are discussed in depth. Figure 10-5 illustrates how the triple originates from the root subject and includes the container object.

In this case, an RDF statement is extracted from the example, but no useful data is reached. Little can be done with an empty RDF container, and two more steps are needed to reach literals that contain names of the flies.

RDF containers

Containers are a list of resources or literals. They are a form of RDF resource. There are three different container types: `bag`, `sequence`, and `alternative`. `Bag` is an unordered list of items, whereas `sequence` is an ordered list of items. They both allow duplicate values. `Alternative` is a list of values that could replace a particular property in a resource. `Sequence` is the most popular container for use in Mozilla

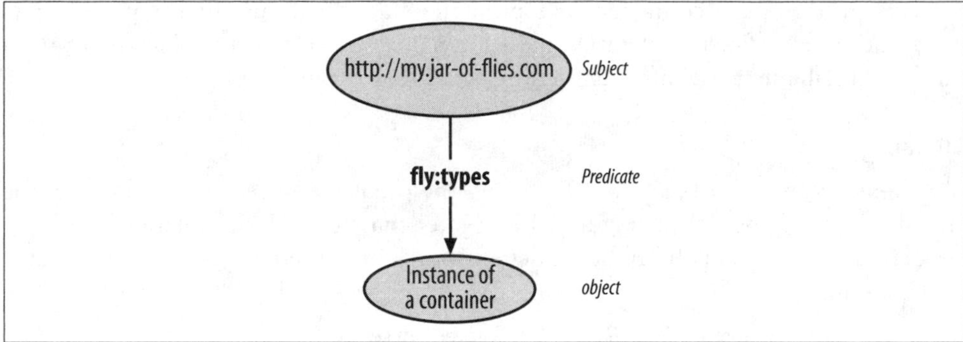

Figure 10-5. The first statement of the graph, with labeled parts

applications because it frequently uses ordered lists of data. A container's graphical definition is an entire separate statement about its type and the items it contains. In Figure 10-6, you can see the type of the container defined in the RDF statement with the property `rdf:type`. The remaining properties are the container's items.

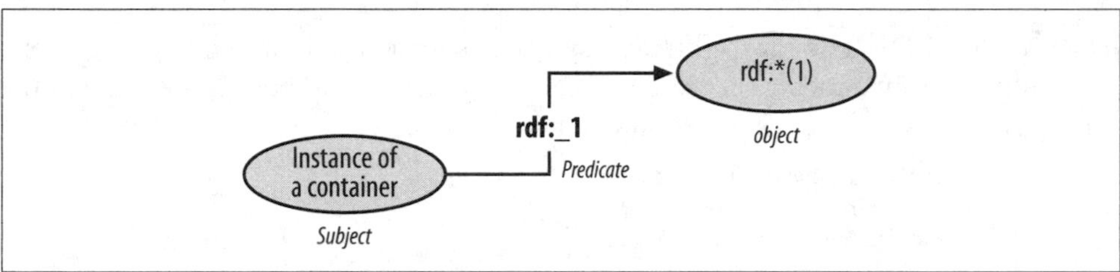

Figure 10-6. The second statement of the graph, with labeled parts

Once the container is defined, you can examine its collection of elements. At this point in the RDF code, direct comparisons can again be made from the code to the graph:

```
<rdf:Bag>
  <rdf:li>
    <rdf:Description ...
```

Here, the `<rdf:li>` tag is similar to the `<li>` tag in HTML, which stands for "list item." Moving from code to graph, the new representation is shown in Figure 10-6.

In Figure 10-6, the subject is the instance of the container. This statement does not begin from `rdf:Bag` because that resource is only a type definition. The actual items in the container originate from the instance created in memory by any RDF processor, including Mozilla's.

Mozilla's RDF processor fills in the `rdf:*(1)` of the resource identifier in Figure 10-6 with a hashed value. The same is true for the container's resource identifier. The actual values come out as something like `rdf:#$omhkm1`, though the values change each time the RDF document is loaded.

Objects inside of the container have properties identified automatically as `rdf:_1`, `rdf:_2`, etc., as defined by the RDF model specification. However, RDF applications such as Mozilla may use different identifiers to differentiate list objects.

Literals

The final statement in Example 10-1 allows the predicate to reach the text data, the literal "horse" shown in Figure 10-7. Note that the `about` reference on the `Description` is fictitious RDF, but it demonstrates the difference between a resource and a literal.

```
<rdf:Description about="rdf:*(1)" fly:name="Horse"/>
```

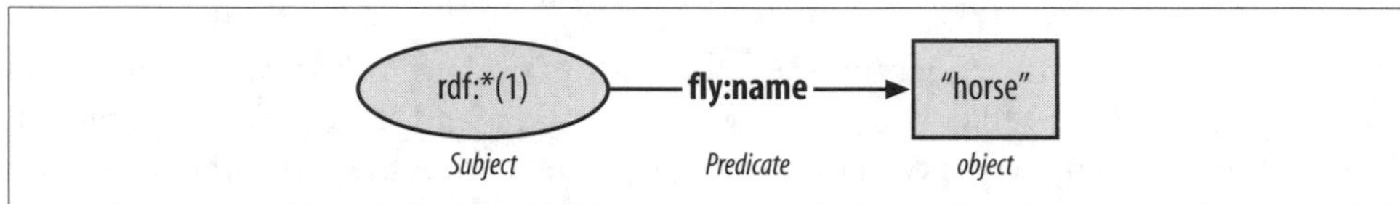

Figure 10-7. The third statement of the graph, with labeled parts

The previous RDF code for the literal is syntactic shorthand. Using this type of shortcut can make RDF much easier to read. The previous code snippet is the same as the longer and more cumbersome one shown here:

```
<rdf:Description about="rdf:*(1)">
  <fly:name>Horse</fly:name>
</rdf:Description>
```

The shorthand version of this statement can be useful when you have a lot of data or when you want to use one syntax to show all relationships in the graph.

The RDF syntax and RDF graphs

Figure 10-8 shows the entire RDF graph for the RDF file in Example 10-1. This graph was compiled by combining the concepts you've seen in Figures 10-5 through 10-7.

As you can see, the statements fit together quite nicely. Four resources originate from the container, and one is the container type definition. The other two properties are numbered according to their order in the RDF file.

Building an RDF File from Scratch

Now that you understand the basic principles of a simple RDF file, this section steps through the creation of an RDF file from information found in regular text:

> There is a jar with the name urn:root. Inside of it there are two types of flies listed as House and Horse.

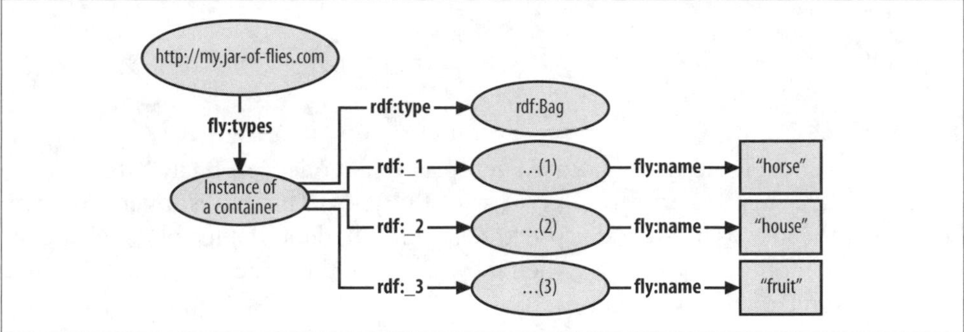

Figure 10-8. The full graph

> There are three Horse flies. The Face Fly, coded in green, is officially identified as "musca autumnalis". The Stable Fly, coded in black, has the identification "stomoxys_calcitrans." The red-coded Horn Fly, located in Kansas, is identified as "haematobia_irritans."
>
> There are also three house flies. "musca_domestica," coded in brown, has the name "Common House Fly." A gray fly named "Carrion Fly" has the ID "sarcophagid" and is found globally. Finally, The "Office Fly," coded with white, is prevalent in the Bay Area.

You can use the techniques described here to model the data you want in your application: spreadsheet-like rosters of people, family trees, or catalogs of books or other items.

Identify namespaces

The new RDF file will have three namespaces including the RDF namespace. The result is two different data types that are connected in an RDF graph. For the sake of the example, one namespace is not in the standard URL format. Here is how the RDF file namespaces are set up:

```
<?xml version="1.0"?>
<rdf:RDF xmlns:rdf="http://www.w3.org/1999/02/22-rdf-syntax-ns#"
         xmlns:fly="http://xfly.mozdev.org/fly-rdf#"
         xmlns:location="fly-location#">
</rdf:RDF>
```

Root resource

This file's root resource is an `urn:root`, which is the conventional name for root nodes in Mozilla's RDF files. When rendering RDF files, defining a root node for processing the document can be useful—especially when building templates. This root node can be entered as the first item in the file:

```
<?xml version="1.0"?>
<rdf:RDF xmlns:rdf="http://www.w3.org/1999/02/22-rdf-syntax-ns#"
         xmlns:fly="http://xfly.mozdev.org/fly-rdf#"
         xmlns:location="fly-location#">
```

```
    <rdf:Description about="urn:root">
    </rdf:Description>
  </rdf:RDF>
```

Root sequence

Next, a generic tag needs to be used to specify a sequence of "fly" data. As in Example 10-2, `<fly:list>` is used as a list of fly types. This tag is a generic name because of the way XUL templates process lists of RDF data. If a list of data has sub-lists, as in the following examples, then they must use the same tag name to recurse correctly for the data they contain.

Example 10-2 represents all the information given in the first paragraph of the text example: "There is a jar set up with the name *urn:root*. Inside of it there are two types of flies, listed as House and Horse."

Example 10-2. RDF root sequence

```
<?xml version="1.0"?>
<rdf:RDF xmlns:rdf="http://www.w3.org/1999/02/22-rdf-syntax-ns#"
         xmlns:fly="http://xfly.mozdev.org/fly-rdf#"
         xmlns:location="fly-location#">
  <rdf:Description about="urn:root">
    <fly:list>
      <rdf:Seq>
        <rdf:li>
          <rdf:Description ID="House" fly:label="House"/>
        </rdf:li>
        <rdf:li>
          <rdf:Description ID="Horse" fly:label="Horse"/>
        </rdf:li>
      </rdf:Seq>
    </fly:list>
  </rdf:Description>
</rdf:RDF>
```

An RDF sequence resides with its list of resources inside `<fly:list>`. Here, shorthand RDF specifies a label with the `fly:label` attribute. The `ID` attribute within this sequence is actually a pointer to the main definition of the resource described by an `about` attribute of the same value. The `about` attribute includes a `#` in its identifier, much like HTML anchors use `<a href="#frag">` to refer to `<a name="frag">`. For example, `ID="Horse"` points to `about="#Horse`" elsewhere in the file, allowing you to add to the description of any element with new properties and resources.

Secondary sequences and literals

The `Horse` and `House` resources need to be defined next. Example 10-3 shows the creation of `Horse` from the second paragraph. The process for creating `House` is almost identical.

Example 10-3. The Horse sequence

```
<rdf:Description about="#Horse">
    <fly:list>
      <rdf:Seq>
        <rdf:li>
          <rdf:Description about="musca_autumnalis"
                           fly:label="Face fly"
                           fly:color="green"/>
        </rdf:li>
        <rdf:li>
          <rdf:Description about="stomoxys_calcitrans"
                           fly:label="Stable Fly"
                           fly:color="black"/>
        </rdf:li>
        <rdf:li>
          <rdf:Description about="haematobia_irritans"
                           fly:label="Horn Fly"
                           fly:color="red"
                           location:location="Kansas"/>
        </rdf:li>
      </rdf:Seq>
    </fly:list>
  </rdf:Description>
```

Here the shorthand RDF definition continues to use only the attributes. Again, a `<fly:list>` is defined and the items inside it are listed. The listed values have multiple attribute values, all of which are RDF literals. In longhand with RDF showing all literals, the last item would be written out as follows:

```
<rdf:li>
   <rdf:Description about="haematobia_irritans ">
      <fly:label>Horn Fly</fly:label>
      <fly:color>red</fly:color>
      <location:location>Kansas</location:location>
   </rdf:Description>
</rdf:li>
```

The two different namespace literals are both resource attributes. `haematobia_irritans` is used as the resource identifier because it is a unique value among all data.

Laying out the data in the same pattern gives you the final, full RDF file in Example 10-4.

Example 10-4. Entire RDF file

```
<?xml version="1.0"?>
<rdf:RDF xmlns:rdf="http://www.w3.org/1999/02/22-rdf-syntax-ns#"
         xmlns:fly="http://xfly.mozdev.org/fly-rdf#"
         xmlns:location="fly-location#">
  <rdf:Description about="urn:root">
    <fly:list>
      <rdf:Seq>
        <rdf:li>
          <rdf:Description ID="House" fly:label="House"/>
```

Example 10-4. Entire RDF file (continued)

```
        </rdf:li>
        <rdf:li>
          <rdf:Description ID="Horse" fly:label="Horse"/>
        </rdf:li>
      </rdf:Seq>
    </fly:list>
  </rdf:Description>
  <rdf:Description about="#Horse">
    <fly:list>
      <rdf:Seq>
        <rdf:li>
          <rdf:Description about="musca_autumnalis"
                           fly:label="Face fly"
                           fly:color="green"/>
        </rdf:li>
        <rdf:li>
          <rdf:Description about="stomoxys_calcitrans"
                           fly:label="Stable Fly"
                           fly:color="black"/>
        </rdf:li>
        <rdf:li>
          <rdf:Description about="haematobia_irritans"
                           fly:label="Horn Fly"
                           fly:color="red"
                           location:location="Kansas"/>
        </rdf:li>
      </rdf:Seq>
    </fly:list>
  </rdf:Description>
  <rdf:Description about="#House">
    <fly:list>
      <rdf:Seq>
        <rdf:li>
          <rdf:Description about="musca_domestica"
                           fly:label="Common House Fly"
                           fly:color="brown"/>
        </rdf:li>
        <rdf:li>
          <rdf:Description about="sarcophagid"
                           fly:label="Carrion Fly"
                           fly:color="gray"
                           location:location="Worldwide"/>
        </rdf:li>
        <rdf:li>
          <rdf:Description about="musca_oficio"
                           fly:label="Office Fly"
                           fly:color="white"
                           location:location="California, Bay Area"/>
        </rdf:li>
      </rdf:Seq>
    </fly:list>
  </rdf:Description>
</rdf:RDF>
```

Example 10-4 shows the RDF data used in several template examples in Chapter 9. Example 9-4 includes the *10-4.rdf* datasource, as do many of those templates. You can copy the data out of Example 10-4 and into a file of the same name to use as a datasource.

The Mozilla Content Model

One theme of this book—and a general goal of the Mozilla development environment—is that developers can create real applications using many of the same technologies they use to create a web page. The Gecko rendering engine, sitting at the heart of Mozilla and happily rendering web content, XML files, XUL interfaces, and whatever else they can support, is what makes this type of development possible. But how does Gecko know what to render and how? How can RDF data be handed over so that Gecko knows how to draw it?

When a browser uses the same engine to draw everything—its own interface as well as the various kinds of content it supports—that engine treats everything as content. Gecko needs a way to understand all the various parts of the Mozilla browser itself—such as the sidebar, the toolbars, and the mail folders and mail messages—as resources it can render and display in the Mozilla chrome. This approach to the Mozilla application interface is called the content model.

In Mozilla's content model, XUL documents and other interface resources are transformed into RDF when they are read. Each chunk of content is represented as a separate RDF datasource (see the next section, "Datasources," for more information) and is then fed to the XUL Content Builder and rendered as the actual bits on the screen, as Figure 10-9 shows.

As you can see in Figure 10-9, the content model can be complex. The XUL documents in Figure 10-9 are files such as *navigator.xul*, which defines the main browser window's basic layout; the RDF documents include files like *help-toc.rdf*, which defines the Mozilla Help viewer's table of contents. The list of mail folders and accounts shown in Example 10-5 are part of the built-in data that Mozilla renders into browser content.

Whatever the source, the content model gets everything processed in-memory as RDF so that any data can be combined and formatted into XUL or other interface code. All sources of RDF data are called datasources.

Datasources

A datasource is a collection of related, typically homogenous, RDF statements. A datasource may be a single RDF file like *localstore.rdf*, a combination of files, or RDF structures that exist only in memory (as discussed later).

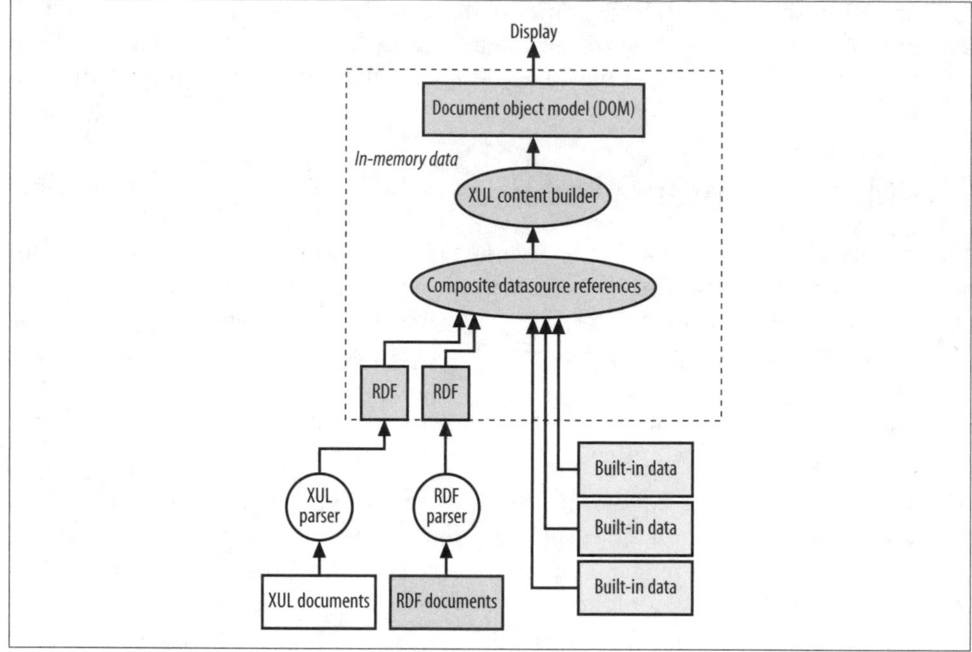

Figure 10-9. Diagram of Mozilla's content model

In Mozilla, datasources represent the messages in your email inbox, your bookmarks, the packages you installed, your browser history, and other sets of data. Datasources can be combined easily (or "composed," which is where the term "composite datasource" comes from).

A datasource example: mailboxes

Several datasources describe all the folders and messages in Mozilla's email. A root datasource called `msgaccounts` describes which mail servers and accounts are present. Separate datasources then represent each account separately. These datasources are composed to create the entire email storage system. The higher levels of this content structure look like Example 10-5.

Example 10-5. Content model of email datasources

```
msgaccounts:/
+-- http://home.netscape.com/NC-rdf#child -->
    imap://oeschger@imap.netscape.com
    |     +-- http://home.netscape.com/NC-rdf#IsServer --> "true"
    |     +-- http://home.netscape.com/NC-rdf#child -->
    |         imap://oeschger@imap.netscape.com/INBOX
    |     +-- http://home.netscape.com/NC-rdf#TotalMessages --> "4"
    |     +-- http://home.netscape.com/NC-rdf#IsServer --> "false"
    |     +-- http://home.netscape.com/NC-rdf#MessageChild -->
    |         imap_message://oeschger@imap.netscape.com/INBOX#1
    |     +-- http://home.netscape.com/NC-rdf#MessageChild -->
```

Example 10-5. Content model of email datasources (continued)

```
    |       imap_message://oeschger@imap.netscape.com/INBOX#2
    |    +-- http://home.netscape.com/NC-rdf#MessageChild -->
    |    etc...
    |
+-- http://home.netscape.com/NC-rdf#child -->
    mailbox://oeschger@pop.netscape.com
    |    +-- http://home.netscape.com/NC-rdf#IsServer --> "true"
    |    +-- http://home.netscape.com/NC-rdf#child -->
    |        mailbox://oeschger@pop.oeschger.com/INBOX
    |    +-- http://home.netscape.com/NC-rdf#TotalMessages --> "2"
    |    etc...
```

Each direct child of the root *msgaccounts:/* is a mail server. This portion of the graph shows two Mozilla email accounts that are the primary children: *imap://oeschger@imap.netscape.com* and *mailbox://oeschger@pop.netscape.com*. These two accounts are entirely different datasources that can exist on their own. The content model for email actually extends much lower than what is represented in this outline. It uses RDF to represent the data all the way into the actual message lists.

Types of datasources

As you may have already inferred, email accounts are not actually RDF files. Mozilla provides a custom RDF map of all email accounts and messages and the content model represents the accounts and their relationships to one another as RDF so they can be integrated and rendered properly. The interface to this custom mail RDF map makes it possible to display a list of messages and mailboxes in a <tree> template.

Another example of a datasource, the *in-memory-datasource*, doesn't come from an actual RDF file. When an in-memory datasource is created, it doesn't contain data. However, data can be inserted into it and stored in memory until the datasource is destroyed. In-memory datasources frequently represent ephemeral data like search results. Other basic datasource types are described in Table 10-2.

Table 10-2. Types of datasources

Type	Description
Local datasource	A local datasource is an RDF graph contained in an RDF/XML file on a local disk. All RDF files in the chrome registry (e.g., *all-packages.rdf* in the *chrome* directory, which keeps track packages installed in Mozilla) are local datasources.
Remote datasource	RDF can be accessed locally or remotely. A remote datasource is an RDF/XML file stored on a server and accessed with a URL.
In-memory datasource	An in-memory datasource exists only in memory during a Mozilla session. In-memory datasources are built with *assertions*, statements that build an in-memory data model by adding resources, properties, and value to those.
Built-in datasource	These unique, prefabricated datasources represent something used often in Mozilla, such as a built-in *filesystem* datasource and a *history* datasource.
Composite datasource	A composite datasource may be a combination of any of the datasources previously listed. RDF allows you to merge different graphs.

RDF Components and Interfaces

Once you are comfortable using XUL templates to display RDF data (see Chapter 9), you should explore the various ways to create and change that data. In Mozilla, data is generally RDF, since all data in Mozilla is either represented formally in RDF or passed through the RDF-based content model for display. Use the tools described in this section to manipulate RDF and the data it represents.

Mozilla has a great set of interfaces for creating, manipulating, and managing RDF, and it also provides ready-made RDF components that represent datasources used in Mozilla. Think of RDF interfaces as ways to manipulate RDF directly and of RDF components as sets of the interfaces already associated with a particular kind of data, such as bookmarks. Interfaces tend to deal with the RDF model itself, without regard to the kinds of data being handled, while RDF components give you control over specific Mozilla data. See the next two sections for more information on RDF interfaces and components.

What Is an RDF Component?

An RDF component may implement any number of the general RDF interfaces described here, in addition to special interfaces for accessing and controlling the data the datasource represents. For example, `@mozilla.org/rdf/datasource;1?name=internetsearch` is an RDF component used to control Mozilla's internet searching facility. In Mozilla, a component can act as a library of code specific to a given set of data or domain. The `internetsearch` component is instantiated and used to recall text entered in a previous search:

```
var searchDS = Components.classes["@mozilla.org/rdf/
datasource;1?name=internetsearch"]
      .getService(Components.interfaces.nsIInternetSearchService);

searchDS.RememberLastSearchText(escapedSearchStr);
```

This RDF component implements an interface called *nsIInternetSearchService*, which is selected from the component and used to call the `RememberLastSearchText` method. Although you can also use the `getService` method to get one of a component's RDF interfaces (e.g., by using `getService(Components.interfaces.nsIRDFDataSource)`), doing so is seldom necessary in practice. RDF components are tailored to the datasources they represent and usually provide all the access you need to access that data directly. Example 10-6 lists RDF components in Mozilla.

Example 10-6. RDF-specific components built into Mozilla

```
@mozilla.org/rdf/container;1
@mozilla.org/rdf/content-sink;1
@mozilla.org/rdf/datasource;1?name=addresscard
@mozilla.org/rdf/datasource;1?name=addressdirectory
@mozilla.org/rdf/datasource;1?name=bookmarks
```

Example 10-6. RDF-specific components built into Mozilla (continued)

```
@mozilla.org/rdf/datasource;1?name=charset-menu
@mozilla.org/rdf/datasource;1?name=composite-datasource
@mozilla.org/rdf/datasource;1?name=files
@mozilla.org/rdf/datasource;1?name=history
@mozilla.org/rdf/datasource;1?name=httpindex
@mozilla.org/rdf/datasource;1?name=in-memory-datasource
@mozilla.org/rdf/datasource;1?name=internetsearch
@mozilla.org/rdf/datasource;1?name=ispdefaults
@mozilla.org/rdf/datasource;1?name=local-store
@mozilla.org/rdf/datasource;1?name=localsearch
@mozilla.org/rdf/datasource;1?name=mailnewsfolders
@mozilla.org/rdf/datasource;1?name=msgaccountmanager
@mozilla.org/rdf/datasource;1?name=msgfilters
@mozilla.org/rdf/datasource;1?name=msgnotifications
@mozilla.org/rdf/datasource;1?name=smtp
@mozilla.org/rdf/datasource;1?name=subscribe
@mozilla.org/rdf/datasource;1?name=window-mediator
@mozilla.org/rdf/datasource;1?name=xml-datasource
@mozilla.org/rdf/delegate-factory;1?key=filter&scheme=imap
@mozilla.org/rdf/delegate-factory;1?key=filter&scheme=mailbox
@mozilla.org/rdf/delegate-factory;1?key=filter&scheme=news
@mozilla.org/rdf/delegate-factory;1?key=smtpserver&scheme=smtp
@mozilla.org/rdf/rdf-service;1
@mozilla.org/rdf/resource-factory;1
@mozilla.org/rdf/resource-factory;1?name=abdirectory
@mozilla.org/rdf/resource-factory;1?name=abmdbcard
@mozilla.org/rdf/resource-factory;1?name=abmdbdirectory
@mozilla.org/rdf/resource-factory;1?name=imap
@mozilla.org/rdf/resource-factory;1?name=mailbox
@mozilla.org/rdf/resource-factory;1?name=news
@mozilla.org/rdf/xml-parser;1
@mozilla.org/rdf/xml-serializer;1
```

From this list, components used often in the Mozilla source code include bookmarks, history, mail and news folders, and address books.

Special URIs

Mozilla's built-in datasource components have special URIs for access. Here is the format used to determine the URI from the component reference:

Component:

```
@mozilla.org/rdf/datasource;1?name=SomeName
```

Datasource URI:

```
rdf:SomeName
```

The URI is also accessible as a datasource property:

```
foo-ds.URI
```

What Are RDF Interfaces?

RDF interfaces are interfaces in Mozilla designed to manipulate RDF structures and data. They typically deal with RDF generally, rather than specific sets of data (as in the case of components). A common use for an RDF interface in JavaScript, shown in Example 10-7, is to use *nsIRDFService* to retrieve or assert the root node of an RDF datasource.

Example 10-7. Creating a root node

```
// get the nsIRDFService interface and assign it to RDF
RDF = Components.classes[`@mozilla.org/rdf/rdf-service;1'].
      getService(Components.interfaces.nsIRDFService);
// call the GetResource method from the interface
rootResource = RDF.GetResource('urn:root');
```

Like all Mozilla interfaces, RDF interfaces (shown in Table 10-3) are defined in IDL and can be accessed through XPCOM. The examples in this section use JavaScript and XPConnect to access the components for simplicity, but you can also use these interfaces with C++, as they are often in the actual Mozilla source code. Most interfaces deal with datasources, which drive the use of RDF in Mozilla.

Table 10-3. Mozilla's built-in RDF interfaces

RDF interface	Description
nsIRDFService	Mostly used for retrieving, datasources, resources, and literals. It also registers and unregisters datasources and resources.
nsIRDFCompositeDataSource	Allows the addition and removal of a datasource from a composite datasource (which may be empty).
nsIRDFDataSource, nsIRDFPurgeableDataSource, nsIRDFRemoteDataSource	Mostly used for adding, removing, and changing triples in a datasource. It provides the means to change the graph.
nsIRDFNode, nsIRDFResource, nsIRDFLiteral	Provide an equality function. Values for resources and literals can be retrieved. Objects of these types are retrieved from `nsIRDFService`.
nsIRDFContainer	Provides vector-like access to an RDF container's elements.
nsIRDFContainerUtils	Provides container creation and other container-related functions.
nsIRDFObserver	Fires events when data is changed in a datasource.
nsIRDFXMLParser, nsIRDFXMLSerializer, nsIRDFXMLSink, nsIRDFXMLSource	Used for working with RDF/XML. Functions are provided for parsing files and serializing content.

The sheer variety of RDF interfaces may seem overwhelming, but all interfaces serve different purposes and are often used in conjunction with one another. In your particular application space, you may find yourself using some subsets of these interfaces constantly and others not at all. This section describes some of the most commonly used functions. You can look up all of interfaces in their entirety at *http://lxr.mozilla.org/seamonkey/source/rdf/base/idl/*.

nsIRDFService

If you will do any sort of RDF processing, you need to use the *nsIRDFService* interface. It provides the basics for working with datasources, resources, and literals, and is useful when you process RDF data. *nsIRDFService* can be initialized by using the getService method of the rdf-service class:

```
RDF = Components.classes[`@mozilla.org/rdf/rdf-service;1']
      getService(Components.interfaces.nsIRDFService);
```

Once the service is available, it's ready to go to work. Even though no datasource is created yet (in this particular example), the RDF service can still get resources and literals, as shown in the next section.

Getting a resource

Once a resource is created (e.g., with the identifier urn:root in Example 10-7), it needs to be added to a datasource:

```
rootResource = RDF.GetResource('urn:root');
```

When a resource is already registered under the given identifier (see "Registering and unregistering datasources," later in this chapter for more information about RDF registration), then GetResource returns that resource.

Getting an anonymous resource

Anonymous resources are resources with no resource identifier. Here is the creation of a new anonymous resource and a test of its anonymity:

```
anonResource = RDF.GetAnonymousResource();
// This would be true. Checking is not necessary, just here for example.
isAnon = RDF.isAnonymousResource(anonResource);
```

Typically, these resources are turned into containers, as shown in the next section. Anonymous resources exist when names are not needed and a simple reference to that resource is all that is required.

Getting a literal

The GetLiteral function returns the given name in the format of a literal, which you can then use to assert into an RDF graph as a resource.

```
myName = RDF.GetLiteral('Eric');
```

Variations on this function are GetIntLiteral and GetDateLiteral.

Registering and unregistering datasources

If you create a Mozilla application that uses the same datasource or RDF resources in different ways, you may want to register the datasource with Mozilla. When you register a datasource, you register it as a component in Mozilla (see "Component

Manager" in Chapter 8 for more information on Mozilla's component model), which means it can be accessed and used as easily as any other XPCOM component, and from anywhere in Mozilla.

To register a datasource, call the RegisterDatasource method of the RDF Service. In this example, the datasource already exists and is assigned to a variable named *myDatasource*:

```
RDF.RegisterDataSource(myDatasource, false);
```

In this case, *myDatasource* is the datasource name, and the false parameter specifies that this datasource is not replacing a datasource with the same name. Once a datasource is registered with the component manager in this way, it can be retrieved by name and associated with another instance:

```
secondDatasource = anotherRDF.GetDataSource("My Datasource");
```

To unregister a datasource from the RDF Service, pass the datasource into the UnRegisterDataSource function:

```
RDF.UnRegisterDataSource(myDatasource);
```

Once it's unregistered, a datasource is no longer available to other instances of the RDF Service. Registered resources work the same way as datasources in the RDF Service: if a resource is registered with the RDF Service, then it is available in every instance of RDF Service. To get two different instances of the same registered datasource and unregister its use:

```
newResource = RDF.GetResource('my.resource');
RDF.RegisterResource(newResource,false);
notNewResource = RDF.GetResource('my.resource');
RDF.UnRegisterResource(notNewResource);
```

If you register resources and datasources, be sure to use the *overwrite* Boolean variable on RegisterDataSource and RegisterResource to avoid overwriting existing datasources.

Getting a remote datasource

Finally, *nsIRDFService* provides a useful method that loads a datasource from a remote server, which is a process that occurs asynchronously. Compared to forthcoming discussions about datasource loading, GetDataSource is a real shortcut:

```
remoteDatasource = RDF.GetDataSource('http://books.mozdev.org/file.rdf');
```

Remember that RDF files requested in this way must be set with the text/rdf MIME type on the web server to load properly.

nsIRDFCompositeDataSource

When you work with multiple datasources, you can make things easier by grouping them, which *nsIRDFCompositeDataSource* allows you to do. This functionality aggregates data in a number of Mozilla's applications. To get this interface, invoke:

```
composite_datasource
   = '@mozilla.org/rdf/datasource;1?name=composite-datasource';
compDataSource = Components.classes[composite_datasource]
   getService(Components.interfaces.nsIRDFCompositeDataSource);
```

Once you have the interface, adding and removing datasources from the composite is easy. You can also enumerate the datasources by using the `getNext` method. Example 10-8 demonstrates how to add, remove, and cycle through datasources.

Example 10-8. Manipulating datasources

```
compDataSource.AddDataSource(datasource1);
compDataSource.AddDataSource(datasource2);
compDataSource.AddDataSource(datasource3);
compDataSource.RemoveDataSource(datasource1);
allDataSources = compDataSource.GetDataSources();
datasource2 = allDataSources.getNext();
datasource2.QueryInterface(Components.interfaces.nsIRDFDataSource);
datasource3 = allDataSources.getNext();
datasource3.QueryInterface(Components.interfaces.nsIRDFDataSource);
```

In Example 10-8, `allDataSources` is an *nsISimpleEnumerator* returned by the `GetDataSources` method on the composite datasource. `datasource1` is removed from the composite, and then the remaining datasources are cycled through. This step provides a way to iterate through a collection of datasources. *nsIRDFCompositeDatasource* also inherits the many functions of *nsIRDFDataSource*; refer to the section "nsIRDFDataSource" for more information.

nsIRDFDataSource

The *nsIRDFDataSource* interface is large, with twenty functions and one attribute (`URI`), so it's one of the most common interfaces used to manipulate RDF data. *nsIRDFDataSource* contains all the components in Example 10-6 with "datasource" in their contract IDs, along with other common components:

```
@mozilla.org/browser/bookmarks-service;1
@mozilla.org/related-links-handler;1
@mozilla.org/browser/localsearch-service;1
@mozilla.org/registry-viewer;1
@mozilla.org/browser/global-history;1
```

The *nsIRDFDataSource* interface is meant to handle some of the core interaction with the datasource. APIs such as `URI`, `GetTarget`, `Assert`, and `Change` are helpful for working on the RDF graph itself. For example, the `@mozilla.org/rdf/datasource;1?name=in-memory-datasource` RDF component demonstrates the use of the *nsIRDFDataSource* interface. When this component is created, it's a blank datasource in memory, into which objects are inserted, changed, and removed. You can access the *nsIRDFDataSource* interface from the RDF component by first constructing an RDF graph in the in-memory datasource:

```
mem = '@mozilla.org/rdf/datasource;1?name=in-memory-datasource';
datasource = Components.classes[mem].
             createInstance(Components.interfaces.nsIRDFDataSource);
```

Of the twenty functions (found at *http://lxr.mozilla.org/seamonkey/source/rdf/base/idl/nsIRDFDataSource.idl*) in this interface, we show only a handful here:

- Assertion and removal
- Changing values
- Moving triples
- HasAssertion
- GetTarget
- GetSource

The main purpose of the *nsIRDFDatasource* interface is to work with RDF triples inside a datasource, allowing you to change that datasource's RDF graph.

Assertion and removal

Recall from the "RDF triples: subject, predicate, and object" section, earlier in this chapter, that triples are RDF statements in which the relationship between the subject, predicate, and object is more strictly defined. In the interface code, a triple's elements are all typically defined as resources rather than plain URIs, which means they can be asserted into a datasource in the particular sequence that makes them meaningful as parts of a triple:

```
rootSubject = RDF.GetResource('urn:root');
predicate = RDF.GetResource('http://books.mozdev.org/rdf#chapters');
object = RDF.GetResource('Chapter1');
datasource.Assert(rootSubject,predicate,object,true);
```

Once you assert the statement's elements into the datasource in this way, the datasource contains the triple. The `truth` value parameter in the last slot indicates that the given node is "locked" and thus cannot be overwritten.

Removing a triple from the datasource is as easy as adding it. If you try to remove a triple that doesn't exist, your request is ignored and no error messages are raised. To unassert a triple in the datasource, use:

```
rootSubject = RDF.GetResource('urn:root');
predicate = RDF.GetResource('http://books.mozdev.org/rdf#chapters');
object = RDF.GetResource('Chapter8');
datasource.Unassert(rootSubject,predicate,object);
```

Changing values

Changing values in a datasource is also very easy. Assert and change a literal in the datasource as follows:

```
subject = RDF.GetResource('Chapter1');
predicate = RDF.GetResource('http://books.mozdev.org/rdf#title');
object = RDF.GetLiteral('Mozilla as a Platform');
datasource.Assert(subject,predicate,object,true);
newObject = RDF.GetLiteral('Mozilla is a cool Platform!');
datasource.Change(subject,predicate,newObject,);
```

If working with triples seems hard in the template generation, their use in these examples—where adding to and changing the parts is so easy—may make things clearer.

Moving triples

Moving a triple in a datasource also requires some simple code. This example moves the asserted triple in the previous section:

```
newSubject = RDF.GetResource('Chapter99');
// Moving from Chapter1 to Chapter99
datasource.Move(subject,newSubject,predicate,object);
```

HasAssertion

This next example checks if the previous statement still exists in the datasource.

```
datasource.HasAssertion(newSubject,predicate,object,true);
```

This function is useful when you create new statements and resources and want to make sure you are not overwriting pre-existing resources.

GetTarget

The `GetTarget` method returns the resource's property value (i.e., the object). Given the RDF statement "(Eric) wrote (a book)," for example, the `GetTarget` method would input "Eric" and "wrote" and get back the object "a book." Once again, the example code is based on the previous examples:

```
object = datasource.GetTarget(newSubject,predicate,true);
objects = datasource.GetTargets(rootSubject,predicate,true);
// objects is an nsIEnumeration of the object and its properties
```

In addition to `GetTarget`, as seen above, a `GetTargets` function returns an object and its properties in an enumeration. This function can be very handy for quick access to resources with fewer function calls.

GetSource

`GetSource` is the inverse of `GetTarget`. Whereas `GetTarget` returns an object, `GetSource` returns the subject attached to an object. Given the RDF statement "(Eric) wrote (a book)" again, in other words, the GetSource method would input "wrote" and "a book" and get back the statement subject "Eric."

```
subject = datasource.GetSource(object,predicate,true);
subjects = datasource.GetSources(object,predicate,true);
// subjects is an nsIEnumeration of the subject and its properties
```

When you create RDF statements with assertions or work with in-memory datasources, it is often difficult to remember the shape of the graph, which statements exist about which resources, or which objects are attached to which subjects. These "getter" methods can help you verify the shape of your graph.

nsIRDFRemoteDataSource

The "nsIRDFService" section (earlier in this chapter) showed how to load a datasource from a remote server simply. If you want control over that datasource, you can manage it by using the *nsIRDFRemoteDatasource* to set up a remote datasource:

```
xml = '@mozilla.org/rdf/datasource;1?name=xml-datasource';
datasource = Components.classes[xml].
             createInstance(Components.interfaces.nsIRDFRemoteDataSource);
datasource.Init('http://books.mozdev.org/file.rdf');
datasource.Refresh(false);
```

In this example, the Init and Refresh methods control the datasource on the server. In addition to these methods, you can call the Flush method to flush the data that's been changed and reload, or you can check whether the datasource is loaded by using the loaded property:

```
if (datasource.loaded) {
  // Do something
}
```

Built-in datasources that implement *nsIRDFRemoteDataSource* (and other necessary interfaces) and do their own data handling include:

```
@mozilla.org/rdf/datasource;1?name=history
@mozilla.org/browser/bookmarks-service;1
@mozilla.org/autocompleteSession;1?type=history
@mozilla.org/browser/global-history;1
@mozilla.org/rdf/datasource;1?name=bookmarks
```

nsIRDFPurgeableDataSource

Using the *nsIRDFPurgeableDatasource* interface allows you to delete a whole section of an existing in-memory datasource in one fell swoop. This means that all relatives—all statements derived from that node—are removed. When you work with large in-memory datasources (such as email systems), the using interface can manipulate the data efficiently. The Sweep() method can delete a section that is marked in the datasource.

```
datasource.
   QueryInterface(Components.interfaces.nsIRDFPurgeableDataSource);
rootSubject = RDF.GetResource('urn:root');
predicate = RDF.GetResource('http://books.mozdev.org/rdf#chapters');
object = RDF.GetResource('Chapter1');
datasource.Mark(rootSubject,predicate,object,true);
datasource.Sweep();
```

In this instance, a statement about a chapter in a book is marked and then removed from the datasource. You can also mark more than one node before sweeping.

nsIRDFNode, nsIRDFResource, and nsIRDFLiteral

These types of objects come from only a few different places. Here are all the functions that can return the resource of a literal:

```
nsIRDFService.GetResource
nsIRDFService.GetAnonymousResource
nsIRDFService.GetLiteral
nsIRDFDataSource.GetSource
nsIRDFDataSource.GetTarget
```

nsIRDFNode is the parent of *nsIRDFResource* and *nsIRDFLiteral*. It is not used often because it's sole function is to test equality:

```
isEqual = resource1.EqualsNode(resource2);
```

The other two interfaces inherit this function automatically. `EqualsNode` tests the equivalency of two resources, which can be useful when you try to put together different statements (e.g., "Eric wrote a book" and "[This] book is about XML") and want to verify that a resource like "book" is the same in both cases.

nsIRDFResource

Like *nsIRDFNode*, *nsIRDFResource* is a minimalist interface. Here are the functions and the property available in a resource from the *nsIRDFResource* interface:

```
resource = RDF.GetAnonymousResource();
// get the resource value, something like 'rdf:#$44RG7'
resourceIdentifierString = resource.Value;
// compare the resource to an identifier
isTrue = resourceEqualsString(resourceIdentifierString);
// Give the resource a real name.
resource.Init('Eric');
```

nsIRDFLiteral

A literal's value can be read but not written. To change the value of a literal, make a new literal and set it properly:

```
aValue = literal.Value;
```

Note that `aValue` could be a string or an integer in this case. The base type conversion, based on the data's format, is done automatically.

nsIRDFContainerUtils

This interface facilitates the creation of containers and provides other container-related functions. It provides functions that make and work with a sequence, bag, and alternative. (The functions work the same way for all types of containers, so only sequence is covered here.) To create an instance of *nsIRDFContainerUtils*, use the following:

```
containerUtils = Components.classes['@mozilla.org/rdf/container-utils;1'
                 getService(Components.interfaces.nsIRDFContainerUtils);
```

Once you create an anonymous resource, you can create a sequence from it. Then you can test the type of the container and see whether it's empty:

```
// create an anonymous resource
anonResource = RDF.GetAnonymousResource();
// create a sequence from that resource
aSequence = containerUtils.MakeSeq(datasource,anonResource);
// test the resource
// (all of these are true)
isContainer = containerUtils.isContainer(datasource,anonResource);
isSequence = containerUtils.isSequence(datasource,anonResource);
isEmpty = containerUtils.isEmpty(datasource,anonResource);
```

Note that the sequence object is not passed into the functions performing the test in the previous example; the resource containing the sequence is passed in. Although `aSequence` and `anonResource` are basically the same resource, their data types are different. `isContainer`, `isSequence`, and `isEmpty` can be used more easily with other RDF functions when a resource is used as a parameter:

```
object = datasource.GetTarget(subject,predicate,true);
if(RDF.isAnonymousResource(object))
{
  isSeq = containerUtils.IsSeq(datasource,object);
}
```

The RDF container utilities also provide an indexing function. `indexOf` is useful for checking if an element exists in a container resource:

```
indexNumber =
   containerUtils.indexOf(datasource,object,RDF.GetLiteral('Eric'));
if(index != -1)
   alert('Eric exists in this container');
```

nsIRDFContainer

This interface provides vector-like access to an RDF container's elements.* The *nsIRDFContainer* interface allows you to add, look up, and remove elements from a container once you create it.

* A vector, for those who don't know, is a flexible and more accessible version of the array data structure.

Adding an element to a container

You can add an element to a container in two ways. You can append it to the end of the list with `Append` or insert it at a specific place in the container:

```
newLiteral = RDF.GetLiteral('Ian');
aSequence.AppendElement(newLiteral);
// or
aSequence.InsertElementAt(newLiteral,3,true);
```

The second attribute in `InsertElementAt` is where the element should be placed. The third attribute specifies that the list can be reordered. This method is useful for working with ordered containers such as sequences. If this locking parameter is set to false and an element already exists at that location, then the existing element is overwritten.

Removing an element from a container

Removing an element from a container works much the same as adding one. The difference is that a reordering attribute is included on `RemoveElement`. If this attribute is set to false, you may have holes in the container, which can create problems when enumerating or indexing elements within.

```
newLiteral = RDF.GetLiteral('Ian');
aSequence.RemoveElement(newLiteral,true);
// or
aSequence.RemoveElementAt(newLiteral,3,true);
```

If you use the `indexOf` property of `nsIRDFContainer`, you can also use `GetCount` to learn how many elements are in the container. The count starts at 0 when the container is initialized:

```
numberOfElements = aSequence.GetCount();
```

Once you have the sequence, the datasource and resource the sequence resides in can be retrieved. In effect, these properties look outward instead of toward the data:

```
seqDatasource = aSequence.DataSource;
seqResource = aSequence.Resource;
```

Like many methods in the RDF interfaces, this one allows you to traverse and retrieve any part of the RDF graph.

nsIRDFXML Interfaces

The RDF/XML interfaces are covered only briefly here. Besides being abstract and confusing, these interfaces require a lot of error handling to work correctly. Fortunately, a library on mozdev.org called *JSLib* handles RDF file access. The *JSLib* XML library does the dirty work in a friendly manner. See the section "JSLib RDF Files," later in this chapter, for more information.

nsIRDFXMLParser and nsIRDFXMLSink

nsIRDFXML is the raw RDF/XML parser of Mozilla. Used by Mozilla, its main purpose is to parse an RDF file asynchronously as a stream listener. Though this subject is beyond the scope of this book, the interface provides something interesting and useful. The `parseString` function allows you to feed *nsIRDFXMLParser* a string and have it parse that data as RDF and put it into a datasource, as Example 10-9 demonstrates.

Example 10-9. Parse an RDF/XML string into a datasource

```
RDF = Components.classes['@mozilla.org/rdf/rdf-service;1'].
       getService(Components.interfaces.nsIRDFService);
// Used to create a URI below
ios = Components.classes["@mozilla.org/network/io-service;1"].
      getService(Components.interfaces.nsIIOService);
xmlParser = '@mozilla.org/rdf/xml-parser;1';
parser = Components.classes[xmlParser].
        createInstance(Components.interfaces.nsIRDFXMLParser);
uri = ios.newURI("http://books.mozdev.org/rdf#", null);
// Entire RDF File stored in a string
rdfString =
  '<rdf:RDF xmlns:rdf=http://www.w3.org/1999/02/22-rdf-syntax-ns#' +
  'xmlns:b="http://books.mozdev.org/rdf#">' +
  '<rdf:Description about="urn:root">' + // Rest of file ...
parser.parseString(datasource,uri,rdfString);
// Parsed string data now resides in the datasource
```

The RDF/XML data that was in the string is a part of the datasource and ready for use (just like any other RDF data in a datasource). The `uri` acts as a base reference for the RDF in case of relative links.

nsIRDFXMLParser uses *nsIRDFXMLSink* for event handling. The interfaces are totally separate, but behind the scenes, they work together with the incoming data. Example 10-10 shows how a series of events is created in an object and then used to handle parser events.

Example 10-10. Setup nsIRDFXMLSink with event handlers

```
var Observer = {
   onBeginLoad: function(aSink)
   {
     alert("Beginning to load the RDF/XML...");
   },
   onInterrupt: function(aSink) {},
   onResume: function(aSink) {},
   onEndLoad: function(aSink)
   {
     doneLoading(); // A function that does something with the datasource
   },
  onError: function(aSink, aStatus, aErrorMsg)
```

Example 10-10. Setup nsIRDFXMLSink with event handlers (continued)

```
  {
    alert("Error: " + aErrorMsg);
  }
};
```

Once the event handlers are set up, you can use *nsIRDFXMLSink*:

```
sink = datasource.QueryInterface(Components.interfaces.nsIRDFXMLSink);
sink.addXMLSinkObserver(observer);
```

The events are then triggered automatically when the datasource is loaded up with data, allowing you to create handlers that manipulate the data as it appears.

nsIRDFXMLSerializer and nsIRDFXMLSource

These two interfaces are meant to work together. *nsIRDFXMLSerializer* lets you init a datasource into the xml-serializer module that outputs RDF. However, *nsIRDFXMLSource* actually contains the Serialize function. Here's how to serialize a datasource into an alert:

```
serializer = '@mozilla.org/rdf/xml-serializer;1';
s = Components.classes[serializer].
createInstance(Components.interfaces.nsIRDFXMLSerializer);
s.init(datasource);
output = new Object();
output.write = new function(buf,count)
{
  alert(buf); // Show the serialized syntax
  return count;
}
   s.QueryInterface(Components.interfaces.nsIRDFXMLSource).Serialize(output);
```

As in the previous example with *nsIRDFXMLParser*, Example 10-10 does not use RDF data from a file. The serialized data is passed directly to an alert, which then displays the generated RDF.

Template Dynamics

Once you learn how to create templates and modify datasources, the ultimate in template mastery is to apply datasources to a template dynamically.

This process is done through the database property of a XUL element that contains a template. The object returned by this property has only two methods, AddDataSource and RemoveDataSource. A separate builder.rebuild function is also available for refreshing the template's display, but you probably won't need it once the template automatically updates itself. The addition and removal of a datasource to a <tree> template is demonstrated here:

```
tree = document.getElementById('tree-template');
tree.database.AddDataSource(someDatasource);
```

```
// tree will now update its display to show contents
tree.database.RemoveDataSource(someDatasource);
// tree will now be empty
// Optional, use only when tree is not updating for some reason
tree.builder.rebuild();
```

You can add and remove any datasource as long as the template actually matches the data inside it. Also, multiple datasources can be applied to the same template with no problems, which allows you to aggregate data from different places, such as contact data, work information, and computer hardware information (e.g., "Eric uses a Compaq with the serial number 1223456-1091 to write his book and he sits on the fourth floor of the Acme Building, which is the Bay Area branch of Acme Enterprises.)

Template Dynamics in XBL

Putting templates inside XBL can be a useful organizational scheme. Here is a basic implementation of a widget that creates a list of people based on names listed in an attribute:

```
<people names="Brian King,Eric Murphy,Ian Oeschger,Pete Collins,David Boswell"/>
```

Obviously, the comma is used as the delimiter for this list. The constructor element in Example 10-11 uses JavaScript to break up this string.

Example 10-11. Binding with in-memory datasource and <listbox> template

```
<?xml version="1.0"?>
<bindings xmlns ="http://www.mozilla.org/xbl"
xmlns:xul="http://www.mozilla.org/keymaster/gatekeeper/there.is.only.xul">
  <binding id="people">
    <implementation>
      <constructor>
      <![CDATA[
        // Read the Names into an Array
        names = document.getAnonymousNodes(this)[0].getAttribute('names');
        names = new String(names);
        namesArray= names.split(',');
        // Initialize the RDF Service
        rdf = Components
             .classes['@mozilla.org/rdf/rdf-service;1']
             .getService(Components.interfaces.nsIRDFService);
        // Initialize a Datasource in Memory
             inMemory = '@mozilla.org/rdf/datasource;1?name=in-memory-datasource';
        datasource = Components.classes[inMemory].
           createInstance(Components.interfaces.nsIRDFDataSource);
        // Create the Root Node and an Anonymous Resource to Start With
        root   = rdf.GetResource('urn:root');
        people = rdf.GetAnonymousResource();
        // Insert the People resource into the RDF graph
        datasource.Assert
          (root,
           rdf.GetResource('http://www.mozdev.org/rdf#people'),
```

Example 10-11. Binding with in-memory datasource and <listbox> template (continued)

```
          people,true);
        // Initialize Methods needed for Containers
        rdfc = Components
              .classes['@mozilla.org/rdf/container-utils;1']
              .getService(Components.interfaces.nsIRDFContainerUtils);
        // For the People resource, make a Sequence of people
        peopleSequence = rdfc.MakeSeq(datasource, people);
        for(i=0;i<namesArray.length;i++)
        {
          // Create a Person, with a Unique Number, for example
          person = rdf.GetResource(i);
          // Insert the Person's name into the RDF graph underneath number
          datasource.Assert
            (person,
             rdf.GetResource('http://www.mozdev.org/rdf#name'),
             rdf.GetLiteral(namesArray[i]),true);
          peopleSequence.AppendElement(person);
        }
        list = document.getAnonymousNodes(this)[1];
        list.database.AddDataSource(datasource);
      ]]>
      </constructor>
    </implementation>
    <content>
      <xul:box id="names" inherits="names" flex="0"/>
      <xul:listbox datasources="rdf:null" ref="urn:root" flex="1">
        <xul:template>
          <xul:rule>
            <xul:conditions>
              <xul:content uri="?uri"/>
              <xul:triple subject="?uri"
                       predicate="http://www.mozdev.org/rdf#people"
                         object="?people"/>
              <xul:member container="?people" child="?person"/>
              <xul:triple subject="?person"
                       predicate="http://www.mozdev.org/rdf#name"
                         object="?name"/>
            </xul:conditions>
            <xul:action>
              <xul:listitem uri="?person">
                <xul:listcell>
                  <xul:description value="?person "/>
                  <xul:description value="?name"/>
                </xul:listcell>
              </xul:listitem>
            </xul:action>
          </xul:rule>
        </xul:template>
      </xul>
    </content>
  </binding>
</bindings>
```

In Example 10-11, everything you need to display a datasource dynamically is present. The only difference between this dynamically generated version and a static RDF-based template is the `datasources="rdf:null"`, which specifies that the template does not refer to an actual datasource. Data that is edited, rearranged, or changed in a different way is often displayed dynamically in the UI with templates in this manner.

JSLib RDF Files

Working with actual RDF files is not easy. However, JSLib (*http://jslib.mozdev.org*) provides an RDF file library that can help you develop an RDF-based application. The library provides many types of error checking, as well as a friendly abstraction away from the RDF/XML interfaces of Mozilla (see "nsIRDFXML Interfaces," later in this chapter). Example 10-12 shows some common uses of the `RDFFile` class in JSLib. This functionality can be used in situations in which you have data in RDF that you want to pull out "manually" and use piece by piece (rather than as a whole datasource in a template).

Example 10-12. Creating and modifying an RDF file using JSLib

```
var rdfFileURL = 'chrome://jarfly/content/jar.rdf';
var gTreeBody = null;
var gListbox = null;
var gRDF = null;
function onload()
{
  fileUtils = new FileUtils();
  path = fileUtils.chrome_to_path(rdfFileURL);
  if(navigator.platform == "Win32") {
    path = path.replace(/\//g,"\\");
    // Only needed on Windows, until JSLib is fixed
  }
  gRDF = new RDFFile(path,'jar:flies','http://mozdev.org/fly-rdf#');
  gTreeBody = document.getElementById('tb');
  gTreeBody.database.AddDataSource(gRDF.dsource);
  gListbox  = document.getElementById('list');
  gListbox.database.AddDataSource(gRDF.dsource);
  rebuildLists();
}
function rebuildLists()
{
  gTreeBody.builder.rebuild();
  gListbox.builder.rebuild();
}
function update()
{
  name      = document.getElementById('nameField').value;
  color     = document.getElementById('colorField').value;
  quantity  = document.getElementById('quantityField').value;
  seqNumber = -1;
```

Example 10-12. Creating and modifying an RDF file using JSLib (continued)

```
  del       = false;
  replace   = false;
  if(document.getElementById('delete').checked)
    del = true;
  if(document.getElementById('replace').checked)
    replace = true;
  var seqLength = 0;
  if(gRDF.doesSeqExist('types'))
  {
    seqLength = gRDF.getSeqSubNodes('types').length;
    //if(del)gRDF.removeSeq('types',false);
  }
  else
    gRDF.addSeq('types');
  for(i=0;i<seqLength;i++)
  {
    tempItem = 'types:_' + (i+1);
    if(gRDF.getAttribute(tempItem,'name')==name)
      seqNumber = gRDF.getAttribute(tempItem,'number');
  }
  if(seqNumber == -1)
  {
    item = 'types:_' + (seqLength+1);
    gRDF.setAttribute(item,'name',name);
    gRDF.setAttribute(item,'number',seqLength+1);
  }
  else
  {
    item = 'types:_' + seqNumber;
    gRDF.setAttribute(item,'number',seqNumber);
  }
  if(color!='')
    gRDF.setAttribute(item,'color',color);
  if(quantity!='')
  {
    gRDF.setAttribute(item,'quantity',quantity);
    gRDF.setAttribute(item,'dead',calcDead(quantity,replace));
  }
  if(!del)
    gRDF.addNode(item);
  else
    gRDF.removeNode(item);
  gRDF.flush();
  onload();
}
function calcDead(quantity,replace)
{
  if(!replace)
  {
    v = parseInt( (quantity * Math.random()) * 0.13 );
    return (v.toString());
  }
  else
```

Example 10-12. Creating and modifying an RDF file using JSLib (continued)

```
    return 0;
}
function changeC(color)
{
  document.getElementById('colorField').value=color;
}
function changeQ(quantity)
{
  document.getElementById('quantityField').value=quantity;
}
```

This example contains a datasource that represents a collection of flies. These flies are built up dynamically with JavaScript objects from the RDF library, which represent the datasource itself (`gRDF = new RDFFile`), methods that view and update the data (`if(gRDF.getAttribute(tempItem,'name')==name`), and utilities that make work with RDF files easier (`path = fileUtils.chrome_to_path(rdfFileURL)`).

Example 10-13 initializes and updates a file after it changes.

Example 10-13. Initialization

```
var rdfFileURL = 'chrome://jarfly/content/jar.rdf';
var gTreeBody = null;
var gListbox = null;
var gRDF = null;
function onload()
{
  fileUtils = new FileUtils();
  path = fileUtils.chrome_to_path(rdfFileURL);
  if(navigator.platform == "Win32") {
    path = path.replace(/\//g,"\\");
    // Only needed on Windows, until JSLib is fixed
  }
  gRDF = new RDFFile(path,'jar:flies','http://mozdev.org/fly-rdf#');
```

In Example 10-13, the file URL is set to an RDF file in the chrome area. Note that both a `<tree>` and a `<listbox>`, which display the same data in different ways, will be updated with the same datasource. The `onload` function is called after the main XUL document is loaded. A class called `FileUtils` is initialized, which will create a path to the RDF file. If the file doesn't already exist, JSLib automatically creates it.

Finally, the `RDFFile` is created by using the path and a root resource identifier, and the "xFly" namespace is used for the data references. Example 10-14 shows that the RDF file is ready to have its data added and deleted.

Example 10-14. Data updating

```
function update()
{
  ...
  var seqLength = 0;
  if(gRDF.doesSeqExist('types'))
```

Example 10-14. Data updating (continued)

```
{
  seqLength = gRDF.getSeqSubNodes('types').length;
  //if(del)gRDF.removeSeq('types',false);
}
else
  gRDF.addSeq('types');
for(i=0;i<seqLength;i++)
{
  tempItem = 'types:_' + (i+1);
  if(gRDF.getAttribute(tempItem,'name')==name)
    seqNumber = gRDF.getAttribute(tempItem,'number');
}
if(seqNumber == -1)
{
  item = 'types:_' + (seqLength+1);
  gRDF.setAttribute(item,'name',name);
  gRDF.setAttribute(item,'number',seqLength+1);
}
else
{
  item = 'types:_' + seqNumber;
  gRDF.setAttribute(item,'number',seqNumber);
}
if(color!='')
  gRDF.setAttribute(item,'color',color);
if(quantity!='')
{
  gRDF.setAttribute(item,'quantity',quantity);
  gRDF.setAttribute(item,'dead',calcDead(quantity,replace));
}
if(!del)
  gRDF.addNode(item);
else
  gRDF.removeNode(item);
gRDF.flush();
onload();
```

Example 10-14 contains a modified version of the `update` function. First, the function checks to see if a sequence called `types` is in the RDF file. If not, it creates one. Next, it appends an item to the sequence using `type:_+(seqLength+1)`. The same type of container setup was described in the section "nsIRDFContainer," earlier in this chapter.

The `update` function then adds the color, quantity, and "dead" properties of that new item in the sequence. Next, it ensures that you actually want to add the item to the RDF file and flushes it out if not. It then recalls the `onload` function to update the template display.

These are the basics of using `RDFFile`. As you can see, using JSLib for RDF is often much easier than trying to implement a similar setup on your own. More information about `RDFFile` and the other JSLib libraries can be found at *http://www.jslib.mozdev.org/*.

Manifests

The package descriptions, generally called *manifests*, use RDF to describe new packages and files to Mozilla. They can be added seamlessly because RDF provides a platform-like environment that facilitates the installation and use of new Mozilla software.

All packages, including the ones that come preinstalled with Mozilla (such as the browser, the MailNews component, and the en-US language pack), have manifests describing them in terms of their relation to other packages. The manifests are typically files called *contents.rdf*, but they may also be called *manifest.rdf*. Example 10-15 presents a *contents.rdf* file that describes a new skin for Mozilla.

Example 10-15. Skin manifest

```
<?xml version="1.0"?>
<RDF:RDF xmlns:RDF="http://www.w3.org/1999/02/22-rdf-syntax-ns#"
  xmlns:chrome="http://www.mozilla.org/rdf/chrome#">
<!-- List all the skins being supplied by this theme -->
<RDF:Seq about="urn:mozilla:skin:root">
  <RDF:li resource="urn:mozilla:skin:modern/1.0" />
</RDF:Seq>
<!-- Modern Information -->
<RDF:Description about="urn:mozilla:skin:modern/1.0"
  chrome:displayName="Modern"
  chrome:author="themes@mozilla.org"
  chrome:name="themes@mozilla.org/modern/1.0">
<chrome:packages>
  <RDF:Seq about="urn:mozilla:skin:modern/1.0:packages">
    <--RDF:li resource="urn:mozilla:skin:modern/1.0:aim"/ -->
    <RDF:li resource="urn:mozilla:skin:modern/1.0:communicator"/>
    <RDF:li resource="urn:mozilla:skin:modern/1.0:editor"/>
    <RDF:li resource="urn:mozilla:skin:modern/1.0:global"/>
    <RDF:li resource="urn:mozilla:skin:modern/1.0:messenger"/>
    <RDF:li resource="urn:mozilla:skin:modern/1.0:navigator"/>
  </RDF:Seq>
</chrome:packages>
</RDF:Description>
</RDF:RDF>
```

As you can see, the manifest is divided up into sections. After the preamble, where the XML processing instruction and the namespace declarations are made, an RDF sequence lists all the themes defined or supplemented (since you can create a package updated for only one Mozilla component, such as the browser) by this package. This section contains only one `RDF:li`—the modern theme.

The next section gives more information on the theme, such as the author, the theme name, and a description. The `chrome:packages` structure that completes the manifest describes the packages to which this theme should be applied. All major components of the Netscape browser are listed in this example—including the AIM client that is not a part of Mozilla—but is skinned by themes such as Modern.

RDF and Dynamic Overlays

Manifests can also add new menu items to existing Mozilla menus. When you add a new package to Mozilla, you should make it accessible from within the browser application, where users can access it easily. This is where RDF and dynamic overlays come in.

The RDF you provide in your package makes it possible for the chrome registry, discussed in Chapter 6, to find, understand, and register your new files. Packages must be registered if they are to be skinned, localized, or accessed using the special tools Mozilla provides (e.g., the chrome URL or XPConnect to the XPCOM libraries). If you do not register your package by providing the necessary RDF manifests, it cannot be accessed except as a disparate collection of files in the browser's main content window, which is not what you want.

You can add overlays in Mozilla in two ways: import them explicitly by using an overlay processing instruction at the top of the XUL file into which items in the overlay file are to be "composed," or use RDF to register and load overlay files at runtime. This latter method will be used here to add an "xFly" item to the Tools menu of the Mozilla suite of applications.

Example 10-16 shows the *contents.rdf* manifest format that alerts Mozilla of the presence of an overlay, its target in the Mozilla application, and the package of which it is a part.

Example 10-16. Overlay for a sample application menu

```
<?xml version="1.0"?>
<RDF:RDF xmlns:RDF="http://www.w3.org/1999/02/22-rdf-syntax-ns#"
         xmlns:chrome="http://www.mozilla.org/rdf/chrome#">
  <RDF:Seq about="urn:mozilla:package:root">
    <RDF:li resource="urn:mozilla:package:help"/>
  </RDF:Seq>
  <RDF:Description about="urn:mozilla:package:help"
        chrome:displayName="xFly Application"
        chrome:author="xfly.mozdev.org"
        chrome:name="xfly">
  </RDF:Description>
  <!-- Declare overlay points used in this package -->
  <RDF:Seq about="urn:mozilla:overlays">
    <RDF:li resource="chrome://communicator/content/tasksOverlay.xul" />
  </RDF:Seq>
  <RDF:Seq about="chrome://communicator/content/tasksOverlay.xul">
    <RDF:li>chrome://xfly/content/xflyOverlay.xul</RDF:li>
  </RDF:Seq>
</RDF:RDF>
```

The manifest in Example 10-16 names the file *xflyOverlay.xul* as an overlay. Then it names *tasksOverlay.xul* as the base file into which the contents are placed. In this case, the overlays can overlay other overlay files arbitrarily. An overlay can define new content anywhere in the application. Overlays are often responsible for putting new items in menus. As long as the target and overlay ids match, any two RDF datasources are merged. You can try this example by putting a single new menu item in an overlay structure like the one shown in Example 10-17. Save it as *xflyOverlay.xul* in the *xfly* content subdirectory and use the manifest information in Example 10-16 as part of the packaging process described in Chapter 6.

Example 10-17. Overlay for an xFly menu item in the browser

```
<?xml version="1.0"?>
<overlay id="xflyMenuID"
        xmlns:html="http://www.w3.org/1999/xhtml"
        xmlns="http://www.mozilla.org/keymaster/gatekeeper/there.is.only.xul">

  <menupopup id="tools_menu">
    <menuitem label="xfly xml editor"
        oncommand="toOpenWindowByType('mozilla:xfly, 'chrome://xfly/content/');" />

</menupopup>

</overlay>
```

The menupopup in Mozilla with the ID "tools_menu" gets a new menu item when this overlay is processed and its content included.

CHAPTER 11
Localization

This chapter describes how to use Mozilla's internationalization (I18N) and localization (L10N) technologies to make applications usable by people around the world. Because the Mozilla community (and the Internet community in general), is global, it is vital to be able to cross language barriers by localizing your application and making it available to a wider audience.

In this chapter, you are given step-by-step instructions on how to change the visible text for your application in the XUL interface and how to handle nonstatic strings that arise from dynamic string handling in other areas of your application code.

While the basic technologies that are used are not new, Mozilla is innovating in areas such as Unicode support and quick access language pack installs. The information in this chapter about the internationalization (*http://www.mozilla.org/projects/intl/index.html*) and localization (*http://www.mozilla.org/projects/l10n/mlp.html*) projects will give you a solid foundation for what is possible in your own application.

Localization Basics

Before learning how to localize your Mozilla application, it's useful to run through some of the high-level goals and features of the Mozilla internationalization and localization projects. First, here are some definitions:

Internationalization (I18N)
: The design and development of software to function in a particular locale. The shorthand term, I18N, refers to the 18 letters between the initial "i" and final "n."

Localization (L10N)
: The modification of software to meet the language of a location and the adaptation of resources, such as the user interface (UI) and documentation, for that region. L10N is an acronym for localization and refers to the 10 letters between the initial "l" and final "n."

Locale

"A set of conventions affected or determined by human language and customs, as defined within a particular geo-political region. These conventions include (but are not necessarily limited to) the written language, formats for dates, numbers and currency, sorting orders, etc.," according to the official Mozilla document found at *http://www.mozilla.org/docs/refList/i18n/*.

Locale in the context of this chapter is related specifically to the display of text in the user interface. The focus will be on UI localization of XUL files and strings contained in JavaScript and C++ files, as well as the methods employed for localization.

Here are some main features of the Mozilla internationalization capabilities, which are relevant to the user front end application level:

- Mozilla is Unicode-enabled for Latin-based languages, Cyrillic, Greek, Chinese, Japanese, and Korean. Mozilla widgets and HTML rendering can support the input and display of these languages. Unicode-enabling for other languages and character sets is an ongoing process.
- Mozilla can be easily localized into different languages, even if not supported by the underlying operating system.
- Most Mozilla localization work involves translating strings as entities in Document Type Definition (DTD) format and properties file format (an idea taken from Java), which are based on open standards.
- Localization can be done once and run on Windows, Macintosh, Unix, and other platforms—something we have come to expect from the Mozilla framework. This is a great time saver, and indeed a cost saver if you come at it from that perspective.
- Mozilla supports BIDI, the display and input of text in a bidirectional format for such languages as Arabic and Hebrew, yet the capabilities for this in the UI were not mature when we were writing this book.
- The UI locale DTD files use UTF-8 as the default encoding for translated items. Mozilla then maps to Unicode or non-Unicode fonts, depending on which platform you're running on or what fonts you installed in your system. You are encouraged to encode your DTD files as UTF-8 when possible.

Recalling the architecture of the XPFE toolkit described in Chapter 2, the locale component can be easily plugged in and out of the application that you are working on without impacting any other components. This functionality is ideal, for instance, for people with linguistic skills and less experience with technical issues to become involved in a Mozilla-related project.

For the Developer

Many available resources show you how to help localize an existing application into a specific language or to find out how to add localization support to your own application.

The Mozilla Localization Project hosts various localization teams and provides help whenever possible. The Mozilla community includes a discussion group that uses many languages to discuss Mozilla development issues. The *netscape.public.mozilla.l10n* and *netscape.public.mozilla.i18n* newsgroups are a great place to discuss these issues with other developers.

When developing an application, some words and phrases that developers like to hear (according to the Mozilla organization, at *http://www.mozilla.org/projects/l10n/xul-l10n.html*) are: standards compliant, simple, leveragable, portable, extensible, separable, consistent, dynamic, valid, parser friendly, invisible (part of the XUL authoring process), and efficient. The following sections will help you understand how these terms and goals impact the chosen technologies and how to use those technologies. The ultimate aim is to help you localize your application easily.

Files and File Formats

Here are the main file types you'll see when learning about locale and that you will use when localizing your Mozilla application. A good home for all of these resources is in the *locale* area of the application *chrome*.

DTD (.dtd)
: Files containing entities that host the strings from XUL content files.

Property (.properties) or string bundles
: Files containing strings that are accessed by JavaScript, C++, and possibly other scripting or component files.

RDF
: RDF files are described in XML syntax, so use entities.

HTML and text
: Suitable for long text, HTML and XML documents and other content that needs to be localized.

The next two sections will help you start localizing your application. The sections focus on DTD files and string bundles, which are the core formats for XUL-localizable content. Before getting started, here is a review of some general principles that might help you design and implement the locale component.

UI Aesthetics and Principles

To put locale in context, this section looks at some issues you may encounter when localizing your Mozilla application. Some are universal principles and others are unique to the environment. This reference is by no means exhaustive, but it contains some scenarios and tips the authors came across in their experience with locale in Mozilla.

Space management

One of the guiding principles in UI design is for your interface to not get too crowded. Although estimates are not specific, it is wise to leave about 30 percent expansion space in your window and dialogs. To achieve this flexibility, you have to ensure that the XUL window has ample space in the first place for all the widgets to fit.

More specifically, the application needs to have space for widgets to expand or contract without detracting from the overall look and feel. Intuitive use of the XUL box model (refer to Chapter 3 for more information) and correct choice of widgets goes a long way in achieving this goal.

The factors that can cause this space to be filled include using languages/character sets that are more verbose than the one that was there originally, and the users changing their font size settings. Some safeguards that have been built into Mozilla already handle this problem. Much of it is done in CSS, but other methods are available. The section "Language Quirks," later in this chapter, outlines one of these methods.

Help system

If you choose to integrate a Help system into your application, a localizable resource will be most content. Opinions differ within technical writing circles, but having screenshots in your documents is generally not considered advantageous. For example, they can get out of date easily in the constantly evolving world of software, or they need to be retaken frequently when new features are added to the UI.

Tooltips

Tooltips are a sometimes overlooked yet valuable way of relaying information to the user. They can be used as an alternative to a help system if you are looking for something simpler. They can also expand an explanation of something that was annotated in the UI text. Sometimes text can have multiple meanings in context, and expanding it with a tooltip can clear up any confusion. In an editor or multifile browser, for example, you might have a find button. A tooltip can clear up the confusion about whether the results of the action searches in the current file or in all files.

Most XUL widgets support tooltips. Implementation is as straightforward as adding a `tooltip` attribute to the widget with an associated value. For it to be localizable, it must be in the form of a DTD entity.

```
<tab id="config" label="&config.label;" tooltip-"&config.tooltip;" />
```

The "Inserting Entities" section, later in this chapter, provides more information on the rationale for using entities and how to insert them into XUL content.

Grammar

In any user interface, there is limited screen space. When possible, however, provide complete or near-complete sentences. These sentences are better than using text based on phrases or acronyms. They provide meaning to the translator and clearer instructions to the user.

Commenting

Commenting was mentioned before, but is worth stressing again. The translators may have not even seen the software that you are working on, but you hope that is not the case! Commenting is very useful for giving context and flagging strings that should not be commented. You can comment your HTML, XML, or DTD files by wrapping it in a `<!-- comment -->` block.

```
<!--NOTE to Translators: Do NOT change the next string -->
<!ENTITY appName.label "My Application">
```

Note that a bundle file uses the # notation at the beginning of each line to signify a comment.

```
# This text is used in the view menu for launching the page choices dialog
pageChoices=Go To...
```

Web resources

Localizable resources are not only strings of text that need to be translated into different languages; they are any variable information that is liable to change over the lifetime of your application. The handling of URLs is a case in point. You may have references interspersed throughout your UI that point to web resources. These references can be explicit listings or widgets that, once activated, launch a client to bring you to a certain location.

Images are another resource commonly used in documentation. A tutorial on your application may have screenshots of the UI in action. If you do use images, keep an eye out for localizable content in them.

DTD Entities

Entities in XUL work the same way as they do in any other XML application. They are used to reference data that was abstracted from the content. This process encourages reuse of data, but in the context of Mozilla's XPFE, it is used to extract visible text in interface widgets. This extraction ensures that the content can remain untouched during the localization process.

Inserting Entities

Example 11-1 shows how to put DTD entities into your XUL code by using attribute values for the text of a menu item (`label`) and the keyboard access shortcuts (accesskey). The syntax requires that an entity be placed in quotes as the value of the attribute. This is a useful example because it highlights the localization of a widget label, which is common to many widgets, and a supplementary attribute, which, in this case, is an accesskey.

Example 11-1. XUL menu with entity references for text and accesskeys

```
<menu label="&menuFile.label;" accesskey="&menuFile.accesskey;">
  <menupopup>
    <menuitem accesskey="&menuNew.accesskey;" label="&menuNew.label;"
        oncommand="doNew();"/>
    <menuitem accesskey="&menuOpen.accesskey;" label="&menuOpen.label;"
        oncommand="doOpen();"/>
    <menuseparator />
    <menuitem accesskey="&menuClose.accesskey;" label="&menuClose.label;"
        oncommand="doClose();"/>
    <menuitem accesskey="&menuSave.accesskey;" label="&menuSave.label;"
        oncommand="doSave()"/>
    <menuitem accesskey="&menuSaveAs.accesskey;" label="&menuSaveAs.label;"
        oncommand="doSaveAs"/>
    <menuseparator />
    <menuitem accesskey="&menuPrint.accesskey;" label="&menuPrint.label;"
        oncommand="doPrint();"/>
    <menuseparator />
    <menuitem accesskey="&menuExit.accesskey;" label="&menuExit.label;"
        oncommand="doExit();"/>
  </menupopup>
</menu>
```

Note that each entity in Example 11-1 has a text value associated with it in the DTD entities declarations. The entity that appears on the menu is `&menuFile.label;`. Note that this entity mirrors the correct syntax for referencing a value, which is: `&get.text;`.

The entity reference (or name, in this context) must be preceded by an ampersand (&) and end with a semicolon (;). The period is optional, but conventional. Typically, the period separates the entity's element or target (`menuFile`) from the type of entity (`label`). Refer to the"Programming and Localization" section later in this chapter for more information on naming conventions.

For some widgets, including `<description>` and `<label>`, the entity can be placed inside the element tags, as opposed to being values of attributes.

```
<description>&explanation.text;</description>
```

Table 11-1 represents the DTD files that accompany the XUL content in Example 11-1. Two languages, English and Spanish, are separated into different files. These files have the same name as the DTD file referenced in the XUL file that contains the entities. However, each file for every different language exists in a separate locale folder. Each entry, or entity, in the DTD file has a name that matches the name referenced in the XUL and a value to be filled in for that entity. The value is enclosed in quotes. When generating these files, you will need to create the file only once and copy it to a different directory where you can replace the values in the entities. A good tool would carry out this process for you. Refer to the "Localization Tools" sidebar later in the chapter for more information.

Table 11-1. Entity definitions for the XUL menu

English DTD	Spanish DTD
<!ENTITY menuFile.label "File">	<!ENTITY menuFile.label "Archivo">
<!ENTITY menuNew.label "New">	<!ENTITY menuNew.label "Nuevo">
<!ENTITY menuOpen.label "Open...">	<!ENTITY menuOpen.label "Abrir Archivo...">
<!ENTITY menuClose.label "Close">	<!ENTITY menuClose.label "Cerrar">
<!ENTITY menuSave.label "Save">	<!ENTITY menuSave.label "Salvar">
<!ENTITY menuSaveAs.label "Save As...">	<!ENTITY menuSaveAs.label "Salvar Como...">
<!ENTITY menuPrint.label "Print...">	<!ENTITY menuPrint.label "Imprimir...">
<!ENTITY menuExit.label "Exit">	<!ENTITY menuExit.label "Salir">
<!ENTITY menuFile.accesskey "f">	<!ENTITY menuFile.accesskey "a">
<!ENTITY menuNew.accesskey "n">	<!ENTITY menuNew.accesskey "n">
<!ENTITY menuOpen.accesskey "o">	<!ENTITY menuOpen.accesskey "o">
<!ENTITY menuClose.accesskey "c">	<!ENTITY menuClose.accesskey "c">
<!ENTITY menuSave.accesskey "s">	<!ENTITY menuSave.accesskey "s">
<!ENTITY menuSaveAs.accesskey "a">	<!ENTITY menuSaveAs.accesskey "a">
<!ENTITY menuPrint.accesskey "p">	<!ENTITY menuPrint.accesskey "i">
<!ENTITY menuExit.accesskey "x">	<!ENTITY menuExit.accesskey "r">

Figure 11-1 shows the resulting XUL menus. There can only be one value for each entity and only one language taking precedence, or appearing in the UI, at a time.

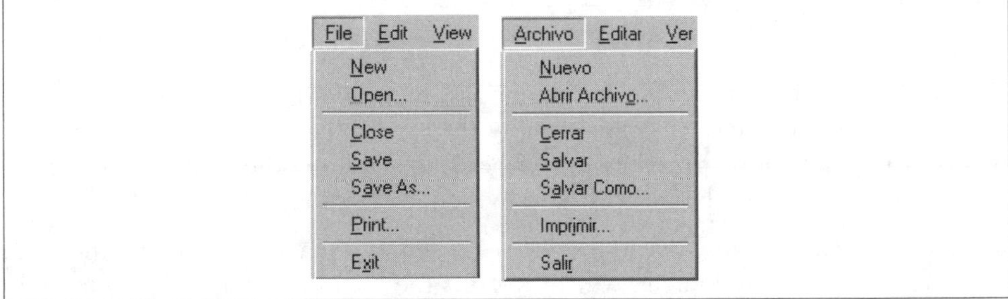

Figure 11-1. Localized menus in English and Spanish

This example presents only two languages, but theoretically, you can have as many languages as you require. The locale-switching mechanism and the chrome registry must determine which one should be used, which is explained later in the section "The Chrome Registry and Locale."

External and Inline Entities

You may ask, how are the entities accessed? You can associate the DTD with your XUL file in two ways. The first is internally, which involves wrapping the strings in a DTD data type enclosure by using the `DOCTYPE` declaration.

```
<!DOCTYPE window [
  <!ENTITY windowTitle.label "Greetings">
  <!ENTITY fileMenu.label "File">
]>
```

The second is an external DTD file, which is associated with your XUL that also uses the DOCTYPE declaration, and a reference pointing to the file:

```
<!DOCTYPE window SYSTEM "chrome://xfly/locale/xfly.dtd">
```

The node referenced in the DOCTYPE declaration is usually followed by the XUL document's root node. In this case, it is window, but can be other elements like page or dialog (however, it is not actually validated so it can be any value).

If you have a small application, the DTD files can reside in the same folder as your XUL files, but putting them into their own locale directory within your chrome structure is good practice.

Consider the main Editor window in Mozilla. Its declaration in Example 11-2 is flexible enough to associate multiple DTD files with your content.

Example 11-2. The Editor's Doctype definitions

```
<!DOCTYPE window [
  <!ENTITY % editorDTD SYSTEM "chrome://editor/locale/editor.dtd" >
  %editorDTD;
  <!ENTITY % editorOverlayDTD SYSTEM "chrome://editor/locale/editorOverlay.dtd" >
  %editorOverlayDTD;
  <!ENTITY % brandDTD SYSTEM "chrome://global/locale/brand.dtd" >
  %brandDTD;
]>
```

The declaration first stores the document associated with the chrome URL in an associated parameter entity. It then simply uses it. XML does not have a one-step way of storing and using the entity as in other languages. In other words, the declaration is the equivalent of the import foo in Python, or #include "foo.h" in C.

Certain localizable resources lend themselves to reuse. It makes sense to use the same strings across different content, which explains the inclusion of a DTD file in more than one XUL document. In Mozilla, this includes brand information, build ID numbers, and help resources.

Which is more appropriate to use: internal or external entities? Using the external approach is preferable because the content (XUL) does not have to be touched during the translation process. If someone opts to create a tool to extract and/or insert strings, their job would be much easier if they had to parse one less file type. This may remove context somewhat, but it can be overcome by actively commenting the DTD file.

String Bundles

String bundles are flat text files that contain text for the UI that is accessed in JavaScript, C++, and theoretically any language that fits within the Mozilla framework. These bundles are strings that can be presented visually to the user via some functionality in the application at any time. This may be anything from a dynamically changing menu item to an alert box, or from a URL to a placeholder that is filled depending on the context in which it is accessed. The bundle files are given an extension of *.properties* and they commonly reside in the locale directory with the DTD files.

A user interface can use one or more string bundles, each of which is defined in a `<stringbundle>` element and surrounded by a `<stringbundleset>` element. Example 11-3 contains the bundles used by the Mozilla browser.

Example 11-3. String bundles used by the Mozilla browser

```
<stringbundleset id="stringbundleset">
    <stringbundle id="bundle_navigator"
        src="chrome://navigator/locale/navigator.properties"/>
    <stringbundle id="bundle_brand"
        src="chrome://global/locale/brand.properties"/>
    <stringbundle id="bundle_navigator_region"
        src="chrome://navigator-region/locale/region.properties"/>
    <stringbundle id="bundle_brand_region"
        src="chrome://global-region/locale/region.properties"/>
    <stringbundle id="findBundle"
        src="chrome://global/locale/finddialog.properties"/>
</stringbundleset>
```

As you can see from their names and their locations in the chrome, each bundle serves a different purpose. They include a file that contains the bulk of the strings for the browser (*navigator.properties*), a file that includes branding strings, and a couple of files for regional information. This model is useful if you need to output many strings to the UI from your source code and would like to organize them into meaningful groups.

Inside a Bundle

A string bundle (*.properties*) file has a very simple format. It contains one or more lines that have the identifier associated with the localizable string. The format of a string bundle string with an identifier is:

```
Identifier=String
```

The format for comments in a bundle file requires the hash notation (#). Comments are useful for notifying translators of the context of strings, or flagging a string that should be left as is and not localized. Comments in properties files are formatted in the following manner.

```
# DO NOT TRANSLATE
applicationTitle=xFly
```

Spaces in bundles are treated literally—spaces between words are observed, with the exception of the start and the end of the string.

The next section shows the methods and properties specific to the `<stringbundle>` element that are available to you when you use it. The implementations are contained in the binding for the element.

String Bundle Methods and Properties

Defining your bundle in XUL and then creating the file with the values is only half the story. This section shows how to extract the values from the bundle and place them in UI. The language of choice in these examples is JavaScript. This process is necessary when you have to change values in the UI because DTD entities can not be updated dynamically.

Methods

Our bundle is defined in XUL like this:

```
<stringbundle id="bundle_xfly"
    src="chrome://xfly/locale/xfly.properties"/>
```

To access the methods of the bundle object in your script, you have to get a handle on the XUL element by using its `id`. First declare the variable globally that will be holding the bundle:

```
var xFlyBundle;
```

Then assign the variable to the bundle. A good place to do this is in the load handler function of your XUL window, or in the constructor for your binding if you are using it from there:

```
xFlyBundle = document.getElementById("bundle_xfly");
```

Now that you have access to the bundle, you can use the available methods to retrieve the strings. The two main functions are `getString` and `getFormattedString`.

getString. The most straightforward string access method, `getString`, takes one parameter (namely the identifier of the string) and returns the localizable string value for use in the UI:

```
var readonly = xFlyBundle.getString(`readonlyFile');
alert(readonly);
```

The string bundle entry looks like this:

```
readonlyfile=This file is read only
```

getFormattedString. This function takes an extra parameter—an array of string values, which are substituted into the string in the bundle. Then the full string with the substituted values is returned:

```
var numFiles = numberInEditor
numFilesMsg = xflyBundle.getFormattedString("numFilesMessage", [numFiles]);
```

You can have more than one value replaced in the string, each one delimited within the square brackets by using a comma:

```
fileInfo = xflyBundle.getFormattedString("fileInformation",
 [fileName, fileSize]);
```

The string bundle entry looks like this:

```
flyFileInformation=The file is called %1$s and its size is %2$s
```

The %x numerical value refers to the ordering of the values to be substituted in the string. The type of the value is determined by the dollar ($) symbol. In this case, there are two possibilities—$s is a string value and $d is an integer value.

Properties

Some binding properties that are exposed to your script accompany the methods. These properties are not often needed for routine retrieval of string values, but are useful to know nonetheless if you ever need to discover or share the meta information related to your bundle and locale.

stringBundle. This property is the string bundle object that queries the *nsIStringBundleService* interfaces and initializes the XPCOM interface, making methods available to it. It is the direct way of getting a string from a bundle:

```
var appBundle = document.getElementById("bundle_app");
return appBundle.stringBundle.GetStringFromName("chapter11");
```

src. This property is the attribute used to get and set the properties file that will be used as a string bundle:

```
var appBundle = document.getElementById("bundle_app");
dump("You are using the properties file " + appBundle.src);
```

Creating Your Own Bundle

The implementation for setting up your string bundle just described is hidden from the XUL author. You only need to point at the bundle you want to use by using the source attribute. There is however, an alternative way to do this if you do not favor using <stringbundle> or would like to extend that binding.

The alternative is to use utility routines that come bundled with Mozilla and are contained in a string resources JavaScript file: *strres.js*. With this file, creating a bundle is a three-step process.

1. Include the JavaScript file:

```
<script type="application/x-javascript"
   src="chrome://global/content/strres.js"/>
```

2. Set up your bundle:

```
var bundle =
   srGetStrBundle("chrome://mypackage/locale/mypackage.properties");
```

3. Access the strings:

```
var greeting = bundle.GetStringFromName( "hello" );
```

The result retrieves the string corresponding to "hello" in your bundle file and is the equivalent of the `getString` call when using the XUL bundle method.

If your chrome is independent of Mozilla's chrome and you do not want to use their UI files, you can create the bundle directly by using the *nsIStringBundleService* XPCOM interface, as seen in Example 11-4.

Example 11-4. Creating the bundle via XPConnect

```
var src = 'chrome://packagexfly/content/packagebundle.properties';
var localeService =
    Components.classes["@mozilla.org/intl/nslocaleservice;1"]
    .getService(Components.interfaces.nsILocaleService);
var appLocale =  localeService.GetApplicationLocale();
var stringBundleService =
    Components.classes["@mozilla.org/intl/stringbundle;1"]
    .getService(Components.interfaces.nsIStringBundleService);
bundle = stringBundleService.CreateBundle(src, appLocale);
```

The first step is to get the application locale—the language that is currently registered with the chrome service. This is done via the `nsILocalService` component. The *nsIStringBundleService* is then initialized and the `CreateBundle` method is called, returning an instance of *nsIStringBundle* that provides access to the methods for querying strings.

Programming and Localization

This section provides little nuggets of information, not necessarily related, that show how to work around common problems when programming locale-related information in your application. It strays a little from the main path of string replacement and translation, and the topics vary from recommended naming conventions for your string identifiers to locale in XBL bindings and what tools you can use to be more productive.

Naming Conventions

The decision of what to call your code internals emerged more than once in this book. In Chapter 8, you decided the name of the component IDL interface IDL file and its associated implementation. In locale, it is the entity names and string identifiers contained in bundles.

Naming conventions in localization are useful because they provide some context to the translator. In this spirit, it is good for the reference to be as descriptive as possible. You can choose your route for naming or stick with the way that Mozilla does it. Examining the files in the Mozilla source base, common naming conventions for entities include the following:

```
id.label
id.tooltip
id.text
id.accesskey
id.commandkey
```

Certain XUL widgets can contain multiple localizable resources, including a text `label` or `description`, a `tooltip`, and an accesskey. A button is a prime example:

```
<button id="flyBtn" label="&flyBtn.label;" accesskey="&flyBtn.accesskey;"
    tooltip="&flyBtn.tooltip;" />
```

The naming convention is consistent, using the value of the `id` attribute appended by the name of the UI feature. The attribute and name are delimited by a period. Not only does using this value flag the resource as being associated with a certain widget, but it also permits logical grouping in the DTD:

```
<!ENTITY flyBtn.label "Fly Away">
<!ENTITY flyBtn.accesskey "f">
<!ENTITY flyBtn.tooltip "Click here to take to the air">
```

Naming string identifiers in bundle files fits less into a pattern like that in DTDs, and in the Mozilla, source files may appear random. If a pattern must be found, you could look at two things: filenames and identifier descriptions.

In a filename, the association of a single *.properties* file is with a logical part of the application. If a string appears in a certain dialog or window, you know where to go to translate the strings or add more strings. Example files in the Mozilla tree worth examining include *editor.properties*, *commonDialogs.properties*, and *wizardManager.properties*.

With identifier descriptions, the text used on the identifier describes what the text actually refers to. The goal is to be as descriptive as possible by using as brief text as possible:

```
dontDeleteFiles=Don't Delete Files
```

The descriptor is the same as the value, although in a different format. The opportunity was taken here to be as descriptive as possible.

Breaking Up the Text

Under certain circumstances, you may need to pop up your own alert messages as XUL dialogs. Some messages may involve multiple lines of text that need to be put on new lines. There is no natural delimiter that breaks up the text contained within `<description>` or `<label>` elements in XUL, so following are a couple of tricks to get around this problem.

Method 1: Multiple <description> elements

First, create the placeholder in your XUL where the generated elements will be inserted:

```
<vbox id="main-message" flex="1" style="max-width: 40em;"/>
  <!-- insert elements here -->
</vbox>
```

The script in Example 11-5 generates the needed text elements, fills in the text, and appends all the items to the containing box.

Example 11-5. Using multiple <description> elements

```
var text = window.arguments[0];
var holder = document.getElementById("main-message");
var lines = text.split("\n");
for (var i = 0; i < lines.length; i++) {
  var descriptionNode = document.createElement("description");
  var linetext = document.createTextNode(messageParagraphs[i]);
  descriptionNode.appendChild(linetext);
  holder.appendChild(descriptionNode);
}
```

The text is passed into the window that is used for the message. It presumes that the `\n` delimiter is used to signify a new line in the text and is split thus. Then it loops through each line, creating a description element for each line and populating it with a text node with the message inside. Then each element is appended to the main container that lives in the XUL file.

Method 2: HTML <br> tag

For this example, create the XUL placeholder similar to the example in Method 1, and then slot the script in Example 11-6 into your load handler.

Example 11-6. Using the HTML break tag

```
var text = window.arguments[0];
var holder = document.getElementById("main-message");
var lines = text.split("\n");
var descriptionNode = document.createElement("description");
for (var i = 0; i < lines.length; i++) {
  var linetext = document.createTextNode(messageParagraphs[i]);
```

Example 11-6. Using the HTML break tag (continued)

```
  var breakNode = document.createElement("html:br");
  descriptionNode.appendChild(linetext);
  descriptionNode.appendChild(breakNode);
}
holder.appendChild(descriptionNode);
```

This way is similar to the code in Example 11-5, with some notable differences. First, there is only one <description> element created outside the loop for each new line. In that loop, the break occurs when an HTML <br> element is inserted after a piece of text.

With both methods, you need to put some sort of width constraint on the window at the level where you want the text to wrap. Method 1 is recommended because it is a true XUL solution, but the second method is also a good example of mixed markup in a XUL document (HTML).

Anonymous Content and Locale

Entities are everywhere. Well, not quite everywhere. However, as entity references and DTD constructs are part of the XML language, they can be used for localization purposes in other files in your package, such as RDF and XBL files.

In the case of XBL, it is common for binding content to inherit its locale information from the base widget. Take the Example 11-7 as a case in point. Here is the bound element in the XUL document; the binding for the bound element is shown:

```
<article id="artheader" class="articleheader" title="Common Garden Flies"
author="Brad Buzzworth"/>
```

The attributes of note here are `title` and `author`, both user-defined, because they contain the localizable values that will be used in the binding.

Example 11-7. Binding with attribute inheritance

```
<binding id="articleheader">
  <content>
    <xul:hbox flex="1">
      <xul:label class="flybox-homeheader-text" xbl:inherits="value=title"/>
      <xul:spacer flex="1"/>
      <xul:label class="flybox-homeheader-text" xbl:inherits="value=author"/>
    </xul:hbox>
  </content>
  <implementation>
    <property name="title">
      <setter>
        <![CDATA[
          this.setAttribute('title',val); return val;
        ]]>
      </setter>
      <getter>
```

Example 11-7. Binding with attribute inheritance (continued)

```
        <![CDATA[
          return this.getAttribute('title');
        ]]>
      </getter>
    </property>
    <property name="author">
      <setter>
        <![CDATA[
          this.setAttribute('author',val); return val;
        ]]>
      </setter>
      <getter>
        <![CDATA[
          return this.getAttribute('author');
        ]]>
      </getter>
    </property>
  </implementation>
</binding>
```

The binding in Example 11-7 illustrates a binding whose content inherits its locale from the bound element. The attributes used on the bound element, namely `title` and `author`, are descriptive, enabling the author to be specific about what they are setting a value to. The rest is taken care of in the binding, where the `inherits` attribute sets the value on the anonymous content to the value of the more descriptive attributes on the bound element. You can retrieve the values or set them by using the getter and setter.

Localizable Resources in HTML

As a web application, Mozilla permits seamless integration of web content, both local and remote, in many formats. If you have verbose text that just needs to be displayed somewhere in the framework of your application, HTML or XML content may be ideal for this purpose. Through the use of XUL content widgets, such as `<iframe>` and `<browser>`, you have ready-made frames to slot your content into:

```
<iframe src="xFly.html" flex="1"/>
```

Therefore, a simple modification of *xFly.html* with a local language leaves the main application untouched. Some other uses of HTML or XML content include an "About" dialog/page, Help pages, a wizard interface, or a getting started/introduction page.

Localizable Resources in RDF

Strings to be converted in RDF content can take more than one form. You can use entities directly in your RDF file or have the text inline in your node descriptions. Whichever method you choose, you must ensure that the file is installed in the right place in the tree and registered correctly for the application to pick up on it.

Localization Tools

To translate your XUL interface strings, just change the text that corresponds to your entity reference or string bundle value. For a small application, this step should be simple, but for large applications, it can be a big task.

The good news is that tools are available to help localize your applications. The most popular tool is MozillaTranslator, which is discussed in more detail in Appendix B.

There is also a handy command line utility for Unicode conversion called nsconv, bundled in the Mozilla *bin* folder in any distribution. (If you are unfamiliar with Unicode, the section "XPFE and Unicode" later in this chapter provides more information.) Although it is broken at the time of this writing, it is worth mentioning. Let's look at a simple conversion of ASCII text to UTF-8:

```
<!ENTITY PrintPreviewCmd.label    "Print Preview">
```

Replace the string in the entity with the Spanish version:

```
<!ENTITY PrintPreviewCmd.label    "Presentación preliminar...">
```

Then run the conversion.

```
> nsconv -f ascii -t utf-8 foo.dtd bar.dtd
```

The accented characters are converted into the Unicode for you:

```
<!ENTITY PrintPreviewCmd.label   "Presentaci&#243;n preliminar...">
```

Using the NCR or CER value as well is also acceptable, if appropriate. A NCR is an entity that contains a hex (`a`) or decimal (`a`) value, while a CER is also an entity containing an abbreviation (`é`). This assumes, though, that you know what the code is! String bundles accept only one form of encoding, which is known as `escape-unicode`. If using nsconv, the name for this encoding is `x-u-escaped`.

Various third-party conversion tools that do the same thing are available. A freeware editor called Unipad that lets you import multiple types of native encoding documents and then save as Unicode. Unipad is available from *http://www.unipad.org/*.

As an XML markup, RDF can handle inline entity definitions. These entity definitions have been covered thoroughly in the chapter so far. Example 11-8 looks at localizable strings contained directly in RDF node descriptions. This example is taken from the Help table of contents in the Mozilla tree.

Example 11-8. RDF Description node with localizable text

```
<rdf:Description about="#nav-doc">
  <nc:subheadings>
    <rdf:Seq>
      <rdf:li>
        <rdf:Description ID="nav-doc-language"
                nc:name="Language and Translation Services"
                nc:link="chrome://help/locale/nav_help.html#nav_language"/>
```

Example 11-8. RDF Description node with localizable text (continued)

```
      </rdf:li>
    </rdf:Seq>
  </nc:subheadings>
</rdf:Description>
```

The text in the `nc:name` attribute is the text that will be changed. Note that this issue of text in RDF is separate from the topic of using RDF as the mechanism in the chrome registry to register your locale and set up a switching mechanism. This difference is addressed in the next section.

The Chrome Registry and Locale

Your application is built and you're ready to upload your shiny new Mozilla program to your server for download. The last piece of the puzzle, locale versions, has been put in place. With the structures that Mozilla has in place, it no longer has to be an afterthought. Once you have the translated files, you need to make the decision about how you want to distribute your language versions, the languages you want to make available to the users, and the level of customization that you want to give to them.

In this section, we look at how the Mozilla application suite handles the chrome's locale component. Then you see how to apply these chrome registry structures and utilities on a more generic level for your application.

The Directory Structure

A typical application chrome structure looks like the directory structure in Figure 11-2. A folder for each language is under the *locale* directory. The general format is that each language has a unique identifier based on country code and the region. This conforms to the ISO-639 two-letter code with ISO-3166 two-letter country code standards.

The W3C site has good resources that provide information about the ISO-639 and ISO-3166 standards at *http://www.w3.org/International/O-HTML-tags.html*.

For example, the unique identifier for Scots, Great Britain, is *Sc-GB*. The first code, *Sc*, is for the Scots (Scottish) dialect, and the second code, *GB*, is for the country code for Great Britain. This is the standard that Mozilla follows.

The folder that is registered is the language folder, which is what has to be changed on an install. Thus, the URL *chrome://package/locale* actually points to *package/locale/en-US* or whichever language is turned on at the time. The language folder may in turn include subfolders that contain logical units for your application.

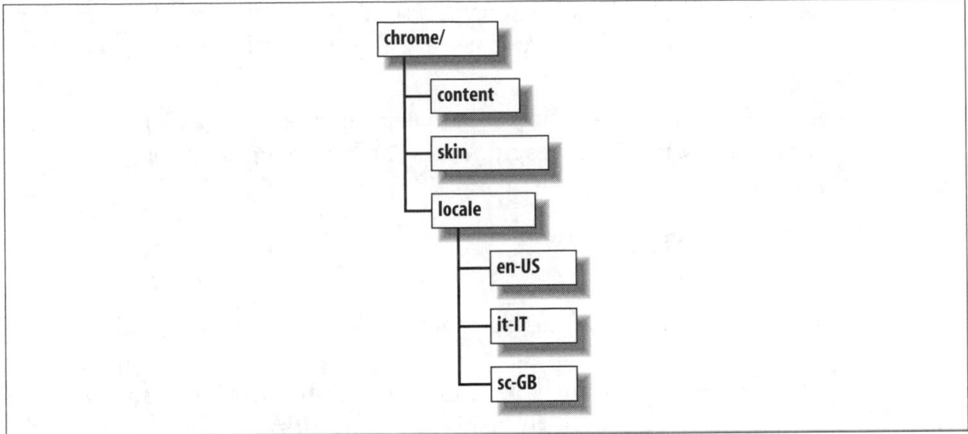

Figure 11-2. Locale's placement in typical chrome layout

Interaction with the Chrome Registry

As pointed out in Chapter 6, your packages directories need to be registered as chrome with the chrome registry. The first step is to ensure that the entry for your package component is in the file *chrome.rdf* in the root chrome directory.

A *resource:/* URL points to the folder for your files to be picked up and recognized by the chrome mechanism and accessed via *chrome://* URLs in your application code. The locale is no exception.

```
<RDF:Description about="urn:mozilla:locale:en-US:xfly"
    c:baseURL="resource:/chrome/xfly/locale/en-US/">
    c:localeVersion="0.1.0.0"
  <c:package resource="urn:mozilla:package:xfly"/>
</RDF:Description>
```

A built-in versioning system in the chrome registry uses *c:localeVersion* descriptor, if you plan on distributing multiple language packs for your application. Other descriptors are available if you choose to use them: display name (*c:displayName*), internal name (*c:name*), location type (*c:locType*), and author (*c:author*).

Distribution

Language distribution may not be an issue for you. If, for example, your application were only going to be localized into a finite number of languages, bundling each of them up with the main installer would be most convenient. If, however, the need for new language versions arises at various intervals in the release process, you need to find a way to make them available and install them on top of an existing installation.

For example, as more people from various locations in the world are becoming aware of the Mozilla project, they want to customize it into their own language. Here are the steps that you need to take to set up your version.

1. Register as a contributor and set up the resources that you need, if any (web page, mailing list). This will ensure that you are added to the project page on the mozilla.org site.
2. Get a copy of Mozilla to test either via a binary distribution or by downloading and building your own source (see Appendix A for more information).
3. Translate the files.
4. Package your new files for distribution.
5. Test and submit your work.

Step 4, the packaging of the new language pack, is discussed next. Mozilla's Cross-Platform Install (XPI) is the ideal candidate for achieving this packaging. This method is discussed extensively in Chapter 6. This distribution method provides great flexibility and has the benefit of being native to Mozilla, thus bypassing the search for external install technologies for your application.

The anatomy of an install script

Example 11-9 presents a script that is based on the Mozilla process that distributes localized language packs. It presumes that there is a single JAR file for the language that is installed and registered in the Mozilla binary's chrome root.

The XPI archive consists of the JAR file in a *bin/chrome* directory and the *install.js* file, together in a compressed archive with an *.xpi* extension. Simply clicking on a web page link to this file invokes the Mozilla software installation service and installs your language. For convenience, inline comments in Example 11-9 explain what is happening.

Example 11-9. The locale XPI install script, install.js

```
function verifyDiskSpace(dirPath, spaceRequired)
{
  var spaceAvailable;
  spaceAvailable = fileGetDiskSpaceAvailable(dirPath);
  spaceAvailable = parseInt(spaceAvailable / 1024);
  if(spaceAvailable < spaceRequired)
  {
    logComment("Insufficient disk space: " + dirPath);
    logComment("  required : " + spaceRequired + " K");
    logComment("  available: " + spaceAvailable + " K");
    return(false);
  }
  return(true);
}
// platform detection
function getPlatform() {
  var platformStr;
  var platformNode;
  if('platform' in Install) {
    platformStr = new String(Install.platform);
    if (!platformStr.search(/^Macintosh/))
```

Example 11-9. The locale XPI install script, install.js (continued)

```
      platformNode = 'mac';
    else if (!platformStr.search(/^Win/))
      platformNode = 'win';
    else
      platformNode = 'unix';
  }
  else {
    var fOSMac  = getFolder("Mac System");
    var fOSWin  = getFolder("Win System");
    logComment("fOSMac: "  + fOSMac);
    logComment("fOSWin: "  + fOSWin);
    if(fOSMac != null)
      platformNode = 'mac';
    else if(fOSWin != null)
      platformNode = 'win';
    else
      platformNode = 'unix';
  }
  return platformNode;
}
// Size in KB of JAR file
var srDest = 500;
var err;
var fProgram;
var platformNode;
platformNode = getPlatform();
// --- LOCALIZATION NOTE: translate only these ---
// These fields are changeable in this generic script
var prettyName = "Irish";
var langcode = "ie";
var regioncode = "GA";
var chromeNode = langcode + "-" + regioncode;
// --- END LOCALIZABLE RESOURCES ---
// build the paths and file names for registry and chrome:// url access
var regName     = "locales/mozilla/" + chromeNode;
var chromeName = chromeNode + ".jar";
var regionFile = regioncode + ".jar";
var platformName = langcode + "-" + platformNode + ".jar";
var localeName = "locale/" + chromeNode + "/";
// Start the installation
err = initInstall(prettyName, regName, "0.1.0.0");
logComment("initInstall: " + err);
fProgram = getFolder("Program");
logComment("fProgram: " + fProgram);
// Check disk space using utility function at the start of the script
if (verifyDiskSpace(fProgram, srDest))
{
  err = addDirectory("",
  "bin",
  fProgram,
  "");
  logComment("addDirectory() returned: " + err);
```

Example 11-9. The locale XPI install script, install.js (continued)

```
  // register chrome
  var cf = getFolder(fProgram, "chrome/"+chromeName);
  var pf = getFolder(fProgram, "chrome/"+platformName);
  var rf = getFolder(fProgram, "chrome/"+regionFile);
  var chromeType = LOCALE | DELAYED_CHROME;
  registerChrome(chromeType, cf, localeName + "global/");
  registerChrome(chromeType, cf, localeName + "communicator/");
  registerChrome(chromeType, cf, localeName + "content-packs/");
  registerChrome(chromeType, cf, localeName + "cookie/");
  registerChrome(chromeType, cf, localeName + "editor/");
  registerChrome(chromeType, cf, localeName + "forms/");
  registerChrome(chromeType, cf, localeName + "help/");
  registerChrome(chromeType, cf, localeName + "messenger/");
  registerChrome(chromeType, cf, localeName + "messenger-smime/");
  registerChrome(chromeType, cf, localeName + "mozldap/");
  registerChrome(chromeType, cf, localeName + "navigator/");
  registerChrome(chromeType, cf, localeName + "necko/");
  registerChrome(chromeType, cf, localeName + "pipnss/");
  registerChrome(chromeType, cf, localeName + "pippki/");
  registerChrome(chromeType, cf, localeName + "wallet/");
  registerChrome(chromeType, pf, localeName + "global-platform/");
  registerChrome(chromeType, pf, localeName + "communicator-platform/");
  registerChrome(chromeType, pf, localeName + "navigator-platform/");
  if (platformNode == "win") {
    registerChrome(chromeType, pf, localeName + "messenger-mapi/");
  }
  registerChrome(chromeType, rf, regionName + "global-region/");
  registerChrome(chromeType, rf, regionName + "communicator-region/");
  registerChrome(chromeType, rf, regionName + "editor-region/");
  registerChrome(chromeType, rf, regionName + "messenger-region/");
  registerChrome(chromeType, rf, regionName + "navigator-region/");
  if (err == SUCCESS)
  {
    // complete the installation
    err = performInstall();
    logComment("performInstall() returned: " + err);
  }
  else
  {
    // cancel the installation
    cancelInstall(err);
    logComment("cancelInstall due to error: " + err);
  }
}
else
{
  // if we enter this section,
  // there is not enough disk space for installation
  cancelInstall(INSUFFICIENT_DISK_SPACE);
}
```

By changing some values of the changeable fields, you can tailor this script to handle the install in any directory in the chrome (*cf*) that you want and register the chrome URL (*localeName*) for use. The rest is handled by the built-in functionality in XPI provided by such functions as `initInstall` and `performInstall`.

Switching languages

The mechanism for switching languages can take many forms. Mozilla switches languages by updating an RDF datasource when a language pack is installed. The UI for switching languages in Mozilla is in the main Preferences (Edit → Preferences). Within the preferences area, the language/content panel (Appearance → Languages/Content) interacts with the chrome registry when loaded, reading in the installed language packs and populating a selectable list with the available language identifier. Selecting one language and restarting Mozilla changes the interface for the user. Example 11-10 is a simple script for switching locales.

Example 11-10. Locale-switching script

```
function switchLocale(langcode)
{
  try {
    var chromeRegistry = Components.classes["@mozilla.org/chrome/chrome-registry;1"].
getService(Components.interfaces.nsIChromeRegistry);
    chromeRegistry.selectLocale(langcode, true);
    var observerService = Components.classes["
        @mozilla.org/observer-service;1"].
        getService(Components.interfaces.nsIObserverService);
    observerService.notifyObservers(null, "locale-selected", null);
    var prefUtilBundle = srGetStrBundle
        ("chrome://communicator/locale/pref/prefutilities.properties");
    var brandBundle = srGetStrBundle
        ("chrome://global/locale/brand.properties");
    var alertText = prefUtilBundle.GetStringFromName("languageAlert");
    var titleText = prefUtilBundle.GetStringFromName("languageTitle");
    alertText = alertText.replace(/%brand%/g,
        brandBundle.GetStringFromName("brandShortName"));
    var promptService = Components.classes["
        @mozilla.org/embedcomp/prompt-service;1"].getService();
    promptService = promptService.QueryInterface
        (Components.interfaces.nsIPromptService)
    promptService.alert(window, titleText, alertText);
  }
  catch(e) {
    return false;
  }
  return true;
}
```

The language code is passed in as a parameter to the `switchLocale` JavaScript method in Example 11-10. The locale is set via the `nsIChromeRegistry` component, which uses a method named `selectLocale`. This locale selection is located in the first few lines, and the rest of the code prepares and shows a prompt to the user. This prompt reminds you to restart Mozilla to ensure that the new locale takes effect.

Localization Issues

This section aims to dig a little deeper into the issues of UI aesthetics and principles, in order to provide some background into the underlying encoding of documents in the XPFE framework. The main portion is taken up by a discussion of Unicode. There is some background to what Unicode is, how Mozilla uses it, and some practical conversion utilities to ensure that your files are in the correct encoding.

XPFE and Unicode

Unicode is a broad topic and we cannot hope to give you anywhere near a full understanding of what it is. However, a brief introduction will highlight its importance in the software world and show how it is used as one of the internationalization cornerstones in the Mozilla project.

For more in-depth information, refer to the book *The Unicode Standard, Version 3.0* by the Unicode Consortium, published by Addison Wesley Longman. Another useful reference is *Unicode: A Primer* by Tony Graham, published by M&T Books.

Unicode is an encoding system used to represent every character with a unique number. It is a standard that came about when multiple encoding systems were merged. It became clear that keeping separate systems was hindering global communication, and applications were not able to exchange information with one another successfully. Now all major systems and applications are standardizing on Unicode. Most major operating systems, such as Windows, AIX, Solaris, and Mac OS, have already adopted it. The latest browsers, including Mozilla, support it. This quote from the Unicode Consortium (*http://www.unicode.org/unicode/standard/WhatIsUnicode.html*) sums it up the best:

> Unicode enables a single software significant cost savings over the use of legacy character sets. Unicode enables a single software product or a single web site to be targeted across multiple platforms, languages and countries without re-engineering. It allows data to be transported through many different systems without corruption.

There are seven character-encoding schemes in Unicode: UTF-8, UTF-16, UTF-16BE, UTF-16LE, UTF-32, UTF-32BE, and UTF-32LE. UTF is an abbreviation for Unicode Transformation Format. The size of the character's internal representation can range from 8 bits (UTF-8) to 32 bits (UTF-32).

One of Unicode's core principles is that it be able to handle any character set and that clients supporting it provide the tools necessary to convert. This conversation can be from Unicode to native character sets and vice versa. The number of native character sets is extensive and ranges from Central European (ISO-8859-2) to Thai (TIS-620).

The default encoding of XUL, XML, and RDF documents in Mozilla is UTF-8. If no encoding is specified in the text declaration, this is the encoding that is used. In the Mozilla tree, you will usually see no encoding specified in this instance and UTF-8 is the default. To use a different encoding, you need to change the XML text declaration at the top of your file. To change your encoding to Central European, include:

```
<?xml version="1.0" encoding="ISO-8859-2" ?>
```

Language Quirks

The size and proportion of your windows can come into play when you know your application will be localized into more than one language. In some languages, it takes more words or characters, hence more physical space, to bring meaning to some text. This is especially the case in widgets that contain more text, such as when you want to provide usage guidelines in a panel.

One solution that Mozilla uses in at least one place is to make the actual size of the window or make the widget into a localizable entity.

```
<window style="&window.size;" ...>
<!ENTITY  window.size            "width: 40em; height: 40em;">
```

The translator or developer can anticipate the size based on the number of words or preview their changes in the displayed UI. If there is an overflow, they can overflow or do the reverse in the case of empty space.

As you begin to localize your application, especially if it is a web-related application, you will encounter words and phrases that have universal meaning and may not require translation. If you translate the whole Mozilla application, for example, you'll find that some words or phrases remain untouched. These items include terms that are used for branding, or universal web browsing terms, such as Bookmarks, Tasks, and Tools. In some instances, the choice to translate some of these terms is purely subjective.

CHAPTER 12

Remote Applications

Remote applications developed with Mozilla use an application without having to endure a full download process. Given the fundamental similarities of Mozilla and standard web content, a remote Mozilla application can work much like a regular web page. For example, you can point people to your project at *http://www.foobar.com/myApp.xul*, and if they use Mozilla (or a browser that is built with Mozilla, such as Netscape 7), the browser window becomes the application. Serving an application in this way allows you to use most features of a locally installed Mozilla program and gives you unique options that aren't otherwise available. These options are discussed in this chapter.

This chapter explores this alternative distribution method and compares it to how an installable application is built. Generally, there is no difference between these two types of applications other than how they are delivered. However, you should be aware of the difficulties encountered when using remote applications.

One of the most important aspects of remote applications for Mozilla is the XPFE environment, or more specifically, the use of XUL/XBL, JavaScript, and CSS. Using the XPFE in remote application development offers more possibilities than, for example, just embedding Gecko into your application. It is the focus of this chapter.

Directions in Remote Application Development

Currently, remote Mozilla applications are not prevalent because development focuses on making the client applications as stable and efficient as possible. Therefore, this area of Mozilla development is largely speculative. This chapter argues that remote applications are worth looking at more closely.

One advantage a remote Mozilla application has over a client application is that a developer doesn't have to worry about an installer. Also, all users have access to the latest version of your application. Because the application is stored centrally on a server instead of on the local computer of everyone who tries your program, when you update it, you make an update available to all users.

Remote software applications might be hosted in a centralized point on the network, on multiple nodes, or on any random node in a Peer to Peer (P2P) fashion. It's even possible to have a whole suite of remote Mozilla applications hosted on several computers combined into one coherent package. Figure 12-1 shows one scenario for a simple distributed Mozilla application.

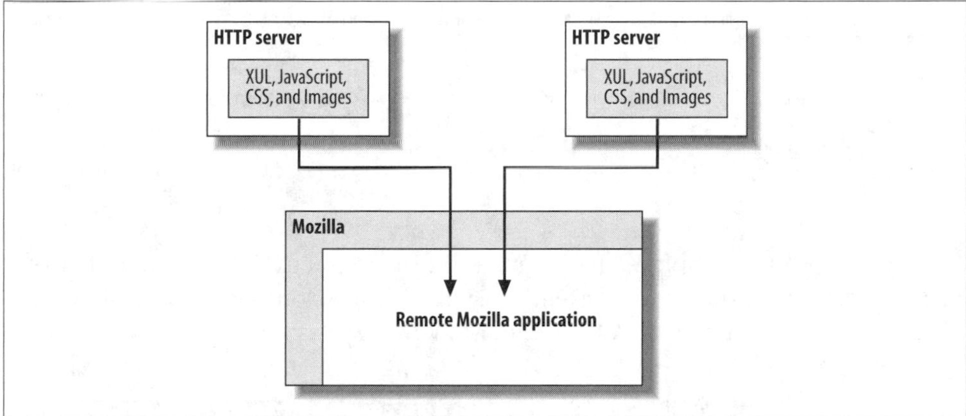

Figure 12-1. Distributed remote Mozilla application

Currently, one of the remote application's biggest disadvantages is that it has very restricted JavaScript privileges. Here, privileges refer to the ability to carry out certain functionalities on the local system. As many high-profile "worm" viruses emerge routinely these days, security restrictions on downloadable scripts and applications are understandable. Some of the most high-profile malicious scripts access the local file system. This is not a problem unique to the Mozilla environment, but it is something to be aware of when planning and implementing a remote application.

To improve security, Mozilla automatically limits what JavaScript has access to on your computer when the executed scripts come from a computer other than the local one. One workaround uses signed scripts, as described in the "Creating Signed Remote Applications" section later in this chapter. You can also have users set a special preference to enable universal XPConnect privileges to both local and remote files. To learn how to open up the security sandbox in this way, see the section "Expanded Privileges in Mozilla" later in this chapter.

Basic Remote Application Example

The simple XUL file in Example 12-1 uses the user's local skin information to create a toolbar-type interface for a file that can be loaded from the server. This successful effect depends on whether your server is configured with the correct Multipart Internet Mail Extension (MIME) type (see the later section "Server Configuration"). The id on the buttons are taken from the navigator skin, so the look of the remote file changes when the user switches themes and remains consistent with the look of the browser itself.

Example 12-1. Remote XUL example

```
<?xml version="1.0"?>
<?xml-stylesheet href="chrome://global/skin/" type="text/css"?>
<?xml-stylesheet href="chrome://navigator/skin/" type="text/css"?>
<window id="remote_example"
    xmlns="http://www.mozilla.org/keymaster/gatekeeper/there.is.only.xul"
    title="Simple Remote Example">
  <hbox>
    <button label="XFlies" class="button-toolbar" id="page-proxy-button"/>
    <button label="Reptiles" class="button-toolbar" />
    <button label="Bugs" class="button-toolbar" />
  </hbox>
</window>
```

As you can see in Example 12-1, the markup of a remote XUL file is like that of a XUL file that is part of a local system's installed application. Figure 12-2 shows the XUL file presented using both Classic and Modern themes.

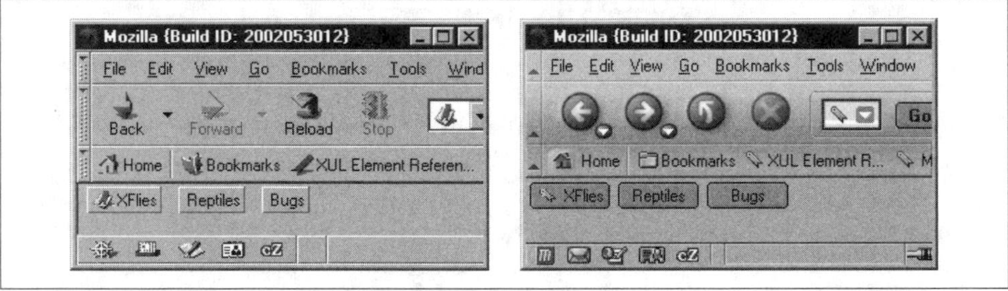

Figure 12-2. Remote XUL file-accessing skin

The XUL in Example 12-1 is minimal, but it does show that the *chrome://* URLs are accessible to the remote file and that the CSS and image resources available in the chrome's skin subdirectories can be accessed remotely. The image on the first button is picked up from a local JAR file, as accessed through chrome by using the button's `page-proxy-button` id. A more elegant application would use toolbars, menus, and other widgets to create a full-featured application UI.

Case Study: Snake (a.k.a. Hiss-zilla)

In this section, we look at an application that is stripped down and based on a basic concept but still useful. This application shows the potential of remote application development. This case study discusses a full-featured game that is played over the Internet. Figure 12-3 below shows a sample screenshot of Hiss-zilla.

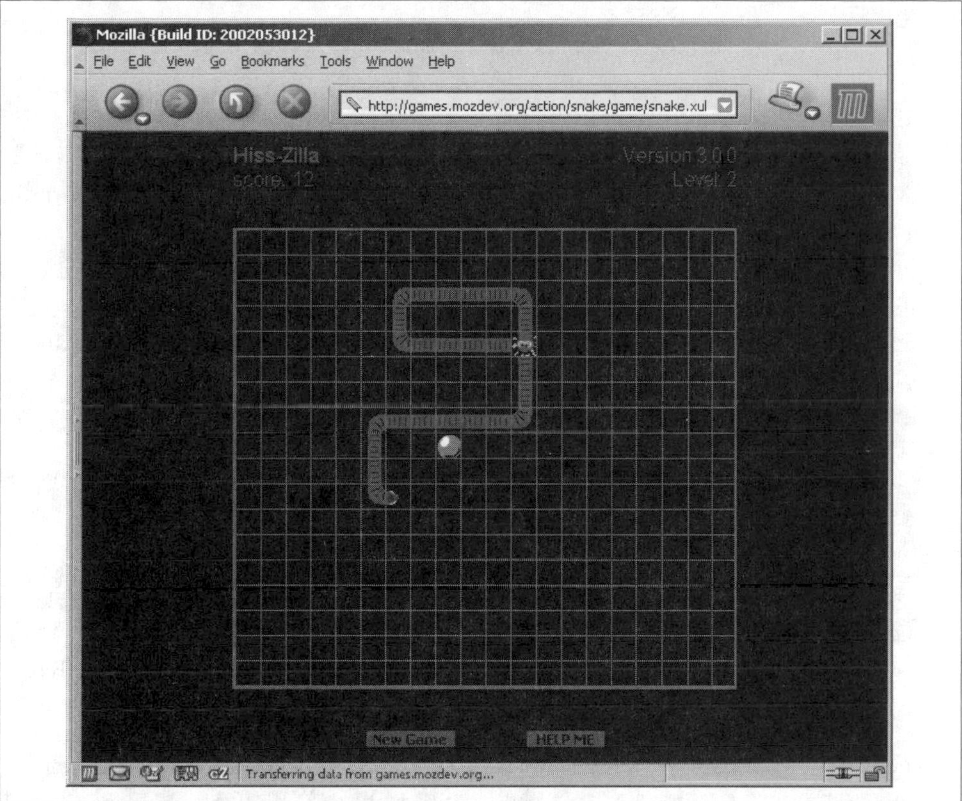

Figure 12-3. Hiss-zilla, a remote game

A direct link to a remote XUL file provides access to the game, as seen in the location bar of the browser in Figure 12-3. The game's rules are straightforward. Click on the New Game button or use N on the keyboard to begin, use arrow keys to change direction, and use the character P to pause the game. To play a game of Hiss-zilla or to take a closer look at the code, see the project page *http://games.mozdev.org/action/snake/*.

The complete package includes all files associated with an XPFE application, including a XUL file, a stylesheet, images, and JavaScript files. The files and their descriptions are as follows:

snake.xul
: Contains the window definition and the top level of the application with the game grid, visual text, and application buttons.

snake.js
: Contains the functionality for the game including the snake's movement and the eating of the food.

snake.css
  Contains styling for the UI features and inclusion of some images.

screen.js
  Enables full screen mode in the game.

Image files
  Miscellaneous images that represent parts of the snake's body as it moves in different directions and the food that it eats.

The Snake application will be developed further later in the chapter in the context of signed scripts. You will see new features that allow you to run the game in full-screen mode and to store the scores. These features illustrate different concepts relevant to remote applications.

Mozilla Gaming

Hiss-zilla is not the only example of a game created with Mozilla. Others, such as Mozinvaders, Mozteroids, PAGMAN, and Xultris use JavaScript and Mozilla's rendering engine to recreate two-dimensional arcade games from the 80s and early 90s. Links to most games are available at *http://games.mozdev.org/*.

Many of these games were created to see how far the application development capabilities of Mozilla could be pushed. PAGMAN in particular was designed as a test case to see what was possible; the result was almost identical to the original PacMan game. The creation of PAGMAN was documented in an article that provides more information about how the game came about and was developed. You can find the *Building a Game in Mozilla* article at *http://www.oreillynet.com/pub/a/network/2000/06/30/magazine/mozilla_game.html*.

Although all of these games are freely available as open source projects, not all of them work with Mozilla 1.0. Many were created while Mozilla was still in development, so games that worked on pre-1.0 releases of Mozilla need additional development to work today. The good news is that if you are just dying to play Mozteroids or Xultris, you can take what you have learned in this book and update the projects so everyone can enjoy them.

Setting Up XPFE for Remote Applications

Remote Mozilla applications are limited because they cannot access and use some of the rich functionality provided in XPCOM interfaces. Unless you make the privilege change described in this section, access to XPCOM via XPConnect in your web page or remote application is forbidden. This privilege modification set up by the remote application developer grants complete access to the Mozilla functionality, to resources in the chrome, and to the host system via the Mozilla components that handle such tasks as File I/O. Of course, making this change means that the files on your server could be read, written to, or deleted, which is why rights are restricted by default. We recommend that you grant this extended privilege only when you do not have valuable data on the server or if you have taken steps to ensure that the data cannot be accessed.

The privilege, called Universal XPConnect, can be turned on from the Privilege Manager, which is a property of the `netscape.security` object. Example 12-2 shows a script that turns this privilege on and then uses new found privilege to create XPCOM component instance.

Example 12-2. Enabling universal XPConnect

```
<script type="application/x-JavaScript">
netscape.security.PrivilegeManager.enablePrivilege("UniversalXPConnect");
var Simple=new Components.Constructor("@mozilla.org/js_simple_component;1", "nsISimple");
var s = new Simple();
for(var list in s)
document.write(list+"<br>\n");
</script>
```

You can also turn on this privilege in your profile user preference file with the following line:

```
enablePrivilege("UniversalXPConnect");
```

A script with this kind of plate-cleaning power can only be run successfully when it's executed locally, as from a local XUL file with a `<DEFANGED_script>` element. To open up XPConnect remotely with JavaScript like this, you have to use a signed script (see the section "Creating Signed Remote Applications" in this chapter).

Once this privilege is enabled, remote XUL applications can run as if they are local. Remote files can use any Mozilla component, reuse skin resources, XBL widgets, and whatever else the browser uses.

Server Configuration

Proper configuration of the XUL MIME type on your web server is necessary to serve remote Mozilla applications successfully. The trick is to ensure that the server recognizes the XUL file type and knows how to serve it properly. By default, most web servers serve files with such unrecognized extensions as *text/plain*. By adding the type *application/vnd.mozilla.xul+xml* to your server's configuration, you can make sure that the server matches the file extension and sends this MIME type in the HTTP header to the browser. To serve up static XUL pages from your web server, you need to add this line to your *mime.types* file if it hasn't been added already:

```
application/vnd.mozilla.xul+xml  <TAB> xul
```

This is how you can configure Apache MIME types to serve static XUL pages. Note that the *mime.types* file requires that you separate the type from the suffix. The format is:

```
mime type <tab> extension.
```

After the type is added to the server, the browser recognizes this header as an XUL file and parses, renders, and creates the appropriate DOM. If your server isn't configured to recognize this MIME type, then users see the contents of your file as source only—a plain text complete with all the formatting.

Now that your web server is configured correctly, you can add a sample XUL file (such as the file in Example 12-3) to your web site to make sure things are running properly. You should name the file *remote.xul* and save it in your web site's root directory for testing.

Example 12-3. A sample static XUL file

```
<?xml version="1.0"?>
<!DOCTYPE window>
<window
  id = "remote"
  xmlns = "http://www.mozilla.org/keymaster/gatekeeper/there.is.only.xul"
  title = "A Remote Image"
  style = "min-width:282px; min-height:137px;"
  orient = "vertical">
  <image src="http://books.mozdev.org/screenshots/logo5.gif" />
</window>
```

You can now view this window by launching it as a chrome file from Mozilla as follows:

```
./mozilla -chrome http://my.domain/remote.xul
```

Or you can also load it up by simply entering the URL in your browser location bar as follows::

```
http://my.domain/remote.xul
```

Generated Content

Today part of the Web is driven by dynamically generated content. This content is primarily stored in databases, which is used by an application or middle layer to format the data to HTML. The web server then sends the content to the browser. The browser receives the web page as the end result and has no knowledge that the page was generated on the server—just that it is a properly formatted HTML file. By using these same conventional principals, we can send generated or database-driven XUL, CSS, or JavaScript to Mozilla. Because XUL is a document that creates a UI, this widget drawing capability opens up a whole new world to web application development.

If you are a web developer creating database-driven applications, you will quickly see the limitations of using a simple markup like HTML—for example, being constrained to the content area of a browser for which you cannot manage all of the application interface's "real estate." Using a browser window for your application is a common enough practice, but you still don't have the application-level widgets of most client-side applications when you use HTML. This section shows that using XUL files created by scripting languages allows you to create windows and applications that move out of the browser window and into the full-featured application space. Mozilla's origins, after all, are as a web browser and suite of Internet applications, and the latest technologies in the XPFE toolkit go that extra step to allow the presentation of UI information over the wire.

Generating Content with Scripting Languages

This section discusses the basic mechanics of server-generated content. In most cases, the actual content is static—although the server application creates the page dynamically, the content itself is not input. It is also not created dynamically by other methods, such as using JavaScript to manipulate the client's document after it loads from the server.

To generate server-generated content, you need to use a scripting language. We explore the use of three different options: PHP, Perl, and Python. PHP is probably the most natural language for this application because it has its origins in serving up dynamic HTML, but you can play around with your favorite language and determine whether it has the appropriate capabilities for this environment. To use various scripting languages with Mozilla, you need a working knowledge of their capabilities; the scope of this book doesn't provide programming information for the selected scripting languages.

PHP

When users of your application may not have configured their browser to support the correct MIME type, you can use the PHP header function to send the browser the correct type.

Remember that when using XUL with PHP, you need to edit your *php.ini* file on the server and change the default configuration to:

```
short_open_tag  =   Off
```

By default, this configuration is set to "On." When "Off," this setting tells the PHP interpreter to parse only the files with escape tag identifiers, such as `<?php ?>` (and not `<? ?>`, which are used by XML). This process is separate from the XML parsing process that occurs when Mozilla receives and tries to render the generated content. If you don't change the *.ini* file, you will see an error like this:

```
Parse error: parse error in /usr/local/share/doc/apache/remote_xul.php on line 2
```

This error occurs when PHP sees your XUL syntax as invalid PHP code.

Once PHP is properly configured to handle XUL files, you're ready to go. To start out with something simple, use the code in Example 12-4 to produce a simple XUL window with the xFly logo by using PHP. Be sure to save the file with a *.php* extension.

Example 12-4. Using PHP to generate the correct XUL MIME type

```
<?php header( "Content-type: application/vnd.mozilla.xul+xml" ); ?>
<?xml version="1.0"?>
<!DOCTYPE window>
<window
    id      = "remote"
    xmlns   = "http://www.mozilla.org/keymaster/gatekeeper/there.is.only.xul"
    title   = "A Remote Image"
    style   = "min-width:282px; min-height:137px;"
    orient = "vertical">
  <image src="http://books.mozdev.org/screenshots/logo5.gif" />
</window>
```

Also remember that a space below the PHP tag results in a parse error in Mozilla. The next example shows the PHP header and the XML declaration at the start of the PHP file. The space between the two renders it invalid:

```
<?php header( "Content-type: application/vnd.mozilla.xul+xml" ); ?>
<?xml version="1.0"?>
```

After PHP parses its content on the server, the rest of the document is sent to Mozilla on the client. Put this file (`remote_xul.php`) somewhere in your document root on the server with PHP installed and launch it from Mozilla like this:

```
./mozilla -chrome http://my.domain/remote_xul.php
```

The window defined in Example 12-4 now appears, displaying the image. You can take advantage of this relatively straightforward technique to serve up more feature-rich user interfaces, inclusive of buttons, menus, and any other pieces of XUL that are needed.

Perl

Although PHP is rising in popularity, Perl is still a very popular web-scripting language. Perl is often used to drive back end web applications with CGI scripts. To process Perl scripts, no extra configuration is needed once you have the Perl interpreter set up to run in a web server environment. If, for example, you're already using Perl to serve up dynamic HTML pages, you're all set. Otherwise, you should grab a distribution of Perl (*http://perl.com/*) and set up the paths to the binary files in your server scripts. This procedure is done by placing the path in the header, otherwise known as the *shebang line*. This script usually takes a form similar to `#!/usr/local/bin/perl` or `#!/usr/bin/perl`. You must also make sure that the server knows where the Perl executable is, which involves including the path to it in the systems `PATH` environment variable. Depending on the platform and the web server you use, other environments may need to be set.

Example 12-5 shows a simple CGI script that generates a minimal amount of XUL for display in the browser. Perl is useful for this task because you can set up several possible scripts and call selected ones, depending on what choices the user makes. You can even have different forks in the same script that displays different widgets or data. For example, imagine that your remote XUL application is an online travel planner. You would display maps, information, and links to resources based on the user's geographic location or preferences for destinations they entered earlier.

Example 12-5. A simple Perl-generated XUL file

```
#!/usr/bin/perl
print "Content-type: application/vnd.mozilla.xul+xml";
print qq{
<?xml version="1.0"?>
<!DOCTYPE window&gt;
<window
  id = "remote"
  xmlns = "http://www.mozilla.org/keym
  style = "min-width:282px; min-height:137px;"
  orient = "vertical">

  <image src="http://books.mozdev.org/screenshots/logo5.gif"/>
</window>
};
```

In Example 12-5, the MIME type must be specified as part of the first line in the CGI script after the *shebang line*, and rest of the script is the XUL code used by Mozilla. Although this example does not display real dynamic content (such as the kind you get from CGI forms or other user-supplied data), it shows how you can interpolate dynamic data into a simple CGI application model.

Python

Like Perl, Python provides modules that make it easy to create CGI applications that generate content dynamically. Python is already an important language in the Mozilla environment because of the *PyXPCOM* bindings discussed in Chapter 8.

If Python is a language that you like to code in, using it in a remote XUL environment would also make sense. Python combines the features of a lower-level language like object-oriented class and function design with the flexibility and simplicity of a scripting language. The latter feature (ease of use) is relative to a language like C++. Example 12-6 shows how to use Python to create a simple form consisting of three checkboxes.

Example 12-6. A Python-generated dynamically updated form

```
#!/usr/local/bin/python
import cgi
form = cgi.FieldStorage()
print """Content-type: application/vnd.mozilla.xul+xml\n
<?xml version=\"1.0\"?>
```

Example 12-6. A Python-generated dynamically updated form (continued)

```
<!DOCTYPE window>
<window
  id = "remote"
  xmlns = "http://www.mozilla.org/keymaster/gatekeeper/there.is.only.xul"
  title = "listbox"
  style = "min-width:282px; min-height:137px;"
  orient = "vertical">
 <box>"""
print `  <checkbox label="%s" />' % form['op1'].value
print `  <checkbox label="%s" />' % form['op2'].value
  print `  <checkbox label="%s" />' % form['op3'].value
  print """</box>
  </window>"""
```

In this example, the CGI module is loaded with the Python `import` statement, and the form object is initialized so that data input to the page in the form of URL `?name=value` pairs create the XUL content dynamically.

Example 12-6 takes a URL, such as *http://www.brownhen.com/cgi-bin/xulgen?opt1=peter?opt2=paul?opt3=mary*, and displays a checkbox for each value of the named form fields. The content type is printed before the XUL content to tell the web server what to pass when the script produces its output.

Generating Content from a Database

One of the important facets of dynamically generated content is interaction with a database to store and retrieve values for the user. For example, a public forum or subscription-based service could have a client that is written in XUL and requires authentication of users. Having such a client could require some form of database lookup. This section covers a simple example that uses data stored in a database to generate a XUL tree. We will use PHP to retrieve the data from the SQL-driven database and format it into XUL. Theoretically, this database could be any relational model, such as Oracle or MySQL.

Example 12-7 generates a simple tree listing with the columns "User" and "Project." The SQL script creates a table called "sample" and then inserts value pairs into the table. To use this type content generation, your database must be set up to handle table creation and dynamic updating via SQL calls.

Example 12-7. SQL script with User and Project data

```
# table to be inserted into database
CREATE TABLE sample (
  User char(16) NOT NULL default '',
  Project char(32) NOT NULL default ''
);
INSERT INTO sample VALUES ('Bob','moz_bob');
```

Example 12-7. SQL script with User and Project data (continued)

```
INSERT INTO sample VALUES ('Joe','skinner');
INSERT INTO sample VALUES ('Bret','bretzilla');
INSERT INTO sample VALUES ('Sally','mozstream');
```

The code in Example 12-7 creates a table with two fields, "User" and "Project." It then inserts four records into the newly created table in the database by using INSERT INTO calls. Now the script has tangible data to query.

Example 12-8 shows the creation of a simple XUL tree with PHP and a MySQL database. The "User" and "Project" columns display the data in the table.

Example 12-8. XUL generated from database

```
<?php header( "Content-type: application/vnd.mozilla.xul+xml" ); ?>
<?xml version="1.0"?>
<?php
  // connect code
  $host           = "127.0.0.1";
  $user           = "nobody";
  $database       = "test";
  $password       = "mypass";
  $connect        =  mysql_connect($host, $user, $password);
  mysql_select_db($database);
  $query          = "SELECT * FROM sample ORDER BY User";
  $result         = mysql_query($query, $connect);
  $e              = mysql_error();
  if($e)
    print  "ERROR:projects: $e";
  $row            = mysql_num_rows($result);
?>
<!DOCTYPE window>
<window
  id = "remote"
  xmlns = "http://www.mozilla.org/keymaster/gatekeeper/there.is.only.xul"
  title = "A Remote Image" style = "min-width:282px; min-height:137px;">
  <image src="http://books.mozdev.org/screenshots/logo5.gif" />
  <hbox>
    <tree>
      <treecols>
        <treecol id="userCol" label="User" />
        <treecol id="projectCol" label="Project" flex="1"/>
      </treecols>

      <treechildren>
        <?php
          // generate data from db
          for($i=0;$i<$row;$i++) {
            $user    = mysql_result($result, $i, "User");
            $project = mysql_result($result, $i, "Project");
            print "<treeitem container=\"true\" open=\"true\">\n";
            print "<treerow>\n";
            print "<treecell label=\"".ucwords($user)."\" />";
            print "<treecell label=\"".ucwords($project)."\" flex=\"1\"/>";
```

Example 12-8. XUL generated from database (continued)

```
            print "</treerow>\n";
            print "</treeitem>\n";
          }
        ?>
      </treechildren>
    </tree>
    <spacer flex="1" />
  </hbox>
</window>
```

The PHP header method is placed at the top of the file to properly format the output as XUL. The PHP MySQL APIs prepare the code for connection to a MySQL database. Finally, a loop is used to print out the stored data's `treerows` and `treecells`.

This kind of operation provides insight into the possibilities of using remote XUL when you have information stored in a database. Many web applications already do this via HTML forms and other mechanisms, but Mozilla's XPFE toolkit provides a richer widget set than HTML to display and retrieve information (see the section "Form Controls" in Chapter 3).

Some XUL widgets are created specifically to display complex tabular data such as `<tree>`, and some widgets provide user selection such as `<checkbox>`, `<radio>`, and `<textbox>`, plus the CSS used for controlling presentation. All of these widgets can be generated on the fly from the database and used to accept user-inputted information.

Localizing Remote Applications

Unfortunately, localizing remote applications is a not as straightforward since there is no *http:* protocol equivalent for *chrome:*-included locales. You could use *HTTP/1.1* content negotiation to serve the users-preferred language, but Mozilla 1.0 does not read DTD files over the wire. To overcome this problem, use server-side page processing. For example, this code includes the DTD by using PHP:

```
<!DOCTYPE window [
<?php require(PROJECT_PATH."/online/locale/xfly.dtd"); ?>
]>
```

Therefore, the served page looks like this:

```
<!DOCTYPE window [
<!ENTITY fileMenu.label        "File">
<!ENTITY fileMenu.accesskey    "f">
...
]>
```

The only caveat for this approach is that you need a method to filter the entities, depending on which language is loaded. Obtaining a method could be done by reading in the locale and outputting the entities or by calling a separate script. This overhead is not necessarily high, as multiple files exist for multiple languages in a client distribution. A remote application would require the same process, but in a different format.

Certificate Authorities and Digital Signatures

Instead of changing the Universal XPConnect privileges (see "Setting Up XPFE for Remote Applications" earlier in this chapter), you could create signed remote applications that can be granted access to users' computers. A signed application means that the application has a digital signature, which verifies that a file or group of files was created by the person or organization from which you download and that they are trustworthy. In essence, if you trust the person or organization signing the files, then you trust the files themselves.

Digital signatures originate from a certificate authority (CA), an organization that claims responsibility for any digital signature it creates. CAs act as gatekeepers by allowing only people who the organization trusts to create digital signatures. Large CAs like Verisign, whose certificates come preinstalled in many web browsers, enforce validity through large fees. For example, if you can afford $600, then you are an organization with whom the CA would be glad to associate. That $600 then also buys your application respectability with user's web browsers. You can see the CAs that come with the Mozilla browser by going to Privacy & Security → Certificates in your preferences panel and then by selecting the Manage Certificates option. Of the different types of CAs—there's a type for SSL connections, for example, and another one for S/MIME—the Netscape Object Signing certificate is what matters for signed applications.

Fortunately, to get your remote applications signed by a CA, you don't have to pay for a Verisign Netscape Object Signing CA because other options are available. You can use the MozDev CA, for example, and even create your own. The next section tells you how use Mozilla tools to become your own certificate authority so you can sign your own applications and those of other Mozilla developers. The "Creating Signed Remote Applications" section later in this chapter uses the MozDev CA to discuss both avenues.

Mozilla Network Security Services (NSS)

The Mozilla Network Security Services tools, which are described in detail at *http://www.mozilla.org/projects/security/pki/nss/*, allow you to become your own Netscape Object Signing CA. By becoming your own Netscape Signing CA, you can distribute signing certificates to Mozilla application developers. You can obtain the tools via a simplified distribution of NSS for Windows and Linux at *http://certs.mozdev.org*. These tools allow you to become a CA and to package signed remote Mozilla applications. Finally, the commands for CertUtil work the same way on Windows, Linux, and any other OS on which you run CertUtil.

CA Certificates, Signing Certificates, and the Certificate Chain

A certificate represents an organization in a official digital form. It provides fields for the organization's name, contact information, date of issue, and an expiration date. There are also two keys: a private and a public key.

To become a CA, you need to create two certificates for yourself: a "root certificate" and a "distribution certificate." Once you set up these certificates, you can issue signing certificates, which create digital signatures. Figure 12-4 shows the chain of relationships between certificates.

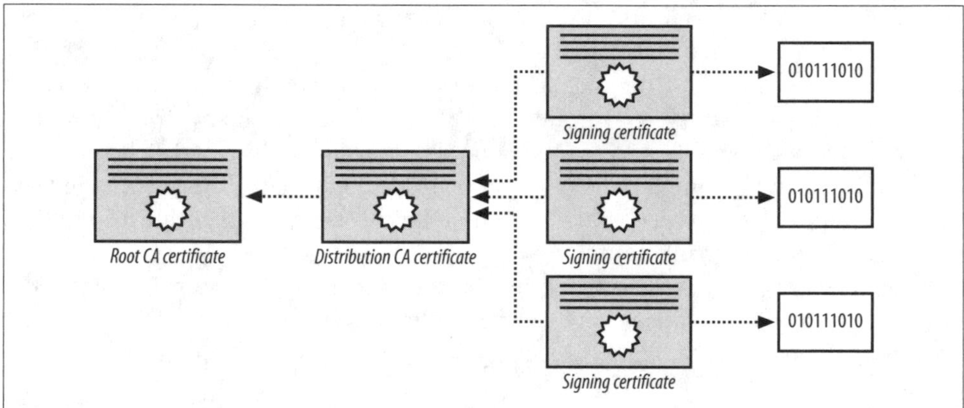

Figure 12-4. A Netscape Object Signing certificate chain

The distribution certificate is based on the root certificate's public key. You can then create signing certificates from the distribution certificate, using its public key that it handles automatically by NSS. Finally, the digital signatures derived from the signing certificate can sign applications using NSS.

Setting Up a Certificate Authority

Using the CertUtil tool that comes with NSS, you need to create a root certificate and a distribution certificate for yourself to become a CA. The CertUtil tool is located in the NSS installation's *bin* directory and can be run from anywhere in a console window. In the next few sections, we walk through the steps necessary to accomplish this process.

Creating a certificate database

Mozilla comes with a prefilled certificate database that contains information about certificates from Verisign and other CAs (found in the file *cert7.db* in the user profile directory), which you can modify. However, starting with a blank database is better because it avoids the possibility of corruption.

At the prompt, create a new database by using the -N and -d options for CertUtil:

```
C:\NSS\bin>certutil -N -d .
```

Enter a password for the database. You need to reenter this password every time you issue or change certificates. CertUtil creates the files *cert7.db*, *key3.db*, and *secmod.db* in the same directory as CertUtil. You can delete the *key3.db* and *secmod.db* files because they do not pertain to certificate creation or modification.

Creating the root CA certificate

The root certificate is the foundation for the certificate chain and should not be shared with anyone outside your organization. You may want to consider storing the database or exported certificate on a floppy disk for safe keeping. If it gets lost or stolen, you need to make a new one and all your users will need to use new certificates and resign their applications.

Once you create *cert7.db*, CertUtil can process the Root CA Certificate into it, using the following and substituting the name of your CA for mozdev.org:

```
C:\NSS\bin>certutil -S -s "CN=mozdev.org, O=mozdev.org" -n "mozdev.org"
-t ",,C" -x -d . -1 -2 -5
```

Enter a password at the prompt and proceed by making the menu choices shown in Example 12-9.

Example 12-9. Creating a root certificate

```
Generating key.  This may take a few moments...
                  0 - Digital Signature
                  1 - Non-repudiation
                  2 - Key encipherment
                  3 - Data encipherment
                  4 - Key agreement
                  5 - Cert signing key
                  6 - CRL signing key
                  Other to finish
5
                  0 - Digital Signature
                  1 - Non-repudiation
                  2 - Key encipherment
                  3 - Data encipherment
                  4 - Key agreement
                  5 - Cert signing key
                  6 - CRL signing key
                  Other to finish
9
Is this a critical extension [y/n]?
n
Is this a CA certificate [y/n]?
y
Enter the path length constraint, enter to skip [<0 for unlimited path]:
Is this a critical extension [y/n]?
```

Example 12-9. Creating a root certificate (continued)

```
n
                              0 - SSL Client
                              1 - SSL Server
                              2 - S/MIME
                              3 - Object Signing
                              4 - Reserved for futuer use
                              5 - SSL CA
                              6 - S/MIME CA
                              7 - Object Signing CA
                              Other to finish
7
                              0 - SSL Client
                              1 - SSL Server
                              2 - S/MIME
                              3 - Object Signing
                              4 - Reserved for futuer use
                              5 - SSL CA
                              6 - S/MIME CA
                              7 - Object Signing CA
                              Other to finish
9
Is this a critical extension [y/n]?
n
```

The mozdev.org Root CA Certificate resides in *cert7.db*. You can export it to a file for safekeeping as follows:

```
C:\NSS\bin>certutil -L -d . -n "mozdev.org" -a -o mozdev.cacert
```

This code will yield an ASCII representation of the certificate.

Creating a distribution CA certificate

Next you must create a distribution certificate. This certificate will be installed into the user's Mozilla web browser so Mozilla can verify related signed remote Mozilla applications. Start the certificate by typing the following code at the prompt and substituting the name of your CA for "mozdev.org":

```
C:\NSS\bin>certutil -S -n "certs.mozdev.org"
-s "CN=certs.mozdev.org, O=certs.mozdev.org" -c "mozdev.org" -v 96
-t ",,C" -d . -1 -2 -5
```

Enter a password at the prompt and make the menu choices shown in Example 12-10.

Example 12-10. Creating a distribution certificate

```
Generating key.  This may take a few moments...
                          0 - Digital Signature
                          1 - Non-repudiation
                          2 - Key encipherment
                          3 - Data encipherment
                          4 - Key agreement
```

Example 12-10. Creating a distribution certificate (continued)

```
                        5 - Cert signning key
                        6 - CRL signning key
                        Other to finish
5
                        0 - Digital Signature
                        1 - Non-repudiation
                        2 - Key encipherment
                        3 - Data encipherment
                        4 - Key agreement
                        5 - Cert signning key
                        6 - CRL signning key
                        Other to finish
9
Is this a critical extension [y/n]?
n
Is this a CA certificate [y/n]?
y
Enter the path length constraint, enter to skip [<0 for unlimited path]:
Is this a critical extension [y/n]?
n
                        0 - SSL Client
                        1 - SSL Server
                        2 - S/MIME
                        3 - Object Signing
                        4 - Reserved for futuer use
                        5 - SSL CA
                        6 - S/MIME CA
                        7 - Object Signing CA
                        Other to finish
7
                        0 - SSL Client
                        1 - SSL Server
                        2 - S/MIME
                        3 - Object Signing
                        4 - Reserved for futuer use
                        5 - SSL CA
                        6 - S/MIME CA
                        7 - Object Signing CA
                        Other to finish
9
Is this a critical extension [y/n]?
n
```

Note the differences between this process and that used to create the root certificate. The distribution certificate is not self-signed, so to create it, you must reference the mozdev.org Root CA Certificate in the initial command. Also, the `-v 96` option indicates that the certificate is good for 96 months.

Once you've created the distribution certificate, export it using the following command (for which "certs.mozdev.org" is the name of your CA):

```
C:\NSS\bin>certutil -L -d . -n "certs.mozdev.org" -a -o certs_mozdev.cacert
```

Keep track of the resulting file because you will need to upload it to your web site later so browsers can install it.

Issuing Signing Certificates

Once you create the two root and distribution certificates for your organization, you are a certificate authority, much like VeriSign. You decide who gets the privilege of a signing certificate and issue them accordingly. Signing certificates should not be reused for different people. When you want to give out a signing certificate, you should create a new one by using CertUtil and make a copy of the exported certificate for yourself to keep and catalog.

To create a signing certificate, use the following command and substitute the name of your CA for "mozdev.org":

```
C:\NSS\bin>certutil -S -n "certs.mozdev.org/signing"
-s "CN=certs.mozdev.org/signing, O=certs.mozdev.org" -c "certs.mozdev.org" -v 96 -t
",,C" -d . -1 -2 -5
```

Enter a password at the prompt and make the menu choices shown in Example 12-11.

Example 12-11. Create a signing certificate

```
Generating key.  This may take a few moments...
                          0 - Digital Signature
                          1 - Non-repudiation
                          2 - Key encipherment
                          3 - Data encipherment
                          4 - Key agreement
                          5 - Cert signing key
                          6 - CRL signing key
                          Other to finish
0
                          0 - Digital Signature
                          1 - Non-repudiation
                          2 - Key encipherment
                          3 - Data encipherment
                          4 - Key agreement
                          5 - Cert signing key
                          6 - CRL signing key
                          Other to finish
5
                          0 - Digital Signature
                          1 - Non-repudiation
                          2 - Key encipherment
                          3 - Data encipherment
                          4 - Key agreement
                          5 - Cert signing key
                          6 - CRL signing key
                          Other to finish
9
Is this a critical extension [y/n]?
```

Example 12-11. Create a signing certificate (continued)

```
n
Is this a CA certificate [y/n]?
n
Enter the path length constraint, enter to skip [<0 for unlimited path]:
Is this a critical extension [y/n]?
n
                         0 - SSL Client
                         1 - SSL Server
                         2 - S/MIME
                         3 - Object Signing
                         4 - Reserved for futuer use
                         5 - SSL CA
                         6 - S/MIME CA
                         7 - Object Signing CA
                         Other to finish
3
                         0 - SSL Client
                         1 - SSL Server
                         2 - S/MIME
                         3 - Object Signing
                         4 - Reserved for futuer use
                         5 - SSL CA
                         6 - S/MIME CA
                         7 - Object Signing CA
                         Other to finish
9
Is this a critical extension [y/n]?
n
```

In Example 12-11, the *certs.mozdev.org/signing* certificate references the *certs.mozdev.org* CA certificate. The Digital Signature option is also set so a signed remote Mozilla application can be compiled from the certificate.

Export the signing certificate with the following command:

```
C:\NSS\bin>certutil -L -d . -n "certs.mozdev.org/signing" -a
-o eric.cacert
```

You can send the resulting file to the person who requested the Signing Certificate. That person can then use it to create signed remote applications, as described later in this chapter in the "Signing the application" section.

Distributing Distribution Certificates

The distribution certificate (*certs_mozdev.cacert* in Example 12-10) must be installed into a user's Mozilla web browser before she can use signed applications that come from certificates you've distributed. It's best to state clearly on the web site hosting these signed remote Mozilla applications that the distribution certificate is needed. If you distribute many different signing certificates, and they are used by all signed remote Mozilla applications, then all applications can use that same distribution certificate (as they do with Verisign's and other certificate authorities).

To allow users to install the distribution certificate, create a link to the certificate file on your web page:

```
<a href="certs_mozdev.cacert">Install the MozDev CA Certificate</a>
```

Also make sure that your web server uses the MIME type `application/x-x509-ca-cert` for *.cacert* files.

If the web server is set up correctly, the user will get a dialog box that looks like Figure 12-5. Tell the user to select the options for "web sites" and "software developers."

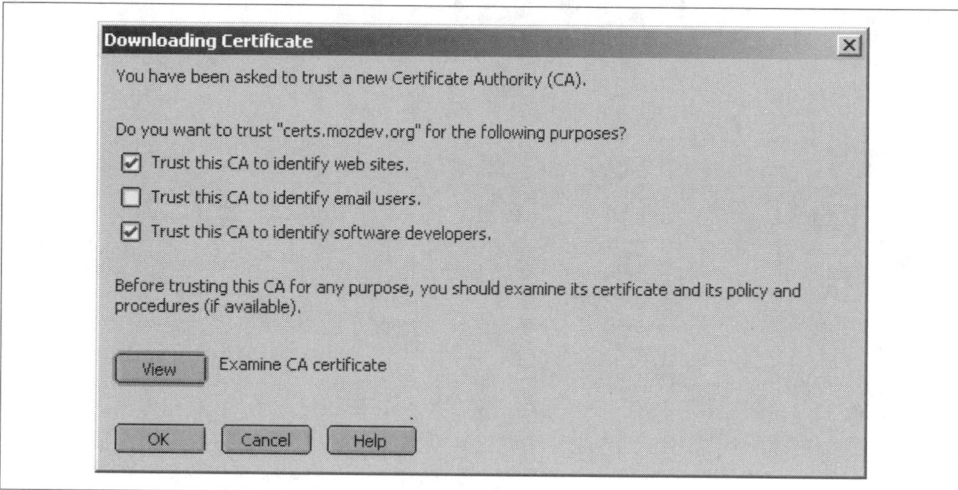

Figure 12-5. Downloading a certificate window

After the certificate is installed, it will appear in the Certificate Manager, as shown in Figure 12-6. The Certificate Manager can be accessed via the global Mozilla preferences (Edit → Preferences → Privacy & Security → Certificates). Mozilla is then ready to run signed remote Mozilla applications bearing signatures from your certificate authority.

Creating Signed Remote Applications

Security in Mozilla's web browser is designed to meet today's advanced scripting needs in a secure manner. Mozilla is a much more secure browser than past Netscape 4.x and Internet Explorer releases because it has a better sense of what remote scripts can and cannot do.

Because of Mozilla's approach toward potentially insecure applications, if you decide to serve up your own application remotely, remember that you will not have automatic access to the chrome in the way you do when you have a registered, locally

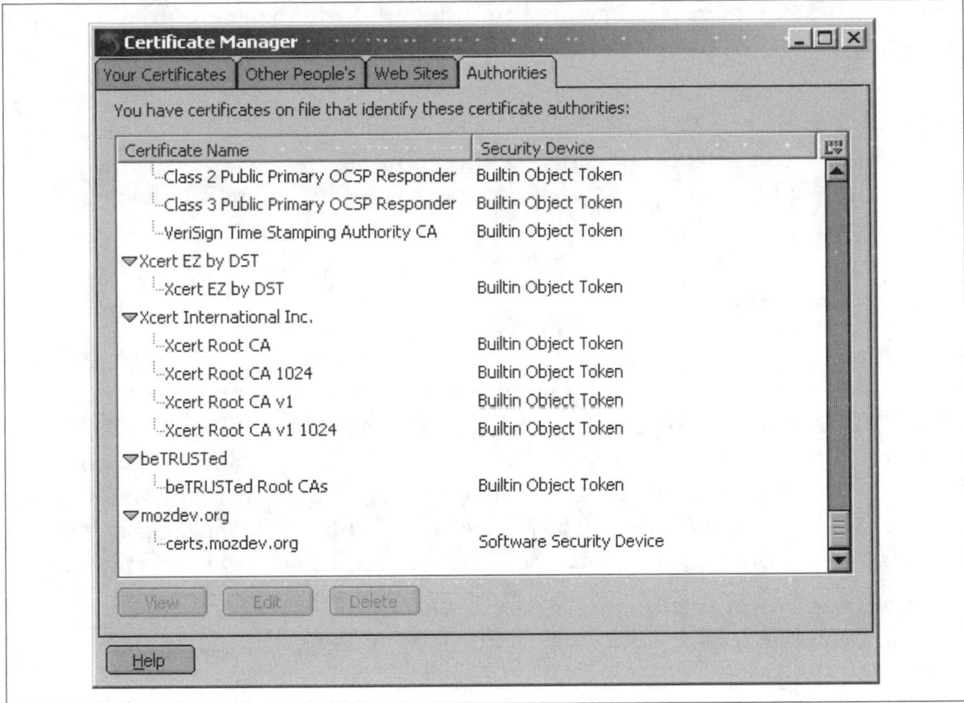

Figure 12-6. Certificate manager with a certs.mozdev.org CA certificate

installed Mozilla application. Unless you sign your application or have the user turn on a special preference (see "Setting Up XPFE for Remote Applications"), services like XPConnect will not be available.

In Mozilla, you can bundle any number of files into a JAR archive (which, you'll recall from Chapter 6, is just a zip file with a JAR suffix) and designate the archive as an object that can be signed. This designation makes it very easy to produce an entire signed and secure remote Mozilla application because it stores your application in a single file type that Mozilla already treats as a separate package.

This section provides an overview of the signed script technology and shows you how to create signed applications that live on the server but take full advantage of the user's local chrome, including Mozilla components.

certs.mozdev.org CA Certificate

Before users can load signed applications, a CA certificate must be installed into their installed copy of Mozilla. Once this certificate is installed in a browser, all MozDev-signed applications can work with this certificate. This setup makes things easier on users who access many of these signed applications because they do not have to install a new certificate for each one. Also, if the user wants to use applications from other certificate authorities, they need to install a distribution certificate from that certificate authority.

Installing the certificate is easy. Just provide the users with a regular link on a web page—for example, *http://certs.mozdev.org/certs_mozdev.cacert*. When loading this page, a dialog box pops up and asks the user to install the certificate. See the "Distributing the application" section later in this chapter for more information about this process.

Signing Certificates

As a Mozilla application developer, you can obtain a common MozDev signing certificate and release a signed application that puts your application on par with other signed MozDev applications. If you consider your application mission-critical, however, you should go to a trusted CA such as Verisign. Mozilla already supports the VeriSign Netscape Object Signing CA, and discriminating users may find it more acceptable. A few other CAs listed in Mozilla's Certificate Manager may support Netscape Object Signing, so researching these options further may be worthwhile.

To get a *certs.mozdev.org/signing* certificate, send email to *cert-request@mozdev.org*. In return, you will receive a *.cacert* file that will be used to sign your remote Mozilla application.

SignTool (part of the NSS tool sets) takes a directory of files, zips them up into a JAR archive (refer to the section "Signing the application" later in this chapter to see how to do this), and signs the archive using the certificate you specify.

SignTool comes with the latest release of NSS, Version 3.4.1. On *http://certs.mozdev.org*, limited functionality versions of NSS contain SignTool for Windows and Linux that you can use instead for the processes in this book.

Use CertUtil to set up a database for SignTool. Next, run some commands to set up the certificate environment:

```
C:\NSS\bin>certutil -N -d .
C:\NSS\bin>certutil -A -n "certs.mozdev.org/signing" -t ",,C"
-i eric.cacert -d .
```

The first command creates an empty *cert7.db* file where certificates can be stored. The second imports your Signing Certificate into the database. SignTool can use only certificates that reside in a database, which is the reason for this process.

Creating and Signing the Application

When someone obtains a private key (which is part of a Signing Certificate), they can encrypt their scripts and produce a public key. The relationship of the private key and the public key is called a private-public key pair. Using this relationship, you can create a signed Mozilla application and make it available to users in three steps:

1. Build the application itself, including the XUL, CSS, JavaScript, and whatever else you use to create the Mozilla application.

   For this section, let's assume that you already created the XUL and JavaScript for the application and have all the files and directories together.
2. Archive and sign the application. SignTool takes care of both steps simultaneously, putting your application files in a JAR with a digital signature to validate everything.

   The signing process described next in "Signing the application" deals entirely with SignTool.
3. Distribute your application (see the later section "Distributing the application").

Signing the application

Security is not simple. Security technologists and vendors work hard to make sure that evildoers cannot abuse their encryption schemes, keys, and other tricks. Tools like SignTool can hide some of this complexity from you. When you sign an application, you create a digital signature in the archive that is based on the relationship of the files being signed, as Figure 12-7 illustrates.

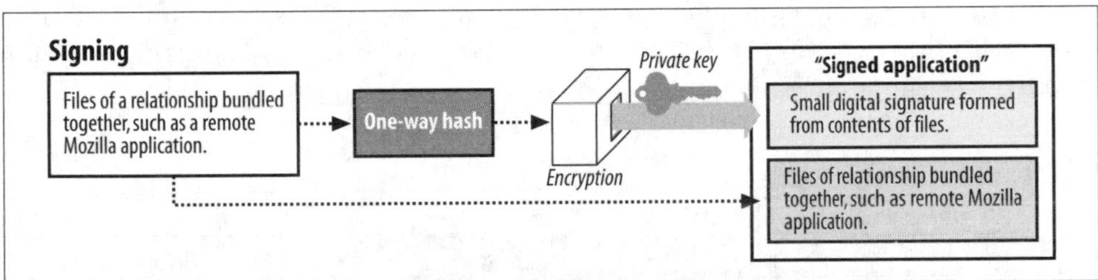

Figure 12-7. SignTool's processes for creating a signed application

SignTool automates these steps for you, so you don't worry about them. However, knowing these processes and seeing how these transactions take place can be useful, especially since using signed applications with Mozilla doesn't always work as expected and long-term directions for signed applications in Mozilla are uncertain. This uncertainty makes long-term deployment of signed remote Mozilla applications a risky option.

To start off your remote Mozilla signed application development, you can do something as simple as place one XUL and one JavaScript file in a single directory. Then move it into a NSS *bin* directory such as *C:\NSS\bin* and issue the command:

```
C:\NSS\bin>signtool -d . -k"certs.mozdev.org/signing"
-p"password_of_database" -Z"myapp.jar" myappfiles/
```

The -d option is where the certificate database resides and -k is the certificate name.

Distributing the application

Once the file is created from the `-Z` option (e.g., *myapp.jar* from the example above), you can put it online. On the application's web page, note that the application is signed and put a link to *http://certs.mozdev.org/certs_mozdev.cacert* so users can install the necessary MozDev certificate if they do not have it.

To access the application online, you must use a special URL format. This format looks like *jar:http://certs.mozdev.org/myapp.jar!/myapp.xul* and points into the JAR at the main application file. This URL is difficult to type, so it may be wise to link it for user access or set up a redirected URL to that address, as shown in Example 12-12.

Example 12-12. Sample redirect into a signed application

```
<HTML>
<HEAD>
  <META HTTP-EQUIV="REFRESH" CONTENT="0;
        URL= jar:http://certs.mozdev.org/sample.jar!/sample.xul">
</HEAD>
</HTML>
```

Receiving a Signed Application

As shown in Figure 12-8, when Mozilla receives a JAR, it must check it for validity before displaying the contents. A public key in *certs_mozdev.cacert* must be used along with the digital signature to make sure that the contents are not tampered with and that the signature is valid.

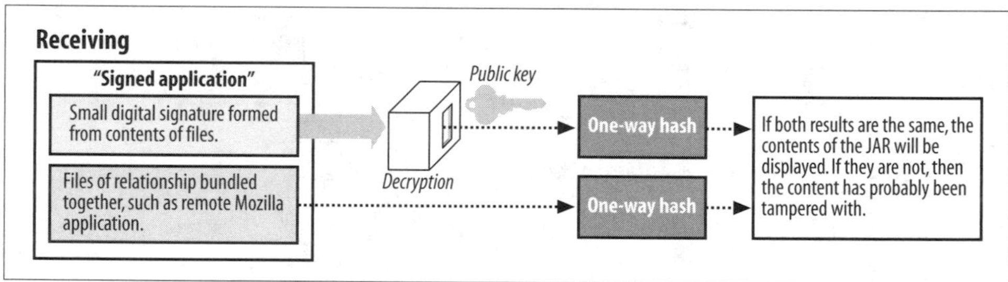

Figure 12-8. Receiving a signed application

When you are developing a signed remote Mozilla application, clear a JAR's cache before trying to reload an updated version of it. Clearing the cache can be done most easily by restarting Mozilla. If you or your users do not do clear it, the consumer of the application will probably wind up with a blank screen.

Expanded Privileges in Mozilla

While the security aspect of signed objects is nice, the ability to make remote Java-Script do just about anything is even better for web developers because it avoids the perceived complexity of languages like C++. Also, JavaScript, along with Perl and PHP, has always been a preferred language in the web environment.

Knowing that Internet Explorer no longer has a huge advantage when it comes to remote browser-based applications is also nice, since JavaScript and XPCOM in Mozilla provide a framework very similar to ActiveX. They also provide web page scripting in which you can create and use components from a web page or web application.

Table 12-1 shows the expanded privileges available to signed scripts. Signed applications are granted these privileges as a matter of course.

Table 12-1. Expanded privileges available to signed scripts

Privilege	Purpose
UniversalBrowserRead	Reads sensitive browser data. This reading allows the script to pass the same origin check when reading from any document.
UniversalBrowserWrite	Modifies sensitive browser data. This modification allows the script to pass the same origin check when writing to any document.
UniversalXPConnect	Gives unrestricted access to browser APIs using XPConnect.
UniversalPreferencesRead	Reads preferences using the `navigator.preference` method.
UniversalPreferencesWrite	Allows you to set preferences using the `navigator.preference` method.
CapabilityPreferencesAccess	Allows you to read/set the preferences that define security policies, including which privileges are granted and denied to scripts. (You also need *UniversalPreferencesRead/Write*.)
UniversalFileRead	Handles `window.open` of *file://* URLs. Makes the browser upload files from the user's hard drive by using `<input type="file">`.

The JavaScript features require expanded privileges and the target used to access each feature. Unsigned scripts cannot do the following:

- Use an *about:* format URL other than *about:blank*; requires *UniversalBrowserRead*.
- Use the history object to find out what other sites the user visited or how many other sites the user visited in this session. Doing so requires *UniversalBrowserRead*.
- When using navigator object, get the preference value by using the preference method. Getting such a value requires *UniversalPreferencesRead*.
- Set the preference value using the preference method; getting this value requires *UniversalPreferencesWrite*.
- Add or remove the directory bar, location bar, menu bar, personal bar, scroll bar, status bar, or toolbar. These are done using the window object and require *UniversalBrowserWrite*.
- Use the methods and properties in the Table 12-2 under the indicated circumstances.

Table 12-2. Expanded privileges available to signed scripts

Method / property	Description
`EnableExternalCapture`	Captures events in pages loaded from different servers. Follow this method with *captureEvents*.
`Close`	Unconditionally closes a browser window.
`moveBy, moveTo`	Moves a window off of the screen.
`Open`	• Creates a window smaller than 100 x 100 pixels or larger than the screen can accommodate by using *innerWidth*, *innerHeight*, *outerWidth*, and *outerHeight*. • Places a window offscreen by using *screenX* and *screenY*. • Creates a window without a titlebar by using `titlebar=no`. • Uses *alwaysRaised*, *alwaysLowered*, or z-lock for any setting.
`resizeTo, resizeBy`	Resizes a window smaller than 100 x 100 pixels or larger than the screen can accommodate.
`innerWidth, innerHeight`	Sets the inner width of a window to a size smaller than 100 x 100 or larger than the screen can accommodate.

This snippet of code shows how to use the privilege manager in JavaScript:

```
netscape.security.PrivilegeManager.
      enablePrivilege("UniversalBrowserWrite");
window.titlebar=no;
```

You can pass any privilege listed in Table 12-1 to the `enablePrivilege` method, which is accessed through the `netscape.security.PrivilegeManager` object. This object is recognized globally. In this example, the code hides the titlebar via the window object.

Security is extremely important, so it is important that some means of granting special privileges to trusted scripts for accessing Mozilla components be available. In essence, signed scripts are Mozilla's version of ActiveX.

The parallels become even more apparent when you consider access to XPConnect as one of the security model's main boundaries. Just as ActiveX makes COM available in IE, signing makes XPCOM available in remote Mozilla applications. Given all that is possible in XPCOM, this chapter leaves what can be archived with remote Mozilla applications and XPConnect up to your imagination.

Signed Remote Snake Game

In this section, we look at an enhanced version of the Snake game presented earlier in the chapter. The enhanced version uses XPConnect to provide a total full-screen display of the game on the Windows platform as a remote application.

How to Expand Mozilla to Full Screen

The best way to expand Mozilla to a full screen mode is through full-screen functions provided in an instance of *navigator.xul*. These functions run in the Windows build of Mozilla via the Full Screen item in the View menu. These functions also work in Linux and Mac, but do not provide 100% full-screen mode, as some menus and titlebars still show.

The problem here is the current window's *navigator.xul* document, which needs to be accessed to get these full-screen functions. A document loaded in that window just can't use something like *window.parent* to get to it, so another route must be found.

This route runs through the *nsIWindowMediator* interface by the way of XPConnect. It gives access to the current browser window's *navigator.xul* document's window object. Example 12-13 includes the code for this window access process, along with the functions used to create the full-screen effect.

Example 12-13. Function for switching screen modes

```
netscape.security.PrivilegeManager.enablePrivilege("UniversalXPConnect");
const MEDIATOR_CONTRACTID="@mozilla.org/appshell/window-mediator;1";
const nsIWindowMediator=Components.interfaces.nsIWindowMediator;
var windowManager=
    Components.classes[MEDIATOR_CONTRACTID].getService(nsIWindowMediator);
var hideSidebar=true;
var isRegular=true;
function switchScreen()
{
  if(isRegular)
  {
    try {
      netscape.security.PrivilegeManager.enablePrivilege("UniversalXPConnect");
      mainWindow = windowManager.getMostRecentWindow("navigator:browser");
    }
    catch(e) {
      alert(e);
    }
    if(mainWindow.sidebar_is_hidden())
      hideSidebar=false;
    if(hideSidebar)
      mainWindow.SidebarShowHide();
    mainWindow.BrowserFullScreen();
    window.fullScreen=true;
    window.locationbar.visible=false;
    window.toolbar.visible=false;
    isRegular=false;
  }
  else
  {
    try {
        netscape.security.PrivilegeManager.enablePrivilege("UniversalXPConnect");
      mainWindow = windowManager.getMostRecentWindow("navigator:browser");
    }
    catch(e) {
      alert(e);
    }
```

Example 12-13. Function for switching screen modes (continued)

```
    window.locationbar.visible=true;
    window.toolbar.visible=true;
    if(hideSidebar)
      mainWindow.SidebarShowHide();
    mainWindow.BrowserFullScreen();
    isRegular=true;
  }
}
```

windowManager, which is spawned by XPConnect, creates the *mainWindow* variable. By using the getMostRecentWindow function for navigator:browser, the Mozilla application window you currently use becomes available. Next, tests are made in code for the window status determine if it is regular or full screen. Appropriate action can then be made by calling the SidebarShowHide function.

As you can see in Example 12-13, code for hiding the toolbar and location bar is also present. This code is accomplished not by the *mainWindow* created through XPConnect, but by the existing window object:

```
window.locationbar.visible=false;
window.toolbar.visible=false;
```

Using both the mainWindow and window objects allows the creation of a full-screen remote Mozilla application by allowing XPConnect privileges. Figure 12-9 shows the result on Windows—a total full screen for a signed remote Mozilla game!

Mozilla's XML Extras and SOAP

Mozilla has built functions called XML Extras that allow the use of XML as data in both JavaScript and C++. Such functions are an XML Serializer, XMLHttpRequest, XML Parser, SOAP-based RPC, and XML Persistence. You can find more information about these functions, along with examples, at *http://www.mozilla.org/xmlextras/*.

The following sections assume that you are familiar with SOAP and .NET. If not, some good O'Reilly books available on these subjects can help get you started.

Mozilla, SOAP, and .NET

In this section, SOAP is used to access data in a .NET web service, therefore allowing the Snake game to have features such as a saved game score, a retrieved game score, and a list of high scores.

As of Mozilla 1.0, the SOAP functions of Mozilla do not work in signed scripts. This bug will be corrected in the future. All JavaScript using SOAP functions in this section is loaded externally of the signed JAR. These SOAP functions do not require enhanced privileges.

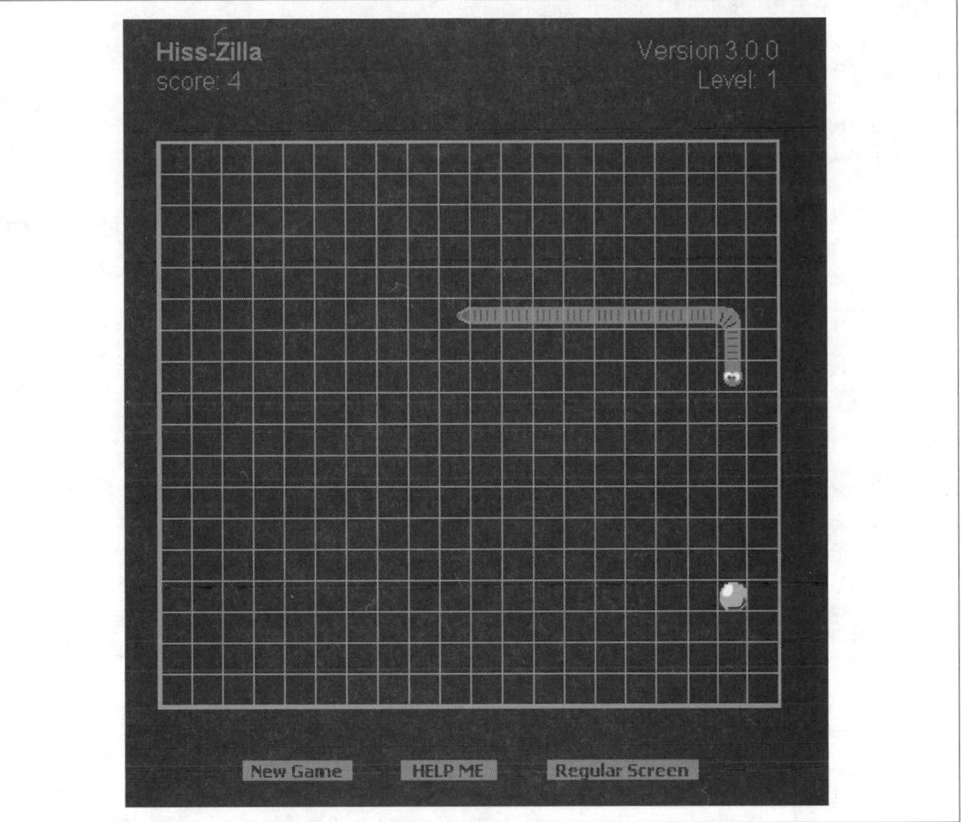

Figure 12-9. Snake game in full-screen mode on Windows

Setting Up a .NET Web Service

The easiest way to create a .NET web service is through Visual Studio.NET, which provides a template for creating these services. Example 12-14 shows a bare minimum of C# code used to compile the functions that return a value to the Snake game.

Obviously, a full implementation would need a database to store these scores. For this section, seeing how the interfaces work for these SOAP functions is more important.

Example 12-14. Minimal .NET web service

```
using System;
using System.Collections;
using System.ComponentModel;
using System.Data;
using System.Diagnostics;
using System.Web;
```

Example 12-14. Minimal .NET web service (continued)

```
using System.Web.Services;
namespace SnakeService
{
    [WebServiceAttribute (Namespace="uri:SnakeScore")]
    public class SnakeService : System.Web.Services.WebService
    {
        public SnakeService()
        {
            InitializeComponent();
        }
        #region Component Designer generated code
        private IContainer components = null;
        private void InitializeComponent(){}
        protected override void Dispose( bool disposing )
        {
            if(disposing && components != null)
            {
                components.Dispose();
            }
            base.Dispose(disposing);
        }
        #endregion
        [WebMethod]
        public string SaveScore(string PlayerName, string Score)
        {
            return "Save of score successful.";
        }
         [WebMethod]
        public string GetScore(string PlayerName)
        {
            int Score = 990;
            return Score.ToString();
        }
        [WebMethod]
        public string GetHighScores()
        {
            return "EDM 1000,SLK 200,BRP 10";
        }
    }
}
```

The most important part of Example 12-14 is the `WebServiceAttribute` because it sets up a URI reference to the `SnakeService` object. When a request is sent from the Snake game to the .NET `SnakeService`, `uri:SnakeScore` becomes the name for the object providing functions for getting and setting the game's score.

In Example 12-14, all the parameter and return values are of the `string` type. Considering the brevity of this example, expanding it would not be hard. Functions using other objects and database connections would really make it a true web application.

.NET WSDL

.NET automatically generates WSDL interfaces inside a web service. Mozilla SOAP doesn't need to reference a WDSL file to make SOAP transactions.

Example 12-15 is a portion of the WDSL that .NET generates and is the specific portion that relates directly to sending raw SOAP calls to the `SnakeService`. Also, only the definitions for the `GetScore` function are in this abbreviated definition.

Example 12-15. Abbreviated WSDL as produced by .NET web service.

```
<?xml version="1.0" encoding="utf-8"?>
<definitions
   xmlns:http="http://schemas.xmlsoap.org/wsdl/http/"
   xmlns:soap="http://schemas.xmlsoap.org/wsdl/soap/"
   xmlns:s="http://www.w3.org/2001/XMLSchema" xmlns:s0="uri:SnakeScore"
   xmlns:soapenc="http://schemas.xmlsoap.org/soap/encoding/"
   xmlns:tm="http://microsoft.com/wsdl/mime/textMatching/"
   xmlns:mime="http://schemas.xmlsoap.org/wsdl/mime/"
   targetNamespace="uri:SnakeScore"
   xmlns="http://schemas.xmlsoap.org/wsdl/">
  <types>
    <s:schema elementFormDefault="qualified"
              targetNamespace="uri:SnakeScore">
      <s:element name="GetScore">
        <s:complexType>
          <s:sequence>
            <s:element minOccurs="0" maxOccurs="1" name="PlayerName"
                       type="s:string" />
          </s:sequence>
        </s:complexType>
      </s:element>
      <s:element name="GetScoreResponse">
        <s:complexType>
          <s:sequence>
            <s:element minOccurs="0" maxOccurs="1" name="GetScoreResult"
                       type="s:string" />
          </s:sequence>
        </s:complexType>
      </s:element>
    </s:schema>
  </types>
  <message name="GetScoreSoapIn">
    <part name="parameters" element="s0:GetScore" />
  </message>
  <message name="GetScoreSoapOut">
    <part name="parameters" element="s0:GetScoreResponse" />
  </message>
  <portType name="SnakeServiceSoap">
    <operation name="GetScore">
      <input message="s0:GetScoreSoapIn" />
      <output message="s0:GetScoreSoapOut" />
    </operation>
```

Example 12-15. Abbreviated WSDL as produced by .NET web service. (continued)

```
  </portType>
  <binding name="SnakeServiceSoap" type="s0:SnakeServiceSoap">
    <soap:binding transport="http://schemas.xmlsoap.org/soap/http"
                  style="document" />
    <operation name="GetScore">
      <soap:operation soapAction="uri:SnakeScore/GetScore"
                      style="document" />
      <input>
        <soap:body use="literal" />
      </input>
      <output>
        <soap:body use="literal" />
      </output>
    </operation>
  </binding>
  <service name="SnakeService">
    <port name="SnakeServiceSoap" binding="s0:SnakeServiceSoap">
      <soap:address
         location="http://localhost/SnakeService/SnakeService.asmx" />
    </port>
  </service>
</definitions>
```

The most important thing to notice in this WSDL is the `soapAction`. In Example 12-15, `uri:SnakeScore/GetScore` is defined as the identifier for the `SnakeScore` object's `GetScore` function. This identifier makes the call to this function in Example 12-19.

SOAP Call XML Formats

When .NET and Mozilla serialize SOAP calls, they produce different XML formats. The namespace prefixes differ, and Mozilla produces more of these namespaces in its version of the SOAP message. However, the code comparison in Examples 12-16 and 12-17 mean fundamentally the same thing. Thus, .NET and Mozilla are able to communicate.

Example 12-16. XML format for SOAP calls of Mozilla

```
<env:Envelope
   xmlns:env="http://schemas.xmlsoap.org/soap/envelope/"
   xmlns:enc="http://schemas.xmlsoap.org/soap/encoding/"
   env:encodingStyle="http://schemas.xmlsoap.org/soap/encoding/"
   xmlns:xs="http://www.w3.org/1999/XMLSchema"
   xmlns:xsi="http://www.w3.org/1999/XMLSchema-instance">
  <env:Header/>
  <env:Body>
    <a0:SaveScore xmlns:a0="uri:SnakeScore">
      <PlayerName xsi:type="xs:string">EDM</PlayerName>
      <Score xsi:type="xs:string">10</Score>
    </a0:SaveScore>
```

Example 12-16. XML format for SOAP calls of Mozilla (continued)

```
  </env:Body>
</env:Envelope>
```

Example 12-17. .NET format for SOAP calls of Mozilla

```
<soap:Envelope
   xmlns:xsi="http://www.w3.org/2001/XMLSchema-instance"
   xmlns:xsd="http://www.w3.org/2001/XMLSchema"
   xmlns:soap="http://schemas.xmlsoap.org/soap/envelope/">
  <soap:Body>
    <SaveScore xmlns="uri:SnakeScore">
      <PlayerName>EDM</PlayerName>
      <Score>10</Score>
    </SaveScore>
  </soap:Body>
</soap:Envelope>
```

Realizing these formatting differences in Examples 12-16 and 12-17 is important because if you develop with SOAP by using .NET and Mozilla, you are bound to run across variations in your future software projects. Luckily the W3C has set a standard that Mozilla and Microsoft adheres to.

Adding SnakeService SOAP to Snake

Developers use built-in methods to just write JavaScript and use SOAP easily. There is no need for enhanced privileges because nothing could affect the client adversely. However, there are some limitations on how SOAP JavaScript is used.

Mozilla sets one level of security with the SOAP function by requiring that the web service and the JavaScript file that makes the SOAP functions access that service be on the same domain. For example, you will not encounter problems when running everything as localhost (as shown in the examples). If you try to move the JavaScript files to mozdev.org, though, they will no longer work.

Another limitation of the SOAP functions is that they can't be used directly in XUL documents. However, a hack, discussed in the next section, can get around this limitation.

Make SOAP Functions Work in XUL Documents

The best way to circumvent the SOAP-in-XUL-documents problem in Mozilla 1.0 (and probably 1.1) is to initially load the JavaScript file containing the SOAP functions from an HTML file, as shown in Example 12-18.

Example 12-18. Preloading scores.js into cache with an HTML association

```
<html>
<head>
```

Example 12-18. Preloading scores.js into cache with an HTML association (continued)

```
  <script src="http://localhost/nss/bin/scores.js"></script>
</head>
<body>
  <script>
window.location.href="jar:http://localhost/nss/bin/snake.jar!/scores.xul";
  </script>
</body>
</html>
```

As stated earlier, *scores.js* (containing the SOAP functions) must exist outside the JAR file. It is loaded up into cache with this HTML document, and then the page redirects to the XUL file that has the SOAP function user interface. That JavaScript file is already loaded up in cache and will work fine.

Remember that doing this is a hack, but later versions of Mozilla that fix the SOAP-in-XUL-document problem would still not break this code.

Examining SOAP Functions for Snake

Example 12-19 shows how to create two functions (`SaveScore` and `SaveScoreResponse`) to handle SOAP transactions with the previously examined .NET web service.

Example 12-19. SaveScore SOAP function

```
const soapVersion  = 0; // Version 1.1
const object       = "uri:SnakeScore";
const transportURI = "http://localhost/SnakeService/SnakeService.asmx";
// SAVE PLAYER SCORE

function SaveScore()
{
  var Score = window.opener.document.getElementById("currentscore").getAttribute("value");
  var PlayerName  = document.getElementById("saveInitials").value;
  var method  = "SaveScore";
  var headers = new Array();
  var params  = new Array(new SOAPParameter(PlayerName,"PlayerName"),
                new SOAPParameter(Score,"Score"));
  var call = new SOAPCall();
  call.transportURI = transportURI;
  call.actionURI = object+"/"+method;
  call.encode(soapVersion,method,object,headers.length,headers,params.length,params);
  var currentRequest = call.asyncInvoke(SaveScoreResponse);
}
function SaveScoreResponse(resp,call,status)
{
  // Display confirmation
  // Part of content of SOAP message returned
  alert(resp.body.firstChild.firstChild.firstChild.data);
}
```

The object defined here is the same as the namespace defined in Example 12-14. Again, this snake score object (uri:SnakeScore) is simply an identifier to that exact web service. The transportURI is the location of the web service. As you can see here, it runs localhost along with the files for the Snake remote Mozilla application. Moving into the actual SaveScore function, a PlayerName is pulled from a <textbox> in the XUL.

The method is the name of the function in the .NET web service with which this code will communicate. headers is an empty array because no SOAP headers are needed for this simple example. Two SOAPParameters are also defined here in an array, and they are just simple strings. Moving on down the code in Example 12-19, a new SOAPCall() is defined into the call variable. Two URIs are set up for this SOAPCall object: call.transportURI and call.actionURI, which combines an object and a method into one string. The next two lines, encode and asyncInvoke the SOAPCall and the encoded XML message, as shown in Examples 12-16 and 12-17, are sent to the .NET web service. When a response is received, the SaveScoreResponse function is called.

Currently, a hack is used in SaveScoreResponse so a DOM property accesses the XML of the returned SOAP message. This implementation is not the best way, but the optimal way doesn't currently work. Here is an easy version of the code:

```
ret = resp.getParameters(false, new Array());
alert(ret[0]);
```

If you put this code in SaveScoreResponse and it works, it could replace the code in Examples 12-16 and 12-17. You need to play around with these different SOAP functions and see what works for you. Again, the code just shown does not work in Mozilla 1.0, but will hopefully work in all future versions of Mozilla.

Example 12-20 shows the code for GetResponse and GetHighScores. Compare the JavaScript code to the code and WSDL in Examples 12-14 and 12-15 to see how they all work together.

Example 12-20. Code for GetScore and GetHighScores

```
// GET PLAYER SCORE
var ScoreElement; // Make this accessible to GetScoreResponse
function GetScore()
{
  ScoreElement = window.opener.document.getElementById("currentscore");
  var PlayerName = document.getElementById("getInitials").value;
  var method  = "GetScore";
  var headers = new Array();
  var params  = new Array(new SOAPParameter(PlayerName,"PlayerName"));
  var call = new SOAPCall();
  call.transportURI = transportURI;
  call.actionURI = object+"/"+method;
  call.encode(soapVersion,method,object,headers.length,headers,params.length,params);
  var currentRequest = call.asyncInvoke(GetScoreResponse);
}
function GetScoreResponse(resp,call,status)
{
```

Example 12-20. Code for GetScore and GetHighScores (continued)

```
  ScoreElement.setAttribute("value",resp.body.firstChild.firstChild.firstChild.data);
  alert("Your score has been reinstated. You can now return to the game.");
}
// GET HIGH SCORES
function GetHighScores()
{
  var method  = "GetHighScores";
  var headers = new Array();
  var params  = new Array();
  var call = new SOAPCall();
  call.transportURI = transportURI;
  call.actionURI = object+"/"+method;
  call.encode(soapVersion,method,object,headers.length,headers,params.length,params);
  var currentRequest = call.asyncInvoke(GetHighScoresResponse);
}
function GetHighScoresResponse(resp,call,status)
{
  alert(resp.body.firstChild.firstChild.firstChild.data);
}
```

Figure 12-10 shows how the XUL interface to these functions in Example 12-20 is designed. Here the score is replaced with "990," as this number is pulled from the code shown in Example 12-14.

Looking Forward

This chapter focuses on just one of many new trends outside of the original project mandate that emerged in the Mozilla developer community. Now that Mozilla 1.0 is released, its future direction will be shaped by the community itself, and Mozilla will become whatever the community would like it to be.

Remote applications are definitely one area of Mozilla development that will get more attention as Mozilla matures. Other areas that will probably also be noticed include development tools (some existing development tools are discussed in Appendix B), embedding, SVG support, and XSLT support.

Remember that Mozilla is open to new ideas and is always looking for contributions. If you can think of a way to improve Mozilla, or if you think of something that should be added, become a part of the community and help expand the possibilities of Mozilla and all Mozilla applications.

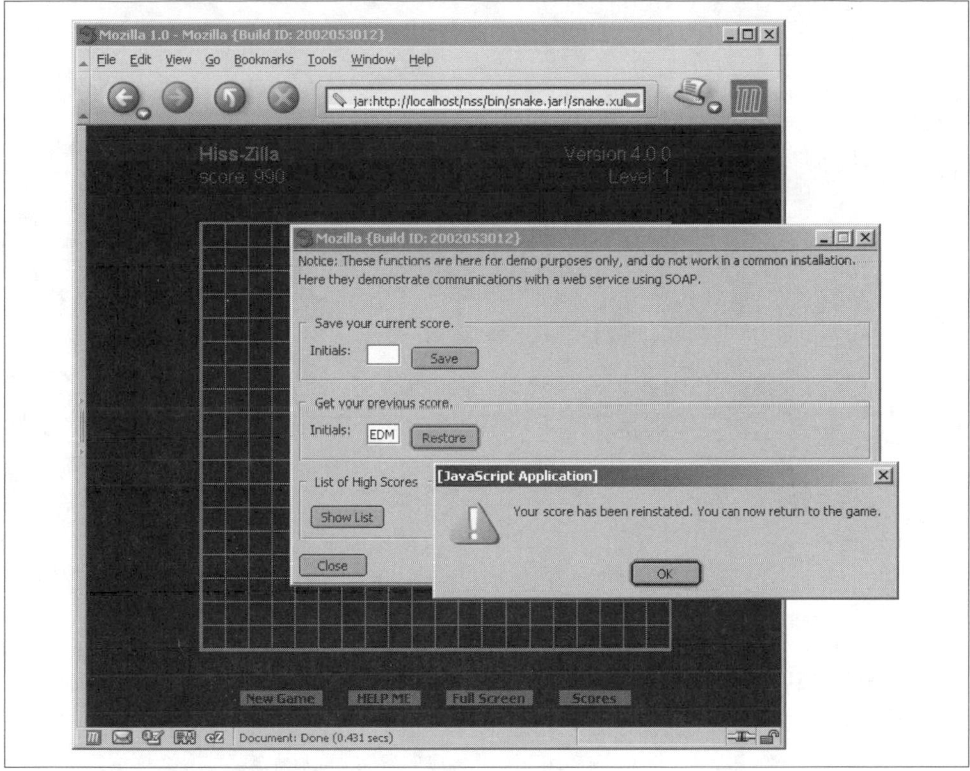

Figure 12-10. Result of using the GetScore function

APPENDIX A

Getting and Building the Mozilla Source

One of the best things about using Mozilla as an application development framework is that you don't need to get involved with the Mozilla source code to create a Mozilla application. A simple Mozilla binary that you download and install is the only development platform you need. You can create and use most procedures and samples described in this book with a precompiled version of the browser.

The best way to get a working version of Mozilla quickly is to download a precompiled binary for your platform. If you go to the mozilla.org homepage, you will find links to Mozilla's most recent stable milestone build for each platform and a link to the nightly development snapshot builds. These binaries come as compressed archives or with an installer, and you can use either to run Mozilla on your computer within a few minutes. These binaries don't include the source for Mozilla (unless you count the XUL, CSS, and JavaScript that made up the front end, which are always available), so read on if you want to obtain the code.

Under the relevant license terms, the Mozilla source code is freely available to anyone who has an Internet connection and a desire to explore. You may want to look at this code out of curiosity or dive into the code as you figure out how it works and can be improved. Whatever your reasons are for looking at the Mozilla source, it is not much more difficult to get the code and build it yourself than it is to download the precompiled binaries. To get started, you need to know a few things about how to get and use the source.

Getting the Source Code

You can get the Mozilla source code in a few different ways. Depending on what you are interested in doing, one method may work better for you than another. This appendix provides basic information about how to get the source, but you can also find information about this topic on the Mozilla site at *http://www.mozilla.org/source.tml*.

If you want to look at the source code and don't intend to recompile it, experiment with it, or update it at all, the best way to get at the source is to browse the Mozilla code base with Mozilla Cross Reference (LXR). As you can see in Figure A-1, LXR is a web-based source code browsing tool located at *http://lxr.mozilla.org*. LXR is also hooked up to other tools, such as Bonsai (*http://bonsai.mozilla.org*) and the various tinderboxen (*http://tinderbox.mozilla.org/showbuilds.cgi*). Together, these tools create a powerful code maintenance system that is used widely by Mozilla developers.

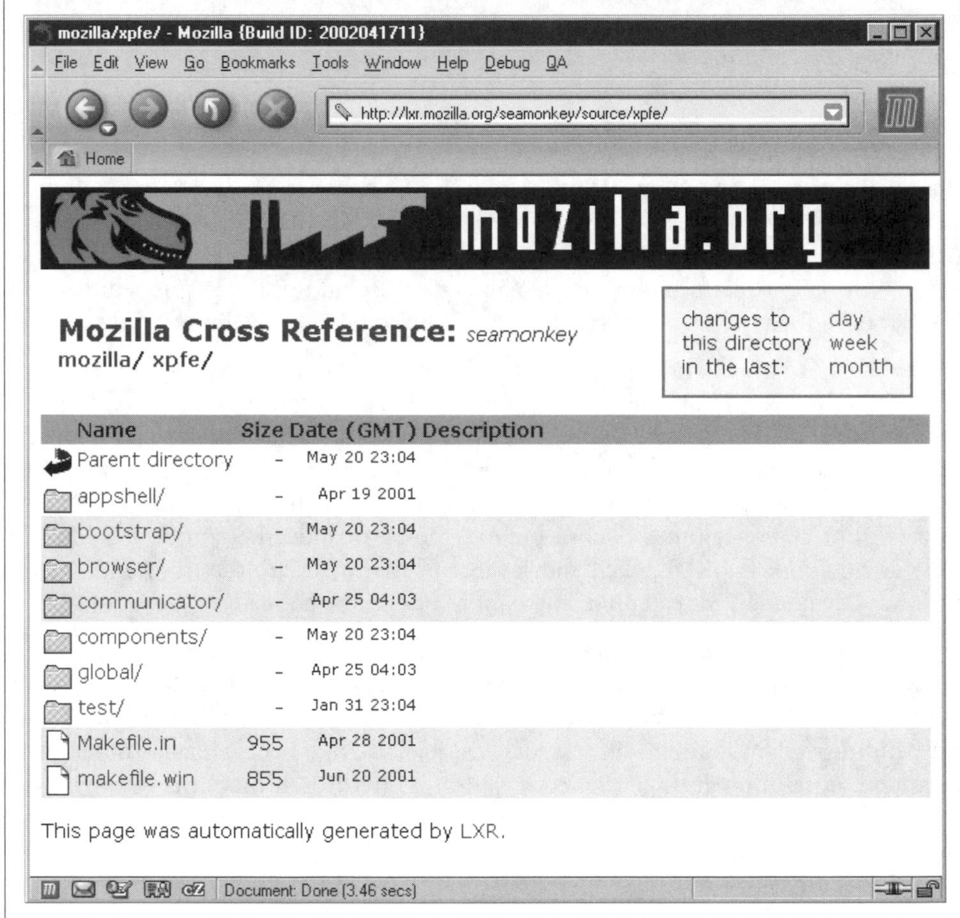

Figure A-1. Mozilla Cross Reference code browsing tool

Downloading the Source with FTP

If you would like to get your hands on the code directly, use either File Transfer Protocol (FTP) or Concurrent Versioning System (CVS) to grab the source from the Mozilla site. Many people prefer to start by grabbing an archive of the source code by FTP and then working with CVS as they modify the code.

If you're sure you won't check your work back into Mozilla and you just want to get the source, using FTP is the easiest way to do so. The main FTP server is at *ftp://ftp.mozilla.org/* (a list of FTP mirrors is available on the mozilla.org site). To download a particular version of Mozilla, go to either */pub/mozilla/nightly/latest/* or */pub/mozilla/releases/*, depending on which build you would like to have.

When you download the source from the releases directory, you get the code for the most recent Mozilla milestone. These releases are versions of Mozilla that have been tested and approved by developers at mozilla.org. Milestones come out about once a month and have some implied stability. The code in the "latest" directory is for the version of Mozilla currently under development. This code is not tested and stability is not guaranteed. In fact, the latest code may not even work if something that was checked in recently breaks Mozilla.

Downloading the Source with CVS

Grabbing the source with CVS requires additional steps to get things set up properly, but for many, it's worth the effort. If you would like to contribute your own changes back to the community, you must understand how CVS works. Pulling the source in this manner is a good way to start learning about Mozilla development.

For a quick understanding of CVS, you can obtain a copy of the *CVS Pocket Reference* (O'Reilly). To pick up a binary distribution of CVS if it isn't already installed, go to *http://www.cvshome.org/downloads.html*, where you'll also find links to documentation.

Using CVS requires logging into the Mozilla site by using a CVS client, checking out the source code, modifying the source code locally, and then checking the code back into the tree. Anyone is free to check out the code, but you need special permission to check in the changes you make to the source. This chapter discusses only how to check out the source with CVS.

You first need a CVS client. Free CVS clients are available for most operating systems, including WinCVS on Windows and MacCVS for the Mac. Linux has a command-line CVS client that should come standard on most Linux distributions. Here are instructions for using the Linux command-line client to check out the source code:

1. Set the *CVSROOT* variable:

```
$ setenv CVSROOT :pserver:anonymous@cvs-mirror.mozilla.org:/cvsroot
```

2. Log in as *anonymous@cvs-mirror.mozilla.org* using the password "anonymous":

```
$ cvs login
CVS password: anonymous
```

3. Check out the build Makefile:

```
$ cvs checkout mozilla/client.mk
U mozilla/client.mk
```

4. Run the Makefile script to get the files:

```
$ cd mozilla
$ make -f client.mk checkout
```

On Windows, the command-line interface used to obtain the Mozilla source is very similar. You just need to make a few small changes to the steps above for a Windows install. Here are the steps listed for comparison:

1. Set the *CVSROOT* variable:

```
> set CVSROOT :pserver:anonymous@cvs-mirror.mozilla.org:/cvsroot
```

2. Log in as *anonymous@cvs-mirror.mozilla.org* using the password "anonymous":

```
> cvs login
CVS password: anonymous
```

3. Check out the build Makefile:

```
> cvs checkout mozilla/client.mk
U mozilla/client.mk
```

4. Run the Makefile script to get the files:

```
> cd mozilla
> make -f client.mk checkout
```

In Step 1, set the *CVSROOT* environment variable using the `set` command. Use the GNU *make* utility (*make*) on Windows just as you would on Unix.

Building using nmake is no longer supported on the Mozilla development trunk, though there is a document describing this process for developers using older branches at *http://www.mozilla.org/build/win32-nmake.html*.

Before you pull the source code, check the tree status in the relevant Tinderbox. Grab the source only if the tree is green (success) or yellow (building). Do not pull the source on red, which indicates that the build is broken.

To pull the Mozilla source code on Macintosh, use a client like MacCVS, which automates much of the CVS process for you. Mac OSX users can use the standard command-line CVS client and pull the source using a method similar to checking out the source in a Unix environment. Also be sure to include the required resources—XML Perl modules, MacPerl, or the CodeWarrior development environment—which are all listed later in Table A-1.

The MacCVS client works with session files, which have all the information and settings you need to pull Mozilla. The settings are listed on the mozilla.org Mac build page, which even has a ready-made session file that you can download into the client. Once you set your tools up and configure your session file for MacCVS, you can pull the Mozilla source by choosing "Check Out Default Module" from the MacCVS Action menu. Like the Macintosh build process, pulling the source on Macintosh involves the interaction of a series of Perl scripts. The *PullMozilla.pl* script, located with the other Macintosh build scripts in *mozilla/build/mac/build_scripts*, can drive your MacCVS client—starting it up and pointing to the right source, setting the proper variables, and so on. For more information on the Macintosh build scripts, see *http://www.mozilla.org/build/mac-build-system.html*.

Working with Branching

Branches are distinct Mozilla source code trees that are "cut" to carry out a specific purpose or used for a milestone release. Developers cut branches when making large architectural changes that could make the main tree unstable. Branches in this context allow freer changing and testing off the main trunk. To work with branches, set the *MOZ_BRANCH* environment variable:

```
> setenv MOZ_BRANCH=MOZILLA_1_0_BRANCH
```

The value changes according to the repository with which you work. All other steps can remain the same in the process.

To find out more about using CVS to get Mozilla source and to learn about what else you can do with CVS, go to *http://www.mozilla.org/cvs.html*.

Building the Source Code

Now that you have the Mozilla source code, what do you do with it? Unlike the Mozilla binaries that are available for download, you can not start using Mozilla once you have all the source code on your computer. Before you can start using the source, you need to set up your working environment and then build Mozilla.

For the Mozilla source to compile on your computer properly, two main aspects of your build environment must be set up. These aspects are the necessary tools and the proper environment variables. You would expect such a large code base to require a large number of tools, but there aren't so many. Table A-1 lists the tools you need to build and run the source code. All information here is presented in more detail at *http://www.mozilla.org/build/*, including links for getting the tools.

Table A-1. Platform tools used to build the Mozilla source code

Linux	Windows	Macintosh
egcs 1.0.3 (or higher), gcc 2.95.2	Microsoft Visual C++ Version 6.0 or later (with service pack 3)	Code Warrior Pro 7 (including Plugin SDK)
GTK+ / Glib 1.2.0	Cygnus toolkit for Windows (the build page lists the specific components)	Menu Sharing Toolkit 1.4
GNU make 3.74	Netscape Wintools (modified versions of gmake, shmsdos, and uname)	ToolServer

Table A-1. Platform tools used to build the Mozilla source code (continued)

Linux	Windows	Macintosh
Perl 5.005 (or higher)	Perl5 for Win32	MacPerl
		cpan-mac distribution
		Perl AppleEvents module
		Perl Launch module
zip 2.3 (or higher)	Zip for Win32	Compress:Zlib module
		Archive::Zip module
LibIDL 0.6.3 (or higher)		(Required for static build)
		XML::RegExp
		XML::Parser
		XML::DOM
Autoconf 2.12 (optional)		

The Linux environment is usually set up by default with all the tools listed for that platform; it therefore requires less time to retrieve and set up programs. Linux distributions usually come with a native compiler that is compatible with the Mozilla build system. Most build time is used compiling the C++ source code—the language most files are written in. Therefore, the compiler is the central component of the build system. Linux uses egcs or gcc, Windows uses Microsoft Visual C++, and Macintosh uses Metroworks Code Warrior. The latest version of CVS for each platform accompanies all tools listed in Table A-1.

You can set various environment settings for each platform to configure and optimize your build environment. Most settings are optional and some are essential. One essential is the *CVSROOT* variable, which tells the CVS server where to look for the tree's home or root. The next section looks at the differences between the Unix, Windows, and Macintosh platforms.

Unix Environment

Unix is probably the easiest platform to configure. In fact, because it's a developer's platform, it is designed to work with little or no user interaction. In the source tree, script is provided to do all the work for you. To run it, you need only the following steps:

```
> cd mozilla
> ./configure
```

Running this command gathers all necessary system information and the list of Makefiles needed to compile the source. This command needs to be run only when a Makefile is added or removed from the tree. After this, it is sufficient to compile Mozilla by launching gmake with no arguments.

Alternatively, you can use the Unix Build Configurator, an online tool (*http://webtools.mozilla.org/build/config.cgi*) that lets you change certain settings if you run into any obstacles when building. It allows setting external package configuration, a choice of Mozilla components, and debugging and optimization options. Once this setting is made, let Mozilla take over via the client.mk script:

```
> gmake -f client.mk
```

One useful post-build setting is the ability to run Mozilla from any directory (rather than just *dist/bin*). To test this option, use MOZILLA_FIVE_HOME to point to the full path, to the *dist/bin*, or wherever your executable resides.

Windows Environment

The setup is different on Windows and requires more interaction on the user's part, mostly in setting up environment variables. Table A-2 lists these variables and expected values. Note that some values are optional.

Table A-2. Windows environment variables used to build Mozilla

Variable	Value	Description
MOZ_BITS	32	Specifies whether you use a 16-bit or 32-bit operating system.
MOZ_DEBUG	1 (optional)	Set only if you want a build with debug information. Remove this variable to enable it by default.
MOZ_SRC	<path to top of source tree>	The directory into which you uncompress or check out the Mozilla source. Ensure that the path does not end with a trailing slash (\).
MOZ_TOOLS	<usually the Cygwin root directory>	The directory where gmake is installed, usually placed there by the wintools.zip package (refer to Table A-1).
WINOS	%OS_TARGET% (see the OS_TARGET variable)	An abbreviation for the operating system that is also used internally by the OS. Windows 2000 takes a value of WINNT. It matches the top-level directory on the filesystem that contains all OS files.
OS_TARGET	WINNT (or WIN95)	A Mozilla representation of the OS_TARGET variable
_MSC_VER	1200 (or 1100 for VC++ 5)	The version of the Microsoft Visual C++ runtime environment running on your machine. The value of 1200 is Version 6, the most reliable version.
DISABLE_TESTS	1 (Optional)	Set only if you do not want to build test directories and binaries. Remove this variable to leave it enabled by default.
MOZ_DISABLE_JAR_PACKAGING	1 (Optional)	Set only if you want to turn off compression into the chrome structure's JAR files. Remove this variable to leave it enabled by default.
MOZ_CONFIG	<path to config file>	This variable is required only for gmake builds.
PATH	%PATH%;%MOZ_TOOLS%\bin;c:\cygwin	The PATH variable is an existing variable that needs the Cygwin root and binary directories appended. The operating system looks at this variable when looking for program executables and DLLs.

You can set these variables either by using the set command for per session variables or the System → Advanced → Environment Variable panel in Control Panel to set them more permanently.

Once your environment is set and the tools are in place, you can begin the build. Go to the *mozilla* directory in the source code and from there, run the make script (*client.mk*) with the necessary arguments:

```
>make -f client.mk build_all
```

Once your environment is set and the tools are in place, building can begin. Go to the *mozilla* directory in the source code and from there, run the make script (*client.mak*) with the necessary arguments:

```
> nmake -f client.mak build_all
```

Table A-3 lists these arguments and what they do. Leaving out this compile flag starts an incremental build or a fresh build if there is no previous build available.

When building incrementally, try to use the provided make script instead of the cvs checkout and `build_all` commands. The latter command can lead to inconsistencies in file versions and may re-download files that you do not even need to your tree.

Table A-3. Make flags

Flag	Function
`pull_all`	Gets only the source code.
`build_all`	Builds only the existing source code.
`pull_and_build_all`	Retrieves the source code and then builds it.
`pull_and_build_ all_dep`	Does a dependent build after retrieving the source code. The source tree is not accessed in a dependent build.
`pull_ clientmak`	Pulls only the latest version of the build file *client.mak*.
`clobber_all`	Deletes all files produced from a previous build to enable a completely fresh build.
`Pull_xpconnect`	Retrieves the XPConnect module. You can retrieve other modules this way, including *nspr* and *psm*.

To rebuild without pulling the tree, use:

```
> make -f client.mk build_all_depend
```

To get or update the source code and not build, use:

```
> make -f client.mk checkout
```

Macintosh Environment

In terms of environment setup, necessary resources, and actual compile time, the Mac OS is the least straightforward of the three major platforms Mozilla builds on. There are several different kinds of Mac builds at mozilla.org, but this section focuses on just two: the Classic Mac OS 9's standard build, which has been the default for a long time, and Mac OS X's Code Fragment Manager (CFM).

Mac OS X builds are becoming more popular as the platform is adopted more widely. Better performance and native Unix build system tools have boosted developer support for Mozilla on Mac OS X. However, the Macintosh is by far the most resource hungry of all platforms Mozilla builds on. The minimum specification includes 1 GB of disk space and 128 MB of memory, but you will probably need even more in reality.

To compile the source, check out the module *mozilla/build/mac/build_scripts*. Once the download is complete, go to the folder and run *BuildMozilla.pl* for an optimized build or *BuildMozillaDebug.pl* for a debug build. Running the CodeWarrior environment during or before running build scripts is useful. When you run the build script, you will be asked for the location of CodeWarrior, if it is not already running. You can change some build options through a local preferences file, which can be found in the system preferences folder for system variables or at the root of the Mozilla tree for tree-specific variables. You can find more information on fine-tuning the build at *http://www.mozilla.org/build/mac-build-system.html*.

When the compile is complete, you need to take an extra step to start it. Mozilla needs certain things set properly so it can gather the information it needs at runtime. Traditional Mac OS systems have no concept of environment variables per se, but one alternative is to use a startup file called *NSPR Logging* that comes with Mozilla in the same directory as the application. Its lines are in the following format:

```
ENV:NSPR_LOG_MODULES=nsComponentManager:5
ENV:NSPR_LOG_FILE=xpcom.log
```

Dragging this file onto Mozilla starts the application with those settings. You can edit this file by adding or changing the `ENV` lines or make another file. This modification method is useful for single session settings. For more permanent settings, you can create a file called *ENVIRONMENT* and put it in the same folder as Mozilla. Mozilla picks up the environment variables in the *ENVIRONMENT* file when it runs. The file contents look something like:

```
NSPR_LOG_MODULES=nsComponentManager:5
NSPR_LOG_FILE=xpcom.log
```

The Mac OS X CFM version uses the same build system as OS 9. If you build, you need to adjust the following setting in order to build with Carbon, which is a set of APIs that transition developers from OS9 and earlier releases to the new OS X system architecture:

In your *Prefs* folder, add the following line to the *Mozilla[debug/opt] build prefs* file:

```
options carbon 1
```

For more information on pulling the Mozilla source on OS X, the OS X build process, and other OSX Mozilla resources, see *http://www.mozilla.org/ports/fizzilla/*.

APPENDIX B

Development Tools

This book describes how to create applications using Mozilla. Generally, all parts that go into an application (including XUL, CSS, XBL, and DTD files) need to be built by hand since no complete ready-made development tools or development applications are available that would make these manual processes easier.

Creating all these files by hand is a great way to familiarize yourself with the way Mozilla works, and becoming more familiar with the inner workings of a Mozilla application certainly helps you see how the various parts fit together. Once you are comfortable creating these files by hand, using the platform becomes much easier and Mozilla fulfills its promise as a rich application development framework.

Development tools are important, though, and platforms like Mozilla can't obtain the sort of developer base they deserve until tools that make application creation easier are available. Although some people want to learn everything there is to know about creating applications with Mozilla, many simply want to create something without a lot of fuss.

Mozilla does not yet have a full set of development tools, but currently several development projects help with part of the application creation process. These tools don't make up a full-featured development environment, but they are useful. They also point the way to an area in Mozilla development that has a bright future and is worth watching.

This appendix describes some of the new tools—including XULKit, Patch Maker, the DOM Inspector, the JavaScript Debugger, and MozillaTranslator—that are already becoming a part of the regular repertoire of Mozilla developers. By learning about how to use these tools for your own project, you can radically simplify the application development process, especially when you combine these tools.

XULKit

Much of the manual editing described in Chapters 6, 7, and 8 can be automated with special scripts and templates being developed in the Mozilla source tree's *tools/*

wizards section (these files are referred to collectively as the XULKit and can be found at *http://www.hacksrus.com/~ginda/xulkit/doc/*).

These tools help you develop your Mozilla application by generating as much of the basic content, structure, and packaging of an application as possible, leaving you free to work only on the aspects of your application that you care about. We mention XULKit first because it can make setting up new Mozilla applications a snap.

XULKit is essentially a set of two scripts: *new-from-template.pl*, which creates a new application framework, and *makexpi.pl*, which packages your application once you finish developing it.

new-from-template.pl Script

Though it's not named very elegantly, the *new-from-template.pl* Perl script takes information you provide in the form of a simple text file and uses it to create various parts of a Mozilla application. These parts include the XUL content, which has a basic menubar you can add to; an overlay that puts an item for your application into the Tools menu in the Mozilla browser; CSS for your XUL; and an installation script for the application package. You can base your application off of a couple of different templates, including a sophisticated one that lets you generate XPCOM interfaces for components you wish to use in your application, described below.

Using these scripts, you can add content and logic to your application, restyle it, or build your application however you would like. You can also register the resulting directory with the chrome registry to see it working in your local copy of Mozilla, and when you finish developing it, the application directory is already structured in exactly the way it must be to be checked into the Mozilla source tree's extensions directory (if you want to check it into this common location for applications that become a part of Mozilla). When you want to distribute your application as described in Chapter 6, you can use the other script in the XULKit, *makexpi.pl*, to package your application files into a cross-platform archive that can be installed from a regular web page.

To use the *new-from-template.pl* script, point it at a template that you filled out with your own information. It then generates the basic application code in the appropriate subdirectory structure:

```
new-from-template.pl       -t FILE [-o DIRECTORY] [-f[d]] [-h] [-?]
```

When you run the script, the XULKit creates a new top-level application directory. In this directory, the script creates the three main package directories, and it places some basic content in each one: a CSS file called *mozreg.css* in the *skins* subdirectory, a few XUL files in the *content* directory (including the overlay that defines a new menu item for the main browser that opens this new application), and localizable data in the *mozref.dtd* file in the *locale* subdirectory.

In addition to these files, the XULKit script creates *contents.rdf* files that describe each package, some Makefiles that instruct the Mozilla build process how to integrate this application into the build (which is a later step and not necessary to run the application), and an *install.js* file that executes the installation of this application when it appears in a XPI. (See Chapter 6 for more information about XPI, Mozilla's cross-platform installation file format.)

If you look at Example B-1—*xul-app.tpl*, which comes with the distribution of *new-from-template.pl*—you can see how easy it is to fill out the basic information and create your own template.

Example B-1. Sample application template

```
# load default template for a XUL app
include "${top_wizard_dir}templates/xul-app.tpl"
# short app name (can not contain spaces.)
# until http://bugzilla.mozilla.org/show_bug.cgi?id=75670 is fixed, this needs
# to be all lowercase.
app_name_short=xulsample
# long app name (spaces are OK.)
app_name_long=Sample XUL Application (generated from sample.xul-app.tpl)
# name as it should appear in the menu
app_name_menu=Sample XUL App
# version to tell the .xpi installer
app_version=1.0
# author, used in various chrome and app registration calls
app_author=mozilla.org
# size of the package when installed, in kilobytes.
# this number is used by the install.js script to check for enough disk space
# before the .xpi is installed.  You can just guess for now, or put 1, and fix it
# in install.js before you make your .xpi file.
install_size_kilobytes=1
```

You can adapt the *xul-app.tpl* for your own purposes or use the *sample.xul-app.tpl* that is already filled out. Table B-1 details different options for *new-from-template.pl*.

Table B-1. Options for the new-from-template.pl script

Option	Description
`-d`	Recursively deletes the output directory before starting; requires the `-f` option.
`-f`	Forces file overwriting in the output directory.
`-h`	Displays a description of the specified template with `-o`. The template will not be processed. The template description is taken from the value of the *template_description* variable in the template file. *template_description*s provided by the main template file's template file(s) are not displayed.
`-o DIRECTORY`	Generates the template into the directory specified by `DIRECTORY`. If this directory already exists, *new-from-template.pl* will fail. This failure prevents you from accidentally overwriting an existing application. Use the `-f` option to continue anyway. Use `-fd` to force `DIRECTORY` to be deleted before the template is processed.
`-t TEMPLATE`	Processes the template specified by `TEMPLATE`. This file is usually in the *my/ sub-directory*, ending in *.tpl*.
`-?`	Shows usage information and exits.

XULKit templates

Two different application templates come with *new-from-template.tpl*, each with its own empty and sample versions. Example B-1 shows *sample.xul-app.tpl* in its entirety. The other template, *xpcom-component.tpl*, uses information you supply to create the framework for an XPCOM component. As with *xul-app.tpl*, the template comes with a sample that's already filled out.

This script creates an IDL file, a header file, and a stubbed-out CPP file in an application subdirectory structure you can use to begin coding your XPCOM component. In the *xpcom-component.tpl*, many variables do not need to be changed, but required fields are set aside in the template:

```
# variables the user's .tpl file MUST declare
required_variables = ${component_name}, ${implementation_guid}, \
                     ${interface_name}, ${interface_guid}
```

Using this script, you can fill out a subset of the template with the information XPCOM requires, and XPCOM will generate the basic files you need, as Example B-2 shows.

Example B-2. Sample XPCOM component template

```
# include default values
include "${top_wizard_dir}templates/xpcom-component.tpl"
component_name      = SampleComponent
implementation_guid = c6793b0c-1dd1-11b2-a246-92bf95c9d097
interface_name      = tstISampleComponent
interface_guid      = d03ea960-1dd1-11b2-9682-81ecad6a042a
```

makexpi.pl Script

In addition to the template-generating script described above, a second script takes your working application and creates an installable package, or XPI, out of it. This way, you can distribute it to others in the same way the various components of the Mozilla browser are distributed and installed when you use the Mozilla installer.

This script, *makexpi.pl*, takes an application directory as input and generates an XPI archive. It also manifests for various parts of your application, the installation script that goes inside this archive, and even the installation web page itself. While *new-from-template.pl* is designed to help you start your application, *makexpi.pl* takes your locally developed application and makes it into a package that can be distributed to other users and installed via the Web.

To use *makexpi.pl*, point it at a configuration file that you have edited to point at your application directory:

```
makexpi.pl      [-c <config-file>] [-d] [-r <revision>] [-?]
```

For example, to create a XPI out of your *MyApp* application directory, in which you created a file called *MyApp.conf* that defines the variables *makexpi.pl* needs, execute the script as follows:

```
perl makexpi.pl -c ~/appdev/MyApp/makexpi.conf -r 0.9.9
```

A *makexpi.conf* file defines the variables *makexpi.pl* needs to know about. Example B-3 shows an example of this file.

Example B-3. makexpi.conf file

```
# directory where xpi should be created
workdir     = /home/rginda/src/xulkit/sample-app/
# directory where jar.mn is
mndir       = ${workdir}/sampleapp/resources/
# location of templatized install.js file
installfile = ${xulkit_dir}/templates/xpi/install.js
# directory where mozilla's make-jars.pl and friends are
mozcfgdir   = ${xulkit_dir}/bin/
# name of resulting xpi file
xpifile = ${app_name_short}-${revision}.xpi
```

Table B-2 lists the options that are recognized by *makexpi.pl*.

Table B-2. Options for the makexpi.pl script

Options	Description
`-c FILE`	Specifies the configuration file to use.
`-d`	Doesn't remake the JAR, but packages the existing contents of the *chrome/* directory as an XPI.
`-r REVISION`	Specifies the value of the *${revision}* variable. This specification overrides any value specified in the configuration file and defaults to "0.01". Typically, this number is used in the *install.js* script and as part of the XPI filename.
`-?`	Shows usage information and exits.

When you run the script against the configuration file, you end up with two separate pieces—the XPI in which your application and its installation script are stored and a web page that you can post on a server to guide the XPI's installation. As described in Chapter 6, the web page interacts with the XPI's *install.js* to install and register your application in Mozilla. If you start your application with the *new-from-template.pl* script, then a template-processed version of *install.js* that works with your application is included as *templates/xpi/install.js* as part of the XULKit package.

Using XULKit

Given these two scripts and the templates that go with them, the XULKit encourages and makes the following application development workflow possible:

1. Fill out a *new-from-template.pl* template with your application information.
2. Run the *new-from-template.pl* script to generate the application directory.

3. Register your application in flat mode: as a directory in your local copy of Mozilla.
4. Develop your application: the XUL content, the CSS, the application code in JS, etc.
5. Test the application code.
6. Run *makexpi.pl* against your working application to create an installable package.
7. Put the XPI and the web page up on a server to create an install for your application.

That's it!

Patch Maker 2.0

Patch Maker is a free software program written by Gervase Markham that lets you change and improve Mozilla's user interface by using only a nightly build.

When you don't build the Mozilla source tree yourself, finding and getting to the files that need to be edited in Mozilla can be difficult. However, you can use the various Patch Maker commands in Build Mode to extract files from the right JARs, add them to your Patch Maker project, edit them, and create the patches, all in an integrated and easily traceable way. These patches can then be submitted back to mozilla.org so that developers working in the source tree can apply and test them. See the "Build Mode" section later in this appendix for more information about using Patch Maker in this way.

This process is possible because Mozilla's user interface is written in XUL, JavaScript, and CSS, and interpreted at runtime. Because understanding CVS or compiling code isn't necessary, Patch Maker greatly lowers the barrier to entry for contributing code to Mozilla. Significant patches, such as one used for draggable toolbars, are made using this tool.

Patch Maker runs under Linux and Windows, and is experimental on Mac OS X. The latest version of Patch Maker is at *http://www.gerv.net/software/patch-maker/*. This application can be used in one of two modes. CVS mode is used by developers who develop and maintain code in a CVS tree and make their changes in the tree. Build mode makes it possible to produce patches that fix some bugs in Mozilla without downloading and compiling the source.

CVS Mode

In CVS mode, Patch Maker manages and tracks multiple patches to a bit of software. It uses unique tags (patch references such as bug numbers) to separate patches, knows what files are in each patch, and can perform operations on them. In CVS mode, Patch Maker can greatly speed up the process of creating, diffing, uploading, refreshing, and checking in a patch. CVS mode's basic commands for Patch Maker give you an idea of how developers working in the Mozilla source tree can use it to work more efficiently with patches and diffs. The basic CVS mode commands are described in Table B-3.

Table B-3. Patch Maker's CVS mode commands

Command	Description
`pmlist`	Shows the file list.
`pmadd` <*filename*>	Adds *filename* to the file list.
`pmremove` <*filename*>	Removes *filename* from the file list.
`pmdiff`	Does a cvs `diff -u` of all files in the file list. Extra arguments, such as `-w`, are passed through to diff. This command won't clobber your old diff if the new one has a size of zero.
`pmview`	Brings up your diff in an editor window.
`pmupdate`	Updates CVS on all files in the file list. Extra arguments to this command are passed through to the CVS update.
`pmpatch`	Patches your diff into your CVS tree. Takes a `-R` to back the patch out again.
`pmedit` <pattern>	Brings up files matching the pattern in your editor. The pattern is a glob, not a regexp. If there are no arguments supplied, then all files are opened.
`pmwhich`	Prints the current patch reference.
`pmswitch` <patchref>	Changes Patch Maker to work with a new patch reference. It automatically creates a `pmupdate()` and a `pmpatch()` (which won't have any effect if the patch is already applied.)
`pmgrep` <pattern>	Greps for *pattern* in all of the current patch's files. Good if you can't remember where you put some code.
`pmcopy`	Copies all files in the file list to their positions in your installed Mozilla tree. Takes a `-f` argument to force copying of all the files.
`pmsetpath`	Points Patch Maker to your current Mozilla-built installation's *chrome* directory. Use */usr/src/mozilla/dist/bin/chrome/* if you build yourself.
`pmunjar`	Unjars the chrome in your setpath installation.
`pmexecute`	Runs the executable in the setpath installation. Extra arguments to this command, such as &, are passed through to the executable.
`pmcheckin`	Runs `pmwhich`, `pmupdate`, `pmdiff`, and `pmview` to show what you are about to change, and then asks you if you really want to check in.
`pmcvsadd`	Does a CVS add of all files. Previously added files fail with a harmless message. You need to use this command for new files so the CVS diff will work properly.

See the CVS Mode instructions at the Patch Maker web site for instructions on how to use Patch Maker with your source tree.

Build Mode

The fact that Mozilla's user interface is interpreted at runtime rather than compile time makes it possible to change the interface and see your changes in the browser.

In Build mode, Patch Maker can help you make these changes and apply, package, and send them to the developers who own the interface modules you edit. The Patch Maker's Build mode is a boon for Mozilla developers who do not build the CVS tree, but who want to take part in developing the interface, in the bug-fixing process, and in other aspects of Mozilla development.

In Mozilla-specific mode, which is triggered when you sit in a Mozilla build install point's chrome directory, you can make patches to Mozilla chrome without using a CVS tree. Patch Maker can cope with multiple patches and has a notion of the "current patch"—the one you are working on at the moment. Patches are identified by a patch reference, or patchref, which is any combination of characters that make a legal filename on your platform. Bug numbers make very good patchrefs. You can add and remove files from Patch Maker's internal list of files that comprise the current patch.

Using Patch Maker in Build mode

Here are the steps to use Patch Maker in Build mode (flip the slashes in these paths if you are on Windows):

1. Set up Patch Maker (see the installation instructions at *http://www.gerv.net/software/patch-maker/build-mode.html*).
2. Change to the chrome directory of a Mozilla nightly build.
3. Execute `pmuj` to unjar your chrome.
4. Run Mozilla (**`../mozilla`**) to see if it still works. Turn off the XUL cache in the Debug → Networking preferences and quit Mozilla.
5. Execute **`pms test`**. Patch Maker will tell you that you are working on patch "test."
6. Confirm this with **`pmw`**.
7. Execute **`pml`**. Note that no files are currently in your patch.
8. Execute **`pma content/navigator/navigator.xul`** to add *navigator.xul* to your patch.
9. Execute `pml` again and see if it was added. Experiment with `pma` and `pmr` if you like.
10. Execute `pme`. Notice that *navigator.xul* appears in your editor. Try `pme foo` to make sure you have no files that match "foo."
11. Change *navigator.xul*—e.g., search for "&mainWindow.title;" and replace that string with "MyBrowser." Save this file.
12. Run Mozilla (**`../mozilla`**).
13. You should have a Mozilla titled "MyBrowser."
14. Edit the file again to make it "YourBrowser." Save the file.
15. Press Ctrl-N in your Mozilla window. The new window should be titled "YourBrowser."

16. Execute `pmd` and `pmv`. You should now have an editor window with a unified diff showing the changes you made.
17. You could attach your patch to a Bugzilla bug by fishing the CVS version (*test.diff*) out of your Patch Maker data directory.

The DOM Inspector

The DOM Inspector tool, which is now installed by default in the Mozilla browser and accessible from Tools → Web Development, displays the document object mode of any document or part of the interface and allows you to update that DOM dynamically by changing attribute values, rearranging the structured content, or deleting nodes.

The DOM Inspector reads the DOM of the requested window or document into memory, where you can manipulate it. However, the DOM Inspector does not persist your changes back out to the file from which that DOM was originally loaded.

If you use JavaScript in the interface or to manipulate web pages, then you will recognize what a powerful tool it can be—particularly given how hard it can be to see the interface's object model clearly and figure out which nodes in the DOM correspond to which parts of the displayed interface. The DOM Inspector also allows you to inspect local files and URLs.

To open a file for inspection in the DOM Inspector, choose either File → Inspect a Window or Inspect a URL... and enter the URL of the web document you want to inspect in the dialog. When the DOM Inspector loads a document, it displays the DOM (as shown in Figure B-1 of that document) as a tree structure on the lefthand side and the individual nodes with their attributes and other information on the righthand side.

As you click on the nodes in the tree in the left panel, the DOM Inspector highlights the nodes that are part of the visible interface by pointing them out with a blinking red border. You can peck through the tree in the DOM Inspector and find all parts of the interface.

The DOM Inspector also displays any anonymous content that is part of the window. See Chapter 7 for information about anonymous content and the way it relates to the DOM. The anonymous content nodes that are bound to the window you specify become part of the DOM that the Inspector reads and can be analyzed and manipulated like any other node.

The pull-down widgets to the left of the pane headers let you select which portions of the DOM are displayed in the panels. By default, the DOM nodes are displayed, as shown in Figure B-1, but you can also display the associated stylesheets, the JavaScript objects, the XBL bindings, the document's box model, and other information.

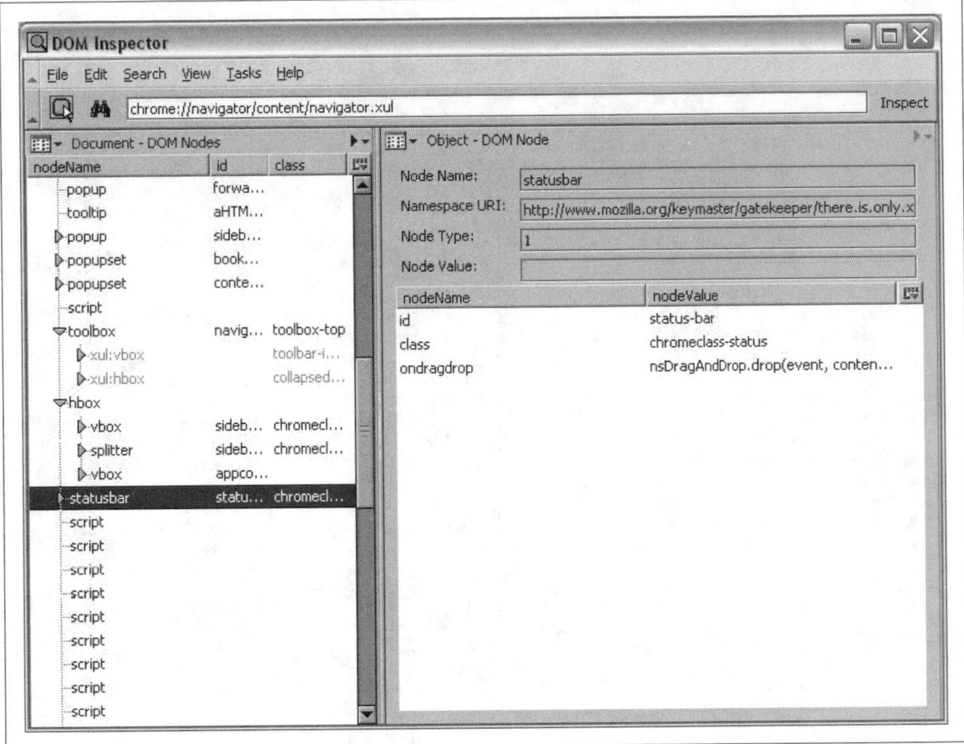

Figure B-1. The DOM inspector interface

The Component Viewer

The Component Viewer is a Mozilla application that displays all components and interfaces available to the XPCOM developer on the Mozilla platform. It is not installed by default in the Mozilla browser, like the DOM Inspector, but you can get binary installations that have it or you can build it from *mozilla/extensios/cview* if you use CVS.

Discovering components and interfaces is actually one of the trickier aspects of developing applications with Mozilla, so this tool can help you when you are at the initial stages of your application development and want to see which XPCOM components and interfaces are available. As shown in Figure B-2, the Component Viewer interface, like the DOM Inspector, has two main panels. The left side shows all components in Mozilla and the right side shows all interfaces.

In XPCOM, a single component can implement more than one interface. Thus, for example, the editor shell component (*@mozilla.org/editor/editorshell;1*) implements *nsIURIContentListener*, *nsIEditorShell*, *nsIEditorSpellCheck*, and others. If you open the interfaces, you will see the various methods those interfaces define. You can also right-click in the component viewer and access a context menu that lets you look up the selected item in LXR, which is the web-based source viewer for Mozilla.

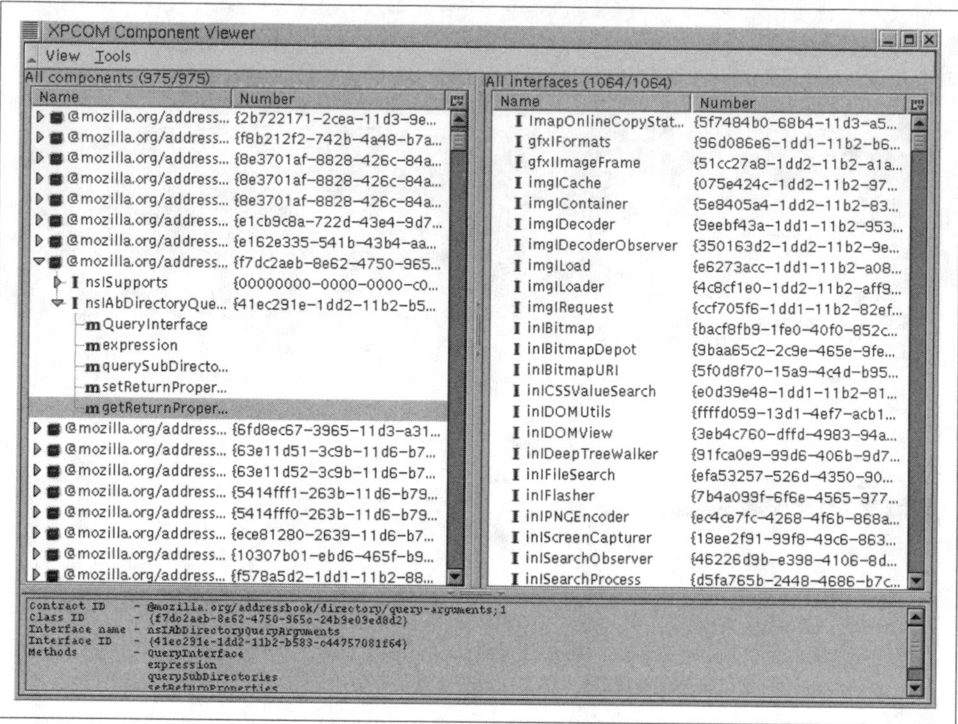

Figure B-2. An interface displayed in the Component Viewer

Venkman: The JavaScript Debugger

Venkman is both a graphical and a console debugger. It is one of the most sophisticated examples of a Mozilla application and an indispensable tool for the many developing applications and web pages that rely on JavaScript. Like the DOM Inspector, you can access the JavaScript Debugger from the Tools → Web Development menu (if it was selected during the Mozilla install process). Figure B-3 shows Venkman in action.

Features such as breakpoint management, call stack inspection, and variable/object inspection are available from both the graphic interface and the console commands. The interactive console allows execution of arbitrary JavaScript code in the context of the target application and in the debugger's own context. Profiling measures the execution time of JavaScript functions during debugging, and pretty printing can re-indent and line wrap a poorly formatted function.

Keyboard shortcuts for the `step` commands are the same as in other common visual debugging environments, and console users should be familiar with Venkman's `break`, `step`, `next`, `finish`, `frame`, and `where` commands.

Venkman consists of eight main interface elements, referred to as "views." These views display information such as local variables, source code, and the interactive

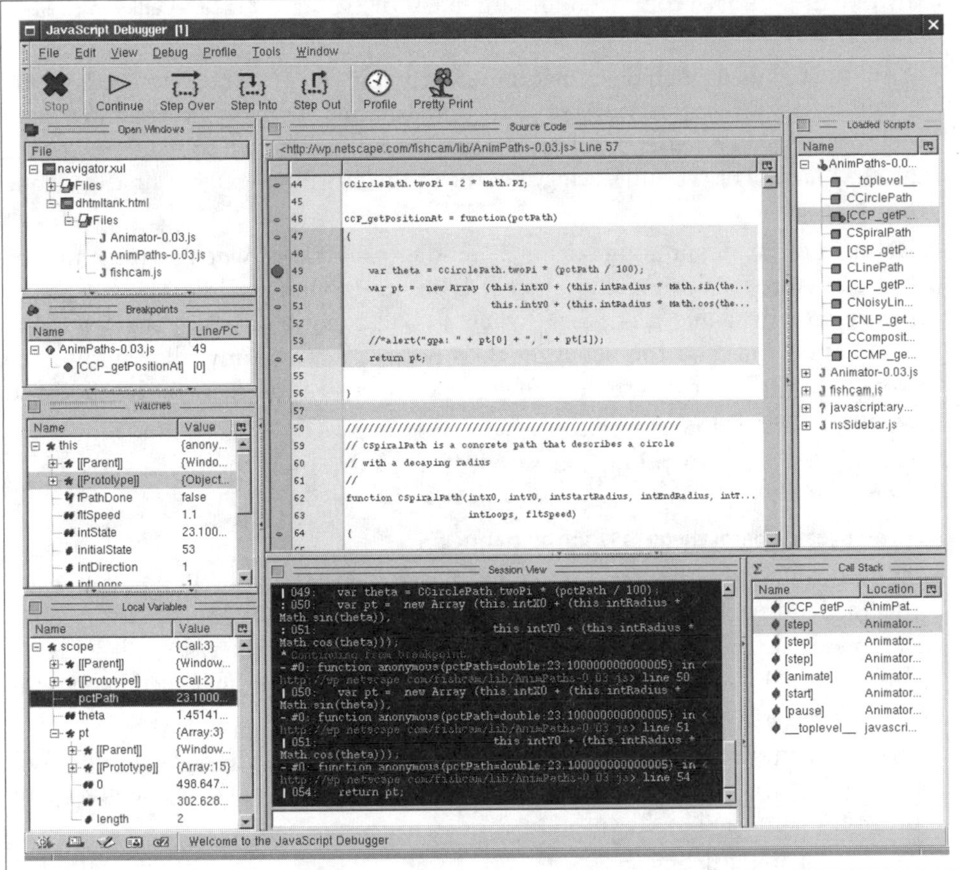

Figure B-3. The JavaScript Debugger

console. They can be detached from the main window to save space on your desktop, or they can be hidden. The Venkman project page at *http://www.mozilla.org/projects/venkman/* describes these views and their modes of operation.

Users can use a JavaScript API to add to the set of commands and views provided with Venkman. These add-ons can be shared among a project team or provided to the general public. The details of that API are not yet documented, but examples are found in Venkman itself. If you install Venkman, *chrome://venkman/content/venkman-commands.js* and *chrome://venkman/content/venkman-views.js* will contain Venkman's default commands and views.

The following sample session introduces you to the basic commands and use of the JavaScript Debugger. This sample session is based on the version of Venkman available at the time the book was written. To find out how to use the latest version of Venkman, read the Venkman walkthrough at *http://www.mozilla.org/projects/venkman/venkman-walkthrough.html*.

1. Invoke the -venkman command-line argument by typing **mozilla -venkman** to start Mozilla.

   You must start the debugger before the scripts it edits can be debugged. If you want to debug the file *navigator.xul*, for example, then Venkman must load before the main browser window. This limitation will either be fixed or worked around later. For the time being, you need to start the debugger first to debug browser chrome.

   Debugging JavaScript components is another example of when scripts must be loaded before the debugger is initialized. Because component registration occurs before command-line processing, when a component changes, it is reloaded at registration time and the debugger does not see it. Currently, the only way to work around it is to start the browser twice: once to re-register the modified component and once to debug it.

2. Launch a browser window and select "Navigator" from the debugger's Tasks menu.

3. Type **break ContextMenu 357** in the debugger.

   The console command break is set and lists breakpoints. The first parameter is the filename that contains the JavaScript you want to break at. The second parameter is the line number. You don't need to specify the entire filename. In this example, we are setting a breakpoint in the function called when the browser wants to create a context menu for web content.

   Or, you could select *nsContextMenu.js* from the Scripts View, locate line 357, and click in the left margin. Setting breakpoints in this way is equivalent to using the break command in the console.

4. Type **break** in the debugger.

   If you don't provide arguments to the break command, all breakpoints are listed.

5. Create a context menu in the Navigator window.

   A right-click in the content area creates a context menu. You should have hit the breakpoint you just set. The debugger should have displayed "Stopped for breakpoint," along with the filename, line number, and snippet source code where it stopped from.

6. Type **step** in the debugger.

   This command executes the line of JavaScript we're stopped on and stops again before the next line is executed. The step command is also available via the "Step Into" button on the toolbar and is bound to the F11 key.

   In addition to Step In, which executes a single line of JavaScript and stops, Step Over steps over a impending function call and returns control to the debugger when the call returns. Step Out executes until the current function call exits. At this point, you should be at line 359, `this.onTextInput = this.isTargetATextBox(elem);`.

7. Type **`props this`** in the debugger.

   The `props` command lists an object's properties. The letters and dashes before the values are the flags for that value. The flags are enumerated in Figure B-3, previously shown.

8. Step one more time.
9. You should be in the `isTargetATextBox` function call now.
10. Type **`frame`** in the debugger.

    When used without arguments, the `frame` command shows you the source code for the current frame (with a few lines of context).

11. Type **`scope`** in the debugger.

    The `scope` command lists the current frame's local variables. In this case, there are two locals: node and attrib. The node property is an argument to the function, while attrib is a local variable. The scope is also visible in the Stack View. Open the `[isTargetATextBox]` frame and the scope node below it.

12. Type **`where`** in the debugger.

    The `where` command lists the current call stack. The `frame` command can be used to change the current frame to any frame listed here. For example, to view variables in the code that called `isTargetATextBox`, type **`frame 1`**, and **`scope`**. To return to the top frame, type **`frame 0`**.

13. Type **`eval window._content`**.

    The `eval` command evaluates arbitrary JavaScript in the current frame. Running the `eval` command on `window._content` itself isn't very useful, so you'll have to think of something more creative.

14. Type **`break`**.

    The `break` command, when used without arguments, lists the current breakpoints by index.

15. Type **`clear 0`**.

    The `clear` command clears breakpoints. In this example, we clear by breakpoint number, which we got from the `break` command in the previous step.

16. Type **`cont`**.

    The `cont` command continues execution. The context menu should pop up as it always does.

MozillaTranslator

Chapter 11 provides information about how to make a Mozilla application usable in many different languages. Localizing an application can be simple if your application is small. For large applications, though, localizing can be a long and complicated process. Fortunately, interested and enthusiastic developers created a tool that makes this process easier.

MozillaTranslator is a program written in Java that reads in a package, provides an interface for changing the strings, and when finished, repackages the files for distribution. It is sophisticated enough to read JAR archives and output cross-platform installers (XPI). This type of solution is ideal for nontechnical people who translate the interface strings.

MozillaTranslator is more than just a program for inputting translated strings. The web site (*http://www.MozillaTranslator.org/*) has resources for setting up projects, uploading language packs, and finding the latest news on localization issues among other features.

To get to the point at which you can input your translated strings, you need to take some introductory steps. After downloading and installing MozillaTranslator, follow these steps:

1. Select File → Manage Products.
2. Press Add in the dialog to add a package.
3. In the window that comes up, give the project a label (for your own use) and point to the *chrome\en-US.jar* file within your Mozilla build (replace the path with your own Mozilla application locale path).
4. Exit the dialog.
5. Select File → Update Product.
6. Select Edit → Chrome View once the update has finished. You should see the component structure shown in Figure B-4. You can then choose fields in which to view the chrome view window.

At this point, you can edit the text straight from the chrome view. Another option is to bring up an edit window for a selected phrase, which supplies all possible editable fields in one window. An advanced search feature exists if you look for a piece of text in multiple files. When your strings are all done, packaging and preparing your language pack for distribution is as straightforward as selecting the Export → Jar File/XPI Install from the menus.

MozillaTranslator has the adaptability to handle any application locale, once you point it at the correct resources. Make sure that your files are packaged in the correct format—namely, a JAR file. MozillaTranslator can handle all localizable resources: DTDs, string bundles, HTML, and RDF files.

Missing Parts

The tools highlighted so far are just some of the pieces needed to form a full-featured Mozilla development environment. Currently, several different areas of the application creation process would benefit greatly from a dedicated development tool. Some of the different types of needed tools are listed below.

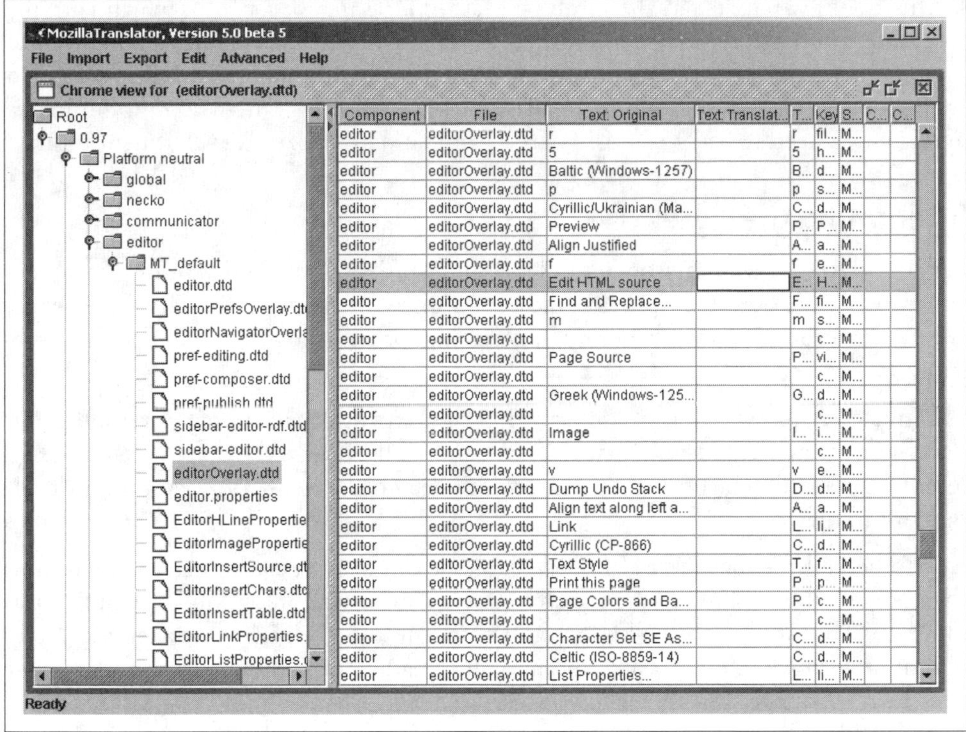

Figure B-4. Chrome view in MozillaTranslator

Visual XUL Editors

XUL is a simple markup language that is similar to HTML. Some people prefer to create HTML code by hand, but others use programs that generate HTML code for them by using a simple point-and-click interface. The creation of a user-friendly XUL editing program would greatly simplify the creation of Mozilla applications and would allow many more people to start their own development projects.

So far, there have been at least a couple of attempts to create such a tool. A few projects, such as Vixen (*http://www.mozilla.org/projects/vixen/*) and XULMaker (*http://xulmaker.mozdev.org*), have started to create a visual XUL editor. So far, however, there isn't a tool that allows someone to quickly create a user interface without creating XUL and CSS code by hand.

Toolkits and Libraries

Mozilla applications currently have a lot of duplication due to a lack of standard libraries and toolkits. Different types of applications still need to do very similar things, so having common programming routines and interface widgets would greatly reduce the amount of time different developers spend recreating frequently needed parts of an application.

In this book, we discussed the JSLib project (*http://jslib.mozdev.org*), which is trying to create a repository of versatile functions that any Mozilla application can reuse. For a project like this to work, however, it needs to be widely available and accepted by the developer community. To ensure its wide availability, these common libraries and toolkits need to become a core part of the standard Mozilla development tools.

Integrating the Pieces

Popular development environments like Microsoft's Visual Studio bring together a cohesive set of tools; they provide the tool framework in which much of the setup, code generation, directory structure, linking, and other drudgery is handled automatically.

When used together, the tools described in this appendix can make your application development process easier. However, currently, all of these tools are located in different places and none of them interact with one another to provide a seamless development framework.

Even when all the tools do become available, it will be necessary to integrate each of these together to create a single development environment for Mozilla application builders. This single tool will allow you to create the shell of an application easily and fill it with XUL, CSS, JavaScript, and all other parts of a Mozilla application that can then be packaged easily when you are done.

APPENDIX C

Programmer's Reference

This appendix is an easy-to-use reference that contains information about XUL elements, XBL elements, and event attributes. Details about how each element and event works within a Mozilla application are covered in the rest of the book; to learn how to use XUL or XBL, read Chapter 3 and Chapter 7.

Once you know how to use XUL and XBL, this reference allows you to look up all available tags and elements quickly. Each entry listed below includes a brief description of the element or event, its purpose, what attributes the element or event has, and what other related elements or events you can look at to get more information.

XUL Element Set

XUL isn't yet identified as a specification, and the language is still changing. The elements and attributes given here represent a stable subset of the XUL widget set. XML allows you to define new elements and attributes arbitrarily (which is partly what makes a powerful extension like XBL possible) in your markup. Although it's discouraged in practice, Mozilla application developers—even those working on the Mozilla source itself—often use this flexibility to manage data in one-off attributes. For example, you may find XUL buttons in the source with attributes like "loading," which is not part of the XUL specification. In fact, XBL's presence, XML's flexibility, and DOM interfaces blur the distinction between valid XUL and other XML markup. This reference tries to document all widgets in the XUL 1.0 release, any additional attributes these elements have, and their use in Mozilla application development.

All XUL elements have the attributes shown in Table C-1.

Table C-1. Common XUL element attributes

Attribute	Description
`align`	Specifies how child elements are aligned: baseline, center, end, start, or stretch
`allowevents`	(Boolean) Specifies whether events should be passed to the child elements
`class`	The element class of the ; often used for class-based style rules
`collapsed`	(Boolean) Specifies whether the element is collapsed or displayed; defaults to false
`container`	(Boolean) Specifies whether the element can have child elements
`containment`	Used in templates; points to RDF property represented by this XUL element
`context`	Points to the context menu that this element should use
`datasources`	Used in templates; points to the RDF data that gets processed
`debug`	Used for debugging XUL; adds borders to make the element and its layout easily visible
`dir`	Specifies the direction of the children: normal or reverse
`empty`	(Boolean) Used for template; specifies that the container has no children
`equalsize`	Specifies whether the children should be of the same size: always or never
`flex`	Provides an integer or percent value that specifies the flexibility of an element relative to its siblings within a container
`flexgroup`	Provides an integer that can group elements and give them the same degree of flexibility
`height`	Specifies an element's height
`hidden`	(Boolean) Specifies whether the element is displayed; defaults to `false`
`id`	A unique identifier for the element
`insertafter`	Names the ID of the element after which this element should be overlaid; this attribute works only in overlays
`insertbefore`	Names the ID of the element which this element should be overlaid before; this attribute works only in overlays
`left`	Specifies an element's position within a container in pixels to the left
`maxheight`	Specifies an element's maximum height
`maxwidth`	Specifies an element's maximum width
`minheight`	Specifies an element's minimum height
`minwidth`	Specifies an element's minimum width
`observes`	Points to a broadcasting element whose state this element observes
`ordinal`	(Integer) Specifies the element's order within the parent
`orient`	Shows the element's orientation: vertical or horizontal
`pack`	Shows how children should be distributed within this container: center, end, or start
`persist`	Shows which of the element's attributes should be persisted/stored for reuse
`position`	Shows the element's position within a list (e.g., menuitems in a menu)
`ref`	Specifies the RDF data root to begin processing (used in templates)
`style`	Provides style rules for the current element
`template`	Specifies an existing template to use for this content (used in templates)
`tooltip`	Specifies a pop up or tooltip ID to be used for this element

Table C-1. Common XUL element attributes (continued)

Attribute	Description
tooltiptext	Specifies text to be displayed in the element's tooltip (doesn't require a separate tooltip attribute)
top	Shows the current element's position within a container in pixels from the top
uri	Specifies the root in the XUL where content processing begins (used in templates)
width	Specifies an element's width

action

Child element in a XUL template structure that draws content for matched data

Additional Attributes

None.

Description

The `action` element defines the content drawn into the XUL when the rules defined in a template's `conditions` structure are met. The content to be drawn is an `action` element's child.

See Also

`template`, `rule`, `condition`, `binding`

arrowscrollbox

Container box for scrolling contents

Additional Attributes

None.

Description

A box with arrows that allow scrolling through its contents. The box scrolls when the user's mouse hovers over the arrows. It is commonly used in large menus that overflow a provided space.

See Also

`autorepeatbutton`, `scrollbox`

autorepeatbutton

Provides arrows for a scrolling area

Additional Attributes

`scrolldir`

Description

This element is used to internally bind the `arrowscrollbox` element and it surrounds a `scrollbox` area to provide the navigation arrows. The `scrolldir` attribute, which can have a value of up or down, determines the direction of the arrows.

See Also

`arrowscrollbox`, `scrollbox`

binding

Child element in a XUL template that optionally matches in the data

Additional Attributes `predicate`, `object`, `subject`, `template`, `rule`, `condition`, `action`, `bindings`

Description

In contrast to the `rule` element, which must match to trigger the action, `binding` allows you to create an optional rule for data matching.

See Also `action, template, rule, condition, bindings`

bindings

Substructure in a XUL template that collects the optional binding rules

Additional Attributes None.

Description

Individual bindings must be defined with a `bindings` parent to be a part of a valid XUL template.

See Also `action`, `template`, `rule`, `condition`, `binding`

box

Generic container and layout element

Additional Attributes None.

Description

This element can contain any type of content and any number of elements. Its default orientation is `horizontal`, unless otherwise overridden by the `orient` attribute, and the contents are laid out in the order they appear in the file. The `box` is the basic layout unit in a XUL interface. Many, if not most, XUL elements inherit from `box`.

See Also `hbox`, `vbox`

broadcaster

Notifies elements when a change occurs in the UI

Contained by `broadcasterset`

Additional Attributes `checked`, `accesskey`, `oncommand`, `value`, `label`, `disabled`

Description

A `broadcaster` acts as a host for other elements, detecting changes that occur in the UI and notifying those elements of the changes via attribute changes. The elements that use it are said to observe the broadcaster. The observed attribute is typically the oncommand attribute, but can be any attribute.

See Also `broadcasterset`, `command`, `observes`

broadcasterset

Container for broadcaster elements

Contains `broadcaster`

Additional Attributes None.

Description

The purpose of this nonvisible element is to group a set of broadcasters logically. The XUL document can contain one or multiple sets.

See Also `broadcaster`, `commandset`

browser

Web-content container

Additional Attributes `src`, `name`, `content`, `onclick`, `type`, `disablehistory`, `disablesecurity`

Description

A content widget or frame used to load in web content for read-only viewing. This element is used by the main Mozilla browser, so it handles HTML, XML, and plain text. To load a page, set the `src` attribute to a URL. Other features include the attachment of a context menu that uses the `context` attribute and various methods and properties exposed for web navigation and display.

See Also `editor`, `iframe`

button

A widget that activates some functionality when pressed

Additional Attributes `accesskey`, `dir`, `disabled`, `dlgType`, `group`, `image`, `label`, `orient`, `type`, `value`

Description

A `button` typically gives the user an option to click it to carry out JavaScript code routine(s). This code can be a function call or inline script and is contained in the `onclick` attribute or the `oncommand` event handler. It can optionally have an image associated with a URL contained in the `image` attribute or by using the `list-style-image` CSS property. There are various types of buttons, determined by the type attribute, including `checkbox`, `menu`, `menu-button`, and `radio`. Leave this out for a normal button.

See Also `autorepeatbutton`, `toolbarbutton`

caption

Provides heading for a groupbox element

Contained by `groupbox`, `radiogroup`

Additional Attributes None.

Description

This element is most commonly used to provide a text label for a `groupbox` by setting the `label` attribute. However, it is flexible about other content it can contain, such as checkboxes or radio buttons.

See Also `description`, `groupbox`, `label`, `radiogroup`

checkbox

Indicates a specified feature's on/off state

Additional Attributes `accesskey`, `label`, `checked`

Description

A `checkbox` appears as a small box that can be checked on or off. When checked on or off, the `checked` attribute is set to `true` or `false`. It can be set initially for a default value. To associate text with a `checkbox`, set the `label` attribute.

See Also `radio`

colorpicker

Widget used to choose a color

Additional Attributes `onchange`, `type`, `id`, `palettename`

Description

When activated, this widget presents a choice of colors to the user in a grid format. The user selects a color by clicking on it. The `palettename` attribute determines the displayed colors. Three values for this attribute represent three types of palettes: standard, grey, and web.

JavaScript Methods and Properties

`color`

column

A column in a grid

Contained by `columns`

Additional Attributes None.

Description

column is a column entry in a grid, of which there can be one or more contained in a columns element. The content of cells in a column is determined by the children of each row element.

See Also columns, grid, row, rows

columns

Container for the number of columns in a grid

Contains column

Additional Attributes None.

Description

The children of this element are one or more column elements, the number of which determines the actual number of grid columns.

See Also column, grid, row, rows

command

Defines functionality that can be called from multiple sources

Contained by commandset

Additional Attributes disabled, accesskey, observes, label, checked

Description

The command element provides a place to organize functionality used in more than one place in the interface—from a context menu, a keyboard shortcut, and a regular menu, for example. The element is identified and shared by using its ID value and an interested element's (i.e., a menu that wants the command) observes attribute. It also typically calls a JavaScript command from its oncommand event handler.

See Also commands, commandset

commands

Container for a group of command sets

Additional Attributes None.

Description

commandsets no longer need to be contained within a commands element. Still, the commands group can help you organize your code and user overlays to import commands, especially related sets.

See Also command, commandset

commandset

A container for multiple command elements

Contains `command`

Additional Attributes `oncommandupdate`, `commandupdater`, `events`

Description

An invisible, document-level element that acts as a logical grouping for commands or other command sets.

See Also `command`, `commands`

conditions

Defines the conditions within a template rule

Contains `content`, `member`, `triple`

Additional Attributes None.

Description

Within a `template`, the `conditions`, `action`, and sometimes the `bindings` elements comprise a single rule. The children of the `conditions` element must be matched to the processed data for that rule's action to make content.

See Also `template`, `rule`, `action`, `member`, `triple`, `content`

content

Binds variables in a template

Contained by `conditions`

Additional Attributes None.

Description

The `content` element is the portion of a template's `conditions` element that associates a variable, often representing a URI (e.g., `<content uri="?uri"/>`) with the data.

See Also `template`, `rule`, `action`, `conditions`, `member`, `triple`

deck

Box container that displays one child element at a time

Additional Attributes `selectedIndex`

Description

deck uses the attribute selectedIndex to determine which child element to display. The others are hidden until they are displayed by index. deck is often used dynamically via the DOM to cycle through child elements, such as buttons.

See Also stack

description

Holder for block of text that can wrap to multiple lines

Additional Attributes crop, onmouseover, onmouseout, value

Description

The description element replaces <html:label> and other HTML-namespaced elements to wrap text in XUL interfaces. Text in a description can be defined as content with the open and close tags or provided in the value attribute. Note that the text does not wrap when placed in the value attribute.

See Also caption, label

dialog

Root element for secondary XUL window

Additional Attributes ondialogaccept, ondialogcancel, ondialoghelp, onunload, onload, title, buttons, windowtype, persist, y, x, screenY, screenX

Description

dialog is a version of the window element built for displaying a secondary dialog window in the application. Like window, dialog is the root element in a XUL file. Event handlers such as ondialogaccept and ondialogcancel are included as conveniences for handling user input.

See Also window, page

dialogheader

Styled text heading for UI panel

Contained by dialog

Additional Attributes title, description

Description

This is a formatted horizontal panel that contains text specified by the title attribute. This element is the heading that appears at the top of the right panel in the Mozilla global preferences dialog.

See Also window, dialog

editor

Content area for editable web content

Additional Attributes `src`

Description

This high-level widget edits text and HTML. `contentDocument` is a reference to the document contained within the editor.

JavaScript Methods and Properties

`contentDocument`

See Also `browser`, `iframe`

grid

Widget for laying out content in a structured tabular fashion

Contains `rows`, `columns`

Additional Attributes None.

Description

The number of column elements that are placed in rows determines the number of columns and the content for each row is placed in the `row` element. The number of row children must correspond to the number of columns.

See Also `column`, `columns`, `listbox`, `row`, `rows`, `tree`

grippy

Visible widget used on a grippy bar to expand or collapse a UI region

Contained by `splitter`

Additional Attributes None.

Description

`grippy` appears as a child of a `splitter` and provides the little "handle" that opens and closes the `sidebar` and other collapsible elements in the interface.

groupbox

Box with frame surrounding it

Contains `caption`

Additional Attributes None.

Description

The border that appears around and organizes elements in the interface (e.g., in dialogs where selectable elements are grouped together); often comes from a groupbox parent.

See Also `box`

hbox

Box container whose children are laid out horizontally

Additional Attributes None.

Description

The `hbox` element is a shorthand for `<box orient="horizontal">`. It is the preferred way to achieve horizontal orientation in box layout.

See Also `box`, `vbox`

iframe

Web content area

Additional Attributes `name`, `src`, `type`

Description

Like `browser`, `iframe` allows you to display web content, XML, and other data using the `src` attribute, but has less intrinsic browsing functionality available (such as browser history). You can use any number of iframes in a document.

See Also `browser`, `editor`

image

Display of a supported type image

Additional Attributes `src`

Description

The XUL image is analogous to the HTML `<img>` element. The supported types in Gecko are PNG, JPG, GIF, and BMP.

key

Definition for a keyboard shortcut

Contained by `keyset`

Additional Attributes `modifiers`, `command`, `key` , `keycode`, `observes`

Description

A key is often defined with a commandkey and a modifier (e.g., P + Ctrl), and uses an oncommand event handler to fire the given command when invoked.

See Also keyset

---

keybinding

Container for a keyset or group of keysets

Contains keyset

Additional Attributes None.

Description

This element is used in an overlaid file to contain a group of platform-specific key sets. It uses the ID attribute to overlay itself into XUL files that pick up sets of key bindings.

See Also key, keyset

---

keyset

Container for one or more key elements

Contains key

Additional Attributes None.

Description

key elements no longer need to be contained within a keyset parent. Still, keysets can help organize groups of keys—particularly related ones.

See Also key, keybinding

---

label

Simple text display element and label for a control element

Additional Attributes control, for, accesskey, crop, value

Description

This text element can just display text in the UI. Unlike the description element, the text will not wrap. If you use it with a control element (the association occurs through the for attribute, the value of which must match the element's id) such as a textbox, the focus moves to the control element when the label is clicked.

See Also caption, description

listbox

Used for display of a flat list of items

Additional Attributes `datasources`, `sortResource`, `sortDirection`, `rows`, `seltype`, `ref`

Description

`listbox` is a lightweight tabular display widget. Unlike `tree`, it cannot handle nested rows. It does support multiple columns, however. It is easy to use and renders content very quickly.

See Also `listcell`, `listcol`, `listcols`, `listhead`, `listheader`, `listitem`

listcell

Single cell of a listbox

Contained by `listitem`

Additional Attributes `label`, `flexlabel`, `crop`, `disabled`, `image`, `checked`

Description

The `listcell` is the element within a `listbox` that actually displays data.

See Also `listbox`, `listcol`, `listcols`, `listheader`, `listitem`

listcol

Listbox column definition

Contained by `listcols`

Description

This element represents a column in a `listbox`.

See Also `listbox`, `listcell`, `listcols`, `listheader`, `listitem`

listcols

Container for listbox columns (listcol)

Contained by `listbox`

Contains `listcol`

Description

This element contains any number of individual `listbox` columns.

See Also `listbox`, `listcell`, `listcol`, `listheader`, `listitem`

listhead

Container for column header in list boxes (listheader)

Contained by listbox

Contains listheader

Description

The `listhead` element is analogous to the HTML `thead` element, and contains the header cells for an XUL listbox table.

See Also `listbox`, `listcell`, `listcol`, `listcols`, `listheader`, `listitem`

listheader

Text header for listbox column

Contained by listhead

Additional Attributes `sortActive`, `sortDirection`, `resource`, `sortable`

Description

The `listheader` element displays the header text.

See Also `listbox`, `listcell`, `listcol`, `listcols`, `listhead`, `listitem`

listitem

Listbox row definition

Contained By listbox

Contains listcell

Additional Attributes `value`, `description`, `accesskey`, `label`, `context`, `type`, `name`

Description

A `listitem` is a row in a `listbox`. The number of `listcell` children corresponds to the number of columns in the `listbox`.

See Also `listbox`, `listcell`, `listcol`, `listcols`, `listhead`, `listheader`

member

Matches container relationships in which the parent element is given by a container element and the child by a child element

Additional Attributes `container`, `child`

Description

The `member` element is part of the conditional structure in a XUL template. It creates a rule by which parent-child relationships are matched and used as a basis for drawing content in the XUL.

See Also `conditions`, `rules`, `bindings`, `template`

menu

A menu element for containing menu items

Additional Attributes `label`, `accesskey`, `disabled`, `image`, `disabled`

Description

`menu` is the basic menu widget. It's often contained in a `menubar`, but may appear elsewhere. The actual `menuitems` are defined within a `menupopup` that is usually the direct child of `menu`.

See Also `menubar`, `menubutton`, `menuitem`, `menulist`, `menupopup`, `menuseparator`

menubar

Containing element for one or more menus

Contains `menu`

Additional Attributes None.

Description

`menubar` is a special box for containing menus (though it can include other content). By default it has a `grippy` for expanding and collapsing the menubar.

See Also `menu`, `menubutton`, `menuitem`, `menulist`, `menupopup`, `menuseparator`, `grippy`

menuitem

Single selectable choice in a menu

Contained by `menupopup`

Additional Attributes `label`, `accesskey`, `crop`, `image`, `disabled`, `checked`

Description

The `menuitem` is the basic element used to display a single item in a menu (e.g., `<menuitem label="File"/>`).

See Also `menu`, `menubar`, `menubutton`, `menulist`, `menupopup`, `menuseparator`

menulist

Drop-down list of selectable items

Contains menupopup

Additional Attributes None.

Description

The menulist displays a list of menuitems, the selected one of which is displayed in the menulist itself. It is a type of drop-down menu.

See Also menu, menubar, menubutton, menuitem, menupopup, menuseparator

menupopup

Pop-up container for menu items

Contained By menu, menubutton, menulist

Contains menuitem

Additional Attributes popupalign, datasources, onpopupshowing, sortResource, onpopuphiding, sortDirection, context, position, popupanchor, ref

Description

The menupopup contains the actual menu items defined for a menu and acts much like the popup element to show the window with a list of choices.

See Also popup, menu, menubar, menubutton, menuitem, menulist, menuseparator

menuseparator

Line separating menu items

Contained By menupopup

Additional Attributes type

Description

The menuseparator is a line through the menu that divides menu items into different groups. You can use the position attribute on the menuseparator to make sure it appears in a particular place, or you can use the common attribute insertAfter.

See Also menu, menubar, menubutton, menuitem, menulist, menuspopup

observes

Broadcast event and attribute listener

Additional Attributes element, attribute, onbroadcast

Description

The observes element observes the state of a broadcasting element and its attributes. observes can be a separate element, defined as a child of the interested observer, or it can be an attribute on any element that wants to watch changes in a broadcasting element.

See Also broadcaster

---

overlay

Root element in a separate file that contains reusable XUL content

Additional Attributes xmlns, title

Description

Like page, window, dialog, and wizard, overlay is a XUL document's root element. Overlay documents contain content blocks that are overlaid dynamically at runtime into XUL content whose IDs match theirs. For example, a menupopup with the ID "file" and a menuitem child in an overlay adds that new menuitem into any menupopup with the ID "file" that it finds in the base XUL.

See Also page, window

---

page

Root element of XUL file loaded in a content frame

Additional Attributes context, headertitle, onload, onunload, title, xmlns

Description

page is the root element for a XUL document that is meant to be loaded within another XUL document, such as a preference panel.

See Also dialog, overlay, window

---

popup

Box container as child window

Additional Attributes onpopupshowing, onpopuphiding

Description

popup is a pop-up window that can be hooked up to any UI content. It is often used for context menus and invoked by elements that use its ID attribute in their popup or context attribute.

See Also menupopup, popupset

popupset

Container for popup elements

Additional Attributes None.

Description

While not strictly necessary as a container for the popup element, `popupset` helps you organize and overlays groups of popups.

See Also `popup`

progressmeter

Visual progress indicator of a time-consuming operation

Additional Attributes `value`, `mode`

Description

This high-level widget uses its `value` attribute to fill in a meter that usually represents how long a particular task takes. You can change the `value` attribute dynamically to update the fill or set the mode to "undetermined" (as opposed to the default "determined" mode) to display a busy meter that doesn't chart actual progress.

radio

Single on/off choice represented as selectable circle

Contained By `radiogroup`

Additional Attributes `selected`, `group`, `label`, `accesskey`, `value`

Description

Within a `radiogroup` element, a single `radio` widget is selected to indicate user choice. `radio` elements can also be used singularly to check an option on or off in the interface.

radiogroup

Framed box for containing radio elements

Contains `radio`

Additional Attributes `disabled`

Description

The `radiogroup` makes all `radio` elements within it belong to a single group from which only a single element can be selected.

resizer

Window-resizing element

Additional Attributes `direction`

Description

A bar that changes the cursor when hovered over to signify that the bar can be dragged to resize the a window. The `direction` attribute specifies which way the window is resized, and can have values such as `topleft`, `top`, `right`, and `bottomright`. For example, a value of `bottomleft` resizes the window down and to the left.

See Also `window`

row

Container for grid cells laid out consecutively

Contained By `rows`

Additional Attributes None.

Description

`row` is a single row in a `grid`. It is analogous to the `<TR>` element in HTML.

See Also `grid`, `rows`

rows

Definition for grid rows

Contains `row`

Additional Attributes None.

Description

The `rows` element is a child of the `grid` element that contains any number of individual `row` elements. It is a sibling of `columns` within the `grid`.

See Also `grid`, `row`, `columns`, `column`

rule

Defines rules for rendering data as XUL

Contained by `template`

Additional Attributes `rdf:type`, `parent`, `isempty`, `iscontainer`

Description

The children of the rule element define a rule: the conditions stated in the conditions element must be met, the bindings provides optional matching, and the content in the action element is rendered if the rule is matched.

See Also template, action, conditions

---

script

Declaration of script used in XUL file

Additional Attributes src, type

Description

The script element can contain script content (e.g., <script>alert("it")</script>) and can also import scripts in JavaScript files, in which case the src attribute is used. The type for JavaScript is application/x-javascript, and the src attribute may also use *chrome://* type URLs to point at JavaScript in the chrome.

---

scrollbar

Widget for scrolling in a container

Contains scrollbarbutton, slider

Additional Attributes curpos, increment, maxpos, pageincrement

Description

The scrollbar element uses the curpos and maxpos attributes to determine where the scrollbarbutton element is drawn within its length. increment specifies how much the scrollbar should move on user input. pageincrement specifies how many pages it should move.

---

scrollbarbutton

Button used to move position of scrollbar thumb

Contained By scrollbar

Additional Attributes sborient, type

Description

The scrollbarbutton can use its src attribute to point to an image that should be drawn over it.

---

scrollbox

Box for scrolling content

Additional Attributes crop

Description

The scrollbox is a regular box with scrollbars that display automatically when the content inside the box overflows the size of the box itself.

See Also box, hbox, vbox

separator

Bar between elements

Additional Attributes None.

Description

The separator is a general-purpose divider. In menus, use menuseparator.

See Also menuseparator

slider

A scrollbar without buttons

Additional Attributes curpos, increment, maxpos, pageincrement

Description

The slider element provides simpler user input—a thumb button and no arrows—for scrolling large content. Like scrollbar, it uses curpos and maxpos to display its position.

See Also scrollbar, scrollbarbutton

spacer

Blank space separating element

Additional Attributes None.

Description

This element is a general-purpose blank space. The use of a spacer with flex to take up available space within a box and shrink its siblings is a staple of the box layout model that XUL uses.

splitter

Element for dragging and resizing associated elements

Additional Attributes persist, state

Description

Users can drag a splitter to resize an associated element or panel that holds content and click a splitter to collapse the specified element within a box. To specify which element you manipulate with a `splitter`, set this element's `collapse` attribute accordingly: `before` to control the element before it in the parent; `after` to control the element after it.

See Also `grippy`, `toolbar`

stack

Shows children one on top of one another, all at the same time

Description

In contrast to the `deck`, `stack` is a `box` that displays all of its children at once. You can use a `stack` to display elements and blend them together, as when you use different stack children as background images and visual layers.

See Also `deck`, `box`

statusbar

Box container for status elements

Contains `statusbarpanel`

Additional Attributes None.

Description

In Mozilla, the `statusbar` is placed at the bottom of the main windows, where it is hooked up to the `window.status` property and can be used to display status text. It is divided into panels, one of which is the `taskbar` where some main component icons are displayed.

See Also `statusbarpanel`

statusbarpanel

Single unit of a statusbar

Contained by `statusbar`

Additional Attributes `persist`, `label`

Description

`statusbarpanels` are subdivisions of the `statusbar` at the bottom of main browser windows. They can contain other content, text using the `label` attribute and an image using the `list-style-image` CSS style rule.

See Also `statusbar`

stringbundle

Holder of localized properties for use in script

Contained by `stringbundleset`

Additional Attributes src

Description

Like the script element, stringbundle uses the src attribute to locate a file for use. In this case, the files is a string bundle (properties file) that is used for holding localizable strings used in the UI.

See Also stringbundleset

stringbundleset

Container for stringbundle elements

Contains stringbundle

Additional Attributes None.

Description

stringbundleset is an optional container for groups of stringbundle elements. Like commandset use for commands, stringbundle organizes sets of related stringbundles, particularly when those sets are overlaid into the UI.

See Also stringbundle

tab

A single selectable tab of a tabbox

Contained by tabs

Additional Attributes accesskey, crop, disabled, label, image

Description

Individual tabs correspond to panels in the tabbox.

See Also tabbox, tabpanel, tabpanels, tabs

tabbox

Box container for tab panels

Contains tabs, tabpanels

Additional Attributes None.

Description

tabbox is the container in which the tabs and tabpanels are defined. It lays out children like a regular box to the orientation specified, which defaults to vertical. The panels are defined in the tabpanels element.

See Also tab, tabpanel, tabpanels, tabs

tabbrowser

Tabbed holder for a set of web content views

Additional Attributes `contentcontextmenu`, `contenttooltip`

Description

`tabbrowser` derives from the `browser` widget. Like `browser`, it lets you view HTML pages and other content. `tabbrowser` has additional methods on it that manage tabbed windows (e.g., `addTab`, `enterTabbedMode`).

See Also `browser`

tabpanel

A single panel of a tabbox

Contained by `tabpanels`

Contains XUL content

Additional Attributes None.

Description

A `tabpanel` is one of the special `box` elements that correspond to a particular tab within a `tabbox`. It can hold any XUL content to be displayed on a particular tab panel.

See Also `tab`, `tabbox`, `tabpanels`, `tabs`

tabpanels

Container for tabpanel elements

Contained by `tabbox`

Contains `tabpanel`, `box`

Additional Attributes None.

Description

The `tabpanels` container corresponds to the `tabs` element that holds all individual tabs, and is a container for the `tabpanel` associated with that tab. This child panel can be either an optional `tabpanel` element that holds XUL content, or just the XUL content.

See Also `tab`, `tabbox`, `tabpanel`, `tabs`

tabs

Container for tab elements

Contained by `tabbox`

Contains `tab`

Additional Attributes None.

Description

This element is a required container for individual tabs.

See Also `tab`, `tabbox`, `tabpanel`, `tabpanels`

template

A high-level widget used to build content dynamically from data

Contains `rule`

Additional Attributes `xmlns:nc`, `xmlns:chrome`

Description

The `template` element has several `rule` children, each of which defines rules for matching data in a datasource and rendering that data as XUL content. A template is defined within the regular XUL content.

textbox

Accepts text input from user

Additional Attributes `multiline`, `maxlength`, `disabled`, `readonly`, `type`, `size`

Description

`textbox` is a user-input element. Expand it beyond its single-line default by setting `multiline` to `true`. You can also disable it, and set its size.

See Also `label`

thumb

Object used to move content in scrollable area

Additional Attributes `sborient`

Description

The `thumb` element appears in the `slider` and the `scrollbar`.

See Also `scrollbar`, `scrollbarbutton`, `slider`

toolbar

Holder of buttons for quick-access UI functionality

Contains `toolbarbutton`, `toolbarseparator`

Additional Attributes `grippyhidden`, `tborient`, `tbalign`, `tbpack`

Description

Toolbars usually have horizontal orientation at the top of an application window, but this does not have to be the case. You can use the `orient` attribute to set it vertically and run its content down and not across. While the most common content for a toolbar is buttons and menus, it can contain any type of content.

See Also `toolbarbutton`, `toolbarseparator`, `toolbox`

toolbarbutton

Specially adapted button for use in a toolbar

Contained by `toolbar`

Additional Attributes `accesskey`, `dir`, `disabled`, `dlgType`, `group`, `image`, `label`, `orient`, `type`, `value`

Description

This is a button designed especially for a toolbar, with special stylings for this purpose. The current theme determines a `toolbarbutton`'s look. See *toolbar.css* in the theme JARs to view styles and bindings for this common button.

See Also `toolbar`, `toolbarseparator`, `toolbox`

toolbarseparator

Visible separator for elements contained in a toolbar

Contained by `toolbar`

Additional Attributes None.

Description

Like the `menuseparator` in a `menu`, `toolbarseparator` divides elements in a `toolbar`.

See Also `toolbar`, `toolbarbutton`, `toolbox`

toolbox

Optional container for menu bars and toolbars

Contains `menubar`, `toolbar`

Additional Attributes None.

Description

`toolbox` can organize several toolbars into one parent element. `toolbox` inherits from `box`, so you can use box layout attributes to control the positioning and layout of toolbars within.

See Also `menubar`, `toolbar`

tooltip

Pop-up window for context-sensitive help

Additional Attributes noautohide, onpopupshowing, onpopuphiding, position

Description

The tooltip element defines text to be displayed. It is associated by ID with elements that want to use its content in the pop ups they display. However, elements can also use the tooltip attribute to display a tooltip more directly for themselves.

tree

Hierarchical holder of information represented as rows

Contains treecols, treechildren

Additional Attributes multiple, datasources, enableColumnDrag, containment, sortResource, sortDirection, border, seltype, sortActive, flags, context, persist, hidecolumnpicker

Description

The tree element is a high-level widget that displays tabular data. More complex than listbox, tree allows you to define nested content, different views, and data display, and provides methods that sort and manipulate its contents.

See Also treecell, treechildren, treecol, treecols, treeitem, treerow

treecell

A single cell in a tree

Contained by treerow

Additional Attributes src, indent, observes, url, value, label, sortActive, sortDirection, tag, mode, resource, allowevents, properties

Description

The treecell contains the actual content to be displayed in a tree. That content can be in the form of a value for the label attribute. It can also be content in the treecell's start and end tags (e.g., <treecell>data</treecell>).

See Also tree, treechildren, treecol, treecols, treeitem, treerow

treechildren

The main body of a tree; a container for treeitems

Contains treeitem

Contained by tree

Additional Attributes open

Description

The treechildren element defines the subset of the tree where the content is actually contained (in contrast to treecols, which defines aspects of the layout).

See Also tree, treecell, treecol, treecols, treeitem, treerow

treecol

A single column of a tree

Contained by treecols

Additional Attributes sort, resource, primary, sortSeparators, label, sortActive, sortDirection, hideheader, accesskey, type

Description

The treecol typically does not contain content. Instead, it defines the header for the columns whose contents are defined in the treerows.

See Also tree, treecell, treechildren, treecols, treeitem, treerow

treecols

Container for tree columns

Contained by tree

Contains treecol

Additional Attributes None.

Description

This element is a container for a group of treecol elements, or columns, in a tree. A tree should have only one treecols.

See Also tree, treecell, treechildren, treecol, treeitem, treerow

treeitem

A treerow container

Contained by treechildren

Contains treerow

Additional Attributes rdf:type, container, open

Description

The treeitem element is a container for a treerow, and makes treerow a selectable element within the tree.

See Also tree, treecell, treechildren, treecol, treecols, treerow

treerow

A single row of a tree

Contained by treeitem

Contains treecell

Additional Attributes properties

Description

Contained within a treeitem, this element represents a single row of a tree.

See Also tree, treecell, treechildren, treecol, treecols, treeitem

triple

Substructure of a template that matches RDF statements in the data

Additional Attributes predicate, object, subject

Description

The children of triple—predicate, object, and subject—match RDF statements that appear in the data processed in the template.

See Also template, member, content, conditions

vbox

Box container with vertically laid out children

Additional Attributes None.

See Also box, hbox

window

Root element of a top-level XUL window document

Additional Attributes windowtype, xmlns:rdf, xmlns:web, titlepreface, onload, onunload, xmlns, titlemodifier, xmlns:html, title, onclose, titlemenuseparator, contenttitlesetting, y, x, screenY, screenX

Description

The window is an XUL document's basic root element. The contents of a XUL document, including the script elements, commands, keys, and broadcasters, appear as children of the window. Overlays, the XML and stylesheet-processing instructions, and the DOCTYPE declaration appear before and outside a document's root element. The window should have a unique ID and use minimally, the XUL namespace to identify markup elements as XUL: `xmlns="http://www.mozilla.org/keymaster/gatekeeper/there.is.only.xul"`.

See Also `overlay`, `page`

---

wizard

Window used to step though a task

Contains `wizardpage`

Additional Attributes `onwizardaccept`, `onwizardcancel`, `xmlns`, `onwizardfinish`, `xmlns:nc`

Description

Like `dialog`, `wizard` is a specialized version of the `window` root element. It easily creates multistep dialog windows that help users set up accounts, password data, and other customizable information. A `wizard` contains one or more `wizardpages`.

See Also `wizardpage`, `window`, `dialog`

---

wizardpage

A single panel (step) of a wizard

Contained by `wizard`

Additional Attributes `label`, `pageid`, `onpageadvanced`, `onpageshow`, `onpagecancel`

Description

The `wizardpage` can contain arbitrary XUL content. One or more wizardpages are defined in a `wizard` window. The intrinsic functionality of a wizard window allows you to step through `wizardpages` by setting the `onpageshow` and `onpagecancel` event handlers on individual pages and using the `onwizardaccept` and `onwizardcancel` event handlers on the `wizard` parent element.

See Also `wizard`, `window`, `dialog`

XBL Element Set

The XBL 1.0 specification published on the mozilla.org web site appeared to be a beacon for application developers. Because the specification was available early in the development process, XBL seemed to be a tighter, more comprehensible language that was easier to learn and master than XUL. Since then, XBL development has strayed from the specification quite a bit, however, and now people consider XBL as opaque as XUL without good documentation that helps people learn and to create a roadmap for use based on continuing development.

This reference section tries to capture basic elements and attributes in XBL. Because it binds rather than creates content, XBL is smaller and inherently more formal than XUL. Nonetheless, as you will see, the language has quite a bit of range and complexity. Each entry in this section describes the XBL element and its purpose, its position in the hierarchy (i.e., which elements it contains and which elements it is contained by), and lists the element's attributes. Chapter 7 introduces XBL and shows how to use it. However, once you are familiar with the basics of XBL, you can consult this reference to find the XBL items you want.

binding

A single XBL binding

Contains `content`, `implementation`, `handlers`

Contained by `bindings`

Attributes `id`, `extends`, `display`, `applyauthorstyles`, `styleexplicitcontent`

Description

This element defines a single XBL binding that can be attached to a bound document. It enables the creation of self-contained widgets that can contain content, implementation, and handlers. This element must have an `id` attribute value; this value is how it is associated—either through a CSS style rule or a DOM method—to the bound element that acts a placeholder for the binding that is filled out during attachment. The `extends` attribute inherits from a XUL element or another binding.

See Also `bindings`

bindings

An XBL document's root element

Contains `binding`, `resources`, `stylesheet`

Attributes `id`, `type`

Description

This root container can hold one or more bindings, represented by the `<binding>` markup. The Mozilla code base references an XBL document through its name, which has an *.xml* extension. The document `id` has to be unique. The other children of `<bindings>` are `<resources>` and `<stylesheet>`, which contain style and image information to be used by the document's bindings.

See Also `binding`

body

Container for JavaScript code to be executed by an XBL method

Contained by `method`

Attributes `id`

Description

This element is designed as a holder for the method's script. It defines a logical block and differentiates the script from the parameter element, which also lies within the method. Script contained in a method has to be in a body element, which in turn should contain a CDATA section. `<![CDATA[...]]>` escapes JavaScript characters like quotes and slashes that may otherwise conflict with the XML parser.

See Also `method`

children

Insertion point for children of a bound element, or inherited binding

Contained by `content`

Attributes `id`, `includes`, `type`

Description

This element needs to be placed in the binding content at the point where you want to place children of the bound element when the binding is rendered. If the children tag contains its own elements, then that element will be default content. If the element the binding attaches to contains children, the default content is ignored.

constructor

Container for code to be executed when a binding is created

Contained by `implementation`

Attributes `action`, `class`, `id`

Description

This behavior element is contained in the `implementation` element and holds code that will be carried out when the binding attachment first takes place. If you picture a binding as an object, your vision is initialization code. The code can alternatively be contained as the `action` attribute's value.

See Also `destructor`

content

Container for anonymous content to be inserted into a bound document

Contains `children`; any markup content

Contained by `binding`

Attributes `id`

Description

This container for the anonymous binding content is placed at the point where the element using it is in the bound document. `children` is the only XBL element allowed as a child of `content`. All other content is either HTML or XUL, depending on the context in which you use the binding.

destructor

Container for code to be executed when a binding is destroyed

Contained by `implementation`

Attributes `action`, `class`, `id`

Description

Contained in the binding's `implementation`, this element carries out code placed within it when the binding is detached or destroyed. This detachment and destruction occurs when the bound element matches a different style rule, the bound element is removed from the document, or the document is closed or destroyed. The code can alternatively be a value of the `action` attribute.

See Also `constructor`

element

Insertion point for bound elements in anonymous content

Contained by `content`

Attributes `id`

Description

This element allows placement of a bound element at a point in the anonymous content (other than the top level that is the default for it). To use it, place it at the point in the binding content where you want the bound element to be rendered. This element is part of the XBL 1.0 specification, but is not yet implemented.

See Also `content`

field

Holder property for simple data

Contained by `implementation`

Attributes `class`, `id name`, `readonly`

Description

This element is a simple data holder and an alternative to a `property`. It differs from `property` because it does not use a `getter` or `setter`. It is useful for holding static/constant values for use elsewhere in the binding.

See Also `implementation`, `property`

getter

Script access point for an element's property

Contained by `property`

Attributes `id`, `type`

Description

This element executes script when the `property` it is attached to is accessed. This is most commonly used to return the value of the property.

See Also `property`, `setter`

handler

Single event handler for an XBL element

Contained by `handlers`

Attributes `id`, `event`, `action`, `phase`, `attachto`, `button`, `modifiers`, `keycode`, `charcode`, `type`

Description

This element defines an event handler on a binding that reacts to a mouse movement or keyboard press on the binding. Some executed code is contained in the handler. This code can go directly under the element or in the `action` attribute.

The `attachto` attribute determines where the event is received—in the element, document, or window. The default receiver is the bound element. The `phase` attribute has three possible values—capturing, bubbling, and target—that determine which part of the event flow and default is bubbling

The `button`, `charcode`, `keycode`, and `modifiers` attributes act as filters. For example, the value of `button` must match the label of the button that triggers the event.

The section "Event Attributes," later in this chapter, contains a complete list of events.

See Also handlers

handlers

Container for event-handler elements

Contains handler

Contained by binding

Attributes id, type

Description

This element is placed under the binding element and contains the event handlers used by that binding.

See Also handler

image

An image resource in a binding

Contained by resources

Attributes class,id, src

Description

This element preloads images; all included image resources are loaded when the binding is used.

See Also resources, stylesheet

implementation

Container for binding methods and properties

Contains method, property

Contained by binding

Attributes id, name, implements, type

Description

This element holds a binding's `<method>` and `<property>` elements that, as a whole, make up a binding's behavior. The optional `implements` attribute can hold a list of comma-separated XPCOM interfaces that are used by the implementation's methods and properties. The optional `type` attribute represents the scripting language to be used. This attribute defaults to JavaScript, the only implemented language that scripts Mozilla's XPFE.

```
<implementation type="application/x-javascript" implements="nsIAccessibleProvider">
  ...
</implementation>
```

See Also `binding`, `method`, `property`

method

Script function to be accessed on a binding object

Contains `body`, `parameter`

Contained by `implementation`

Attributes `id`, `name`, `type`

Description

This element supplies a single function to the bound element or binding object. The most important attribute is `name`, which calls the method and is compulsory. The method can have the `<parameter>` element define parameters. A `<body>` element contains the code that will be executed.

See Also `body`, `implementation`, `parameter`

parameter

Single paramter declaration for a method

Contained by `method`

Attributes `id`, `name`

Description

Each `<parameter>` element lists a single parameter for a method. The `name` attribute is compulsory and is used by the method code to access the parameter's value.

See Also `method`

property

Definition of a single binding object property

Contains `getter`, `setter`

Contained by `implementation`

Attributes `id`, `name`, `readonly`, `onget`, `onset`, `element`, `attribute`, `property`, `type`

Description

This element defines a bound element's or binding object's property. The name attribute is compulsory because it accesses the property. `<getter>` and `<setter>` child elements are optional and get and set the property value, respectively. The `onget` and `onset` attributes are alternatives. The `element` attribute is a reference to the anonymous content's node `id`. When the property is set, it is also set on that node. The property can be set to `readonly`.

See Also `field`, `getter`, `setter`

resources

Container for list of resources that can be used by a binding

Contains `image`, `stylesheet`

Contained by `binding`

Description

Along with `<content>`, `<implementation>`, and `<handlers>`, this element is one of the binding element's top-level children. It defines the binding's resources. Stylesheets and images are the current resources available to bindings. It is common for a single binding to contain all resources, which another binding can then inherit.

See Also `image`, `stylesheet`

setter

Change a binding property's value

Contained by `property`

Attributes `id`, `type`

Description

This element commonly sets the value of the property, and optionally executes other script for the property.

See Also `getter`, `property`

stylesheet

Captures an external stylesheet for use by anonymous content

Contained by `resources`

Attributes `src`

Description

This element defines a stylesheet to be used by a binding. An element's bound element and explicit children as well as anonymous content can use `stylesheet`. The `src` attribute has a URL value that points to the stylesheet. If you use the `xml-stylesheet` processing instruction on a binding, it can be applied only at a document level. It cannot be applied at a binding level, which is covered by the `<stylesheet>` element.

See Also `image`, `resources`

Event Attributes

Events are built-in constructs that are part of the interaction between JavaScript and HTML. These constructs have been crucial to DHTML for many years. They are designed to capture and handle actions triggered by the user, such as a mouse click or the pressing of a certain key. Event handlers have been brought into the world of XUL/XBL and allow dynamic, interactive Mozilla applications. In XUL, events can exist on any attribute, and typically bubble up through the hierarchy. An event attribute of the empty string generates a JS strict warning (if this is turned on in the user preferences), and removing an event attribute from a XUL event does not remove the event listener (although it does in HTML).

The events are listed in the form `on<eventName>`, which is how events are used as attributes on XUL elements. The attribute contains lines of script or a function call, when a script is too long. Here is an example of an event attribute that carries out a function each time a `menulist` value changes:

```
<menulist id="eventList" editable="true" flex="1" onchange="addEvent(this)">
```

The syntax is different in XBL. Here the event is specified as the value of the `name` attribute, which is attached to the `handler` element. One or more of these elements can optionally be contained in a binding. The given value is the event's name, minus the "on" prefix. The executed code is contained in the body of the handler inline, or in the `action` attribute, as shown in this example:

```
<handler name="focus" action="this.activate()"/>
```

Chapter 7 provides a closer look at events in XBL. All the events listed here are available for use in XUL and XBL.

onblur

Usually used for input element such as a textbox, this event triggers actions when the focus leaves a widget. This action is the opposite of the `onfocus` event.

onbroadcast

This event is activated when the broadcaster attributes being "listened to" are changed. It can be placed on the `observes` element, which is placed in an element that is being listened to, or on an element that uses the `observes` attribute. Refer to Chapter 3 for more information on broadcasters and observers.

onchange

This event is fired when the value of a particular widget's (element) attribute that uses it changes. A menulist selection is one example. It can also be used on an observer when the attribute the observer listens to changes.

onclick

Relevant to any element that can be clicked on, such as a button, this event occurs when the mouse is clicked on an element that uses it. For some widgets that use this event, using `oncommand` attribute (which covers clicking) is recommended to avoid excluding keyboard selection. Here are some commonly used properties associated with this event:

`button`
: This property tells you which mouse button was clicked. Its values are 0 for the left mouse button, 1 for middle button, and 2 for right button.

`detail`
: This property counts how many clicks occur over an element before the mouse is moved. The values for this property start at 1 and increment for every click.

Instead of catching double clicks this way, you can use the `ondblclick` event.

onclose

Usually used to evaluate script when a window is closed with the close button or via a `window.close()` call, this event traps the closure of a widow. If the JavaScript evaluates to "true," the window closes; otherwise, the window remains open.

oncommand

This event is sent when an element is activated. Activation can mean more than one thing. You can activate by selecting a menu item, hitting Enter on the keyboard when an element has focus, or clicking on an element. Use this event if you want to cover the most possibilities available for activation.

oncommandupdate

This event is used on a command set when one of its commands is updated, such as when its disabled attribute changes.

oncontextmenu

This event occurs when a request is made for a context menu—usually a right click, depending on the platform—and is activated before the menu appears. `oncontextmenu` is similar to the `oncreate` and `onpopupshowing` events.

oncreate

Called on a popup element, this event carries out some code before the popup appears. It can be useful for dynamically determining which items appear in the resulting menu.

ondblclick

This event cccurs when there are two consecutive mouse clicks on an element. You could also use the `onclick` event's detail property with a value of 2.

ondestroy

Designed to carry out functions after a pop-up window disappears, this event can be used with a popup or menupopup element.

ondragdrop

When a drag and drop session completes and the user releases the mouse over the element, this event is triggered. The accessed code can acknowledge the drop and carry out an operation after accepting the dragged object.

ondragenter

The `ondragenter` event is sent when the mouse cursor first moves over an element during a drag and drop session. This element differs from the `mouseover` event because it occurs during a drag and drop session.

ondragexit

This element is activated when the cursor moves away from an element during a drag and drop session. It occurs after the `ondragdrop` event.

ondraggesture

The event is triggered at the beginning of a drag and drop session when the user holds the mouse button on the dragged object.

ondragover

When an object is dragged over an element, this event is commonly used by an element to determine whether the drop can occur.

onfocus

This event is triggered when an element receives focus in the UI. When it has focus, it can accept keyboard events. The opposite of `onfocus` is `onblur`.

oninput

Used on `textbox` elements, this event is activated when displayable keys change the text in the box.

onkeydown

This event occurs when the user presses a key on an element that has focus and the key press is not released.

onkeypress

Similar to `onkeydown`, this event occurs on a focused element when a key is pressed. The distinction is that with this event, the key is released soon after being pressed. The check for which key was pressed can be using the `event.keyCode` property.

onkeyup

This event is activated when the key press is released on a focused element.

onload

This event is activated on a XUL window or dialog after it has fully loaded. It should be attached to the elements of the same name. It can also be attached to `image` elements or elements that display images.

onmousedown

This event occurs when a mouse is pressed on an element but not released.

onmousemove

A reoccuring event, this event repeatedly fires when a mouse moves over an element.

onmouseout

When the mouse moves away from an element, this event occurs.

onmouseover

A hover event, this event fires when the mouse initially moves into an element's space.

onmouseup

This event occurs when a mouse is clicked and the button is released on an element immediately afterwards.

onoverflow

Relating to a box or layout element, this event is activated when the content contained in the box is too big for its given size and and "falls over the edge."

onoverflowchanged

This element is called when an element's overflow state changes. This can indicate that it did not have enough space to display it contents fully but does now, or that it does not have enough space and thus overflowed.

onpopuphidden

This event is activated on a popup when the pop-up window is hidden.

onpopuphiding

This event is activated on a popup while it is hidden.

onpopupshowing

This event is activated on a popup just before it opens. It is commonly used to dynamically set the contents of the popup when it is requested in the UI.

onpopupshown

This is event is activated on a popup after it is opened.

onselect

When you activate or select an available option in a widget, this event is fired. This event applies to such widgets as trees and listboxes.

onunderflow

This event can be used in tandem with the `onoverflow` event. It is activated when a layout element's content changes to fit into its given constraints after being in an overflow state.

onunload

This event is activated when a window or dialog closes. It should be used on the root elements of these window documents.

Index

A

We'd like to hear your suggestions for improving our indexes. Send email to *index@oreilly.com*.

D

E

F

G

H

I

J

K

L

M

N

O

P

Q

R

S

T

U

V

W

X

About the Authors

David Boswell has been involved in the Mozilla community for over three years. He started the Mozilla development effort at Alphanumerica and set up the first two Mozilla Developer Meetings. At Alphanumerica, David worked with Pete Collins on a number of Mozilla applications, including Aphrodite, Total Recall, and Chameleon. Pete and David also founded mozdev.org, a site offering free hosting for Mozilla applications. There are currently over 70 development projects hosted on the site. David has written a number of articles about Mozilla, including "Getting Your Work Into Mozilla," as well as a series of articles discussing how to use Mozilla technologies to create a Pacman-like video game. He is currently working for CollabNet on a number of other open source projects.

Brian King has been hacking on Mozilla and related projects since early 1999, when he was working on a European-funded project called Fabula to create software for children that teaches minority languages such as Basque, Catalan, Frisian, Irish, and Welsh. This software was built using Mozilla. Interest bloomed, and he started contributing to the Mozilla Editor and exploring the rest of the vast body of code. He moved on to work at ActiveState, where he was heavily involved in the Komodo project, which is a scripting language IDE that uses the Mozilla application framework. Previously, Brian spent his time as a C++ applications developer, interspersed with some Perl development and XML consultancy. His technical interests include observing and participating in the reshaping of the web environment brought about by XML. He also dabbles in the PHP, Python, and JavaScript languages. Brian is currently a web technologies consultant and is living in Dublin, Ireland.

Ian Oeschger is senior principal writer at Netscape Communications, where mozilla.org was started over three years ago. His abiding interest in language is the basis for some of his more recent infatuations with Python, XML, web application development, and linguistics. He maintains a number of the XPFE documents on mozilla.org, including the XUL and DOM References. Ian has published several articles about XML and Mozilla application development for O'Reilly, and also wrote the themes documentation for Netscape, the XPInstall API Reference, and others. Before getting involved with Mozilla and Netscape, he worked at Oceania, a startup doing XML-based electronic medical records and charting software, owned a small bookstore with his wife, and had more time to write fiction, which he still does when he can.

Pete Collins has been involved with the Mozilla project since April 1999 as a contributor to the editor module. He was also the first external developer to start documenting XUL. His initial efforts were a remote, web-enabled script editor and a community-driven rewrite of the existing Mozilla UI. The project was later named Aphrodite. In January 2000, he joined with David Boswell and the Alphanumerica team. Together, they evangelized Mozilla as a viable application platform through the many projects they created and the Mozilla developer meetings they organized. Currently a software engineer employed by WorldGate, Pete is working on customizing Mozilla for their TV Internet Client Software. He is the cofounder of mozdev.org a site dedicated to Mozilla-based projects. He is a regular Mozilla cvs comitter and owner of various Mozdev projects, including jslib and Chameleon.

Eric Murphy has been doing Mozilla development since spring 2000, starting off with an instant-messenger client called Jabberzilla. He enjoys exploring opportunities for Jabber and Mozilla to work together through new implementations, such as a collaborative whiteboard and real-time web content demonstrations. Eric is looking forward to joining the work force in 2002 with a recent computer science degree from the University of Northern Iowa. Working on Mozilla projects has been a great resume-builder for him and will always be an important part of his life to on which to reflect.

Colophon

Our look is the result of reader comments, our own experimentation, and feedback from distribution channels. Distinctive covers complement our distinctive approach to technical topics, breathing personality and life into potentially dry subjects.

The animal on the cover of *Creating Applications with Mozilla* is a frilled lizard. Native to Australia, the frilled lizard is known for the colorful neck frill that it uses to frighten predators. The frill normally lies in folds around the lizard's shoulders, creating a camouflage. When the lizard is frightened, it activates the frill by opening its mouth wide. This raises the frill, displaying its bright red and orange underside. Frilled lizards eat insects such as cicadas, ants, and spiders. Their population has been greatly diminished by land clearing and being preyed on by cats.

Mary Brady was the production editor and proofreader, and Ann Schirmer was the copyeditor for *Creating Applications with Mozilla*. Mary Anne Weeks Mayo and Claire Cloutier provided quality control. Johnna Van Hoose Dinse wrote the index. Brian Sawyer and Derek Di Matteo provided production support.

Ellie Volckhausen designed the cover of this book, based on a series design by Edie Freedman. The cover image is a 19th-century engraving from the Dover Pictorial Archive. Emma Colby produced the cover layout with QuarkXPress 4.1 using Adobe's ITC Garamond font.

David Futato designed the interior layout. This book was converted to FrameMaker 5.5.6 with a format conversion tool created by Erik Ray, Jason McIntosh, Neil Walls, and Mike Sierra that uses Perl and XML technologies. The text font is Linotype Birka; the heading font is Adobe Myriad Condensed; and the code font is LucasFont's TheSans Mono Condensed. The illustrations that appear in the book were produced by Robert Romano and Jessamyn Read using Macromedia FreeHand 9 and Adobe Photoshop 6. The tip and warning icons were drawn by Christopher Bing. This colophon was written by Linley Dolby.

Other Titles Available from O'Reilly

Web Programming

ActionScript for Flash MX: The Definitive Guide, 2nd Edition

By Colin Moock
2nd Edition December 2002 (est.)
1104 pages (est.), ISBN 0-596-00396-X

This is the only complete, up-to-date reference available for the latest version of ActionScript, Macromedia's programming language for Flash. The book's language reference alone has nearly doubled from the first edition, with over 250 new classes, objects, methods, and properties! Hundreds of new code examples show new Flash MX techniques in the real world—how to draw circles, save data to disk, convert arrays to onscreen tables, create reusable components, and preload variables, XML and sounds.

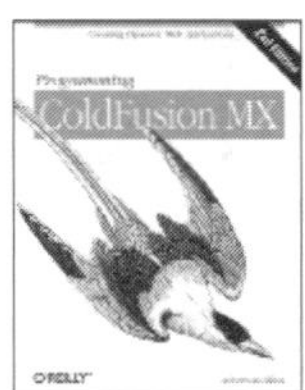

Programming ColdFusion MX, 2nd Edition

By Rob Brooks-Bilson
2nd Edition March 2002 (est.)
1000 pages (est.), ISBN 0-596-00380-3

This exhaustive resource covers everything from ColdFusion basics to advanced topics, so not only is the book ideal for intermediate developers—with topics on sharing application data and accessing databases—*Programming ColdFusion MX* continues to be a one-stop clearinghouse on techniques for the most seasoned ColdFusion developers. Topics include advanced database techniques, working with the Verity search engine, interacting with data sources such as LDAP directories, creating custom tags, integrating ColdFusion with Flash, and calling external objects.

JavaScript: The Definitive Guide, 4th Edition

By David Flanagan
4th Edition November 2001
936 pages, ISBN 0-596-00048-0

To stay on top of their work, web professionals need the most up-to-date, complete reference available on the core JavaScript language, which is growing more and more essential for effective web design and development. This new edition covers JavaScript 1.5, the latest version of the language. The book's comprehensive reference section documents every object, property, method, event handler, function and constructor used by client-side JavaScript.

HTTP: The Definitive Guide

By Brian Totty & David Gourley with Marjorie Sayer, Anshu Aggarwal & Sailu Reddy
1st Edition September 2002
656 pages, ISBN 1-56592-509-2

HTTP: The Definitive Guide gives a complete and detailed description of the HTTP protocol and how it shapes the landscape of the Web. It doesn't stop at a simple listing of the HTTP methods and headers, but explains HTTP in context of the web technologies that it supports. This is a book that every serious web programmer will need on his or her shelf.

Dynamic HTML: The Definitive Reference, 2nd Edition

By Danny Goodman
2nd Edition September 2002
1418 pages, ISBN 0-596-00316-1

Packed with information on the latest web specifications, including HTML 4.01, CSS2, DOM Level 2, and JavaScript 1.5, *Dynamic HTML: The Definitive Reference* also details the latest versions of the major browsers – Internet Explorer 6 and Netscape Navigator 6 and 7. Indispensable, complete, and succinct, this is the must-have compendium for all web developers involved in creating dynamic web content. It contains everything a developer needs to create functional, cross-platform Dynamic HTML web applications.

JavaScript Pocket Reference, 2nd Edition

By David Flanagan
2nd Edition November 2002 (est.)
128 pages (est.), ISBN 0-596-00411-7

This handy guide offers a complete overview of the core JavaScript language and contains summaries of core and client-side objects, methods, and properties. Ideal as an introduction for beginners and a quick reference for advanced developers, the second edition has been revised to cover JavaScript 1.5, the current version of the language. This pocket-sized book is easy to take anywhere and serves as the perfect companion to *JavaScript: The Definitive Guide*.

Web Programming

Webmaster In a Nutshell, 3rd Edition

By Stephen Spainhour & Robert Eckstein
3rd Edition December 2002 (est.)
520 pages (est.), ISBN 0-596-00357-9

This book is the only quick reference available for all core web-related technologies, with material on HTML, CSS, XML, CGI, JavaScript, PHP, HTTP, and Apache. With significant changes to the PHP, CSS, Apache, and JavaScript sections, this edition makes the most essential data accessible for developers, with a fast-paced introduction, detailed reference section, and quick reference guide to each technology.

PHP Pocket Reference, 2nd Edition

By Rasmus Lerdorf
2nd Edition November 2002 (est.)
144 pages (est.), ISBN 0-596-00402-8

Simple, to the point, and compact, the second edition of PHP Pocket Reference is thoroughly updated to include the specifics of PHP 4, the language's latest version. It is both a handy introduction to PHP syntax and structure, and a quick reference to the vast array of functions provided by PHP. The quick reference section organizes all the core functions of PHP alphabetically so you can find what you need easily.

Programming PHP

By Rasmus Lerdorf & Kevin Tatroe
1st Edition March 2002
528 pages, ISBN 1-56592-610-2

Programming PHP is a comprehensive guide to PHP, a simple yet powerful language for creating dynamic web content. Filled with the unique knowledge of the creator of PHP, Rasmus Lerdorf, this book is a detailed reference to the language and its applications, including such topics as form processing, sessions, databases, XML, and graphics. Covers PHP 4, the latest version of the language.

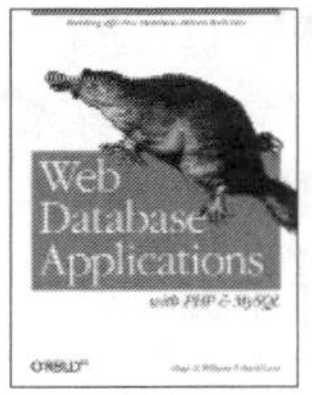

Web Database Applications with PHP & MySQL

By Hugh E. Williams & David Lane
1st Edition March 2002
582 pages, ISBN 0-596-00041-3

This book offers both theoretical and practical guidance for creating web database applications. The detailed information on designing relational databases and the web application architectures that interact with them will be especially useful to readers who have worked with or built database-backed web sites before. The book implements a sample web application using PHP and MySQL on the Apache platform.

PHP Cookbook

By David Sklar & Adam Trachtenberg
1st Edition November 2002 (est.)
600 pages (est.), ISBN 1-56592-681-1

This cookbook has a wealth of solutions for problems that PHP programmers face regularly. With topics that range from beginner questions to advanced web programming techniques, the *PHP Cookbook* contains practical examples—or "recipes"—for any programmer or web designer who uses the scripting language to generate dynamic web content. With each recipe, the authors include a discussion that explains the logic and concepts underlying the solution.

How to stay in touch with O'Reilly

1. Visit our award-winning web site

http://www.oreilly.com/

★ "Top 100 Sites on the Web"—PC Magazine
★ CIO Magazine's Web Business 50 Awards

Our web site contains a library of comprehensive product information (including book excerpts and tables of contents), downloadable software, background articles, interviews with technology leaders, links to relevant sites, book cover art, and more. File us in your bookmarks or favorites!

2. Join our email mailing lists

Sign up to get email announcements of new books and conferences, special offers, and O'Reilly Network technology newsletters at:

http://elists.oreilly.com

It's easy to customize your free elists subscription so you'll get exactly the O'Reilly news you want.

3. Get examples from our books

To find example files for a book, go to:

http://www.oreilly.com/catalog

select the book, and follow the "Examples" link.

4. Work with us

Check out our web site for current employment opportunities:

http://jobs.oreilly.com/

5. Register your book

Register your book at:

http://register.oreilly.com

6. Contact us

O'Reilly & Associates, Inc.
1005 Gravenstein Hwy North
Sebastopol, CA 95472 USA
TEL: 707-827-7000 or 800-998-9938
(6am to 5pm PST)
FAX: 707-829-0104

order@oreilly.com
For answers to problems regarding your order or our products. To place a book order online visit:

http://www.oreilly.com/order_new/

catalog@oreilly.com
To request a copy of our latest catalog.

booktech@oreilly.com
For book content technical questions or corrections.

corporate@oreilly.com
For educational, library, government, and corporate sales.

proposals@oreilly.com
To submit new book proposals to our editors and product managers.

international@oreilly.com
For information about our international distributors or translation queries. For a list of our distributors outside of North America check out:

http://international.oreilly.com/distributors.html

adoption@oreilly.com
For information about academic use of O'Reilly books, visit:

http://academic.oreilly.com

O'REILLY®

To order: *800-998-9938* • *order@oreilly.com* • *www.oreilly.com*
Online editions of most O'Reilly titles are available by subscription at *safari.oreilly.com*
Also available at most retail and online bookstores.